ABSENCE FROM FELICITY

ABSENCE FROM FELICITY

The Story of Helen Schucman
and Her Scribing of
A COURSE IN MIRACLES

KENNETH WAPNICK, Ph.D.

Foundation for "A Course in Miracles"

Foundation for "A Course in Miracles"
R.R. 2, Box 71
Roscoe, NY 12776-9506

Printed in the United States of America

Portions of *A Course in Miracles* © 1975, *Psychotherapy: Purpose, Process and Practice* © 1976, *The Song of Prayer* © 1978, *The Gifts of God* © 1982, used by permission of the Foundation for Inner Peace.

Portions of the *Unpublished Writings of Helen Schucman,* Volumes 1–22, © 1990 Kenneth Wapnick, used by permission.

Cover: photograph by Gloria Wapnick

Library of Congress Cataloging in Publication Data

Wapnick, Kenneth
    Absence from felicity : the story of Helen Schucman and her scribing A course in miracles / Kenneth Wapnick.
        p.   cm.
    ISBN 0-933291-08-6 (pbk.)
    1. Schucman, Helen. 2. Course in miracles. 3. Spiritual life.
I. Title.
BP605.C68S388   1991
299'.93--dc20   91-8916
                                              CIP

FOR HELEN

Into Christ's Presence has she entered now, serenely unaware of everything except His shining face and perfect Love. The vision of His face will stay with her, but there will be an instant which transcends all vision, even this, the holiest. This she will never teach, for she attained it not through learning. Yet the vision speaks of her rememberance of what she knew that instant, and will surely know again. (Adapted from A COURSE IN MIRACLES, workbook Lesson 157.)

CONTENTS

PREFACE 1

INTRODUCTION: A MIDDLE-AGED LAWYER 7

PART I—THE EARLY YEARS

INTRODUCTION 17

Chapter 1: HEAVEN AND HELEN: INTRODUCTION 19

Chapter 2: HEAVEN AND HELEN: THE EARLY YEARS 27

PART II—THE SCRIBING OF *A COURSE IN MIRACLES*

INTRODUCTION 47

Chapter 3: LEADING TO *A COURSE IN MIRACLES*—A (from ca. 1938)
     Preparing for Graduate School 49
     The Subway Experience 52
     Dreams 56

Chapter 4: LEADING TO *A COURSE IN MIRACLES*—B (ca. 1950–1964)
     Psychology—Columbia-Presbyterian Medical Center 83

Chapter 5: LEADING TO *A COURSE IN MIRACLES*—C (1965)
     "There Must Be Another Way" 93

Chapter 6: HELEN'S LETTERS TO BILL (SUMMER, 1965) 133

Chapter 7: THE BEGINNING OF *A COURSE IN MIRACLES* (1965) ... 185

Chapter 8: THE SCRIBING OF *A COURSE IN MIRACLES*—A (1965)
     The Early Weeks: The Miracle Principles 215

Chapter 9: THE SCRIBING OF *A COURSE IN MIRACLES*—B (1965)
     Specific Teachings 249
     Bill's Class 269
     More Specific Teachings 280

Chapter 10: THE SCRIBING OF *A COURSE IN MIRACLES*—C (1965–1972)
Special Messages 293
Bill's Journal 311
Continuation and Conclusion of the Course 324

PART III—THE YEARS FOLLOWING *A COURSE IN MIRACLES*

INTRODUCTION 333

Chapter 11: SUMMER, 1973: THE CAVE 335

Chapter 12: THE EDITING (1973–1975) 359

Chapter 13: HELEN AND BILL: THE SPECIAL AND HOLY
RELATIONSHIP, AND THEIR LATER LIFE WITH
A COURSE IN MIRACLES
Helen, Bill, and I 369
Judith Skutch and the Post-Publication Years 374
Helen's Relationship with *A Course in Miracles* 381

Chapter 14: OTHER SCRIBINGS—A
"Notes on Sound" (1972, 1977) 387
"Psychotherapy: Purpose, Process and Practice"
(1973, 1975) 389
"Clarification of Terms" (1975) 391
"The Song of Prayer" (1977) 393
Special Messages (1975–1978) 393

Chapter 15: OTHER SCRIBINGS—B
THE GIFTS OF GOD: HELEN'S POETRY
The Writing of the Poems 401
The Poems 407
"The Gifts of God" 419

Chapter 16: JESUS: THE WAY, THE TRUTH, AND THE LIFE 423
             Catholicism—Mary 424
             Helen's Ambivalence Towards Jesus 435
                 1. The Journey Home to Jesus 435
                 2. Resistance and Shame 438
                 3. Doubt and Inconsistency 444
                 4. Shopping 445
             Defense Against Jesus and Against Love:
                 Special Hate (Judgment) and Special Love 447
             The Jesus Poems 453

Chapter 17: THE REALITY OF JESUS: INTO CHRIST'S PRESENCE
             "The Song of Prayer": Special Message 461
             "The Song of Prayer": The Pamphlet 471
             Helen and Jesus: The Illusion and the Reality 477
             The Unconscious Priestess 487

Chapter 18: HELEN'S FINAL MONTHS AND REQUIEM 493

                              EPILOGUE

BEYOND HEAVEN AND HELEN: THE PRIESTESS 499

                              APPENDIX

A Course in Miracles - What It Says 507
Dates 513
Indices
    Index of Names 515
    Index of William Thetford 517
    Index of Helen Schucman 518

PREFACE

Helen Schucman, the subject of this book, was the scribe of *A Course in Miracles.*[1] From October 1965 through September 1972, she "heard" the voice of Jesus dictating to her the three volumes that comprise one of the most significant spiritual messages of our time. This book, in part, is the story of this dictation, set in the context of Helen's lifetime search for God.

One afternoon, several years after the Course was completed, Helen and I were sitting on her living room couch, our favorite spot when the weather was not conducive to walking. We began to discuss the distortions about her life and the Course's origins that were already beginning to be heard, and this at a time when she was still very much alive. Imagine, we thought out loud, what would happen after she was gone. Helen, incidentally, seemed rather certain that she would die at the age of seventy-two, that being the number written on her tombstone she had seen in a vision. In point of fact, she died about five months short of her seventy-second birthday. While I do not recall the exact date of our conversation on the couch, it was most likely around two or three years before Helen's death in 1981.

It was mutually understood by us that her unpublished autobiography was hardly a true and accurate account of her life, being rather an overly stylized, literary rendering—her public stance—that did not truly reflect the deeper level of Helen's feelings and experiences. Our one attempt to correct the inaccuracies and edit out the distortions, while an improvement in some places, proved in many others to be even worse than the original. Recounting certain events in her life— especially those of a religious nature, and even more specifically, those events surrounding *A Course in Miracles*— aroused tremendous anxiety in Helen, and her discomfort directly led to an almost fierce over-editing that affected the

---

1. Foundation for Inner Peace, P.O. Box 1104, Glen Ellen, CA: 1975. For those readers unfamiliar with *A Course in Miracles*, it consists of three books—text, workbook for students, manual for teachers—set in the context of a self-study curriculum. A brief summary of its teachings is provided in the Appendix.

1

faithfulness of her life's retelling. It was out of this context, therefore, that I said to Helen that I would write her story, as well as the related events—inner and outer—that preceded, accompanied, and followed her taking down the Course.

Helen agreed that this was a good idea, and then, as one of us would often do, I quoted from our mutually favorite literary work, *Hamlet*. It was from the final scene where Hamlet is dying of the poisoned cup, and his trusted Horatio begins to drink the poison to join his friend in death. Hamlet quickly seizes the cup from Horatio's hands, exclaiming:

> O good Horatio, what a wounded name,
> Things standing thus unknown, shall live behind me!
> If thou didst ever hold me in thy heart,
> Absent thee from felicity awhile,
> And in this harsh world draw thy breath in pain,
> To tell my story (V, ii).

I hardly think this is a harsh world, nor do I experience my surviving Helen as painful, nor did I think that way then. However, I had some premonitions of what the world would do to Helen—"what a wounded name...shall live behind me!"— unable to resist the temptation to sensationalize, mythologize, or otherwise distort her life and experiences. This I knew would only obscure the truth of what was an inspiring and powerful story simply by being what it was, without need to have it conform to Hollywood standards. And so the need for a biography I would write—as I truly held her in my heart—that would more closely reflect Helen's experience: a life dedicated to bringing forth the message of Jesus, and yet a life that was in truth, in Helen's conscious experience at least, an absence from felicity.

Indeed, some distorted accounts of Helen and the origins of *A Course in Miracles* have already begun to appear, and these do not do justice to: 1) Helen's true experience of God and Jesus; 2) the uniqueness of what appeared to be her dual personality of a highly developed spiritual self coupled with an almost equally highly developed ego; and 3) her relationship with William Thetford, that on one level was the direct stimulus and provided the setting for the transmission of the Course. A major purpose of this book, therefore, is to chronicle the unusually ambivalent relationship Helen had with God and Jesus, beginning with her childhood and continuing on through the scribing of the Course to the moment of her death in 1981.

The book, however, is not a conventional biography, for it does not present a complete nor totally linear view of Helen's life. Nor is it a psycho-biography, a genre that has been somewhat in favor in our Freudian age. Echoing *A Course in Miracles*, this book reflects a particular point of view; namely, that the aforementioned conflict in Helen between these parts of her self—wanting to return to God and the fear of such return—is the predominant theme in everyone's life, independent of familial and/or hereditary circumstances. This was a conflict that symbolized both sides of Helen's personality, and reflected the same ambivalence we all share regarding our relationship with God and with the person of Jesus, whose love for us was the closest the world has come to experiencing the resplendent Love of God, our Source.

In chronicling the development of this personal conflict, and its ultimate resolution, I thus am writing everyone's story. The drama of this aspect of Helen's inner life reflects the inner life of all people, seemingly trapped in a Godless world and wandering "uncertain, lonely, and in constant fear" (text, p. 621), yet all the time yearning to hear the Call of the loving God that would lead them back to Him. I therefore, for the most part, do not dwell on Helen's worldly life—the *form*— except insofar as it reflects the underlying *content* of this conflict. Analyzing the ego is fruitless, as the Course repeatedly instructs us. On the other hand, understanding that the entire ego thought system is a defense against our true Self is extremely helpful. Thus, for example, Helen's clear ambivalence towards her parents and organized religion— providing a goldmine of data for a psychologist seeking to find psychodynamic causes for her inner experiences—is here seen as reflective of this deeper God-ego conflict, not its cause.

The ultimate origins of this conflict, however, lie buried still deeper midst ancient scars, born on a raging battlefield of a transtemporal mind far greater than its tiny expression we call Helen Schucman. It is the mind of a larger, post-separation self (called the split mind or ego by *A Course in Miracles*) that is the source of our experienced personal self. Understanding Helen's life therefore provides a model for this ontological God-ego conflict that rages inside all people. As the two sides of this battle are recognized, they can be brought together and transcended at last.

Helen, thus, not only left the world *A Course in Miracles*—in my opinion the world's most psychologically sophisticated account of the mind's subterranean warfare, along with teaching the means for undoing this war against God through forgiveness—but her own life provided a model for its teachings as well. Very few, if any at all, knew fully these two sides of Helen—Hamlet's "Things standing thus unknown"—and it is this complex combination I hope to capture in this book. While Helen would not have wanted what I am to write to have been public knowledge during her lifetime, for reasons that form one of the important themes of this book, I know she would be pleased that I am at this time presenting her story and that of the Course's beginnings. I therefore hope that this book will restore to Helen's reported experience a balance that has been heretofore lacking, and that will record for posterity the wonderful if not painfully human story of a woman who remained absolutely faithful to Jesus, the one she both loved and hated above all others.

And yet, all this being said, the love and hate but veiled the Love in her that existed before time was, and will continue after time ceases to be. For beyond the personal and ambivalent side to Helen, rested a totally different self. In fact, "Self" may be a more appropriate spelling, for this part of her inner life was totally impersonal, and transcended the love-hate relationship with Jesus that in effect *was* her personal self. Almost always hidden in Helen, this other-worldly side nonetheless was the ultimate foundation for her life, and gave it the meaning from which all else must be understood.

This book, therefore, has two principal themes. The first, which predominates, is Helen's love-hate relationship with God and Jesus, what *A Course in Miracles* refers to as the conflict between our right- and wrong-minded selves. The second, which runs throughout as an undercurrent, is the Love of Christ that Helen truly *knew* and was, called One-Mindedness

4

in the Course. Although I shall make reference to this transpersonal Self from time to time, especially in connection with Helen's recurring image of the priestess, I shall leave for the Epilogue a fuller consideration of this aspect of Helen, letting the development of her personal side form the basic contours of this book. At the conclusion of Helen's personal story, I shall then return to this Self, as a composer concludes a symphony with a coda: the final episode that introduces new themes, yet which nonetheless remains intimately connected to the spirit of the music preceding it.

Helen and I shared a deep love for one another, and for Jesus in whose love we knew we were joined, and on behalf of whose Course we had come together. It is my prayer that I am able to convey that love in these pages. In the words that Beethoven inscribed over the opening measures of his choral masterpiece *Missa Solemnis*: "From the heart, may it go to the heart."

Introduction

"A MIDDLE-AGED LAWYER"

I first met Helen Schucman on Saturday night, November 25, 1972. We met at William Thetford's apartment on the upper east side of New York City, and our meeting was arranged by our mutual friend Father Michael. The three of them, along with Bill's roommate Chip, had spent the afternoon at a healing service of Kathryn Kuhlman, the famous faith-healer, and had been impressed, if not worn out, by the intense sincerity of the service. I later learned how unusual it was for Helen to agree to go out in the evening, especially after a tiring day. Looking back on that meeting, I can see a certain inevitability in the circumstances leading up to it.

Brought up in a Jewish home and educated for the first eight grades in a Hebrew parochial school called a Yeshivah, I had left God and Judaism behind at the age of thirteen, determined never to think of religious issues again. There followed a long period of agnosticism that was coupled with a growing and passionate love for classical music, with Beethoven and Mozart heading my personal pantheon of guides that led me ever more deeply to internal experiences that I, in my ignorance during that period, scarcely would have termed spiritual. This period included my graduate education, and very surprisingly, a doctoral dissertation on St. Teresa of Avila, the famous sixteenth-century Spanish mystic. A couple of years later (1970), after the break-up of my first marriage, God "showed up," and I began to feel a personal Presence that was behind these "non-spiritual" experiences. Two years later, after a chain of experiences irrelevant to this book, I found myself visiting a Trappist monastery, the Abbey of Gethsemani in Kentucky, very unexpectedly feeling totally "at home."

The pace of my life now seemed to quicken markedly. I decided while at the monastery that it was God's Will that I become a Trappist monk, as well as a Roman Catholic, though I had no interest in the Church whatsoever, nor any conscious interest in Jesus, its central figure. Upon my return to the hospital where I was employed, I spoke to the Catholic chaplain who baptized and confirmed me within three weeks. In preparation for entering the monastery—Church law decreed I had to wait a year—I decided to leave my job at Thanksgiving and spend the time quietly alone. I felt I should spend part of this time in Israel, and so arranged to go a few days after the holiday. But I am slightly ahead of the story.

Shortly after my baptism in September 1972, the chaplain told me that a priest in his religious order was very anxious to meet me. This was my introduction to Father Michael. The circumstances were far more interesting than this, however. Father Michael was a psychologist, and had done part of his graduate training under William Thetford and Helen Schucman at the Psychiatric Institute, part of the Columbia-Presbyterian Medical Center. The three of them became good friends, and in fact, Michael was one of the very, very few people with whom Helen and Bill shared *A Course in Miracles*, even as it was still coming through.

One day Bill was reading John White's *The Highest State of Consciousness,* an anthology in which an article of mine appeared. This was "Mysticism and Schizophrenia," a paper that was originally meant for my dissertation, and was first published in the *Journal of Transpersonal Psychology.* The article compared and contrasted the mystical experiences of St. Teresa with those of a schizophrenic, the principal point being that schizophrenics were not mystics, and mystics were not schizophrenics. Bill showed it to Michael as an example of a psychologist who took the mystical experience seriously, more of a rare occurrence in the mid-1960s than it is today. When the baptizing chaplain mentioned to Michael that he had recently baptized a psychologist (a phenomenon I think he equated with the imminent announcement of the Second Coming), Michael recognized my name from the article and expressed interest in meeting me.

I called him, set up a time to get together, and he and I soon became fast friends. Shortly before I was to leave for Israel, Michael told me about two psychologists he thought I should meet. And so Michael, Helen, Bill, Chip, and I met that Saturday evening. Most of the time, as I recall, was spent in my telling how I came to be where I now was in my life. Helen shared a couple of her early experiences, and I remember feeling a particularly close connection with her.

At one point in the evening, someone—I think it might have been Michael—mentioned this "book" that Helen had "written," which had to do with spiritual development. Bill pointed to a corner in his living room where his copy of the manuscript of the Course was kept in seven black thesis binders. For some reason I did not feel I should look at them, although it would have been perfectly all right with Helen and Bill if I had done so.

The evening ended and I felt that I had just met two very holy people, although I obviously could not have recognized then the real importance they would have in my life. Michael and I drove Helen home to her downtown Manhattan apartment, and Helen mentioned that the name "Wapnick" was familiar to her, as indeed "Schucman" was to me. We then realized that Helen knew my ex-wife Ruth, who had worked for a while at the Medical Center as a research assistant. I recalled that Ruth had found her immediate supervisor to be quite difficult, and had spoken to Helen, a consultant to the project. Ruth had experienced Helen as very supportive and helpful, as she did Bill. Interestingly enough, this association was within the first year or so of the Course's transmission.

After we dropped Helen off, Michael and I continued to his residence where I spent the night. Before we went to sleep, Michael offered me a copy of "Helen's book" to examine, but again, I did not feel I should look at it. I then went to bed and yet could not fall asleep, a very unusual occurrence for me. Though tired, I tossed and turned for quite some time, trying to figure out why I was having so much difficulty.

Finally I remembered a dream I had had over a year before. In the dream I was with a group of people, who I felt were considerably younger than I. A very wise middle-aged lawyer then walked in, and took me to a different section of the room, which resembled a library, apart from the others. She then presented me with me three questions, only the first of which is relevant here. It asked what I would change, if I could, of any of my childhood experiences. My answer, which proved to

9

be the correct one, was that I would not change anything, since all was the way it should be and the past no longer mattered. I awoke at this point, and then finished the dream in a semiconscious, hypnagogic state. In the dream (which I recognized to be a significant one), the woman-lawyer was a kind of spiritual teacher, for whom I had a great deal of respect, and whose respect and approval I had obviously gained as well.

Lying in bed at Father Michael's, I suddenly realized that the lawyer was Helen. I barely knew her, but at this point already recognized in Helen the powerful presence of a spiritual authority. Obviously, however, I had no way of knowing then just how complex an individual she was. I became quite peaceful, and instantly fell asleep. When I told Michael about it the following morning, he laughed: "Of course Helen would be a lawyer," referring to Helen's keen analytic and logically probing mind.

I left for Israel a few days later, and as it ended up, most of my time was spent in two monasteries. I wrote Helen and Bill separate letters in March, from the Trappist Abbey of Latroun, outside Jerusalem. My letter to Bill survives, but this first letter to Helen is missing. In it, Helen remarked to me later, I referred to my desire to read her book, and spelled it with a capital "B," something I never would have consciously done.

Moreover, while in Israel I had two dreams relating to "Helen's Book." In the first, I was standing on a New York City subway platform. I walked over to a garbage can and there on top was what I knew to be a very holy book, but not one with which I was acquainted. In another dream, I was walking along a beach, and found this same holy book in the sand.

I eventually left Latroun and went to Lavra Netofa, a small and physically primitive monastic community atop a mountain in the region of Galilee, affording a beautiful view of the northern end of the famous Sea. After two months, and feeling very much at home there, I decided to remain on this mountain top for an indefinite period of time. But before nestling in, I thought I should visit the United States to see my family, as well as to look up Helen and Bill. In my letter to Helen announcing my visit, I wrote:

Since I shall be remaining here quite some time, I have decided to come to the United States for about a month before returning here and settling in. I plan to arrive somewhere around the week-end of May 12 [1973]...and I hope we can get together soon thereafter. I also look forward very much to reading your book [here spelled with a lower case "b"][2] while in the States.

I stayed with Michael on my arrival in New York, and shortly afterwards he drove me down to Columbia-Presbyterian. Helen's recollection was that I walked into the door and said, "Hello, here I am; where's the book?" While I know I was anxious to see this material, I doubt if I would have totally forgotten my good manners. I would have at least said, "Hello, *how are you?*" And then, "Where's the book?" But obviously I could not wait to see "Helen's" manuscript.

Helen and Bill had adjacent offices within a larger enclosed area, and they sat me down in Bill's office while he went into Helen's. Helen handed me her two favorite sections—"For They Have Come" and "Choose Once Again"—which thus became my introduction to *A Course in Miracles.* I read eagerly, and could scarcely believe what I was reading. Long a lover of Shakespeare, these extremely poetic sections were to me every bit as beautiful as anything the Bard had written, and yet I remember exclaiming to Helen and Bill that unlike Shakespeare, these words contained a profound spiritual message. I could not envision a more sublime integration of form and content, equaling in my mind the perfection of Beethoven's C-Sharp Minor Quartet.

My memory of the exact sequence of events is hazy, but as I began reading the text from the beginning I quickly recognized the Course as being the most perfect blend of psychology and spirituality that I had ever seen. And I am sure that it did not take me very long to realize that *A Course in Miracles* was my life's work, Helen and Bill were my spiritual family, and that I was not to become a monk but to remain in New York with them instead.

---

2. Throughout the book, my additions to quoted material are indicated by brackets [ ], as opposed to parentheses ( ), which will always be from the quoted material itself.

During this period, which seemed to have a life of its own, extending itself from the original four-week visit to ten, I was dividing most of my time between being with Helen and Bill—together and individually—and my parents. The latter understandably felt considerable discomfort and concern for their "nice Jewish son" who had joined the "enemy camp," and who they felt, moreover, had been abducted by a group of very suspect monks. I also traveled around seeing many friends, including a trip to the Abbey of Gethsemani.

I thus spent a great deal of time with my "new family," going over the entire course of my life, sometimes in great detail. Helen and Bill seemed happy to listen, and it was obviously important for me to share with them who I was, at least who I thought I was. In addition, Helen and I began spending a lot of time together, and it was clear that a real bond had been discovered between us. I also spent time alone with Bill, and felt a closeness with him as well. All in all, I was somewhat surprised by Helen's and Bill's openness to share with me their difficulties with the Course, and the general unhappy state of their lives, not to mention with each other.

Thus the honeymoon period for me did not last very long, as the other aspect of Helen's and Bill's lives also became—painfully at first—quite clear. Helen and Bill were far more complex people than they had originally appeared to be. My initial reactions to them were certainly not inaccurate, simply incomplete. The love I felt for Helen and Bill, their dedication to God and *A Course in Miracles* that I recognized from the beginning, never diminished in my mind. But another dimension in them slowly began to dawn on my awareness, that for a while I attempted to stifle. Here were two kind and wise people, clinical psychologists no less, with whom I was able to speak openly of my relationship with God and Jesus, and find total understanding. Moreover, they were, after all, the two persons responsible for this remarkable book that I was beginning to see was the centerpoint of my life: the culmination of my past journey, and foundation for the rest of my time here.

But I could also see the enormous difficulty both of them experienced living in the world, seeming appearances and professional accomplishments to the contrary. And, above all, I could see the mess their interpersonal relationship was in. In short, the situation was hardly the spiritual Camelot I thought I had wandered into. Rather it was, I was beginning to recognize, a complex hotbed of pain and hatred, paradoxically coupled with Helen's and Bill's genuine dedication to God and the Course, not to mention a love and concern for each other.

This paradox in their relationship, to which I shall return in later chapters, was also reflective of the aforementioned paradox within Helen herself: a phenomenon exhibited in her dissociation of two almost entirely separate selves, what *A Course in Miracles* terms the right and wrong minds, representing God and the ego. This paradox, once again, is the central theme in this book, which itself has three parts. Part I details this conflict within Helen—"Heaven and Helen"—as it was manifest in her early years. It is based principally upon Helen's autobiography, which I present in as corrected a form as I felt the license to do, interspersed with my own comments.[3]

Part II largely describes Helen's meeting Bill and taking down *A Course in Miracles*, and I draw heavily here upon the personal material given to Helen during the early weeks of the Course's scribing. In addition, I cite relevant excerpts from Helen's dreams, as well as from letters Helen wrote to Bill, and notes from Bill's journal.

In Part III I return to the period of my association with Helen and Bill, which basically began in 1973, specifically calling upon my personal reminiscences of Helen to discuss her two sides, and the ultimate resolution of this conflict. Once this duality was transcended, only the unity of her one Self remained. Thus Parts I and II span Helen's childhood years to the fall of 1972 when she completed taking down the Course. Part III of the book covers the final period of her life, 1973–1981, when I was so intimately connected with her.

---

3. Helen and Bill had "appointed" me archivist of all the material related to *A Course in Miracles*, including Helen's original notebooks and all subsequent typings of the Course manuscript. This material has been copyrighted by me under the title "The Unpublished Writings of Helen Schucman, Volumes 1-22." These writings also include Helen's above-mentioned autobiography, correspondence between Helen and Bill, and Helen and me, Helen's dreams, undergraduate and graduate school term papers, etc. I quote extensively from these writings in the chapters to follow.

PART I

THE EARLY YEARS

INTRODUCTION TO PART I

The main title of the chapters of this first Part—"Heaven and Helen"—was taken from a paper Helen had written in graduate school, about ten years before the scribing of *A Course in Miracles* began. The paper fulfilled an "assignment to describe a specific problem in our lives, and how we had finally resolved it." The problem Helen chose was her lifetime's preoccupation with God, and she introduced the paper as follows:

> This is the story of my search for God. It began when I was a very little girl, and ended, comparatively recently, on a somewhat tentative note [obviously written, again, years before the Course]. Whether or not you think I found a solution in the end depends very largely on how you look at the problem itself. You could certainly say that, from one point of view, I did not solve it at all, since on the question of God I came to no conclusions. However, you might also say that the problem was not entirely a religious one from the very beginning, so that solution in religious terms is not really essential. Either way, I did get over a great preoccupation with the whole question, and that, in itself, is a solution of a sort.

Obviously, as Helen herself later observed, that was not the real ending of the story. In her unpublished autobiography, an amalgam of several edited versions to be described presently, Helen looked back on this graduate school assignment and described the paper as having traced her early interest in religion

> through a long series of disappointments to a sense of resignation and defeat...a long and discouraging search for God, and was obviously written from a psychological rather than a religious point of view. That was the conceptual framework at which I had arrived at the time, and the level at which I fully expected to remain both professionally and personally.

This book, on the other hand, is written from the opposite point of view—religious rather than psychological—a view to which of course Helen herself later subscribed.

Part I thus draws largely from Helen's graduate school

paper, which served as the basis for the aforementioned autobiography, and which actually exists in eight and a half—mostly similar—versions: the first being the paper handed in at New York University; four and a half more are Helen's initial edits of the paper for the autobiography (the second part was edited by her twice, hence the half); Helen's and my later combined editing; Helen's retyping of our editing, which contained still other changes (Helen was a compulsive editor); finally, there was another graduate school paper dealing with her early years, totally different from the others in the absence of any religious emphasis, though still containing some religious material. In my quotations here I have chosen the form that was most consistently used by Helen, as well as the material I know, based upon my discussions with Helen over the years, to be closest to her own experience.

Finally, I may note that Helen's experiences—which she relegated to the psychological in writing about them—clearly do *not* fall under any psychiatric classification (the Diagnostic and Statistical Manual of the American Psychiatric Association has no category for authentic spiritual experience, let alone scribing), but rather her reactions to this inner voice of Jesus reflected a lifetime's conflict between two parts of her personality: Heaven or Helen, God or the ego.[4] In other words, for Helen the basic question was: Am I a child of God, or a child of the ego? Her entire personal life reflected a vacillation between these two poles, and we begin our story with an account of this conflict.

---

4. The word "ego" is used in the Course to denote the false self that was made in opposition to, and as substitute for the Self of Christ that God created and which is our true spiritual Identity.

Chapter 1

HEAVEN AND HELEN: INTRODUCTION

Far beyond all the material and psychological circumstances of Helen's life there can be found an underlying
tension that runs throughout, almost from birth, and in its
intensity assumes quasi-cosmic proportions. It was a conflict
between two mutually exclusive identities, and a conflict which
appeared never to be truly resolved, certainly not in the perception of this world. The dynamics of this basic conflict are central to an understanding of Helen's life, both prior to, during,
and following her scribing *A Course in Miracles*. Very shortly
after Jesus began dictating the Course to Helen, he gave her
what was called a "special revelation," which actually reflects
Helen's spiritual Self that I referred to in the Preface. He said
to her:

> You are wholly lovely. A perfect shaft of pure light. Before
> your loveliness the stars stand transfixed and bow to the power
> of your will. What do children know of their creation, except
> what their Creator tells them? You were created above the
> angels because your role involves creation as well as protection.
> You who are in the image of the Father need bow only to Him,
> before whom I kneel with you [a reference to an experience
> Helen had prior to the Course's scribing; *see below*, p. 106].

And yet Helen's own view of herself was quite different, and
she felt most uncomfortable with Jesus' estimation of herself
and could not accept it. In a vision that preceded the actual
scribing of the Course, and which we shall quote in its entirety
in Chapter 5, Helen saw herself kneeling before a very holy
priestess, also a symbol of the true innocence of her Self. For
quite a while Helen was unable to look at the priestess' face, in
fear of the condemnation she was sure she would see there.
Finally, she looked directly at the priestess:

> When I did, I burst into tears. Her face was gentle and full of
> compassion, and her eyes were beyond description....She knew
> nothing about me that warranted condemnation. I loved her so
> much that I literally fell on my knees in front of her.

The opening lines of Lesson 93 in the workbook serve as a powerful summarizing statement of Helen's negative self-concept, a concept on one level all of us share. It was one which she successfully hid from the world, but not as successfully from herself.

> You think you are the home of evil, darkness and sin. You think if anyone could see the truth about you he would be repelled, recoiling from you as if from a poisonous snake. You think if what is true about you were revealed to you, you would be struck with horror so intense that you would rush to death by your own hand...(workbook, p. 159).

This conflict was powerfully experienced by Helen in successive events that occurred in southern France and London, during the period when *A Course in Miracles* was still coming through.

> Before falling asleep [in France] one evening, a sense of unbelievable strength and joy rose up in me, beginning in the chest area and rising up into my throat and out into my arms. For several minutes I felt as if I could easily reach out and touch the whole world and everyone in it. My sense of closeness to them all was intensely joyous.
>
> Later [in London] this happy experience had a fearful counterpart in the form of a startlingly clear sensation of horror. One evening I lay down for a brief rest before getting ready for dinner. Most unexpectedly I was seized by a murderous rage so intense and so completely indiscriminate that I jumped up literally shaking. An ugly, hateful thing seemed to rise up in me and take over my body. These two experiences presented such a shocking contrast that they almost seemed to represent Heaven and hell.

Helen described this latter experience to me as her feeling almost possessed by a hatred so intense she believed at that moment she could have gladly destroyed the entire world, the exact counterpart to the former experience when the love—equally intense in its scope—surged through her and embraced the world. Helen also experienced a similar contrast in the period immediately preceding the beginning of the Course. There, the contrast was between a "good" and "evil" priestess. We shall return to this in a later chapter.

On rare occasions Helen expressed to me the painful reality that she "did not know how to love." She knew that her love for me for example—as we shall discuss in Part III—was greatly distorted by her own needs to control her fear of loss and abandonment, as well as to defend against her underlying hatred for everyone and everything she was dependent on.[5] So sensitive to this dynamic in others, and the tragic personal consequences of this albatross the ego hung around our necks, Helen also knew that she could not let go of these same needs in herself.

The persistent conflict of who she was ran through Helen's entire life as does a theme in a symphony. In undergraduate school Helen wrote a composition—probably an exercise in creative writing—that dealt with a fish who wished to be a bird, and then, on being able to fly, wished he were a fish again, yet throughout retaining a fundamental dissatisfaction with his lot in life. Though written with more than a slight tongue-in-cheek, beginning with its title which was borrowed from Shakespeare's second sonnet, the short story reflects Helen's inability to make up her mind about who she was. It begins and ends with a cute note to her professor.

HE ALL ALONE BEWEPT HIS OUTCAST STATE

There is certainly some sort of explanation due you for this, but all I can say is that I've felt it coming on for some time, and it was bound to happen sooner or later. I'll make it as short as possible.

He All Alone Bewept His Outcast State

Once upon a time, at the bottom of the ocean, there lived a sad little fish, and all day long, he would sit on a rock, and sing to himself in a melancholy way, something like this:

"Oh a bird he can fly 'way up to the sky,
As happy as happy can be;
But a poor little fish, 'though he wish and he wish,
Must always stay down in the sea."

---

5. This is referred to in *A Course in Miracles* as our need for specialness, described briefly in the summary found in the Appendix.

He got sadder and sadder, and all the other little fishes began to worry about him, until, one day, they called a meeting, to decide what they could do for him. And a kind silver flying-fish was so sorry for his sad little friend that he agreed to lend him his wings, so he could try being a bird for a while, and see how he liked it. When the unhappy little fish heard about this, he was so pleased that he very nearly forgot himself, and smiled. Then the flying-fish unhooked his wings, and tied them around his friend's neck, and the sad little fish flew up toward the sky, and sat down to rest on a branch of a willow tree that lived beside a little pond. For a while, he was almost happy, being a bird. But bye and bye, he began to get rather melancholy again, and sang a very sad song to himself, that went something like this:

"Way down in the sea, as snug as can be,
A fish he can swim 'round all day.
He's much happier there than a bird in the air
Who must always be flying away."

He got sadder and sadder, and all the birds who lived in the neighborhood tried to comfort him, but it was no use. And then all of a sudden, he remembered that he really wasn't a bird, so he flew back into the ocean, and returned the wings to the little flying-fish, and explained that he was through being a bird. Then he went sadly to his rock, and sang a sad little song to himself, that went very much like this:

"Oh I want to be, instead of just me,
A bird that can swim in the sea,
Or a fish that can fly up into the sky,
As happy as happy can be."

And there he is now, sitting all by himself on the rock at the bottom of the sea. The other fishes swim by sometimes, and try to cheer him up, but nobody seems to be able to help him any more.

So there it is, and I can truthfully say that I am very, very sorry. It won't happen again.

That same theme of intrapersonal conflict was graphically expressed in several dreams. A representative one, the others to be considered later, concerned a bird that could not make up its mind whether its color was blue or gray, or whether it even was a bird at all. The bird's strange and convoluted mental, as well as behavioral, gymnastics in attempting to deal with its precarious life situation were reminiscent of how Helen herself dealt with her own conflicted life situation. The dream came, incidentally, in 1940, when Helen was thirty-one years old. As was her custom, Helen wrote the dream down as if it were a short story.

The Blue-Gray Bird

This story begins with the line, "Once upon a time there was a blue bird," which is only partially true. It would be more accurate to say, "Once upon a time there was a bird who told everybody that he was a blue bird." In point of fact, he was gray. Since this was perfectly obvious, people got the impression that the bird was somewhat confused, but this was not the case at all.

It seems that the bird lived at the time of the American Civil War, which was often called the war between the blues and the grays....[6] He was especially concerned about the final outcome, but he had no way of predicting which side would win. And so he felt it would be safest to prepare for either eventuality.

"Being a gray bird," he reasoned, "the best thing to do is to adopt the position of being blue. Then, if the grays win, they will say, 'this bird is gray even though he insists that he is blue. As long as he is really gray, what difference does it make what he thinks he is? We will not hurt him.' On the other hand, if the blues win, they will say, 'this gray bird evidently believes that he is blue. As long as he thinks he is, what difference does it make what he really is? We will not hurt him.'"...

Meanwhile, the bird was living in a dry and rotting tree, entirely leafless from endless battles. The branches were broken, the roots were shriveled, and the trunk was tilting perilously. It was, however, the only tree left standing after so many years of war, so the bird did not know where else to go.

In order to maintain his equilibrium in the tree, the bird was compelled to lean increasingly in the opposite direction to compensate for the sagging of the branches. As time went on he became quite lop-sided; so much so that he would no longer

---

6. Here and throughout the book, all ellipses are mine, unless otherwise noted.

have been able to keep his balance in a straight tree, even if he ever managed to find one. This, however, did not concern him too much, since the chances of his finding a straight tree any more were rather remote.

What really bothered him were certain contradictory elements in the whole situation, which he found very difficult to reconcile. He recognized that when a bird is in difficulty, it flies away. Yet here was a bird who, in spite of very difficult living conditions, had not only failed to fly away, but had not even tried to do so....

It was possible, he thought.... that he was not really a bird at all. This, of course, would account for his not flying away. But it would also mean that nobody could seriously regard his basic problem as primarily a difficulty in color perception, which would leave him as poorly equipped to deal with peace as with war.

Perhaps fortunately, under the circumstances, he had to admit as a practical bird that managing to live through the war was probably the most he could handle. Armies from both sides kept appearing from nowhere, and smashing at each other under the tree. The blood-drenched ground shook under them, and the noise was ear-splitting. They were probably unaware of the bird and his tree, but the effects on both were devastating. Knowing that the tree could not possibly last much longer, it was probably pointless to worry about what would become of him in a hypothetical peace.

Helen's way of dealing with her "blue-gray," God-ego identity crisis was essentially to accept the conflict as real, deny the spiritual side that connected her to God, and cope somehow with the issue of her ego self's survival in a "blood-drenched" battlefield of a world in which she knew there was ultimately no hope. The rotting tree in which the bird lived represented Helen's self-concept, and the perilous status of the tree's life reflected her own perceived vulnerability living in the world. The bird's becoming lop-sided in his attempts to compensate for the leaning tree suggested Helen's recognition that her own attempts at adjusting to her perceived life situation were also lop-sided and quite maladaptive. There is, as *A Course in Miracles* would later teach, no way out of such a dilemma, unless the basic conflict itself is raised to awareness and questioned. And it was this questioning that Helen feared, for it meant the end of her world as she knew it, a fear we shall return to in a later chapter. Thus, all her defenses were aimed at keeping this conflict out of awareness, and her ego self secure.

Indeed, as mentioned above, Helen's life was characterized from early childhood by the conflict of these two selves, symbolized in the strongly ambivalent nature of her relationship with God and Jesus, not to mention with the Roman Catholic Church. The following chapter presents a synopsis of these early years, highlighting Helen's "search for God."

Chapter 2

HEAVEN AND HELEN: THE EARLY YEARS

Helen's God-ego conflict was symbolized in the religious attitudes of her parents. As discussed earlier, however, these early experiences and parental attitudes are not causative, but simply reflect the different expressions of this conflict. Helen's chemist-metallurgist father Sigmund Cohn was half-Jewish—his mother was Lutheran—but as uninvolved with religion as one could be, having what certainly appeared to be a totally objective non-interest in the subject. Helen's English mother, Rose, was also half-Jewish—her father having been trained as a rabbi—but she bitterly resented her Jewish roots and spent most of her adult years as a spiritual seeker, being involved in many different, if not always traditional, expressions of Christianity.

During Helen's early years, the family had a German governness, Miss Richardson.[7] Helen and she were quite close, and shared a secret. Miss Richardson was a devout Catholic who said her rosary regularly, and Helen was attracted to the almost magical quality of the blue beads and the prayers that accompanied the daily ritual. However, Miss Richardson told her she could not have a rosary because she was not Catholic. Moreover, every Sunday morning, while ostensibly going to the park, they would go to a Catholic church, which Helen later described as being for her then "one of the most beautiful places I ever saw in my whole life." Again, not being Catholic, Helen was told she could not go in, and so she would wait in the vestibule until Mass was over. Yet Helen yearned to be inside.

> I could see the flowers and the candles and the statues through the little space between the two large doors. Sometimes I heard

---

7. At least this was the name given her by Helen in her autobiography. Helen always had a phobia against using people's correct names (*see below*, pp. 240f), and so in the autobiography no true name is given for anyone, and her parents' names are never stated. I supply the actual names here except for the governness, whose real name I never did learn, although she was not English as Helen had reported.

music and a man's voice saying things I did not understand. There was a lovely smell, too. Once I sneaked round to a little chapel on the side of the church. There was a statue of a lovely lady there [Mary], with light around her head and flowers and candles in the little garden in front of her. Everyone there had beads like Miss Richardson's. I wanted to stay there but decided not to because I was afraid Miss Richardson would not approve because I wasn't a Catholic. But I made up my mind to be a Catholic when I grew up so I could stay as long as I liked.

A Catholic friend of Miss Richardson was also a governness, taking care of a Catholic girl. The girl and Helen became friends, and she spoke to Helen about the advantages of being Catholic, of praying to God and the Blessed Virgin, and receiving what you wanted. Moreover, Helen was told, unless one were Catholic one would burn in hell. Panic-stricken at this thought, Helen spoke to Miss Richardson who suggested she speak to her parents, since children "generally have the same religion as their parents do and maybe they could explain things to me." However, she attempted to comfort Helen by telling her that she need not be afraid of hell because she would pray for her.

Helen did speak with her father about the subject, but was told that he did not believe in God and had no interest in religion, and that he felt that people should decide about religion for themselves. Helen asked him about her mother, who was not home at the time, and he said that she had "some sort of religion," but that he did not know much about it. It was obvious to Helen, however, that he did not think very much of it, and moreover was not particularly interested in it. Helen pressed on, and she and her father had one of the very few "real talks" they ever had. He explained to Helen that one could be religious without believing in hell, a relief to Helen, and that he did not think she had to worry about the subject. At Helen's urging, he then taught her a Jewish prayer, as Helen desperately wanted to be something, and being Jewish would have sufficed. The prayer began with the words: "Lord God of Israel...." Helen quickly forgot the rest. Helen then asked again about her mother's religion, and specifically whether she might become Jewish, but her father simply laughed and said that "it was not likely."

28

Helen seemed satisfied for the moment, and happily returned to her room armed against hell with her new prayer and the knowledge that she was Jewish.

> That night while she [Miss Richardson] said her rosary, I said "Lord God of Israel" over and over to myself. I was very excited about being Jewish. I had suspected for a long time that there was something missing about me, and now that I was Jewish I hoped everything would be all right. I did not mention my religion to my mother, though. Somehow I felt she might not like it.

Helen was about five years old at the time, and a year or so later Miss Richardson returned to Germany, promising Helen to continue to pray for her. Helen kept on reciting her prayer, but her faith in the power of the "Lord God of Israel" to protect her ended abruptly when a feigned stomachache designed to keep her mother from leaving her at night resulted in an emergency (though totally unnecessary) appendectomy. Screaming "Lord God of Israel" as she was being wheeled into the operating room and anesthetized, Helen in characteristic fashion blamed God for the debacle. While recuperating in the hospital, Helen decided there was probably no Jewish God anyway, which was why her father stopped believing in Him, and so there was no longer any point in her being Jewish.

During her hospital stay, Helen and her mother had a relatively rare conversation about religion, with Helen hoping that perhaps she would come up with a religious solution for her. Unlike her atheistic and detached father, Helen's mother was quite willing to speak openly on the subject, as Helen indicates:

> She said she was still searching. But she did believe in God, but she was not sure how yet. She told me all about her religions ever since she was a little girl. I was very much surprised to discover that she had once been mostly Jewish herself. She did not, however, seem to like Jews very much....My mother herself was now a Theosophist. She tried to explain this to me, but I did not get very far with it. She looked calm and happy as she told me about it, and a sort of glow came over her face. I tried to understand what she was saying, but it did not make much sense to me.

In answer to Helen's request, her mother then taught her a prayer.

It was simple and fairly short and she said it to me until I knew it by heart. Then she said she was very glad I was interested in religion and urged me to ask God to help me. She was certain that He would show me the way. She seemed to me to be having trouble in finding the way herself but I did not like to mention this. After all she was trying to help. She said that when we got home we would say our prayer together every evening. I said I thought that would be very nice. We gave it up after a few days. I was not really sorry. I did not want to tell her, but I never really believed the prayer was much good. I completely forgot it myself within a month.

Helen's ambivalence towards God was expressed in another college composition, where the protagonist, six-year-old Elizabeth Jane, sounds very much like the child Helen of the autobiography.

God and Elizabeth Jane

When Elizabeth Jane was six, her father died, and her mother explained that God had taken him home. Now Elizabeth Jane loved God, and was accustomed to having Him do rather unaccountable things, so this didn't especially surprise her. But when she understood that she wouldn't see her father again until she got to Heaven, she felt that, while of course God did only what was right, He owed her some sort of explanation for this. Elizabeth Jane had always believed that God lived near the tall evergreen tree that grew in the garden behind the house, and that, if she ever really wanted to talk to Him about anything, she could find Him there. She went into the garden now.

Elizabeth Jane sat down on the grass, under the evergreen tree, where she waited for God a very long time. She watched the heavy cones that wept from the tree, and listened to the wind that flew through the branches, rattling them against each other. But God did not seem to be in the garden that day. When the sky began to get dark, she got up, and went slowly into the house.

That night, Elizabeth Jane's mother came to kiss her goodnight, and she sat down on the bed and took her daughter in her arms and cried. Then she put her into bed, and kissed her, and told her to remember to say her prayers before she went to bed. Elizabeth Jane nodded gravely. Her mother tucked in the blankets, and said, "Don't forget, darling," in a shaky sort of voice. Elizabeth Jane nodded gravely again.

When her mother had closed the door, Elizabeth Jane lay in bed, and thought about her father, and about the tears in her mother's voice, and about the evergreen tree. Suddenly she remembered her promise to her mother. So she closed her eyes, and folded her hands, and said, "Dear God," and stopped. Then she turned over and went to sleep.

Some time passed in the autobiographical account, and Helen's next mention of religion was in reference to an experience she had at the age of twelve, when the family went to Europe. The last part of the trip was a visit to Lourdes, as Helen's mother was interested in seeing the famous shrine to the Blessed Virgin Mary. Helen was, in her own words, "deeply impressed" by the grotto piled high with thrown-away crutches and braces, and "loved" the statue of the Blessed Virgin standing atop a large rock, which she could see from the balcony of her hotel bedroom. She even bought herself a rosary, a medal of Mary, and a bottle filled with the holy and healing water that flowed from the rock on which the statue stood. Helen and her mother went to Mass at the grotto, and stayed

for a beautiful service afterwards. It was Saturday and there were even more flowers and music and processions than usual. People were praying everywhere. It was all very, very beautiful. I asked my mother if she had ever been a Catholic and she said no. But you could see she was weakening.

Extremely moved by her experiences, and tempted to believe in God again, Helen decided to make a deal with Him. Standing on her balcony that evening, she told God that she would believe in Him and His miracles, and become a Catholic as well, if He would send *her* a miracle.

"Please, God," I said, aloud, "I know I'm not a Catholic, but if all of this is true would you send me a miracle so I can believe in you?"

I had already decided what the miracle should be. I would close my eyes and say three Hail Mary's. Then if I saw a meteor in the sky when I opened my eyes that would be my miracle.... When I opened my eyes the sky was full of shooting stars. I watched in stunned silence, and then whispered, "It's my miracle. God really did send it. Look, oh look! It's my miracle!"

Helen's joy and faith were short-lived, however. As the sky darkened again, she began to rationalize away her miracle: the tour guide had told them of the frequency of meteor showers this time of year—one can be easily fooled by this kind of thing, she reasoned; and, finally, if the shooting stars were really God's doing, then He would have seen to it that she believed in His miracle, which she was fast beginning not to.

> I had become deeply suspicious of the whole thing. I even got a little bit angry about it. Perhaps, I said to myself, the water and the healings and the crutches were all like the meteor shower. People just thought they were miracles. It all could happen that way.

On the other hand, Helen went on, the miracle did happen as she asked; and besides, what if God became angry at her ingratitude and disbelief?

> If there were a God he[8] might not like the way I was taking his miracle. Perhaps I was not being appreciative. If God had taken the trouble to send a miracle especially for me, he might not take kindly to all this skepticism. And if there were a God, then there might also be a hell for people who did not appreciate him.

Unable to resolve her problem, which was rapidly assuming major proportions in her mind, Helen finally decided she did not need to make a decision right away. And there the matter of God, miracles, and the Catholic Church rested, so to speak. However, throughout her life Helen never lost her fascination and attraction for Catholicism. Years later, she reflected on this period:

> When I had been younger I used to drop in to Catholic Churches quite often. I was on friendly terms with the Blessed

---

8. Interestingly enough—in keeping with her atheistic pose during graduate school, which I discuss below—Helen here did not capitalize pronouns relating to God. Later on, however, she was very insistent about the use of capitals for most words associated with the Divine. *See below*, p. 365.

Virgin, but disregarded God entirely. I always went down the side of the church where her statue was.... I liked the Church and the candles and especially the services devoted to the Blessed Virgin. I used to join the singing and bless myself and feel like everybody else.

When I decided to be a great poet [see below] I bought myself a silver rosary and went to a Catholic Church every day. I knelt down like everybody else and recited my rosary, but instead of saying the "Hail Mary's," I said the name of a famous poet instead.... When I ... [decided to be] a great painter I used the names of great painters. In my role as a great singer I recited names of operas on the beads.

As for her mother and the experience at Lourdes, Helen wrote:

My mother had changed her own religion again, but she did not discuss this much with me and I did not like to raise the question myself. I still wore my medal of the Blessed Virgin but I had not reached a definite conclusion about my miracle. I thought of it every once in a while but I always held off taking a firm stand.

Religion, however, once again reared its head about a year after the experience at Lourdes, through the family maid Georgia. Georgia and Helen had been close for some time, but their friendship deepened when the family moved to a smaller apartment after Helen's brother Adolph, fourteen years her senior, married and moved out. Georgia came from Alabama and had no family in New York, so the Cohns, and particularly Helen, became her family. Georgia was a deeply religious Baptist, and Helen developed a strong interest in her religion.

Her church thought hell was real, she told me, but I gathered that she herself believed in a God who was quite friendly and did not go around scaring people with hell-fire and damnation. Besides, although he did not bother his children by making too many unreasonable demands on them he did not let them down, and arranged it so that things always came out all right in the end. This sounded good enough to me. I was none too sure that everything would come out all right myself.

Helen went to Georgia's room every evening to read the Bible. "It was a nice thing to do before going to bed," Helen observed. Then one Sunday Georgia invited Helen to accompany her to church, and Helen could scarcely contain her excitement as they traveled way uptown together.

> Georgia said that God would be waiting for us and she was usually right. Before the service, Georgia took me right up in front of the church and introduced me to the minister, who said "God bless you" to me. Then Georgia and I sat down together and waited for the Lord.
>
> The people in Georgia's church sang songs that were very different from anything I had ever heard. They were simple and lovely little melodies. The people sang them over and over, beginning softly and getting louder and louder each time. It got so beautiful you could burst into tears. A number of people did. But most of them became very happy and began to clap their hands and stamp their feet to the music.[9] Some of them even stood up in their seats or went out into the aisles and began to shout. I could tell they were feeling wonderful even though I could not understand most of the words they were shouting. I was not sure they were even speaking English.[10] It was obvious, though, that they were on friendly terms with God and were accustomed to speaking to Him this way. At first I was surprised by all this. I had always addressed God formally, and hardly with intimacy. I did not know what to make of this approach for a while, and even suspected it might be a mistake. But soon my feet began to tap with the music. A little later I was clapping my hands and still later I was singing out loud just like everyone else.
>
> Georgia was swaying back and forth with her eyes closed, but every once in a while she would look toward me and smile. I was feeling happy and very much at home. Then the minister gave us a wonderful talk. He told us all about God and Heaven and salvation. He said this world was not our real home and wonderful things were waiting for us. Some day, he said, we would all be with the Lord forever. All we needed was faith. Faith was the gift of God and anyone who asked him for it would be given it.... we sang some more and then everyone went outside to shake hands with the minister. When my turn

---

9. This would seem to have been the genesis of Helen's lifetime love of Negro spirituals. *See* p. 417.

10. Helen here was referring to the pentecostal phenomenon of "speaking in tongues," one of the "gifts of the Holy Spirit" described in the New Testament.

came he asked me how I liked the service and I said it was just wonderful. He said I should come again and patted me on the shoulder.

Now that I had been specially invited I went to church with Georgia as often as possible.... In the church I prayed and sang with everybody else, but outside when I tried to talk to God I was never really sure anyone was there to listen. Something was missing. And finally one day I found out what it was. Georgia took me one Sunday to a baptism service. People in long white robes stood at the side of a marble pool in front of the church. The minister, who was now a great friend of mine, stood in the pool and laid each of the people gently back into the water. Afterwards, they walked out of the pool on the other side and joined the ranks of the redeemed. I was very much impressed. Before the ceremony the minister had said, "Those who are to be baptized today have come to fulfill the wishes of the Lord himself. He has told us that we must be baptized to be saved. Unless you are baptized you cannot be pure in heart, and unless you are pure in heart you cannot see God."[11] That's it, I thought to myself. You have to be baptized before you can see God. I had not been baptized. That was what was missing.

Helen discussed this first with Georgia, who fervently recommended this "most wonderful experience of her life."

She said when you get baptized the Spirit of the Lord descends on you and works a miracle in your heart, and afterwards you have a big party. Baptism makes you a real child of God. After all, the Bible says you are supposed to be baptized. Georgia took the Bible and showed me the passage. That was what it said, all right. There was no doubt about it.

Helen made up her mind: she should be baptized. She spoke to the minister, who explained that the baptized are expected to join the church. This presented a problem Helen had not foreseen. The minister suggested Helen give it some thought.

I went home and thought it over. Things were more complicated than I had realized. I had not expected that joining the

---

11. One of Helen's very favorite Bible passages was from John's first letter, 3:2f: "Beloved, now are we the sons of God, and it doth not yet appear what we shall be: but we know that, when he shall appear, we shall be like him; for we shall see him as he is. And every man that hath this hope in him purifieth himself, even as he is pure." *See* pages 35, 196, and 599 in the text.

church was part of being baptized, and I felt that one should at least believe in God before taking a big step like that.

Helen also spoke to a Baptist minister near her home, but was told the same thing: "He would be glad to baptize me and accept me as a church member. Those seemed to be the rules." However, Helen finally found a minister who held a special monthly baptism service, and he agreed to baptize the thirteen-year-old. He suggested, however, that perhaps it would be a good idea for Helen to ask her parents first, especially as her father was Jewish.

Helen complied. Her mother was pleased and promised to buy Helen the pocketbook she had desired, while her father had no feeling whatsoever, other than that he felt Helen should do what she wished. And so Helen returned to the minister, and prepared to be baptized the following Sunday.

> Georgia came to my baptism as my witness and my friend. She helped me get ready and put on my white robe. She was very excited and kept telling me that I was going to have the most wonderful experience of my life. I hoped that she was right. After the ceremony I got dressed and went to the minister's study to get my baptismal certificate while Georgia put my wet things away in a bag we had brought with us....
>
> On the way home Georgia said we should have some sort of party, so she treated me to ice cream and cake and bought me a box of candy afterwards. I enjoyed the party, but when we got home I began to feel sad. It was not really different now that I had been baptized. I went on going to church with Georgia a while longer, just in case. Then I began to go only once in a while, and finally just [stopped altogether].... There was no use. I did not have faith. Georgia said it was probably the work of the devil and suggested that I pray anyway. She also promised to pray for me. God would not let me down, she was sure, now that I had been properly baptized. I was very fond of Georgia. She had been very kind to me. I thanked her for her prayers and let it go at that.

I remember Helen's husband Louis (pronounced *Louie*) once telling me how important a figure Georgia had been for Helen, since she was the one who "had given Helen her religious foundation," and how much Helen had always loved her. Georgia remained with Helen and Louis, incidentally, until around

1970, when she had become almost blind and entered a nursing home. She and Helen remained in contact for a while after, and then Helen lost track of her old friend, one of the very, very few people in her life to whom she exhibited no ambivalence.

Helen's young life seemed to deteriorate from this point. Entering adolescence, an ongoing weight problem suddenly assumed almost cosmic proportions. She became the butt of cruel jokes by her friends, and boys paid little or no attention to her.

> I was pretty miserable and did what I always did when I was miserable. I ate. The more I ate the fatter I got. I began to refuse all invitations and came home right after school and stayed there. I had not found God and it was beginning to look as though I was not wanted much on earth either.

Helen's mother was supportive and tried to be helpful. She had by this time turned her religious interest to Christian Science, and so brought Helen to a "most wonderful" practitioner, one who had "shown her the light."

> I needed a bit of light myself, so I agreed to try the practitioner. My mother gave me a book to read first. It did not make much impression on me one way or the other, and I went to the practitioner more in desperation than in faith. The practitioner spoke a lot about God, gave me a lot of arguments with the glibness born of frequent repetition, but I could not help thinking that by her way of argument you could prove just about anything. I realized very soon that I was up against the same old problem of faith. You have to believe first and find proof afterwards. There was no point in going through all that again.

Eventually, *without God's help*, Helen slimmed down, although her weight was an ongoing problem and concern throughout her life. In her later years Helen was successful in containing her weight, but at great expense of mental energy. She was constantly preoccupied with the invasion of extra calories into her system, and because of all her "fat thoughts," I used to tease her about being the fattest thin person I ever knew.

In general, Helen's high school years and on into college were unhappy ones. Moreover, she had decided at some point that she would make her mark in life by being a great writer,[12] yet there was a serious problem in Helen's writing aspirations—her great fear of putting words down on paper.

> I had no doubt that some day I would be a great writer, probably an internationally famous novelist. I would live by myself and write....In view of my secret goal, the intense difficulty I had in writing anything at all was particularly hard to cope with. Further, I was so sensitive about anything I wrote that even when I finally succeeded in getting something down on paper I was likely to refuse to hand it in. It was difficult to deny that this was not in keeping with my future career as I envisioned it. I finally managed, though shakily, to work it into my role as an intellectual and a great writer-to-be, although I was never too comfortable with it. As an intellectual I was hypercritical and as a writer I was super-sensitive. Some day these attributes would add to my eminence, even though they were hard to handle at present.

In light of Helen's later conflict over scribing *A Course in Miracles*, her early difficulties in writing assume greater interest. While Helen was taking down the Course, Jesus explained this to her:

> Your earlier acute problem in writing things down came from a *much* earlier [i.e., in a past life] misuse of very great scribal abilities. These were turned to secret rather than shared advantage, depriving the ability of its miraculous potential, and diverting it to possession.

More of this later, but to continue now with Helen's autobiography:

> Meanwhile I read a lot of philosophy [Plato was always a favorite of Helen] and became happily involved in systems of thought in general, and logic in particular. Here at last was surety of a kind. Whatever might happen in an uncertain world, one could still go safely from given premises to the proper conclusions....I loved logic and math and anything that

---

12. Helen at other times, as mentioned above, also considered careers as a world famous painter and opera singer; her singing teacher was even able to arrange an audition for a radio program, yet Helen developed laryngitis "which lasted so long that my singing career somehow got laid aside permanently."

gave me the feeling of being a nice, tight, closed system. This I felt I could cope with. I almost had a fit the first time I ran up against inductive math. I felt betrayed by my best friend. I majored in philosophy, which offers excellent opportunities for arguing on both sides of practically any question, and I had a very good time.... [Thus] I played around with syllogisms for years and loved them, but to the business of living I paid as little attention as possible.

Helen's fascination with logic successfully filled her need to manipulate form, without paying particular attention to the underlying meaning or content of her fear of relating to the world. She loved, for example, the idea that one can logically prove anything—whether true or false—once one accepts a beginning premise. This dynamic of "form at the expense of content" was a major component in Helen's massive defensive system against the meaning of God, and was characteristic of her entire life. It is interesting to note, as will be described more fully later, how in *A Course in Miracles* Jesus made use of Helen's syllogistic skills, but shifted the underlying content from Helen's fear to his love.

While a sophomore at New York University, Helen met Louis Schucman, who was a senior working in the library. One of their early encounters involved Helen's pleading with Louis to allow her to keep a reserved book an extra day as she had not yet completed her class assignment. Louis refused at first, but eventually succumbed to Helen's charms and promises to have the book back promptly. Helen took the book, with full intentions of returning it as promised. But while reading it next to an open window, the book "flew" out of her hands into a most inaccessible alley way. She very sheepishly had to inform Louis of what happened, but despite the fiasco of trying to retrieve the book (I believe they eventually did so), they became good friends, finding in each other a suitable partner: intellectuals somewhat uncomfortable with the opposite sex, and, in fact, with the whole "business of living."

Louis proposed to Helen three months later. Helen's father predictably had no opinion on the subject: as he said to Helen, he hardly knew the young man. Helen's mother on the other hand, while having some reservations since Louis was Jewish, nonetheless was enthusiastic, in large part because she was afraid Helen would never receive another proposal.

> My mother asked me if I were sure he was really the right one and I said I was, not really knowing what else to say. Then my mother kissed me and began to arrange for a party. And so, it seemed, we were engaged.

Helen and Louis were married a few months afterwards on May 26, 1933, in a short ceremony held, to please Louis' parents, in a reformed rabbi's office. Shortly before the wedding Helen did a characteristic thing:

> The Sunday before we were married Georgia made a special consecration for us, and...I really appreciated it. I was quite uneasy about the marriage. I went for a thoughtful walk the afternoon before the ceremony, and what with one thing and another I stopped off at a Catholic Church. I did not say any prayers but I lit two candles, one for my future husband and one for me. It seemed like a good thing to do.

The ceremony was over within ten minutes, seemingly to everyone's relief. And then Helen and Louis returned to their respective parents' homes to study for final exams. Many years later, Helen described the wedding in a letter to Bill:

> We had a horrible wedding (I claim I wasn't there), and my brother yelled at me, and my mother said she hoped everything would come out all right even though Jonathan [Louis][13] was a Russian Jew. My father came to the wedding, of course, but he *really* wasn't there. Fortunately, I had to study for an exam and so did Jonathan, so the whole thing blew over quietly.

Louis graduated that spring and went into the book business, his love, while Helen still had two years of school to complete. They lived at first with Helen's parents, as they had no money. The state of being married seemed to have had little or no effect on either of them. Shortly after Helen's college graduation, her mother became very ill. The doctor suggested she be relieved of all household responsibilities, and so Helen's parents moved to a hotel, while Helen and Louis took a small apartment nearby.

---

13. *See* pp. 240f for a discussion of Helen's renaming of Louis.

Georgia was no longer needed by the Cohns, but they felt responsible for her as she was "virtually a member of the family." Since Helen and Louis could not afford a maid, and Helen was totally unable to run a household, Helen's parents continued to pay Georgia's salary so she could work for Helen and Louis: "I was very grateful for this decision. I did not know how to cook, and Georgia was a very old friend and it was nice to have her around."

Helen's marriage to Louis triggered deep-seated insecurities that manifested in excessive and obsessive concerns about his health. And she once again returned to the magic the Catholic Church offered her:

> Now, in order to protect Louis from illness, disaster and sudden death...I began going to the Catholic Church again. This time it became a real prison. I had to go to Mass every day, and to special services in the evening. I made Novenas all the time. I recited prayers over and over, and had to make sure that each one was said exactly as given in the prayer-book. I said prayers all day long....Louis is Jewish. He is not religious, but he has a sincere interest in Jewish things. He didn't like my going to Church all the time, but he didn't interfere.

Helen later told me that Louis' constant fear was that he would wake up in the morning to find that Helen had been baptized a Roman Catholic.

Helen's unhappiness continued, however, as she did not really know what to do with her life. Joining Louis in the bookstore did not really work out well; it was his life, not hers. And then Helen became very ill. Years of compulsive overeating followed by equally compulsive dieting—her weight rising and falling in great rapidity—caused a serious gall bladder condition. For several months Helen delayed the inevitable operation, but nights of screaming nightmares coupled with increased pain forced her finally to accede to entering the hospital. The doctor assured her that the surgery was routine, and that she should be home in a week or so. But Helen did not believe him, and so still again she turned to God for help.

> That evening I sat down and tried to get organized. I did not like the idea of having this operation all by myself. It

would be much easier, I thought, if I believed God would take care of me. There was a chance, I supposed, that he existed after all. Certainly the fact that I did not believe in him had nothing to do with his existence one way or another. In any case, there could be no harm in trying a compromise. I would put the operation in God's hands in case he existed, and if things turned out all right I might even be able to believe in him again. There was nothing to lose by trying. I said the Lord's Prayer, put my operation in the hands of God, and went to the hospital the next day with my medal of the Blessed Virgin around my neck.

The operation, as it turned out, was anything but simple, and Helen barely survived it. She remained unconscious for a long time and was not discharged for over four months. One of Helen's nurses was a very religious Catholic, and seeing Helen's medal, assumed she was too. Later on, the nurse told Helen that she had been praying for her every day, and had offered a Mass of thanksgiving when Helen regained consciousness.

God had been very good to me, she said, and it was a real miracle I had pulled through. She said I ought to be very thankful. I did not see it that way myself. I was very angry about the whole thing and stayed angry about it for years. If this were God's idea of making things turn out all right, I thought, he certainly had a nasty sense of humor. The nurse did not approve of my attitude and said, rather stiffly, that she would continue to pray for me anyhow. God would make me see things properly. She did not think I appreciated all he had done for me....I told the nurse that I could not stop her from praying, of course, but added that I would appreciate her not asking God for another miracle, at least until I was strong enough to cope with this one. I said that, all things considered, I was lucky to have survived it. I was, in fact, willing to wait quite a long time before the next one, and suggested that she tell God there was no hurry. The nurse replied that it was obvious I needed prayers, regardless of how I felt about it, and that she would continue trying to help me in spite of my lack of appreciation for the miracle God had bestowed on me. I felt anything but grateful, and told her so. What I really needed was to feel better and get out of the hospital, and it did not seem likely to me that her prayers would help.

When Helen was finally discharged, her pre-hospitalization depression returned, for she realized that nothing had really changed.

> I was convinced that nobody really cared much about me, a belief that neither my husband nor Georgia could shake. If there were a God, which I very much doubted, probably he did not care much, either. I felt abandoned by earth as well as Heaven.... It was years before it dawned on me that I might have been looking at things the wrong way. Having conceded this much I began to review my life thus far, and among other things I went over my long painful search for God. It was clear that I had got nowhere with that. Admittedly, the fault may have been mine. Perhaps, as the nurse had said in the hospital, I did not look at God properly, and did not appreciate all that he had done for me there. I had had trouble accepting a miracle once before, as I remembered. Maybe I had set up the whole project badly from the very beginning. Nevertheless, people can set up projects only as best they can, and in my way I felt I had tried. There was no point in speculating about how the search might have turned out had I done it differently. If God did exist, which I very much doubted, he might someday bring up the question of religion himself. If he did not exist, well, then that is the way it is. For myself, the project was over.

Five years after Helen's marriage, her mother died "while she was considering the possibilities of Unity [the Unity Church, now thought of as a form of New Age Christianity], but she did not have time to come to conclusions about it. Georgia took care of Helen's father, until he died some years later, and then she returned to Helen and Louis.

Helen closed her term paper this way:

> Of the Old Gods only Georgia remains. She is something of a miracle herself. Her hair is white but otherwise she has changed very little.... She is still very religious, and whenever she goes to church she always says a prayer for my husband and myself. She says the Lord will reveal himself to me yet.
>
> Well, perhaps he will. For myself, I do not think about him very often any more. It's nice to think of Georgia praying for us, though. And I still have my medal of the Blessed Virgin, attached to my key ring, and look at it every once in a while. I

would hate to lose it, somehow. Beyond that, I do not think about God very often any more.

This essentially closes the first part of Helen's life. The split in Helen's mind, so clearly expressed in her conflict with Jesus and *A Course in Miracles*, is foreshadowed in these early years. During the next period, that eventually led Helen to graduate school, preparing her for professional life as a psychologist and the later scribing of *A Course in Miracles*, she had several dreams that also reflected this split. In addition, Helen had a vision that was perhaps the most stunning of her life. This period, including the vision and dreams, is the subject of the following chapter, as we begin Part II.

PART II

THE SCRIBING OF
A COURSE IN MIRACLES

INTRODUCTION TO PART II

The actual scribing of *A Course in Miracles* was foreshadowed by several events—inner and outer—that comprise the first four chapters in this Part. These included Helen's decision to enter graduate school in clinical psychology, the circumstances that led her to the Columbia-Presbyterian Medical Center and meeting William Thetford, and a series of visions, dreams, and psychic phenomena that prepared her for the beginning of the dictation.

The next four chapters discuss the scribing of the Course itself, presenting portions of the personal material that were subsequently deleted from the printed edition. These illustrate, as will be discussed in more detail in the chapters themselves, the intensely personal nature of Helen's relationship with Jesus, and the specific help he provided for her and Bill in understanding the Course theoretically, as well as learning how to apply its principles to their lives.

This Part also presents excerpts from a series of letters Helen had written to Bill during the summer preceding the beginning of the Course's scribing, as well as notes from a journal Bill had kept about one year into the dictation. These reflect the sincerity and dedication with which Helen and Bill approached the task of learning and practicing the Course's teachings on forgiveness. The letters and journal notes remain perhaps the brightest personal light in the sky of their twenty-three-year relationship.

Chapter 3

LEADING TO *A COURSE IN MIRACLES*—A
(from ca. 1938)

Preparing for Graduate School

During the period following her ill-fated gall bladder operation, Helen's misery and depression continued. She even consulted two psychoanalysts. The first, an orthodox Freudian,
did not prove to be very helpful, as Helen basically knew and
understood all that the analyst could offer her. It was also very
difficult for Helen to accept help from anyone, given her fear of
joining. On an even deeper level, however, psychotherapy was
useless to Helen since her neurosis followed another logic, as
we shall see presently and will discuss in greater depth later in
the book. It was during this first analysis that she discussed
her recurring experience of feeling the presence of a man
behind her left shoulder, trying to get her attention which she
steadfastly refused to give. Helen certainly knew the identity
of the man (she would have spelled it with a capital "M"), from
whose crucifixion two thousand years ago a British psychic
once told her she had never recovered. Yet she kept his
identity a secret from her analyst. Without one's understanding her motivated reluctance to turn to Jesus, any
attempts to help Helen would have been pointless and in vain.
Helen's second therapist, a Horneyan analyst, ended up becoming Helen's "patient"; in a subtle reversal of roles, Helen
proved to be very helpful to her.

This period of depression, basically spanning her twenties
and thirties, seemed to end with Helen's decision to return to
school and study for her doctorate in psychology. This is how
she described it in her autobiography:

> When I turned away from my research into Heaven, I
> thought I would try research on earth instead, realizing I had
> better start to search for a better way to spend the rest of my
> life. This, I recognized, might be difficult, since I still knew
> very little about the world, but I felt I might just as well get

started. Georgia still took care of the housekeeping and we had no children to occupy my time.

At first I tried the book business again, but while it was clearly the right place for my husband it was equally clearly the wrong one for me. I began to go there less and less frequently and usually quarrelled with my husband when I did. We just could not seem to get along together in business. I began to feel trapped in a bad situation without a clear-cut idea of how to get out of it. For a time it began to look as though my search for a place on earth might end up as ineffectually as my search for Heaven, even though I was singularly free to do whatever I wanted.... In the course of looking around I found a field of especial interest to me. I realized that I would need an awful lot of training and experience, and I found the prospect rather overwhelming at first. I decided that the time involved did not really matter much, though.... [and] my father did not mind helping with whatever expenses might be entailed.

Louis was very supportive and encouraging to Helen during this period. Indeed, he was always an important figure in Helen's adult life, albeit at times a seemingly secondary one, as I shall discuss later in the book. It was actually Louis who first suggested to Helen that she consider returning to school for a doctorate in psychology. Knowing Helen's intuitive ability to be helpful to people in distress, as she had been with family and friends over the years, Louis recognized the waste involved in her remaining home doing nothing. And yet Helen was reluctant to return to school.

My husband showed exemplary patience during our long and frequent discussions about my potential career, but I was so uncertain that it took years before I arrived at the decision. Even after I had more or less decided to be a psychologist, my efforts were limited for a long time to endless discussion with my husband, writing for course catalogues, and talking about training possibilities with college advisors. Actually I did not really know what psychology was about. I had only a vague sort of notion that it had some of the answers I needed. I finally made up my mind to overcome my fears and enter graduate school...I was determined to get top grades, and studied compulsively, haunted by a strong fear of failing and almost fiercely driven to succeed.... Having failed in the search for Heaven I was grimly determined to succeed on earth.

Yet the story is more interesting than that. Regarding her professional career, Helen had

> planned every step with obsessional care, and made decisions only after wearying and interminable ruminations. Yet it was not my own decisions which dictated the major professional directions I took. For example, I applied to and was accepted into a doctoral program which, unknown to me, had been officially closed to new admissions. A student whom I sat next to in the school cafeteria suggested a potential thesis topic to me, which was of great interest to the head of my department, although I was unaware of it at the time. He not only approved my admission to the program, but agreed to be my chairman.

As Helen was beginning to experience, her professional "choices" from this point on in her life had nothing to do with *her* logic or wishes. Rather, they were based on a decision made on an entirely different level that related to her willingness to become the scribe of *A Course in Miracles*. This decision obviously related directly to Helen's very close relationship with Jesus. Whether or not she chose to accept the fact, Helen was deeply involved with Jesus all of her life, as later chapters will discuss.

In Helen's mind, nonetheless, making the decision to go to New York University and become a psychologist resolved her frustrating and fruitless search for God. She now believed that she was free at last to make her mark in the world. Regarding God, Helen concluded that she had done her best to find Him, but He had not done very well in helping her. And therefore, so much for Him: she was now a rational and objective scientist, and that would be her religion. An extraordinary experience on the New York City subway, however, if she had paid any attention to it, would have indicated to her the folly of such an idea. It demonstrated that in the end Georgia had been right: God *would* reveal Himself to Helen, although, as Helen later wrote, "It took me a long time to recognize it and still longer to accept it. In fact, I was bitterly opposed to the whole idea for quite a while."

51

The Subway Experience

Helen's account of this experience, which begins the second part of the autobiography—the first part being her graduate school paper I discussed above (*see* pp. 17f)—was characteristically somewhat embroidered in the *setting* Helen gave it, though not in the *experience* itself. Rather than edit down Helen's written account without her assistance, I have decided to reproduce it as Helen wrote it (and re-wrote it). My recollection of Helen's recounting this experience to me, incidentally, as well as what is stated in one of the versions of the narrative, was that it occurred many years *prior* to her entering graduate school ("after I had been married some five years or so"), yet it appears in all the other versions of her autobiography while she was attending school. If my memory is indeed correct, as is my understanding of this discrepancy, the shift in date came from Helen's feeling that it was effective from a literary point of view (a frequent concern of hers) to place the experience while she was attending school, rather than earlier. This temporal change would then provide a sharp contrast between the striking religious nature of the experience and the "angry atheism" she adopted during the period she was at New York University. Here then is Helen's description:

> As it turned out, the subject of God was not a closed issue after all. It came up again in a most unexpected way. The first of a long and startling series of episodes took place at a particularly unlikely time. I had shifted from agnosticism to angry atheism, having reached a point where the mere mention of religion or God irritated me. I was heavily armed with "scientific" weapons, prepared and even eager to do battle with ideas even remotely religiously toned. If anyone was intent on pursuing the subject I was apt to become rather insulting, and if I happened to come upon a religious discussion on the radio or TV I would snap the set off sharply, afterwards directing a few choice comments in its direction.
>
> I was also angry at people. The chip on my shoulder kept falling off and I spent a good deal of time and energy looking around for things to get angry at. Naturally, they were not hard to find. People seemed to have developed an exploitative tendency and a lack of consideration the extent of which I had

not previously suspected. I felt increasingly deprived, unappreciated and resentful, but did not suspect that I was actually quite depressed and anxious. I firmly though rather simple-mindedly believed I had overcome religious superstition at last and, arriving at the one remaining area of truth—a rigid and particularly dogmatic experimentalism—was finally looking at things realistically. To borrow a phrase from my own much later notes [actually, the phrase originated from Helen's lips as she awoke one morning, and was related to Bill; *see below*, p. 166], "never underestimate the power of denial." It can indeed obscure the very obvious.

One cold winter evening my husband and I went to visit some friends who lived some distance away. I hated public transportation and avoided it whenever possible. I had been a secret cab-taker for years before I was married, but had generally left the cab a block or so from our building because my father strongly disapproved of cabs except in emergencies. Now I no longer saw any need to apologize for my indulgence. In fact, I felt it was something to which I was actually entitled. I wanted to take a cab that evening, particularly as it was starting to snow. Louis did not share my viewpoint and reminded me, to my great annoyance, that the trip was long and the subway only a block away. I regarded this as an unpardonable insult, but without expressing further objections I marched angrily to the subway, grimly determined to suffer, but not alone.

As we reached the platform a train was just pulling out, and we had to wait some twenty minutes for the next one. I grew angrier and angrier as the time passed. When the next train finally came it was packed, and we had to stand quite a while before we got a seat over a very hot radiator. I was wearing a new fur coat, which I was sure would be ruined. At each station a freezing gale blew in against my hatless head as the doors opened. It also worked havoc with my hairdo, on which I had spent considerable time before leaving home. I grew increasingly convinced I would come down with pneumonia [a constant fear of Helen's], probably in both lungs. As an additional hazard, people were coughing and sneezing all around me, and I could almost see the germs attacking. I was certain by that time that my husband's thoughtlessness would have a fatal outcome. His contented absorption in his newspaper did not help matters, either.

Besides being dangerous, the whole situation was

thoroughly revolting to me. The train smelled of garlic and peanuts, and the people crowded in with us looked dirty and shabby. Across the aisle a child with hands streaked with chocolate had patted his mother's face and coat, leaving smudgy fingerprints all over her. Two seats away another mother was wiping off her dress where her baby had thrown up. A group of older children were making a lot of noise, and one of them picked up a wad of chewing gum from the floor and put it in his mouth. At the far end of the train some old men were arguing heatedly and perspiring freely. I was finding the whole situation increasingly disgusting, and closed my eyes to shut it out, feeling sick to my stomach.

And then a stunning thing happened. It was very brief. The intense emotions associated with it began to fade almost at once, and disappeared entirely in something less than a minute. An accurate account of what happened is impossible. As an approximation, however, I can say that it was though a blinding light blazed up behind my closed eyes and filled my mind entirely. Without opening my eyes, I seemed to be watching a figure of myself as a child, walking directly into the light. The child seemed to know exactly what she was doing. It was as if the situation were completely familiar to her. For a moment she paused and knelt down, touching the shining ground with elbows, wrists, and forehead in what looked like an Eastern gesture of deep reverence. Then she got up, walked to the right side and knelt again, this time resting her head as if leaning against a gigantic knee. The feeling of a great arm [one of "God's everlasting Arms"] reached around her and she disappeared. The light grew even brighter, and I felt the most indescribably intense love streaming from the light to me. It was so powerful that I literally gasped and opened my eyes.

I saw the light an instant longer, during which I loved everyone on the train with that same incredible intensity. Everyone there was unbelievably beautiful and incredibly dear. Then the light faded and the old picture of dirt and ugliness returned. The contrast was truly shocking. It took me several minutes to regain a semblance of composure. Then I reached uncertainly for Louis' hand.

"I don't know how to explain this," I said in a shaky voice, "but a very funny thing just happened. Actually, it scared me a little, and it's very hard to describe. But, well—" I hesitated a moment, and then went on breathlessly, "I saw a great light, and waves and waves of love came out of it, and when I opened my eyes I loved everybody here, just like it loved me. It's all gone now, and I don't understand what happened."

Louis, an omnivorous reader, had read a little on mysticism, although he found the subject was of limited interest. Strangely enough, he did not seem surprised, and patted my hand reassuringly.

"Don't worry," he said, soothingly, picking up his newspaper again. "It's a common mystical experience. Don't give it another thought."

The experience was so startlingly different from Helen's conscious life, that she tried hard to do what Louis recommended:

> I tried to follow his advice and partially succeeded. The episode did not fit into my conscious life, which remained unaffected by it for a long time. However, it hung suspended in a corner of my mind, although I did not give it any serious thought for years.

Incidentally, readers familiar with *A Course in Miracles* will recognize an allusion to this experience in the beautiful passage in the section from the text called "The Forgotten Song":

> Beyond the body, beyond the sun and stars, past everything you see and yet somehow familiar, is an arc of golden light that stretches as you look into a great and shining circle. And all the circle fills with light before your eyes. The edges of the circle disappear, and what is in it is no longer contained at all. The light expands and covers everything, extending to infinity forever shining and with no break or limit anywhere. Within it everything is joined in perfect continuity. Nor is it possible to imagine that anything could be outside, for there is nowhere that this light is not.
>
> This is the vision of the Son of God, whom you know well. Here is the sight of him who knows his Father. Here is the memory of what you are; a part of this, with all of it within, and joined to all as surely as all is joined in you (text, p. 417).

This passage always made Helen uncomfortable, for reasons that for a long time I could never understand, as its beautiful language was such that Helen ordinarily would have loved it. I then one day remembered the passage's connection with the "subway experience," and recognized that the discomfort related to this experience, and not to the passage itself.

During this period preceding her entering graduate school, Helen had a series of dreams which bear on her split self. We have already examined one of these, "The Blue-Gray Bird," but the others are interesting as well, for they reflect directly the underlying conflict in Helen that is one of the central themes of this book. We turn to them now.

Dreams

As I mentioned in the discussion of "The Blue-Gray Bird," Helen wrote down the dreams in a stylized way, as if they were short stories. While the form of the dreams, therefore, has changed, their content of reflecting Helen's inner conflict has remained the same. Moreover, they exhibit a remarkable consistency, even though they span many years.[14] The dreams, incidentally, were not given titles by Helen, but I have supplied them for ease of reference. Moreover, I have occasionally edited them down, with ellipses signifying my omissions (unless otherwise noted), and have also performed some very minor editing on mistakes I know Helen would have wished corrected. She obviously never planned on these dreams being published, which also accounts for the informal nature of the writing.

The Gentleman

The first dream we consider is "The Gentleman," where Helen is confronted by a Gentleman, symbolic of Jesus, hence the capital "G." He offers Helen the choice of joining his world, which among other things has an "economy of great abundance" and "is not an economy of scarcity"; its inhabitants have no needs of any kind. The Gentleman is totally non-confrontive, and exerts no coercion on Helen at all. He merely states the reality of Helen's choice, and allows her total

---

14. Most of these dreams were undated, but their general chronology I believe can be ascertained. Some of them extend beyond her graduate years at New York University, but have been included here for the sake of preserving the continuity of the split-self theme.

freedom to accept or refuse his offer. Characteristically, Helen is uncommitted, and still retains the right to choose her own personal world: "'Thank you for the invitation.'...I haven't made up my mind about coming, but if I do, I'll insist on bringing my own slack suits." This is the dream:

"Wouldn't it be wonderful if it would stay like this all year round?" I say to myself, slipping back my cape and baking happily in the hot sun. "But of course it won't. In just a little while it'll be winter and the snow and cold will come back and I'll freeze to death again. It'll stay like that for months and months, and I'll get colder and colder. I've lived through a lot of winters, but somehow I have a feeling that I won't get through another one." I begin to shiver in spite of the heat, and pull my cape closely around my shoulders.

"Perhaps you'd like to spend the winter underground with us this year?" asks the Gentleman. We are standing in an enormous underground cavern, lit by hundreds of small crystal clusters of lights set in the high, arched ceiling. The lights are so remote that they seem like stars, and the high dome suggests the open sky....

"This place is surely intended for a great many people," I say. "Where is everybody?"

"They haven't come as yet," the Gentleman explains, "but they will. There is no need for them to come here as long as it's still summer. And now tell me," he asks, returning to his first question, "how would you like to spend the winter underground with us?"

"I don't quite know," I say, uneasily. "I'd better think it over first....I'm afraid I'd be dreadfully uncomfortable here."

"You needn't worry about that," says the Gentleman, reassuringly. "You'll be quite safe here...."

"It's not that I doubt your word, of course," I add, hastily.
. . .

The Gentleman laughs pleasantly. "It's quite evident that you do doubt my word," he says, "but it's not likely that you could take anybody's word for anything. Faith isn't one of your strong points, now, is it?..."

"How's the weather here?" I ask next, feeling that this is a really important question for me.

"It's quite warm and very pleasant," says the Gentleman. "In fact, most people come here at first because of the climate.

If they decide to stay, though, and most of them do, they usually do so for better reasons."

"Such as?" I ask, curiously.

"That's hard to explain," says the Gentleman. "It's quite different here; so different that it's hard to get used to at first. You see, the environment itself is perfect, but what you make of it is strictly your own affair. That in itself makes a great difference. But understanding the difference depends on your ability to perceive it, which, of course, nobody can do for you. You may not be able to see any difference at all, which would be most unfortunate. I've been hoping you'll learn in time. But if not, you can always go away. Nobody will detain you."

So far it sounds fair enough to me. However, there are still some further questions to be settled.

"What does one wear down here?" I ask, mentally reviewing my wardrobe.

"You don't have to be concerned with that," answers the Gentleman. "We take care of all such details for you." He leads me into one of the shops. In the open show-cases are piles of curious-looking black slack-suits....

The slack-suits don't particularly appeal to me. However, I examine them, chiefly to be polite.

"How many would I need?" I ask.

"Oh, you won't need more than one," says the Gentleman.

I don't like this at all. One would hardly be enough. I begin at once to figure out some way of getting more, and decide that, since the show-cases are open, it would be easy to steal an extra suit or two without being discovered. As if I had spoken out loud the Gentleman answers, still pleasantly and without criticism, "I told you it was different here. It's quite impossible to steal anything. Ours is not an economy of scarcity. We have plenty of everything. You just take it if you want it. As for the suits, I didn't say you could have only one. I said you'd need only one. You can have as many as you want.... ours is not a money economy. There is nothing you can either steal or buy. We have an economy of great abundance, because where there is scarcity it is very difficult for people to realize that there is nothing worth stealing or buying. You'd better start off by taking as many of everything as you see fit. After a while it will no longer occur to you to take more than you need. There just won't be any sense in doing it."

I am inclined to doubt this, but refrain from saying so. "I have two very pretty blue slack-suits at home," I say. "Do you think it would be wrong to bring them with me?"

"Certainly not," the Gentleman says. "How can it be wrong, if you think they'll make you happier? You won't wear them very long, though." . . .

I am beginning to feel confused. Obviously the Gentleman was right. This place is very different, and I'm not too sure that I'd get along here very well. I've got by in my own world, after a fashion, but this place might be something I couldn't cope with.

"If you don't care about appearances, and if people can't steal or buy anything, how do you manage to get along?" I ask. "I mean, how does one get to be noticed or liked?"

"That's very simple," says the Gentleman. "If you're nice, people will notice you and like you. If not, why then, they won't. It will take a long time for you to be either noticed or liked. You may, in fact, be very nearly invisible to the people here for quite a while, because what you emphasize they won't even see. But still, since you can't stand another cold winter, you can't lose anything by taking a chance. If you like you can regard it as an experiment. You can always go away. It's still summer, so you have plenty of time to think it over. The decision isn't final, either way, so don't get a notion that it's a life and death affair. It really isn't. When the fall comes, see how you feel about it, and then do whatever you like."

We shake hands. "Thank you for the invitation," I say, politely, and go out. I haven't made up my mind about coming, but if I do, I'll insist on bringing my own slack-suits. I don't believe in Utopias. . . .

Again, the final lines reflect, as does the whole dream, the part of Helen's mind that resisted Jesus' offer to enter his world of abundance and peace, referred to in *A Course in Miracles* as the real world. To the end, Helen retained her right to choose to remain exactly where she was, even though she was clearly not happy.

The Hen and the Pot

"The Hen and the Pot," succinctly, if not acerbically, portrays Helen's conflict between a suicidal, death-attracted self and a self that strives for survival. The protagonists are a hungry Helen and a suicidal hen who keeps diving into the cooking pot. The dream closes with a statement of Helen's seemingly perennial situation: "Neither of us moves. It *is* a stalemate, and there is no answer."

I have just placed a large, empty iron pot on the stove. Before I light the flame under it, a small tan hen, who looks something like a female pheasant, flies in through the window and makes a beeline for the pot. She nestles down, tucks her wings in contentedly, and smiles sweetly at me. I am quite surprised at her sudden intrusion, but I do not want to hurt her. I take my hand from the gas-handle, and try to lift her gently from the pot. She is not heavy, and can easily be picked up. However, she makes a desperate and successful effort to re-enter the pot every time she is removed. Finally, I try to reason with her.

"Why do you want to stay in that pot?" I ask. "There's not much sense in persisting in risking getting yourself burned up."

"It's not a matter of sense," the hen answers, with some smugness. "It's an instinct. I do it all the time. I couldn't possibly stop even if I wanted to, and I don't want to, as it happens."

I find this annoying. With some irritation, I say, "You'll have to fly off now. I must fix lunch. And frankly, I don't think much of this whole thing. Look at it this way. There's no water or grease in this pot, and you wouldn't even make a tasty stew. You're all full of feathers, which would merely burn away. Even if you don't care what happens to you, the pot would be ruined. Now be a good bird, please, and go away. I'd really not want to hurt you."

The hen shakes her head. "Instinct is instinct," she replies. "This is my way of life. I'm sorry it's interfering with yours, and I have nothing against you personally. However, since our interests obviously conflict at this point, it's only fair to tell you that I will probably win."

There is a moment of silence, while I try to decide what to do next. This bird is obviously quite serious. I try to appeal to her sympathy.

"Look here," I say, "I have really had it even before you flew in. Do you think that if I told you why I haven't managed to get a bite to eat for almost two days, you might take pity on me and go away?"

"Frankly, I doubt it," replies the hen. "I don't really care about you one way or the other, although I repeat that personal animosity is not involved. You want to eat, and apparently you need this pot for that purpose. I need this pot for my own suicidal tendencies. Unfortunately, the way things look now, neither of us is going to get what we want. You won't turn on the flame, and I won't go away."

"Maybe we can work things out," I say, hoping to resolve this stalemate. "Look here,—I'll get another pot, and you can stay in this one. Will that do?"

"Obviously not," says the hen, indignantly. "If you turn the fire on under another pot, I would have to fly into that one. You don't expect me merely to sit quietly in a cold pot, do you? That wouldn't accomplish anything."

I am now reduced to desperation. "Please be reasonable," I beg the hen. "I've had an awful lot of trouble in this kitchen. The refrigerator broke, and we got a new one but that didn't work either. The gas main or something broke, too, and there was a big mess with the stove. Nothing has been working right until the very minute when you came in. I'm starving to death, and you won't let me cook my lunch. I don't think that's fair. I'm willing to compromise, but I can't let you interfere with me forever."

"It's sweet of you to think I'm giving you a choice," says the hen, "but you really don't understand the situation. I have to do this. It's my life work. It's inappropriate of you even to think of eating at a time like this."

I look silently at the hen for a minute or two, and suddenly jump back, startled by the brief gleam of unmistakable hatred in her round black eyes. Her equanimity returns quickly, and she smiles. Neither of us moves. It is *a stalemate, and there is no answer.*

The stalemate of course is between the two parts of Helen's split mind—the one choosing to live, the other to die—a conflict which at this point in her life shows no indications of being resolved. The next dream presents a similar picture.

The Puppy

In a dream that appears to have occurred during the scribing of *A Course in Miracles*, since there is a written comment on this dream by Bill in the fall of 1966, Helen expressed her same conflict in a tale of an obnoxious yet obviously distraught puppy. On her way to an important appointment, Helen is confronted by a seemingly lost and troubled little dog, who nonetheless, in a manner not too dissimilar to the suicidal hen, and of course to Helen's own ways of surviving as well, obstinately clings to his very maladaptive means of relating.

Though obviously quite annoyed by the puppy's manipulations, Helen nonetheless finds herself unable to resist helping him home (to the pet store across the street). The puppy then seems quite content. But Helen is told by the woman who owns the pet store that he will soon begin to howl once more, and repeat the same process all over again with someone else: "He'll begin to get restless and unhappy and decide to go away.... He just can't seem to make up his mind."

I am running down the street, hoping to catch the train that is just pulling in at the El [elevated subway] station. Before I reach the stairs a long, heart-breaking howl stops me. Huddled miserably in the gutter next to the curb I see a small, black puppy. He fixes his mournful eyes on me and howls again. Something warns me not to get involved with this pup. He looks pathetic enough, but there is also something vaguely objectionable about him. Besides, I am already very late for my appointment,—one I am quite anxious to keep,—and I have no time to waste. I start to run on, determined to ignore the puppy. As I pass him, however, he throws back his head and lets out a really dreadful yelp. The puppy wins. I go over to him and say, soothingly, "There, there. I expect you're lost. Perhaps I can help you."

"It's about time you tried," snaps the puppy, crossly.

"Why, you can talk!" I say, very much surprised. "But that's impossible. Dogs can't talk, you know."

"I can," answers the puppy, a trifle smugly. "I don't do it very often, though. Most of the time I just howl. But today nobody will pay any attention to me, so I think maybe I'd better start talking."

"That's sensible," I say, seriously. "And now that you've decided to talk, perhaps you will be good enough to tell me what you want, so that I can be getting on. I'm very late as it is."

"Very well, then, I'll tell you," says the puppy, suddenly becoming businesslike. "I want my mother."

"I can understand that," I tell him, sympathetically. "Where is your mother?"

The Puppy waves a paw. "She's over there in that pet shop across the street," he says, "and I want to see her right away."

I am pleased to find that the problem isn't going to be too

difficult, after all. "Well, then," I say, "as long as you know where your mother is, you're not really lost. Why don't you just run across the street and find her?" ...

"No," says the puppy. "I wouldn't even consider it."

I remain grimly patient. "If that won't do, perhaps you'd care to suggest something better?" I ask.

"Yes I would," answers the puppy. "I'd suggest you carry me over.... If you're really in such a hurry you'd probably save a lot of time by just picking me up and taking me over without arguing about it so much," the puppy points out, reasonably. "Just consider how much time you've wasted already." ...

"All right, I'll take you," I say, in despair. "Come on let's get it over with." ...

I snatch up the puppy and carry him across the street and into the pet shop. A plain-faced, elderly woman steps out of the shadows in the rear of the shop and comes forward to meet me, wiping her hands on her soiled, white apron. The puppy has settled down comfortably in the bend of my elbow, and seems to have fallen off to sleep. I dump him down on the floor in front of the woman and say, "I think this dog belongs to you. I found him...."

"I know," says the woman, wearily. "You found him sitting in the gutter and howling. So you brought him back. Somebody always does."

"I must say you don't seem very glad to see him," I say, beginning to feel rather sorry for the puppy. "He's very much attached to you. Besides, he understands English quite well and I suspect he's really very sensitive. You ought to be careful what you say in front of him."

The woman sighs. "You don't have to live with him," she says. "It's really dreadful. All he does all day long is howl. He's the most awful nuisance."

"There's no question about that," I agree, heartily.

We both watch the puppy in silence. He is sitting contentedly at the woman's feet, playing happily with her shoe-laces. He looks like a perfectly ordinary puppy, and if he does understand what we've been saying, he gives no sign of it.

"What will he do now?" I ask, after a while.

"Oh, he'll be quite satisfied for a time," the woman answers, "and then the whole thing will start all over again. He'll begin to get restless and unhappy and decide to go away, and then he'll wind up in the gutter somewhere and howl until somebody brings him back again. He just can't seem to make up his mind. If you'd care to wait, you can see for yourself."

"No, thank you," I say, making hastily for the door. "I'll take your word for it."

This dream, too, reflects the two parts of Helen: the one needing help desperately, yet stubbornly refusing to accept it except under her own terms, while the other is totally capable of choosing the Help that is always there. This inner conflict was clearly represented in Helen's own experience, where she was continually in the position of helping people whom she did not particularly care for, and moreover, resented the experienced intrusion on her time and energy. Nonetheless, she almost never refused anyone's call for help. Helen herself commented on this characteristic in herself in her letters to Bill which are presented in Chapter 6.

The Rabbit

While the previous dreams reflect an indecision in Helen's mind—the "stalemate" of "The Hen and the Pot," for example—"The Rabbit" leaves no doubt as to the outcome of the dream's conflict. Here, Helen is dressed as Alice in a setting very much like Lewis Carroll's *Wonderland*. She is confronted by a very argumentative, accusatory, and not-very-pleasant rabbit, more like a district attorney than the white rabbit of Carroll's fantasy. He sees through Helen's defenses, particularly her "face of innocence," wherein she appears to be "an innocent and well-meaning little girl to whom a number of strange things occur, none of them of her own doing."

In a situation not too unlike K's in Kafka's *Trial*, Helen-Alice finds herself trapped in an unfair trial in which she discovers ultimately that she is pitted against herself: the name given to the proceedings actually is "Helen versus Helen." Moreover, she is told that she really will have little to complain about since the quality of the procedures will be beyond reproach: "You are something of a formalist yourself, and I am sure that you will approve of the style." As the "trial" begins, Helen loses "interest in the proceedings since, after all, there is very little doubt of the outcome." Here is the dream, which actually occurred in 1961, after Helen arrived at Columbia-Presbyterian, but still over four years before *A Course in Miracles* began:

I am standing in a large, open field, dressed like Alice in *Wonderland,* and looking up at a very large white rabbit. The rabbit, who appears to have a rather legalistic point of view, is arguing that the whole scene may not be what it seems to be.... He presents his viewpoint quite dispassionately, but his disapproval is obvious.

"Now you claim that all this is a scene directly out of *Alice in Wonderland,* which, as I remember, is a story about an innocent and well-meaning little girl to whom a number of strange things occur, none of them of her own doing." Here the rabbit pauses, with a look of deep suspicion. He coughs slightly, and in fact scornfully, and continues.

"I must say in your favor that you have set the thing up quite well. The scenery is quite authentic, and so are the costumes. There are, however, several details which are open to serious question."...

[Helen responds irritably:] "I can't see any sense in complicating things unnecessarily. This looks like a very conventional *Alice in Wonderland* sketch, taken, in fact, right out of the original illustrations. You would have no reason to suspect it of being anything else if you weren't such a suspicious rabbit. Why should it even occur to you that it isn't just what it seems to be?"

"Oh, the possibility exists that it is," the rabbit hastens to assure me, "but we have to consider all of the angles, you know."

"Why do we?" I protest. "There are probably so many that we would never even find all of them. And I'm not sure that they would be worth the time, even if we could find them."

"Nonsense," answers the rabbit. "You can't be as naive as all that. You know perfectly well that you have to get awfully complicated first, and then become simpler in your approach. You can't possibly do it the other way round."

"I don't believe it," I burst out. "If that were true, most of us would never get out of the complexity. It would be much more sensible to start in by being simple, and then get complicated only if it's absolutely necessary. You could get things bogged down for years and years the other way."

"Yes indeed you could," says the rabbit, somewhat complacently. "Most of us do. Your own chances of escape, in fact, are none too good.... it is true that dressing me up as a white rabbit was your own idea...."

The rabbit looks straight at me as he says this, and the

accusing look is difficult to face. Nevertheless, I cannot help feeling that there is a certain basic injustice in his attitude. I am also becoming increasingly annoyed with the necessity of defending my position, which, I still feel, was not unethical and should not have been regarded in that light from the outset. I am still further irritated by an uncomfortable feeling that I must manage to dispel the rabbit's suspicions, or things will somehow not go well with me.....

[The rabbit says pompously:] "I think we should leave the whole thing to the jury, myself."...

The rabbit brings a little silver bell out of his pocket, and begins to ring it solemnly, with just a shadow of a smile in the corner of his lips. It is not a nice smile.

"Hear ye, hear ye..."[15] he begins.

"Now you wait just one minute," I burst out, no longer concerned with placating him. "I consider this whole thing an imposition, and I won't have anything more to do with you. I don't have to put up with this foolishness, and I don't care what you think of me. I don't really need your approval, and if I did, I probably wouldn't get it whatever I did. I think that's pretty obvious by now. But I don't have to stand trial for something you think I did. I am going to stick to my original interpretation, and you can, and probably will, stick to yours. I just can't help it, and I'm not even going to try to help it any more."

The rabbit pays no attention to me, and merely continues, "Hear ye, hear ye...."[16]

I abruptly drop my defiance. "Very well," I say, "so there will have to be a trial. I'm not afraid of a trial if it's a fair one."

"Oh, don't worry," says the rabbit, with exasperating smugness, "it won't be a fair one."

His remark brings me close to tears. However, I decide to see if I can get some protection even in this most unreasonable situation.

"Don't you think I should at least know something more about the trial?" I ask, desperately. "For example, most cases have names. What will this one be called?"

"Oh, it's been named a long time ago," replies the rabbit, in an off-hand way. "It's called Helen versus Helen. You may not

---

15. Helen's ellipsis.

16. Helen's ellipsis.

like the title, but there was no reason why you should have been consulted."

I am really outraged now. "That's atrocious," I tell him, practically at the point of screaming. "I am definitely not taking both sides of this case. My own position is perfectly clear, just as I stated it at the beginning. You are the one who is taking the other side, and entirely without justice, if I may say so. I refuse to take the responsibility for your distorted viewpoint."

"You may refuse as much as you like, but that's still the name of the case," says the rabbit, regally. "Since your opinion does not really matter, I don't see much point in your continuing to drag this matter out. It will end the same way regardless of what you do, anyway."

"But if it's a matter of Helen versus Helen, I can't possibly win," I tell him tearfully.

"Oh, come, now," says the rabbit, patting my shoulder with an irritating pretense at reassurance. "That depends on how you look at it. You might also say that you can't possibly lose. Why be pessimistic?"

"But you just told me that the trial would not be fair," I cry. "Please don't go through with it. I won't have a chance."

I grab at the rabbit's sleeve, which he gently disentangles from my grasp. Then he continues, almost dreamily, "It won't be fair, that's true. You know it, and perhaps I know it too. But that does not give you the right to attack our well established institutions. I assure you that the trial will sound entirely correct in all ways, and there will be no grounds [on which] to object to the quality of the procedures. You are something of a formalist yourself, and I am sure that you will approve of the style. And so, perhaps, we had better get on with it."

The rabbit turns away abruptly, and waves his paw. "You will note the magnificence of this courtroom," he announces in a grand manner.

I look carefully about me. The scene has not changed at all. "What courtroom?" I ask.

The rabbit disregards this, and continues, with great dignity. "And here is the jury. I assure you that they were very carefully chosen. I think you should say 'how do you do' to them."

I turn in the direction which the rabbit indicates, but I cannot see anyone at all. The rabbit, however, does not pause for my response. He begins his address in a deep, ringing voice. "Ladies and gentlemen of the jury, this is the culprit,—I mean the defendant. It is her outrageous contention that all this is nothing more than a scene out of *Alice in Wonderland*. While this contention is clearly ridiculous, I feel that it is my duty to present her point of view as fairly as possible, in spite of the fact that it is thoroughly repugnant to me, and an insult to your intelligence. It seems that in the month of April in the year 1961, this woman.... ''[17]

I hear the sound of his voice trail away, and become a confusion of sound. I can no longer make out what he is saying, though I am aware that he is making a deeply impassioned appeal to an invisible audience. I lose interest in the proceedings since, after all, there is very little doubt of the outcome.

The pessimism here, as indicated earlier, is Kafkaesque in its relentless presentation of the inevitable outcome. It is thus a painfully accurate portrait of the ego's thought system of victim-victimizer, persecuted-persecutor, in which, seemingly, there is no way out.

"The Greatest Experience of My Life"

We come now to this most curious description of what Helen called "the greatest experience of my life." From the reference to "our book business" we know that it predates, probably by a few years, Helen's entering graduate school. Thus the experience more than likely took place during the 1940s, when Helen was still in her thirties. As she explains below, the experience consists of two dreams and the day that followed. I quote it all first.

> That night I had the greatest experience of my life. In fact, it was my life. It was a short life. It lasted less than twenty-four hours and consisted only of two dreams and the one day that followed them. I was never really alive before that, and I died very shortly afterwards. But when I get to the throne of God and He asks me, "Did anything ever really happen to you while you were alive?" I will remember these dreams and say, "Yes, Lord, something really did."

---

17. Helen's ellipsis.

Dream I

I was sitting very, very sleepily in a heavily-cushioned easy chair.... I was feeling peaceful and untroubled.... In a far-off part of the room a radio was playing undistinguishable music very softly. Without disturbing the great peace of the room, my cousin Harry's voice came gently over the radio, half chanting from the Christian Science Bible;

"Our Father-Mother God all harmonious, hallowed be Thy Name...."[18]

"Christian Science yet," says me, mildly annoyed. "Oh well, he'll stop."

He didn't stop. He just kept on repeating the phrase over and over. After a while it got to be even more soothing than the music, and again I was on the point of falling off to sleep. Then Harry began calling to me,

"Helen, Helen, Helen," he said, in a curiously hypnotic monotone, "just keep on listening to the radio for a while longer, and the Lord God Himself will speak to you. He has a special message for you and you will surely want to hear it." ...

The voice continued undisturbed.

"You know, Helen, you're in a pretty bad way," it whispered. "I wonder whether you realize just how bad it really is?"

"I assure you I do," I said, now awake enough to be irritated. "But still, why all this nonsense? That sort of thing hasn't ever solved anything yet."

The voice merely went on as if I hadn't interrupted. "... You won't have much chance, you know."

"I do know," I said, "and I don't pretend I like it. Still, I'll manage to pull through without that sort of help, and if I don't, well, thank you, but I still wouldn't be interested."

The voice went on, calm, steady and insistent.

"You're quite sure you know what you're up against?"

"I know," I repeated. "And I still say 'No thanks.'"

"But it's so easy," the voice continued, now almost singing. "Here you are after so many, many years of fighting a desperate and almost hopeless battle. And now, besides being pretty badly battered and very, very tired, you have the further handicap of much greater awareness than is likely to make it

---

18. Helen's ellipsis.

easier for you. There isn't much chance you'll get through all right in the end...."

"I can try," I said, with an assurance I didn't feel.

"Look here, Helen," the voice droned on. "Just suppose for a minute that I could give you a strong Power outside yourself,—a Power that would tell you what to do and would solve all your problems for you. You'd be perfectly safe then, wouldn't you? You'd never even think of suicide then."

"But I don't believe in it," I argue. "It's ridiculous. Even the phrase, 'Our Father-Mother God,' why, just think of it. It's infantile. It's not real. I wouldn't even consider it."

"As you wish," the voice says, still imperturbable. "But please allow me just one question. Whatever you may think of it, wouldn't you like such a thing to be true? Don't answer right away; just remember the position you're in, and think my offer over for a while."

As I consider the matter, my determination drops away. "Yes, I'd like it," I said, my own voice growing very quiet now. "My God, yes, I'd like it."

The voice waited for a second or so, and then began again. "So now that's settled, and all you have to do is to pick up those two little pieces of cardboard that are lying on the table beside you, and slip them between your eyes and your glasses. Then just go off to sleep. That's all there is to it. Surely that's nothing to be afraid of?"

I was not entirely reassured, but I reached over and picked up the pieces of cardboard, and put them in front of my eyes. Then I snatched them away again and snapped myself awake. "I won't do it!" I said. "I just won't! It's dark in this room and I can't see very much as it is. With these things in front of my eyes I won't be able to see anything at all. I won't do it!"

The voice from the radio went right on chanting. The fight I put up against falling asleep under its persuasiveness almost split me in half. I woke up freezing.

"So what,—just a nightmare," says me, and went back to sleep.

Dream II

I was climbing slowly and painfully out of an enormous hole in the ground. Against the side of the hole I seemed tiny as a fly. I was pulling myself hand over hand up along a yellow rope that lay loosely along the ground beside the mouth of the hole and dangled down along the side. The rope seemed a risky means of escape, and I was thinking that it would have been much better if at least the rope were tied to something substantial like a good, strong tree. However, it offered the only way out, so there was no choice. It had been a very long way up that rope. I had the impression that I had spent most of my life at the job, and I was getting terribly tired. The walls of the hole were slippery, and I couldn't get a good foot-hold against the side. My hands were hurting very badly. The skin was torn off almost to the bone, and blood was streaming down the rope, making it almost too slippery to hold. I was so exhausted that I wouldn't be able to hold on much longer anyway.

I had been climbing in complete darkness for some time, but it was getting much lighter now. Looking up, I could see a little patch of sky overhead.

"So there's an end to this climb, after all," I thought to myself. "It's nice to know that much, at least. I couldn't be sure of even that until now."

But there was still a very long way to go. I had almost no strength left, and I was getting unbelievably tired. The rope was getting increasingly slippery, my hands wouldn't hold out much longer, and I was dangerously close to passing out. I went slowly on, almost overwhelmed by my growing feeling of hopelessness.

"This can't be worth it," I thought. "It just can't be. Nothing would be. I'll never make it anyhow. It's impossible. Besides, I started on this climb without properly considering the matter in the first place. It's been such a long and dreadful business getting out of this hole, and what proof have I got that it's been worth all this effort? All I know is that somehow or other I decided that it was worth doing, and have acted ever since as though it were. That's nothing but a hunch, and needn't be true. Maybe I've wasted my whole life on an illusion. In any case, there's not much chance that I'll ever be able to get out. And even if I have a chance, how can I be sure that there's anything outside of this hole, after all? I've never been outside, so I can't have any certainty about what's out there. And if there is something outside, why should I ever have assumed that it's something good? For all I know, I'm better off inside the hole than outside it. And so this whole climb may have been undertaken on the basis of false assumptions from the very beginning. It is surely senseless to have opinions and feelings without any knowledge whatever.

So all I'd have to do is to let go of this rope, and then the whole thing would be over and done with. My hands will open by themselves in a little while anyway. And all that would happen is that I'd slide back into the hole again. It's a long way down, I know, and I'd never have the ghost of a chance of getting out again, but I'd land on the cushions at the bottom and go quietly to sleep and never wake up. When I come to think of it, that would be the best thing to do, in view of the fact that even if there is something good outside, and even if I never do get to discover it, even that can't bother me if I'm asleep. On the other hand, if there's nothing out there, or if it's something bad, well, then, I wouldn't ever know that either. Surely this is a sensible solution to the problem, particularly in view of the state I'm in. . . ."[19]

I stopped to think this over. Then, without either letting go of the rope or climbing ahead, I rested for a little and thought, "If I let go now, I'll be finished. I could never get this far again. In one way I'd save my life, but in another way I'd lose it, and this time I'd lose it forever. It's true I don't know what's outside, and it's also true I may not be able to make it. But I'm not dead yet, so I can still try. It's worth it. It's just got to be worth it. And if I don't make it, I'll die trying. People have died gladly for less. . . ."[20]

When I woke up this time I was a mess. I was soaked with sweat, my face was covered with tears, and my nails had dug holes in my palms. I lay in bed for a while and just kept on repeating, "It was worth it; it was. . . ."[21] Then I decided to throw some cold water on my face, and crawled into the bathroom. I washed my face and took a long and thoughtful look at myself in the mirror.

"That's me," I said to myself, in some surprise. "I sure look awful at the moment, but it's really me. Come to think of it, I never felt quite sure before."

I wasn't feeling very sleepy, so I went into the living room. I picked up a book, but I didn't feel much like reading, and anyway I didn't have my glasses with me, so I just sat there looking around the room. Then I noticed a remarkable improvement in my vision. I wasn't wearing glasses, but I could see the little folds on top of the drapes quite clearly from across the room. I went over to the window, and found I could see across

---

19. Helen's ellipsis.   20. Helen's ellipsis.   21. Helen's ellipsis.

the street without any difficulty. And besides that, I felt quite different all over.

"Feels as though something really did happen," I thought. "I know it was only a dream, but it seems to have made a lot of changes."

I sat down to think the thing over. I stayed there a long time, still convinced that something had happened. I couldn't understand it, but the conviction remained. Towards morning, I went back to bed and slept for a couple of hours. Long before I was fully awake I heard myself saying, "It was worth it. Oh yes, it really was."

It's difficult to explain just what was so unusual about the following day. Nothing remarkable or exciting happened. In fact, it was extremely ordinary. But it was different from any other day of my life. After I had washed my face, I noticed a black-head in my chin. I put up my hands to squeeze it out, but changed my mind. "I always give myself a hole in the face doing that," I thought. "And anyway, what's so awful in a black-head?"

Then I brushed my hair, and noticed that it was just a trifle longer on one side than the other. I got the scissors to even it off, and then decided against it. "So what?" I thought. "Why does it have to be even?"

While I was dressing, I kept reminding myself of all the things about myself I didn't like, but they just didn't bother me. "After all," I thought, "I'm a person, which is a very nice thing to be. People don't have to be perfect. They just do the best they can, and some of them are very nice."

It was an unfamiliar attitude for me, and I didn't understand it at first, but it came to me all of a sudden. "It's self respect, that's what it is," I thought. "I wonder where it's been all this time? After all, I've never done anything to be ashamed of."

Then I thought, "I'm getting older and it's beginning to show, too. And some day I'll die."

This idea didn't especially appeal to me, but it wasn't overly disturbing.

"At least I'm alive now," I thought. "As for dying, I threw away my immortality last night, and believe me, it's a pleasure."[22]

---

22. By this Helen meant that she was no longer afraid to die; thus it was unnecessary for her to cling to the defense of believing in immortality.

When Louis came home, I said "hello" sort of friendly-like, never having seen him before, and feeling a little surprised and pleased about him.

"There is another person," I thought. "Isn't that a nice thing?"

After dinner, Louis asked me to start a new catalogue, so I got a pencil and paper, and we started to work out a heading. As I sat down, my whole body felt something very unusual. It felt very nice, but I didn't recognize what it was. Again it came to me all of a sudden.

"I'm resting," I thought. "I don't recognize it because I've never really done it before."

Still later, I felt something else strange. It interfered with my typing, but it was rather pleasant. Then I thought, "I'm getting sleepy. It's late and I didn't sleep much last night, so it's what is supposed to happen. Generally I go to bed when I think it's time for it, and I haven't ever stopped to consider whether I'm sleepy or not, so I never knew before. So I'll go to bed. That's what people do when they're sleepy."

After I was undressed I started to brush my hair in accordance with my inflexible rule that I'm supposed to brush my hair twice a day. This time the routine irritated me, and I decided the hell with it. It suddenly occurred to me that I had never really considered the actual value to a lot of the things I seem to think are absolutely essential. For all I know, hair-brushing may not be necessary at all, and certainly I don't have to do it with such horrible regularity. The next time I do it, I thought, will be when I darned well feel like it.

Louis went off to bed, but it was still quite early for me, and I went into the other room to think over my new situation. It was a mistake, though I started off quite sensibly. First I got to considering the future, which didn't strike me as terrifying, but which certainly did need a bit of planning. Louis and I have been living way above our income for years now, I figured, and no good can come of that, but fortunately it's not too late to do something about it. After all, I thought, our book business is potentially a pretty good business, and has suffered in the past from two great handicaps,—Louis and me. But if we'd quit horsing around so much, and would get our catalogues out on time, which we have never managed to do, they'd pay off all right. They always have. Or I could go on working for Louis and look around for something for myself that might interest me more. That notion I've always had that I wouldn't have time for both isn't really so. I don't know how to do anything, I thought, but I can still find out. Other people do, and I have just as good a chance as anybody else. I've wasted an awful lot of time, and I'm way behind, which are very good reasons for not wasting any more. After all, I thought, I belong to myself now....[23]

That last remark did it. I began to get uneasy about Louis, so I went into the bedroom to cover him up so he wouldn't catch a cold and die. Then I remembered that I hadn't said my prayers all day. I'd somehow forgotten all about them. In fact, I didn't say them even then, but I knew that wasn't really the point. The "big difference" had gone. I put up a bit of a fight against the whole thing, but it was without conviction. I knew I wouldn't win.

So ended the "greatest experience" of Helen's life.

In the first dream, cousin Harry's voice can be symbolically likened to the Voice of the Holy Spirit or Jesus, calmly and defenselessly presenting Helen with the logical arguments why she should at least consider "another way," since hers was not working out too well. In this sense, Harry was not dissimilar from the Gentleman in the earlier dream who also objectively presented his position to Helen. The "way" in this dream consists of Helen's preventing *her* vision from operating (the two pieces of cardboard), the unspoken implication being that she would thereby allow another vision to take its place. Within the dream Helen resists with a "fight...[that] almost split me in half." Setting aside the literalness of the cardboard pieces for the moment, one can denote the same tone and process found years later in Jesus' messages to Helen in *A Course in Miracles*.

In the second dream we are once again in the midst of Helen's titanic struggle against herself. The hole out of which she is trying to climb represents her life: "In one way I'd save my life, but in another way I'd lose it, and this time I'd lose it forever." This statement is parallel in form to the Rabbit's answer to Helen's objection to the trial of Helen versus Helen, a trial she could not win: "Oh, come, now....That depends on how you look at it. You might also say that you can't possibly

---

23. Helen's ellipsis.

lose." The climb up also represents Helen's eventual decision not to give up the struggle—"I can still try. It's worth it. It's just got to be worth it"—reflecting her decision not to die *before* scribing *A Course in Miracles*. In the dream, as indeed in her life, Helen will remain ultimately faithful to her promise to choose life. Nonetheless, this fidelity would not be immediately manifest.

On her awakening from the dreams Helen was decidedly different, almost ecstatically repeating the words: "It was worth it." Her vision had physically improved, her compulsions had disappeared, and her attitude towards Louis was totally changed. Above all, she felt rested, for the first time in her life. The change lasted a full day, culminating in the statement "I belong to myself now," reflecting her experience of freedom from the ego's tyranny over her. Then the aforementioned fear of God's love and peace suddenly returned, and by characteristically excluding Jesus or God from her life once again, Helen fell back into her usual anxiety. Her ego's defenses regained their supremacy.

> The "big difference" had gone. I put up a bit of a fight against the whole thing, but it was without conviction. I knew I wouldn't win.

The hopeless pessimism of this experience finds parallels, again, with the work of Franz Kafka. One of the clearest expressions of this ultimate pessimism, of which I was always reminded in thinking of Helen, is the scene in *The Trial*, sometimes subtitled "Before the Law": A man waits a lifetime to gain admittance through a single door that will lead him to the Law, his goal. Finally, when the man is near death, the doorkeeper tells him, matter of factly: "No one but you could gain admittance through this door, since this door was intended for you. I am now going to shut it."[24] End of story.

Fortunately, as we have seen, there was another thought system present in Helen's mind. This next dream, which came much later in time, reflects this other and positive side to her.

---

24. Franz Kafka, *The Trial* (New York: Alfred A. Knopf, 1960), p. 269.

76

The Witch/Angel

During June of 1975, Helen dreamt of a young woman who was a cross between a witch and an angel. As in the other dreams, this one reflects Helen's internal conflict, here projected onto the figure of this woman. However, the dream seems to look forward to a more favorable resolution of this conflict, as it points to a time when Helen's judgment will not be contaminated, and her considerable gifts more appropriately utilized. This resolution actually reflects the aforementioned transpersonal dimension of Helen's inner life as the priestess, which will be the subject of the Epilogue. Incidentally, Bill typed down the dream from Helen's description of it, hence its stylistic differences from the others. The two parenthetical comments are Bill's.

> A small thin dark-haired and intense woman, who is something like a girl. She is a driven and curious person, but Helen is fond of her, and at the same time not so fond. This woman-girl had some real talents and gifts—a lot of the supernatural about her. While "not evil," her judgment was poor. She could not tell the difference.
>
> In general, she was somewhere between a witch and an angel. Terribly unpredictable. She had lived with Helen but always parted with a big fight. Now, there is no fight, but they have parted as good friends. It was different this time. They couldn't afford it any more. Also, something about keeping a room for her in the future.
>
> In the dream, Helen recognized it was essential that they not have these terrible fights again. Before that she had been hit in the head (by Helen).
>
> This a.m., after awakening, Helen kept seeing priestess figure.
>
> Interpretation of dream very clear to Helen. When time comes that her judgment is sufficiently good, she will be able to use it for the right purpose (interpretation of meaning of "keeping room"). Now, her judgment is too contaminated.

This positive ending, which is much more hopeful of the future, reflects the deeper meaning of Helen's life in terms of her ultimate identification with the priestess-Self.

The Recorder

In 1945 Helen had a dream that on the level of form we could never fully understand, but on another level reflects what I feel to have been the center of Helen's life. It particularly addresses the meaning of Helen's being in the world, and foreshadows in time the decisive instant when Helen did in fact make the right choice. It was the dream's looking forward to Helen's future decision to join with Bill that led me to place it out of chronological sequence, and at the end of this chapter. Here is the dream:

I am standing in a small, rectangular room lined with books from floor to ceiling. There are no windows. A single door, open behind me, leads to a short, dark corridor opening into the gloomy interior of a large and undistinguishable building. In the middle of the room a tall and incredibly ancient man, evidently some sort of clerk, sits on a very high stool, his skinny shoulders hunched over a small, flat-topped desk. His feet are twisted around a rung just below the seat of the stool and his bony knees are drawn up almost to his chin. He is carefully making small, neat entries with a long-handled quill pen in a large, gray-bound ledger. His weak eyes, protected by a green eye-shade, squint near-sightedly at his meticulous figures through thick-lensed spectacles. I edge cautiously into the room, clear my throat unsuccessfully several times, and finally find my voice.

"Forgive me for disturbing you, sir," I begin, very respectfully. "I know you are very busy. But I have a very difficult problem on my mind and I've been hoping you would help me. I understand that everything that is or has ever been in the whole universe is recorded here, so I felt that this would be the logical place to come."

The clerk is mildly annoyed at the intrusion. He continues writing and answers absently, "It is certainly true that I am very busy. However, if you will ask me your question, I will try to answer it."

"But that's just the trouble," I tell him, sadly. "If only I knew the question I could probably find the answer myself. But I haven't the faintest idea what the question is. In fact, that's really the problem."

"I'm afraid I can't help you, then." says the clerk. "Most people who come here know what they want to ask. Your problem sounds impossible and even a little senseless to me. I wouldn't know how or where to look it up."

"It isn't easy, I know," I say, apologetically, "but I thought maybe we might try first under 'K' for 'Knowledge.' If you will be kind enough to show me where you keep the 'K' book, I'll try to find the question for myself." [This is perhaps a foreshadowing of the Course's use of knowledge as a synonym for Heaven.]

"Knowledge isn't to be found in a book," says the clerk, a trifle pedantically. He reaches a gnarled, yellow hand down to the floor, fumbles about beside his stool, and finally comes up with a gray cardboard cylinder about a foot and a half long and some three inches wide. Its ends are sealed off with cardboard discs. He opens one end of the cylinder as he talks.

"I keep 'Knowledge' in this," he explains. "It consists of an infinite number of sheepskin diplomas, rolled one inside the other. I suspect that what you want is somewhere in the middle of this thing, but you would have to peel off the diplomas one by one in order to reach it. Since the number of diplomas is infinite, it is obvious that you could never get to the center. Therefore, you might just as well not bother to begin."

A picture of a heavy, spindle-shaped object about three inches long and a half an inch wide, something like a lead fishing sinker, crosses my mind as he speaks.

"Oh yes, that's where it is!" I cry, very much excited. "But there isn't any need to be side-tracked by the diplomas. All we'd have to do is to shake the container and whatever is at the middle of it will fall out easily."

The clerk is displeased at this. He withdraws the cylinder a safe distance from my eager hand and says, reprovingly, "I cannot permit such unorthodox methods of research. No, I'm very sorry but knowledge will not help you."

He returns the cylinder to the floor and turns away from me in disapproval. I am disappointed and a little chastened, but after a short pause I decide to try again.

"Perhaps we might try under 'I' for 'Information'?" I suggest, hopefully.

"Information merely gives telephone numbers," says the clerk. "That couldn't possibly help you."

"Or maybe 'P' for 'Prurience' [i.e., lasciviousness or lewdness]?" I ask, desperate but still persistent.

"May I remind you, young lady, that research is properly conducted only with an open and unprejudiced mind," says the clerk, severely. "Such a word is indicative of very strong emotional bias. It has no place in your search."

"I'm very sorry," I say, contritely, backing away a little. "I just thought maybe,—" I break off, and then say, this time rather wildly, "What would you think of 'S' for 'Salome'?"

This time the clerk is really angry.

"Now you're being just plain silly," he says, sharply. "I have no time for nonsense and I suggest that you run along."

The clerk's anger frightens me and I try to soothe him back to a reasonable degree of friendliness.

"Please don't be angry with me," I beg him. "I didn't really mean to say it. It just sort of slipped out. Tell you what;—I'll forget about the whole thing if you'd prefer it. Perhaps that would be best, after all."

"It would certainly be wiser," says the clerk, dryly. Then, seeing that I am still unwilling to leave, he adds, firmly, "Well, then, good-bye."

I turn obediently toward the door. The clerk's annoyance and his abrupt dismissal of me have made me acutely uncomfortable. Besides, the whole interview has been dreadfully disappointing. The clerk has been of no assistance. Also he has made it quite clear that my problem, never of much interest to him, is now of no concern whatever. There is no real reason to suspect that he could help me even if he wanted to. And yet the feeling persists that he could somehow help enormously, if only he cared to. I am afraid of angering him further by not accepting my dismissal, but I am also unwilling to let the matter drop on so unsatisfactory a note. I hang about in the doorway uncertainly for a while, shifting miserably from one foot to the other. Then I tip-toe very softly back into the room. At first the clerk pretends not to notice me. At last he shrugs his shoulders in resignation, and says, with forced patience, "Still here, eh?"

"I'm afraid so," I say, in a very small voice. "I know I'm being a terrible nuisance, but I was wondering if you would tell me what you're doing,—that is, if you don't mind very much," I add, quickly.

"I'm making accounts," says the clerk, briefly.

"Whose accounts?" I ask, eagerly, pleased that he has answered me at all.

"Everybody's," answers the clerk.

"I don't understand that," I say. "Could you very kindly explain it to me?"

The clerk sighs. "I suppose I'll have no peace until I do," he says, wearily. "Very well, then. In this ledger is a page of accounts for everybody that lives, and all his actions are recorded on it. Whenever someone dies, I draw a line under the last entry, add up the figures, and get a total. This total I pass on to the proper Authorities."

"I see," I say, much interested. "You mean you decide whether people have been good or bad, and things like that."

"Dear me, no," answers the clerk. "I merely record facts. Good and bad mean nothing to me. They may concern the Authorities, of course. I wouldn't know. It's not my department."

"I was just thinking," I say, speaking very casually, "I mean, well, how would you say my page looks?"

"I wouldn't know yet," answers the clerk, without much interest. "Your account hasn't been closed as yet."

"I know, but there must be some figures on it already. I was sort of wondering what you think about it so far. Do you think it will shape up all right?" I ask, anxiously.

"I never indulge in speculation," replies the clerk. "In my work it would be a waste of time. Over and over I've seen a person suddenly decide to do something very unexpected,— something that changes the whole picture of his accounts. He's quite likely to do it up until the very last minute. Therefore I've given up speculating beforehand. And afterwards, of course, guessing is no longer necessary. I'll tell you one thing, though," he says, wheeling suddenly round toward me and speaking with unaccustomed emphasis, "your final account will be determined very largely on what you decide to do with that shoehorn."

"Shoehorn!" I gasp. "What shoehorn? I don't know what on earth you're talking about."

The clerk looks straight at me.

"I think you do," he says, very quietly. "Oh yes, I think you do. However," he goes on, his voice returning to its former matter-of-factness, "to me it won't matter either way. It seemed charitable to mention it, since I have an idea you don't realize its importance. As for me, I will duly record your decision when you make it and there my concern with the matter will end. And now, if you will excuse me, I'll be getting on with my bookkeeping, after this long and rather futile interruption. Good-bye again."

This time I also say good-bye.

Recall that the dream occurred in 1945, about thirteen years before Helen met Bill, and twenty years before Bill's "There must be another way" speech, which, as we shall see later, was the external stimulus for the scribing of *A Course in Miracles*. While Helen, Bill, and I were never able to decipher the shoehorn symbolism, it seemed to us as if it must somehow refer to Helen's decision to join with Bill, as well as, on another level, her decision not to misuse her scribal ability that would be expressed in the "God Is" vision described below in Chapter 5. (I personally tried, to no avail, to make connections between the shoehorn and the scroll in this vision, exploring all kinds of Hebrew associations, and others as well.) However, Helen's "final account" did seem settled—at last—for her decisions regarding Bill and *A Course in Miracles* did in the end reconcile her "account" with Jesus, who could then gently bring her Home.

Chapter 4

LEADING TO *A COURSE IN MIRACLES*—B
(ca. 1950–1964)

Psychology—Columbia-Presbyterian Medical Center

Helen entered the doctoral program in clinical psychology at New York University's School of Education in the early fifties, and excelled in her studies, finishing at the top of her class. Helen's success was all the more astonishing given her phobia against reading. One could almost have called her a functional illiterate, as I later teased her, because of this phobia. I shall return to her incredible learning ability, especially given this psychological handicap, in Chapter 6.

Helen's difficulty in school was compounded, moreover, by a writer's anxiety that bordered on the extreme, making writing assignments very difficult. Here again I draw upon Helen's autobiography for an account of events belonging to this time period.

> As an undergraduate I had managed to write very few papers, settling for a lower grade, or reading an extra book; anything to avoid writing papers. [In graduate school] I wrote and rewrote them any number of times, and needed Louis' reassurance for each new version. After I had handed them in, I worried incessantly until they were returned. I was always sure that I had written something dreadfully stupid, and the professor would laugh at me when he read it. I always got good marks and favorable comments, which is not surprising in view of how hard I worked. I was not reassured, and each time I was certain of disaster.

This experience of extreme anxiety over the quality of her written work surfaced again, as we shall see, as the scribing of *A Course in Miracles* progressed. Incidentally, Helen's comments here were overly modest. I have in my possession two term papers she wrote—"Psychoanalytic Concepts of a 'Real Self'" and "Psychoanalytic Concepts of 'Basic' Conflict"— which were returned by her professor Dr. William Rockwell with the following comments on each paper respectively:

Dear Mrs. Schucman—One of the joys of being engaged in the activity of teaching is to witness a student striving for, and reaching, a goal in attainment and synthesis in his thinking that is unconditionally admirable. This paper is so good that I hesitate to use current adjectives in describing it. Congratulations upon an excellent job! What about publication? I think it merits it. Let us talk it over some day.

Dear Mrs. Schucman—I don't know if you have ever experienced the pride and joy that comes to a teacher upon an excellent performance by a student. I have such now. This is an exceedingly good job. comments on each paper respectively:

Another professor read this second paper as well, and wrote:

If I may add my comment too, I should just like to say what a very great pleasure indeed it has been to read your paper. You have the sort of mind for which one can have only the deepest admiration and respect.

Helen's professional interest was research as well as retarded children, a population always very close to Helen's heart. In fact, the retarded were probably the only group about whom I never heard Helen say a critical or unkind word. Upon her graduation in June 1957, a grant proposal based upon her doctoral study—"A Study in the Learning Ability of the Severely Mentally Retarded Child"—was approved for funding by a federal agency which had not given funds to the university for over thirty years. The project turned out well and the head of the department offered her a teaching position at the university, based upon the understanding that she was to submit additional research proposals, an activity at which Helen was expert.

The success of Helen's professional career seemed assured, and she had visions of heading up a large research department. The proper launching of this career merely awaited the almost certain approval of her latest grant applications. On the day they were being considered, Helen's anxiety level was beyond even its usual high state, and so she went for a walk in an attempt to calm her nerves and distract her thoughts. To her great surprise, this rational "atheist" found herself in a Catholic church, and to my even greater surprise I lit a candle and prayed for the approval of my grant proposals. Perhaps I felt it was a good time to give God one more chance because I was so desperate. I was not prepared, however, to give him any options as to the outcome. I wanted those proposals funded, and that was that. Even before I finished making my request I knew what the outcome would be. It was as if I were being told that the department I was in was the wrong place for me and I was not to stay there. The grants would not come through and I would have to look elsewhere for a job. This was totally unacceptable to me [Helen later told me that she had informed God her request was "non-negotiable": she *wanted* those grant proposals accepted] and I walked angrily out of the church.

Helen knew she had lost the "battle" and would not get her way. And indeed when she returned home that evening she learned that the grant applications had been turned down, leaving an opening in her professional life that William Thetford and the Columbia-Presbyterian Medical Center would very shortly fill. I do not think that Helen's ego ever forgot (or forgave) this affront to its own importance. In the words of *A Course in Miracles*, Helen always preferred to be right rather than happy (text, p. 573); and she pursued this attitude with a vengeance, choosing ultimately, as we shall see, to sacrifice her happiness and peace of mind in her ego's attempts to maintain control over her life and exclude God.

Helen now was without employment, and did nothing for several weeks except to become increasingly depressed and angry.

I kept on complaining how miserable I was without a job, but I did nothing at all to get one. Actually, I had made excellent professional connections, and was not likely to have to do more than call a few friends. I felt, however, that they should really call me, even though they did not know I was available. Eventually I recognized the unreasonableness of my position. I pulled myself together, made a list of people to call, and began on it the next morning. I had been working in a highly specialized area, and one in which people with training and experience were badly needed. The first person I called [Harold Michal-Smith] gave me a list of very promising leads.

Right after Helen's call, William Thetford, who had himself

recently come to the Medical Center, also called Michal-Smith, asking if he knew of a good research psychologist for a project at Columbia-Presbyterian. Helen was about to call the first name on the list she had received, when Michal-Smith called her back and emphatically told her to forget about the list he had given:

> "You call William Thetford right now. He's the head of the Psychology Department at Presbyterian Hospital. Here's his number. And when you get him, be sure to tell him I said he's looking for you."

Helen did not particularly want to work in a medical setting, nor did the job description sound very appealing. However, because of Michal-Smith's "surprising urgency" she did make Dr. Thetford her first call, and an appointment was set up.

> As I walked into his office a few days later I made the first of a series of silent remarks that I did not understand myself, and to which I paid little attention at the time.
>
> "And there he is," I said to myself. "He's the one I'm supposed to help."
>
> I was to make a somewhat similar remark a few days later, after Bill and I had got to know each other a little better. It was another of those odd, unrelated things that somehow began to break into my consciousness without any connection with my ongoing life. For a brief interval I seemed to be somewhere else, saying, as if in answer to a silent but urgent call, "Of course I'll go, Father. He's stuck and needs help. Besides, it will be only for such a little while!" The situation had something of the quality of a half-forgotten memory, and I was aware only of being in a very happy place. I had no idea to whom I was speaking, but I somehow knew I was making a definite commitment that I would not break. The actual remark, however, meant as little to me as did the previous one in Bill's office at our first meeting.

This "half-forgotten memory" can be understood as Helen's brief awareness of another level of her mind, in which she had agreed ("a definite commitment") to accept her function as the light-bearer, to Bill as well as to the world. This "other level of her mind" is the home of Helen's priestess-Self, which was in constant communion with God.

The job "did not amount to much," with neither an impressive salary nor title. Yet Helen accepted it, ostensibly for the reasons that Columbia-Presbyterian was a prestige institution, she would have time to devote to a consultantship at the Shield Institute for Retarded Children, an organization of which she was very fond, and there would be funds available for special projects she could initiate. In retrospect, though, Helen wrote:

> In view of later events, however, it seems likely that I did not really have much choice in the matter. That was where I was supposed to be.

The position, however, turned out to be even worse than Helen had imagined.

> The job was really ghastly. The hospital did not provide space for the project and it became increasingly clear that the "upper echelon" regarded it more as a liability than an asset. When it was finally housed in a nearby apartment I settled down to the dullest and most difficult situation of my professional life. The job was more than routine; it was actually oppressive. Besides, it was carried out in an atmosphere of suspicion and competitiveness to which I had not been previously exposed. As I got to know Bill better I learned there were serious difficulties in the whole department, where funds as well as interpersonal harmony were depressingly lacking.

As Helen and Bill's friendship grew, Helen learned that Bill, like herself, had ended up at Columbia-Presbyterian somewhat to his own surprise. He had previously been at the Cornell University Medical Center on the other side of Manhattan, working under Harold Wolff, the noted pioneer in the study of psychosomatic medicine. At a professional meeting, Bill was approached by a colleague whom he hardly knew, who insisted that he apply for the position of director of a pre-doctoral training program in clinical psychology, as well as head of the Psychology Department at Presbyterian Hospital. Bill was not interested,[25] being content at that point to remain at Cornell.

---

25. At least that was Bill's recollection. *See*, however, p. 277 below, where in his dictation of the Course to Helen, Jesus' account of Bill's appointment differed from his.

However he did agree at least to come for an interview. Still uninterested in the move, Bill made what he thought was an unreasonable request; namely, that he be appointed as an Associate Professor. Some time later, to his great surprise, Bill was granted his request. Thus in February 1958 Bill became an Associate Professor of Medical Psychology in the Department of Psychiatry. (Later he was promoted to full Professor. Helen came in as an Assistant Professor, and later was promoted to Associate Professor.)

Like Helen, Bill had had more than his share of difficulties in living in the world, despite his rapid professional advancement. In Helen's words:

> When I arrived a few months later there was little doubt that Bill needed help. He looked haggard, and badly needed someone to talk to. His was an unexpectedly difficult assignment.

Thus, on the one hand Helen and Bill were obviously drawn together, as if they both recognized on another level a purpose to their association greater than simply the professional one. Helen felt an unexpected devotion to helping Bill build up the Psychology Department. Their efforts, incidentally, though successful in some areas, failed miserably in others as there was simply no support in the hospital for psychology. However, on the other hand

> there was another source of strain that we both found even more difficult to handle. Bill and I were actually a most unlikely team, and in spite of our shared goal we grated on each other's already jangled nerves a good part of the time.

While I did not know Helen and Bill during this time period, my close friendship and association with them afterwards does not make it too difficult to describe, at least in general terms, the tremendous animosity that existed between them. I shall await later chapters for a presentation of some of the more unhappy details, during the period when I *was* present. Suffice it for now to state that Helen and Bill probably could not have said hello to each other in the morning without it leading to increased friction and tension. Each basically found the other totally responsible for the misery of the other. Helen even once accused Bill, quite directly, of being responsible for all of her difficulties, *even before they had ever met!*

Thus almost from the beginning, their relationship was characterized by an hostility that existed, paradoxically, in the context of a mutual trust and support that defied rational psychological explanation. On some level, the ambivalent nature of this relationship reflected the conflict with God that was present within Helen herself. Moreover, Helen's and Bill's own difficulties with each other mirrored the animosity and belligerence that existed within their department and between theirs and other departments in the Medical Center. Thus Helen and Bill experienced their overall situation as on a professional battlefield, a war in which they both were active if not eager participants.

Even physically they were opposite. Bill was over thirteen years younger than Helen (Helen was 49 when they first met, Bill almost 36), and over a foot taller. Even more to the point were their personalities. Bill tended to be quietly soft-spoken, while Helen was quite assertive and could be abrasive at times. Bill's anger was almost always channeled through passive means, while Helen was directly if not sometimes strongly aggressive. They would argue throughout the day, and then in the evening would often spend another hour or so on the phone going over their mutual grievances, each of them desperately convinced of the correctness of his and her position. Constantly critical of each other, their discussions were seemingly endless.

Their personality differences merely fueled the flames of their animosity. While Helen was taking down the Course, Jesus frequently described these differences in terms of Helen's and Bill's respective uses of denial and projection. We shall return to these in their proper sequence. Finally, there was Bill's homosexuality. Though never particularly active sexually (in a letter to Bill, Helen once referred to him as asexual), Bill's lack of sexual interest in her was perceived by Helen as effectively thwarting her desire to control him sexually. At first Helen had felt attracted to Bill, who later asked her rhetorically how many men to whom she had been attracted was she currently involved with. The answer of course was none, and a sexual form to their intense relationship would obviously have interfered with the transmission of *A Course in Miracles.* Helen, incidentally, despite her occasional sexual attractions to other men, remained faithful to Louis.

Helen described her differences with Bill this way:

> [Bill] had led a rather difficult life, and when I met him he was at a low point in his personal as well as his professional affairs. He was quite vulnerable to anxiety, depressed and somewhat withdrawn. Nevertheless, he retained a persistent spark of inherent optimism and a somewhat wobbly belief that there was a way out which he would somehow manage to find. In contrast, I was anxious to the point of agitation, apt to be sharp-tongued, and worked with an intensity that Bill found positively alarming. I tried to maintain a facade of hopefulness and certainty but the pessimism and insecurity underneath were very close to the surface. Bill and I approached the departmental problems and reacted to pressure in very different ways. Bill was apt to withdraw when he perceived a situation as demanding or coercive, which he frequently did; directions in which his perception was quite biased at the time. He rarely attacked openly when he was angry or irritated, which he frequently was, but was much more likely to become increasingly aloof and unresponsive, and then openly angry. I, on the other hand, tended to become over-involved and then to feel hopelessly trapped and resentful.
>
> Many calls for help were made on me during that period, and my telephone was generally busy all evening, sometimes until very late. I did not refuse to help where I could, even though many calls came from total strangers who had somehow got hold of my name. In fact, I was generally more sympathetic towards strangers and acquaintances than towards those close to me, such as Louis or Bill, toward both of whom I felt considerable resentment. My sense of being imposed on, which had been growing for years, began to reach an explosive potential.

The worsening nature of their own relationship was mirrored in their professional ones. The state of the department worsened and filled with tension, amid an atmosphere of competition, quarreling, and very divisive anger. Regarding her relationship with Bill, Helen wrote in her autobiography:

The relationship between Bill and myself deteriorated steadily. We had become quite interdependent, but we had also developed considerable anger towards each other. Our genuine attempts to cooperate were more than offset by our growing resentments. We began to get much less work done, while experiencing greater and greater fatigue.... It became more and more evident that the best thing for me to do was to leave. However, Bill and I seemed to be trapped in a relationship which, although we hated it in many ways, could not be escaped.

This severe strain of Helen's and Bill's personal and professional relationships became the setting for the sudden turnaround that led to the beginning of *A Course in Miracles*. As the Course would later say, "In crucifixion is redemption laid" (text, p. 518), and we leave this redemption for the next chapter.

Chapter 5

LEADING TO *A COURSE IN MIRACLES*—C
(1965)

"There Must Be Another Way"

As Helen recorded it in her autobiography, a most unexpected change came in June of 1965.

> What happened next is particularly hard to describe, because I had reached a state of mind in which a positive response to it on my part was singularly unlikely. Nevertheless I made one, and from that time on a great change began.

Some time earlier, Helen and Bill had become consultants to an interdisciplinary research project at the Cornell University Medical Center, Bill's former employer. Their responsibilities included an hour-long meeting every week which grew to epitomize all that was wrong in their personal and professional lives. The meetings were characterized by the same backbiting if not savage competitiveness and anger they were accustomed to in their own Medical Center, not to mention in their own relationship. Helen and Bill hated going, feeling both uncomfortable and angry, yet believing that professionally they had no choice.

And so this June afternoon they once again prepared to go, stopping off first at Bill's east side apartment. This time, however, their perennial negative discussion took a different turn.

> [Bill] had something on his mind, but he seemed to be quite embarrassed and found it hard to talk about. In fact, he tried unsuccessfully several times to begin. Finally he took a deep breath, grew slightly red-faced, and delivered a speech. It was hard for him, he told me later, because the words sounded trite and sentimental even as he said them. Nor was he anticipating a particularly favorable response from me. Nevertheless, he said what he felt he had to say. He had been thinking things over and had concluded we were using the wrong approach. *"There must,"* he said, *"be another way."* Our attitudes had become so negative that we could not work anything out. He had therefore decided to try to look at things differently.

93

Bill proposed, quite specifically, to try out the new approach that day at the research meeting. He was not going to get angry and was determined not to attack. He was going to look for a constructive side in what the people there said and did, and was not going to focus on mistakes and point up errors. He was going to cooperate rather than compete. We had obviously been headed the wrong way and it was time to take a new direction. It was a long speech for Bill, and he spoke with unaccustomed emphasis. There was no doubt that he meant what he said. When it was over he waited for my response in obvious discomfort. Whatever reaction he may have expected, it was certainly not the one he got. I jumped up, told Bill with genuine conviction that he was perfectly right, and said I would join in the new approach with him [my italics].

One can truly say that the birth of *A Course in Miracles* occurred that June afternoon in Bill's apartment. In Helen and Bill's joining together to find that other way, an example of what the Course would later call a "holy instant," one finds a shining example of a miracle: "The holiest of all the spots on earth is where an ancient hatred has become a present love" (text, p. 522). The results were not immediately apparent, but nonetheless certain changes, internal and external, did begin to manifest.

Neither of us did very well at the meeting that afternoon, although we both tried. Nor can I truthfully say that we are wholly successful even now, so many years later. I can say, however, that we have kept on trying, and that we have not been wholly unsuccessful either. Many unexpected things have happened since. I will touch on some of the more factual changes which took place first, because these are comparatively easy things to talk about. The other kinds of [internal] experiences, of which there have been a great number [*see below*] will be more difficult to describe. Most of the words I would need to picture them accurately have not been invented as yet.

The facts are simple. The whole climate of the department gradually changed for the better. Bill worked particularly hard on this, determined to turn hostilities into friendships by perceiving the relationships differently. It took considerable effort on his part, but he did succeed eventually. Tensions lessened and antagonisms dropped away. The wrong people left, though on friendly terms, and the right ones came along almost immediately. A new and secure position opened up for me. Although our efforts were sometimes inconsistent and often halfhearted, there is little doubt that they showed results. In time the department became smooth-functioning, relaxed, and efficient. Meanwhile I felt impelled to pick up my earlier friendships which had been broken off for one reason or another. In some cases this was very difficult, especially when the break-up had been accompanied by marked hostility, and I had felt unfairly treated in the course of it. In one case I hesitated for over a year. Yet I vaguely recognized that these reparatory steps were essential. They seemed to be part of a mandatory preparation period.

As the departmental situation improved, Bill turned his attention to straightening out his own social relationships too. We both felt this was crucial. For the most part we did well with these attempts. We had much greater difficulty with our own relationship. We tried to be charitable and understanding toward each other, especially since we had embarked on a new approach which obviously should be extended to ourselves, and one which had already proved to be well worthwhile.

Yet although we became increasingly willing to recognize our impatience and lack of appreciation toward one another, and did make significant improvements in these respects, we continued to experience sudden outbreaks of antagonism toward each other, sometimes for trivial reasons and sometimes for no reason at all. This upset us both very much, for we both realized that this was a serious roadblock to cooperation and to real progress, and one which we would have to overcome.

As we shall see below, on any kind of observable level Helen and Bill never truly succeeded in healing their own relationship. If anything, with the exception of the period that began now, their external relationship seemed to worsen over time.

Concurrent with the changes that Helen and Bill consciously strove to apply to their relationships, a purely internal set of experiences began for Helen as well. It was almost as if Helen had waited all of her life for Bill to make his "There must be another way" speech. This seemed to act as a stimulus that triggered off a long series of inner experiences that can be categorized variously as visions, dreams, heightened imagery, and the psychic.

It was while we were trying to straighten things out between us that another kind of experience began. It may seem somewhat more plausible if I introduce this by mentioning a characteristic of mine which I have had ever since I can remember. When I closed my eyes I would often see very clear mental pictures. They were so much a part of my own awareness that I thought they happened to everyone. The pictures could be of anything; a woman with a dog, trees in the rain, a shoestore window, a birthday cake with lighted candles, a flight of stairs down the side of a cliff. Sometimes I would recognize part of a picture as related to something I had actually seen, but even then there were details I knew had not been there originally. Most of the pictures did not seem to be associated with anything. A few other images I identified as my own imaginary pictures of how someone I was going to see would look, or what a place I was going to visit would look like. Pictures of this kind rarely turned out to be accurate, but they still rose to mind in connection with the people or places originally giving rise to them.

The pictures were particularly sharp just before I fell asleep, but I often became aware of distinct visual images during the day even when my eyes were open, while I talked with someone else and even when I was by myself. In fact, the pictures seemed almost to represent the words or thoughts as corresponding symbols at a different but related level of consciousness. They could come at virtually any time. They did not interrupt or even disturb my overt activities in any way. It was as if there were a constant mental activity going on in the background that could be brought to the foreground at any time I chose to notice it. For years the pictures had been motionless and exclusively black and white, appearing much like a series of "stills," often without any obvious relationship or progression. As our "adventure in cooperation" continued, however, the pictures began to take on color and motion, and soon afterwards frequently appeared in meaningful sequences. So, too, did my dreams, which often continued with themes begun before I fell asleep or with images from dreams of the preceding night.

During the four-month period that preceded the scribing of *A Course in Miracles*, three "more or less distinct and sequential lines" of visions and dream images reached Helen's "startled awareness." Helen observed them as if she were looking at a movie, and so she experienced herself more as an observer in this experience than a participant. This was so even when, as was most often the case, she was looking at herself. It was as if one aspect of her self were observing another.

> Perhaps you could call them all dream material, since they took place when my eyes were closed, either briefly or in sleep. Parts of them came to me during my early attempts to "meditate," a process which Bill was convinced would be helpful to us, but which I did not understand and found vaguely frightening. Bill, however, was reading books on the subject, and I listened to his eager accounts with some irritation. I did not feel that our agreement to try a new approach to problems justified entering into "crackpot" areas. I had believed for some time that charity is a prerequisite for mental health, and one which also tends to prevent ulcers and reduce blood pressure. However, things like ESP, flying saucers, spirits from another world, and Indian mysticism were something else. On the subject of God, I had become an uneasy agnostic.
>
> Over considerable resistance I finally read a bit on meditation, and was by no means optimistic about its possibilities. Still, I felt that closing my eyes for a few minutes several times a day would probably be restful, if nothing else, as I was generally pretty tense and inclined to hypertension. Besides, Bill's enthusiasm struck me as somehow contagious as well as aggravating, and we agreed to try it for a few minutes together during the day, and also to continue separately in the mornings when we woke up, and before going to sleep at night. It was during these times that the first picture sequence began.

Here then is Helen's own account of these experiences, beginning with the priestess vision partially quoted in Chapter 1. The experiences somewhat overlapped each other, but Helen presented them separately in three series for the sake of clarity, as I do here. They reflect a quite different side to Helen, and this first experience in particular reflects the Self beyond the personal that I mentioned in the preface to this book.

Series I

The first of the series began with a picture of an unrecognized female figure, heavily draped and kneeling with bowed head. Thick chains were twisted around her wrists and

97

ankles. A fire rose high above her head from a large metal brazier standing near her on a low tripod. She seemed to be some sort of priestess, and the fire appeared to be associated with an ancient religious rite. This figure came to me almost daily for several weeks, each time with a noticeable change. The chains began to drop away and she started to raise her head. At last she stood up very slowly, with only a short, unconnected length of chain still tied to her left wrist. The fire blazed with unaccustomed brightness as she rose.

I was quite unprepared for the intensity of my emotional reaction to her. When she first raised her eyes and looked at me I was terribly afraid. I was sure she would be angry and expected that her eyes would be filled with condemnation and disdain. I kept my head turned away the first few times I saw her after she stood up, but finally made up my mind to look straight at her face. When I did, I burst into tears. Her face was gentle and full of compassion, and her eyes were beyond description. The best word I could find in describing them to Bill was "innocent." She had never seen what I was afraid she would find in me. She knew nothing about me that warranted condemnation. Yet she did know many things I had never known, or at least had entirely forgotten. I loved her so much that I literally fell on my knees in front of her. Then I tried unsuccessfully to unite with her as she stood facing me, either by slipping over to her side or drawing her to mine. I noticed that she still had a few links of chain around her wrists. That, I felt, was probably the problem.

My next reactions were even stranger. I was suddenly swept away by a sense of joy so intense I could hardly breathe. Aloud I asked, "Does this mean I can have my function back?" The answer, silent but perfectly clear, was, "Of course!" At that I began to dance around the room in an intense surge of happiness I had never felt before. I would not have believed it was possible to experience such happiness as that answer brought with it, and for a little while I kept repeating, "How wonderful! Oh, how wonderful!" There seemed to be no doubt that there was a part of me I did not know, but which understood exactly what all this meant. It was a strangely split awareness, of a kind which was to become increasingly familiar.

The priestess still turns up from time to time [written in approximately 1971; I am not aware of Helen's experiencing her as a visual symbol after that time], but I have never been able to identify completely with her yet. Whenever I see her, though, I am strongly impelled to try. Perhaps I will succeed when Bill and I have finally worked out our relationship once and for all. After all, she still wears just a bit of chain around her wrist, though it does seem to me to be getting smaller.

This vision is interesting for a number of reasons, aside from the obvious one of Helen's experiencing the innocence of Christ, so different from her and our self-perceptions of unworthiness. This experience also reflects Helen's conscious perception of two selves: innocence and guilt, the priestess and her ego self. The priestess was thus an extremely important symbol for Helen, and identification with her came to represent Helen's goal of remembering her eternal innocence. Helen's seeming inability to unite with this innocence in herself reflected the inability in her lifetime consciously to forgive Bill, except for rare moments to be discussed later. And yet, the happy end of the vision does certainly reflect forgiveness, pointing to Helen's priestess-Self with which I shall conclude this book. A later vision involving an ancient scroll found in a cave reflects this same forgiveness, and so we shall postpone any further discussion until then.

Series II

The second series, like the first, came to Helen in "short glimpses rather like daydreams and sometimes in sleeping dreams." The pictures included Bill in what would appear to have been past-life situations. It is not necessary, however, for the reader to believe in reincarnation (*see* the manual, pp. 57f, for example). On one level, Helen did not allow herself to believe in it, though her letters to Bill from this period belie her usual assertion of disbelief. Be that as it may, the subject certainly made her most uncomfortable. But if nothing else, the various images do reflect symbolically the strongly ambivalent nature of Helen and Bill's relationship.

We [Helen and Bill] turned up together in various relationships, although the actual chronology was quite confused. Situations which seemed to be quite ancient often came after almost contemporary ones. Many of the episodes struck me as essentially allegorical even at the time. I saw myself in a boat, frantically rowing but getting nowhere. Looking about, I identified the place as Venice and the boat as a gondola. Nearby a tall thin man, very reminiscent of Bill, was leaning casually against a striped wooden post that protruded from the water. His arms were folded across his chest, and he watched me with mock seriousness. I grew more and more certain he was Bill when I noticed his eyes. He was dressed as a gondolier with gleaming sequins scattered across his shirt. He neither moved nor spoke. Then I noticed the gondola was tied to a wharf with a heavy rope. It was a silly situation; I was working hard at the impossible. Bill still said nothing, but it was evident that he regarded my efforts as amusing. He did not offer to help me, although his smile was not unkind.

The next events in the series are quite vague. Bill turned up as a bull fighter in a spectacular costume, gold from head to foot, and there was a dim impression of an arena in the background. He appeared next as a witch doctor with feathers round his ankles and wrists, dressed in a straw skirt and wearing an imposing headdress of bright feathers and gleaming jewels. I wore a simple homespun dress. We were both black. We were standing facing each other in a clearing in a thick jungle, and I seemed to have come to him for help. He was responding to my appeal with a weird dance, accompanied by loud cries in a language I did not understand. At first I felt this would help me, and briefly experienced a sense of comfort. Then I grew afraid and begged him to stop. He did not seem to hear me through the increasingly loud banging of the crude wooden instruments he was holding and the loud beating of drums in the background. I crept away terrified, holding my hands over my ears in a frantic effort to shut out the noise. I was now in a state of real terror, and did not look back. There was no conclusion.

The next episode involving Bill and me seemed like a story within a story. One theme in particular took about a week before reaching its grim conclusion. It was very clear. I was a priestess in what looked like an Egyptian temple, although I had an idea it was much older. Huge stone statues were vaguely outlined along the sides and back of the building. They [obviously, the statues were of figures] were seated stiffly upright, with arms held tightly at the side and hands pressed against the knees. I could not make them out well because the interior of the temple was dimly lit. Even in the half light I could tell that the temple was enormous and extremely imposing. Although the whole temple seemed to be magnificent, the altar, the only brightly-lit part of the temple, was particularly splendid. A blazing light shone down on it from a source I could not identify. Magnificent jewels glowed all around it, and its smooth, polished stone surfaces reflected the light like mirrors. As the high priestess I was very elaborately dressed, wearing a heavily inlaid jewelled crown from which the large center stone was missing.

In the opening "scene," I was standing at the altar leaning over Bill, who lay on the floor almost naked. I was holding the shaft of a sharp spear. Its point was resting on Bill's forehead between his eyes. Then came an extended series of "flashbacks" of the events that led up to the scene. There had been a slave uprising. I was about to kill Bill, the leader of the revolt, who had stolen the large center ruby from my crown. It was not an ordinary ruby. It gave its wearer magical powers. The thief had to be killed if these powers were to return to me, the savage priestess whose religion was power and enslavement. To revolt against her was to ask for death.

I cannot account for what happened next. I can only say that it was totally out of character and completely unexpected. I felt intense rage and vindictiveness as I prepared to plunge the point of the spear into Bill's head between his eyes. He did not seem to be particularly frightened. He merely looked up at me and waited. I braced myself, ready to bring the spear down, and hesitated just an instant. I knew it was all over with me. *Bill would live and I would die.* As I threw the spear down my death was certain.

In the final episode, I was standing alone on the top step of a wide stairway before an enormous bolted door. I was outside the temple. My crown was gone, and so was my magnificent robe. I was wearing a loose white dress, smudged down the sides and torn at the neck. In front of me was nothing but desert. The wind blew hot dry sand against my face, and I could see whitened bones scattered about in the distance. Mine would soon be among them. I cursed myself bitterly for not killing Bill. I must have been insane. Anger literally shook me as I walked slowly down the stairway, with thirst already biting at my throat and the smell of death in the wind.

The emotional impact of this last episode was intense and long-lasting. I felt the anger long after the images faded, and it later blazed into open fury as I told Bill the story at lunch the next day, particularly when I spoke of the theft of the ruby. It was as if it were happening all over again. A crystal-clear picture of the ruby, beautiful and blood red, rose before my eyes, as I spoke. And for a brief period the scene became reality for me. Again I berated myself for dying for a rebellious slave who was nothing but a common thief. I could barely contain my fury at Bill, who was understandably upset. So was I. The intensity of my anger was quite startling to both of us [my italics].

When Helen and I discussed this episode many years later, I was surprised to find remnants of this specific anger still within her. She described to me one earlier attempt on Bill's part to be nice to her, and she shot back to him that it was "too little and too late!" It seemed largely a result of this experience that Helen felt justified in blaming Bill, as mentioned before, not only for her present woes, but for all of her past ones as well, including the almost forty-nine years she lived before ever meeting him. The extent of her anger, not to mention hatred, was truly alarming, reminiscent of her later experience of hate in London, described above in Chapter 2.

The "one or the other" motif—"Bill would live and I would die"—plays an important role in the ego's thought system, as *A Course in Miracles* would later explain. And it was a most important theme in Helen's ego life as well. It came in different forms. A prominent one, to which we shall return, was that Helen would help others, but always feeling sacrificial, as if she were giving up something of herself. Another form was that it was extremely difficult for Helen to love two people at the same time: psychologically, one had to live, the other die. Important pairs in her life in which this was played out included her parents, her mother and Louis, Louis and Bill, Bill and me, me and Louis. In all of these, Helen's love and attention could be expressed only to one of the two, never to both simultaneously. This dynamic plays an important role in the ego's defense against God's Love, which knows only of total acceptance of *all* His children, without exception and without loss of any kind to anyone.

It took a while before Helen was able to let the next experience in the series come to her mind. She had been sharing these inner events with Bill on a daily level, and "It was almost as though we had to recover a little before going on." Though the next image was also negative in its outcome, it did lack the intensity of the previous one.

Bill, a Franciscan monk dressed in a brown robe and sandals, was walking up and down an arched monastery corridor, intent on a book. The corridor was one of the four sides bordering on a small, well-kept green lawn. There was a lovely fountain in the middle, with birds bathing in the basin and rows of bright flowers around its base and scattered in patches across the grass. The time was uncertain, but the place seemed to be in Spain. I was walking slowly down the corridor toward Bill, dressed in heavy black. My face was veiled, my eyes were cast down, and my hands were clasped as if in prayer. When I reached Bill I knelt before him as a penitent and very humbly asked him for forgiveness. He did not look up. Anger took hold of me, and I rose and accused him of being an over-intellectualized religious without a heart. He did not seem to hear me, merely continuing serenely with his reading. His eyes never left the book. I backed away in angry but helpless frustration. The picture faded out slowly and inconclusively.

This scene is reminiscent of much of what went on in Helen's mind regarding Bill; namely, that he was insensitive to her needs, and moreover, that he was unaware of his own passive hostility.

What followed was a return to the image of this most holy priestess, Helen's true Self.

The next scene, in order of appearance, was so ancient that it seemed to be taking place at the very beginning of time. I was a priestess again, but of a very different kind. This priestess was, in fact, much like the one with the innocent eyes whom I had watched emerging from heavy chains into freedom. *While I was certain this priestess was myself, I was somehow not quite at one with her, just as I could not completely identify with her previous likeness.* She was hidden from the world in a small white marble temple, set in a broad and very green valley. I was not sure that her body was entirely solid. Actually what I saw was little more than an outline of a small, slender woman dressed in white, who never came further into the world than the doorway of a little room containing a plain wooden altar against the far wall. A small flame burned on it, sending up a small, steady column of white smoke. The priestess stayed close to the altar, sitting on a low wooden stool, praying with closed eyes for those who came to her for help.

There were a number of episodes in this series. Sometimes I saw only the green valley outside the white temple. Sometimes there seemed to be no one there, but at other times the valley was filled with a huge column of people marching joyously together in rows that seemed to extend endlessly in both directions. I could feel a deep sense of freedom and unity in each one as he marched ahead to certain victory.

I was not sure of the exact role the priestess had in their happiness, but I knew her prayers somehow made a vital contribution. I was also sure that people came to her for help from all over; some, in fact, from very far away. They did not, however, speak to the priestess directly. They knelt one by one at the ledge that ran around a low wall separating the inner and outer parts of the temple, stating their needs to a man who seemed like a sort of intermediary between the priestess and the world. He stayed in the enclosed space between the priestess and those who came for help. The man conveyed their needs to her.

He played a crucial role in enabling the priestess to fulfill her function, and I insisted for a long time that he was not Bill, although at length I came to concede that he probably was [in a later vision of the same priestess, the man was Jesus; *see below*, pp. 246f]. He was tall and thin, but I could not see his face clearly. When people told him what they needed, he went to the door of her room and said: "Priestess, a brother has come to your shrine. Heal him for me." She never asked for anyone's name, nor for the details of his request. She merely prayed for him, sitting very quietly beside the flame on the altar. It never occurred to her that help would not be granted. She prayed for everyone in the same way, and never really left God's side, remaining peacefully certain of His presence there in the room with her. She never really stepped into the world, and was very quiet and very happy. She was so close to God that she was always aware of Him. *I was sure she was myself, and yet I was not sure. What was certain was that I watched her with great love* [my italics].

The sentences in italics reflect again Helen's recognition that the priestess was herself, and yet at the same time she was not able to identify with her. The other-worldly image of the priestess—"I was not sure that her body was entirely solid";

"She never really stepped into the world"; the fact that she was "hidden from the world" in an inner temple that people could not enter except through an intermediary—suggests that her Self was not really here, but remained totally at one with God's Love. Thus she "never really left God's side, remaining peacefully certain of His presence there in the room with her....She was so close to God that she was always aware of Him." This reflected the state of mind *A Course in Miracles* would later call the "real world," mentioned earlier.

Finally, the priestess' prayer anticipates the first principle of miracles with which the Course begins, that there is no order of difficulty among them (text, p. 1). She prayed for all the people "in the same way" and "never asked for anyone's name, nor for the details of his request," and it "never occurred to her that help would not be granted." For Helen, the priestess was truly the holiest person in the world, and Helen's experience of her was the reminder that she was that Person (Self) as well. A parallel experience in content, though not in form, is described by Helen in a letter to Bill, to be presented below in Chapter 6. This vision involved a laurel wreath (representing Helen's self) disappearing into a light.

The next episode returned Helen to earth, as it were, and to the "more usual" antagonism between her and Bill, this time with Helen cast as the victimizer and Bill as the victim.

> The next episode was a dramatic contrast. Bill and I were now both slaves in what seemed to be mid-19th century America. We were married, but I was quite contemptuous of him. He was much older than I, much darker in skin coloring and deeply religious in what I regarded as a very simple-minded way. I saw no justification for his childlike trust in God. He had a similarly naive trust in me, and for this at least I knew he had no reason. The actual story was unclear, but I dimly sensed part of what was happening. I was beautiful, almost white in appearance, and completely amoral. White men took a liking to me, and I traded favors readily enough. I had managed to make a deal whereby I was to gain freedom by disappearing from the scene with the help of my white "friends." Bill would have to remain behind, a fact which caused me no concern whatsoever. I felt I was much above

him; better educated, much more attractive, and far more sophisticated. I had no use for his simple-minded religious notions. I hid my plans from him until the very end. Then I enjoyed telling him about them. He did not condemn me or attempt to interfere. I turned my back on him and flounced out. But I remember the sadness in his eyes.

This second series ended, most unexpectedly given the preceding pictures, on a "note of achievement and even glory." The characteristic in these episodes of rapid shifts from one dimension of Helen to another, incidentally, was also found in her "normal," everyday experience, as I shall discuss in a later chapter.

I was in a large room on the top floor of a church building. Bill, seated at a large, old-fashioned church organ, was playing Handel's "Hallelujah Chorus," his face glowing with joy. We had finally reached our goal. I was standing at the back of the room, facing a simple brown wooden altar on which two words were written one above the other. I cannot imagine a less appropriate pair of words. The top word was "Elohim," which I did not recognize at the time. Later I found out it is the Hebrew word for God. The other word, "Evoe," I recognized to be the cry of the Greek Bacchantes, the female revellers in the rites of Bacchus.

As I watched, a jagged streak of lightning from the back of the room struck the altar and obliterated the second word entirely. Only "Elohim" remained, its bright gold letters standing out in stark simplicity against the brown background of the altar. The music reached a crescendo and a figure outlined in brilliant light stepped from behind the altar and came toward me. Recognizing him as Jesus I started to kneel, but he came around to my side and knelt beside me at the altar, saying, "I would as soon kneel at your altar as have you kneel at mine." Bill rose from the organ and knelt at his other side. And then a Voice, with which I was to become increasingly familiar, said silently but unmistakably, "That altar is within you." The impact was so intense that I burst into tears and did not regain my composure for some time.

This vision was among the most powerful and meaningful of Helen's life, and reflected the return to her deepest Self through her having chosen, irrevocably, to let go of her ego (symbolized by the word "Evoe"). As that choice for God was made, only His memory would remain in her mind. The immediate effect of that choice, as experienced in this world, was the joining with Jesus and Bill that was the climax of the vision. The choice for God came through her joining with Jesus, who represents the priestess-Self in Helen, the innocence of Christ. This allowed her then to join with Bill, who now is perceived as the image of Helen's innocence, projected from her mind. This innocence came to be symbolized later in the Course by the image of "the face of Christ." Bill was Helen's special learning lesson, and by forgiving him the sins she perceived in him, she would be forgiving her own. Thus she would be able at last to remember her true Self. The climactic message from the inner Voice of the Holy Spirit—"That altar is within you"—meant of course that the external vision merely reflected the inner altar of her mind, where the choice was made.

When in the summer of 1974 I moved to an apartment a block away from Helen, I arranged to have the Elohim altar built for her, exactly to the specifications of the vision, both in size and color. Where the word "Evoe" had been, I had a gold star painted. In *A Course in Miracles* the star is a symbol for Christ, the light-filled presence of God revealed to us through forgiveness and the undoing of the ego. For Helen, a gold star was even more specifically a deeply meaningful symbol for Jesus. As I knew the importance that this vision had for Helen, I thought having the altar in my apartment, in which we would spend a fair amount of time together, would be meaningful to her. Louis certainly never would have wanted it in their apartment, and I am not so sure Helen would have wanted it either.

The altar stood in front of my bed-couch on which we often prayed together, and Helen and I spent many hours in its presence. Helen told me at times she would awaken in the middle of the night, think of the altar in my apartment, and feel a very strong pull coming from it to her. She experienced this pull quite directly as the Love of God, not different from her intense love experiences in the subway or southern France. I also had asked Helen to take down a poem for the altar when I moved in, and she kindly obliged with these two lovely stanzas:

107

Dedication For An Altar

Temples are where God's holy altars are,
And He has placed an altar in each Son
Whom He created. Let us worship here
In thankfulness that what He gives to one
He gives to all, and never takes away.
For what He wills has been forever done.

Temples are where a brother comes to pray
And rest a while. Whoever he may be,
He brings with him a lighted lamp to show
My Savior's face is there for me to see
Upon the altar, and remember God.
My brother, come and worship here with me.
                                        (*The Gifts of God*, p. 93)

Series III

The final series of pictures was longer than the others, and had a plot, as it were. Throughout the sequence a male figure appeared from time to time, always in a helping role. At first Helen had no recognition of him, then thought perhaps he was Bill. But eventually she "was sure he was really Jesus, a realization accompanied by great surprise and even shock." At some point later on when Helen was recounting one of the episodes to Bill, he asked her what Jesus looked like, and she replied: "It's a funny thing, but he looks a lot like you." They both found this surprising, and still later when Helen asked Jesus about it, she heard: "How else would you expect me to look?" The series basically relates Helen's own inner journey, and its stirring yet peaceful conclusion. The "story" began

as I was wandering along the shore of a lake, and coming upon a large deserted boat lying on its side, with a door to its cabin swung open. It was held down by thick ropes attached to a heavy metal anchor sunk deep into the mud that covered much of the boat as well, apparently preventing rescue. It had obviously been abandoned years ago. I somehow knew I was supposed to get it started again, although salvage seemed all but impossible.

I knew I could not possibly release the boat without help but I nevertheless felt impelled to try. I tugged futilely at the

108

ropes, which were so heavy I could hardly lift them. Besides, the mud was so slippery that I kept falling. I called out for help, although I knew that no one was likely to hear me in such a deserted spot. It crossed my mind that I might perhaps telephone for help, but this did not seem likely either as there were no houses anywhere nearby. It was a frustrating situation. I realized the importance of freeing the boat but I was also aware of my complete inability to do so. And then the answer came to me. I had been going about it wrong.

"Inside the boat is a very powerful receiving and sending set," said the internal Voice. "It hasn't been used for a very long time but it still works. And that's the only way you'll ever get the boat started again."

The first episode ended there.

Several rather unclear things happened next. A Man[26] turned up from somewhere, and together we managed to drag the anchor out of the mud, set the boat straight and finally get it into the water. Then it began to move, although the anchor dragged a little at first. The boat gained momentum, however, and seemed to embark on a very definite course, almost on its own power. I had no idea where it was going, but apparently I did not need to know. The Man did know. That was sufficient.

After the boat had gone on for a time the water began to get rough and I was beginning to feel afraid. Fortunately, the Man was in the boat, dressed for trouble in a yellow slicker, helmet and boots. This time I did identify him as Jesus. I was steering uncertainly when he arrived, and he took the wheel from my hand.

"You go over there and sit down," he said firmly but not unkindly. "It's going to be heavy weather for a while. I'll get you through this and then you can steer again."

I was neither surprised nor particularly impressed. I even seemed to have expected him. I sat down uneasily on a bench along the side of the boat.

"If you think there's going to be trouble," I said timidly, "maybe we should use that receiving and sending set that's inside the boat and ask for more help."

"We'll just keep away from that," said the Man, quickly and still more firmly. "You're not ready yet. You'd merely get into

---

26. As will be discussed below, Helen's personal preference was to capitalize nouns and pronouns related to Jesus, although this practice is not followed in *A Course in Miracles*.

trouble. When you're ready to use it, I'll tell you. Meanwhile, don't worry. We'll make it all right."

I watched as the Man adroitly steered the boat through a very narrow passage in which the current was surprisingly strong. A violent storm raged all around us. Rain poured down from a black sky, and enormous waves rose above the sides of the boat and splashed across the deck. Oddly enough, I did not even get wet. Gradually the storm subsided and the boat emerged into quiet waters, and I found the steering wheel again in my own hands. "You can take over, now," he said. "I'll watch."

The Man, still Jesus, had taken off his slicker, and was lounging comfortably in shorts and an open-necked summer shirt. The weather had turned warm and sunny, the water smooth and the boat was easy to steer. We were standing together at the wheel and chatting. I noticed that he wore a gold chain around his neck, with a small unfamiliar gold symbol hanging from it. I thought perhaps it might be a Hebrew letter. Then I remembered something.

"I have one like that," I said, looking at the symbol. "In fact, I'm wearing it right now."

"I know that," replied the Man, smiling.

"The only thing is," I added, "Mine goes the other way."

"I know that, too," said the Man, still smiling. "As a matter of fact, this one is yours as well as the one you're wearing. I'll keep it for you a while longer, though, but I promise to give it to you when you can use it and it will be helpful."

The two symbols, mirror images of each other, were so clear in my mind that I copied them down afterwards. One went from left to right and the other from right to left. Otherwise they were the same. Some time later I ran across a friend who had been a Hebrew scholar, and asked if he recognized them. He was uncertain at first, but finally recognized the symbols. "Of course!" he said, "the symbol of the miracle of the reversal." He had to explain to me that when Moses came down from Mount Sinai where God had given him the ten commandments, the words could be read correctly from either the front or the back of the tablets, even though this was not possible by ordinary means.

An added though parallel explanation, which I supplied Helen when she told me the story and drew the two symbols, was that when they were placed together, the symbols traced the outline of the two tablets. The tablets, along with the ten commandments, represented God's covenant with the Jewish people. I felt that in Helen's vision the two symbols represented the covenant she and Jesus had made with each other to take down *A Course in Miracles.* The symbols closely resembled the Hebrew letter "resh" ("r" in English), and its reversal. Here is how they looked, with the resh on the left:

Helen's account continues:

My reactions to this information were curiously mixed. On the one hand I was delighted and also deeply impressed. On the other hand, however, I was irritated and even angry. It might be more accurate to say I was afraid. I still found it hard to believe that my pictures were more than unrealistic attempts at wish-fulfillment, and I had somehow managed to dismiss much of what I had already seen and heard on that basis. I did not like this sort of thing, and found it very difficult to credit. This, however, was harder to explain away so easily.

Perhaps it was my discomfort that held up the rest of the series for some time, and when the next episode did come it took the form of a dream. In characteristic dream fashion, the boat had turned into a car. I was driving across a bridge in very heavy traffic. I wanted to make a right turn, but I was in the wrong lane and another car was blocking my way. Both of us were crowded in, with cars in front and behind. The situation was one large traffic jam. Apparently, there was no possible way I could safely make the turn, even though it was essential that I do so.

"If I try to turn I'll crash into that car next to me," I thought, "and if he turns right I won't have time to follow before the gap will close and I'll be jammed in again."

I was much distressed about this, and kept trying to think up ways to make the turn. But all of them were inadequate, most of them were disastrous, and one or two would probably turn out to be fatal. And then the solution came to me.

"We'll make it together," I thought, happily. "It won't be

any trouble at all." And so our two cars made the right turn together. It was very easy. "It's funny I never thought of that before," I said to myself as the picture faded.

Next time I found myself back in the boat alone, still aware of having taken the right turn. The boat was moving easily and slowly along a narrow pretty canal. The landscape was quite beautiful and very peaceful. The canal was lined with lovely old trees and green lawns edged with banks of flowers, and there was just enough breeze to help the boat along.

"I wonder if there's buried treasure here," I thought to myself, dreamily. "I wouldn't be surprised if there is. It's just the place for it." Then I noticed a long pole with a large hook at the end, lying on the bottom of the boat. "Just the thing," I thought, dropping the hook into the quiet water and reaching the pole down as far as I could. The hook caught something heavy and I raised it with difficulty. It was an ancient treasure chest, the wood worn from the water, but the metal edges and lock still intact. The bottom was covered with seaweed. I managed to get the chest into the boat and opened it excitedly.

I was bitterly disappointed. I had expected buried treasure, probably jewels or coins, but there was nothing in the chest except a large black book. The binding was like the "spring binders" used for temporarily holding large manuscripts or papers together. On the spine, printed in gold, was the single word "Aesculapius." When I looked it up I found it was the name of the Greek god of healing [here given by Helen in its Roman spelling]. I saw the book again a few nights later. This time there was a string of pearls around it. Neither Bill nor I had any idea what the book stood for until one day, long afterwards, we suddenly realized that the binding looked like the black thesis binders in which we had put the original manuscript of the course for safekeeping.

Helen later told me of still another experience of the "book," in a dream during this same period. She was standing on the ground looking up at a stork flying overhead. Helen wondered what was so special about that, and then the inner Voice said, "Look at what the stork is carrying." And when Helen looked she did not see the expected baby, but rather the black book, this time with a gold cross on the cover. The Voice then said to her, "This is your book."

This important series requires some commentary, although its broad meaning is clear. The "large deserted boat" can be understood as the Atonement journey that Helen at last is ready to undertake: "It had obviously been abandoned years ago. I somehow knew I was supposed to get it started again, although salvage seemed all but impossible." Yet Helen recognized that she could not do it alone; this recognition itself—an expression of the "little willingness" *A Course in Miracles* emphasizes—starts her successfully on the journey. She still attempts to free the boat herself, but understands the futility of her efforts: "I knew I could not possibly release the boat without help but I nevertheless felt impelled to try.... I realized the importance of freeing the boat but I was also aware of my complete inability to do so."

It is explained to Helen that the only way of freeing the boat—beginning the journey—was through the "very powerful receiving and sending set." This symbolized her ancient ability to "hear," or to experience a closeness with Jesus that only comes from a decision to join with love. She, however, was not ready to use it yet; as she was told later in the sequence: "You'd merely get into trouble. When you're ready to use it, I'll tell you." But she was able to let Jesus help her free the boat: "*together* we managed to...finally get it into the water [my italics]." She did not know the course of the boat's voyage, but as Jesus did, her understanding was not necessary. Moreover, he always appeared when help was needed, and his presence began to feel natural to Helen.

The incident with the parallel gold symbols, though opposite to each other, underscores the idea of Helen's joining with Jesus. If my interpretation is correct (*see above*, pp. 110f), their joining together results in the fulfillment of the covenant made between them. The episode with the cars turning together, Helen's joining with the other driver, then reflects the joining with Bill. No longer seeing their interests as separate, if not antagonistic to each other, she happily realizes the solution: "We'll make it together." And so the two cars make the turn as one.

The end of the journey comes in the quiet waters of a canal, whose banks are lined with the green lawns that are reminiscent of the lawns of Heaven representing the real world, the goal of our journey with the Course. And there Helen finds her

113

treasure, not the treasure of the ego, but that of the love in her heart: the manuscript of *A Course in Miracles* that reflects her love for Jesus, and is the fruit of her having joined with him. Again, a most significant experience for Helen.

Having no interest nor belief in psychic phenomena, Helen found these series, as well as other picture images that began to appear, most disconcerting. These images strongly suggested what Helen referred to as "flashbacks of myself in other times and places." As mentioned earlier, one part of Helen found the idea of reincarnation "particularly repellent," and so she later chose to think of these as

> strictly symbolic; the usual shifting dream symbols most familiar to clinical psychologists. I watched them as a spectator, although I had little doubt that they were representations of myself.

It was obvious to her, however, that events were occurring that were difficult to explain away.

> I was so conflicted about the situation that I tried not to think about it at all. The whole thing was quite unsettling. . . . They [the inner events] were consistent, certainly, and rather well organized. Nevertheless, I believed, or perhaps more accurately hoped, that they were merely imaginative. On any other basis I would have become intensely fearful.

In retrospect, it is clear that these inner experiences, at least in part, were preparation for what was to follow, events that would be "truly hard to explain."

Helen's husband Louis found hearing about these experiences most anxiety-producing, and so she told him relatively little. Bill, however, was intensely interested in all of these episodes, and Helen gave him a running account as they occurred. Besides, it was certainly something that involved both of them—together. Like Helen, Bill had no prior interest in, nor knowledge of, psychic phenomena. However, as these episodes unfolded he began to develop a serious interest, being sure that they meant something. Bill began to acquire and read books on the subject, the beginning of his amassing a rather large library, which, as *A Course in Miracles* unfolded, also included an impressive array of books on spirituality and mysticism, East and West. Bill clearly took a much broader and open-minded view of paranormal phenomena than Helen did. He was particularly impressed by the evidence which suggested that minds can reach each other by extrasensory means, and would point out to Helen that "some rather unusual things" had been occurring that clearly could not be accounted for in the usual way. Helen could not disagree with that, despite her enormous anxiety.

Early on, after the third series of inner experiences ended, Bill read a book on the great American psychic Edgar Cayce, written by his son, Hugh Lynn Cayce. Bill was impressed and tried to talk about it with Helen, who agreed to read it, though not without considerable distaste, despite her "determination to remain objective." She did find the book interesting, yet at the same time was

> repelled by what I regarded as its "spooky" and more incredible aspects.... Bill was clearly impressed by the Cayce readings, but, as I told myself, he was apt to be impressed by pretty much anything along those lines. I did not think it strange that he believed the very odd things I told him about, but that was different.

Bill's continued attempts to interest Helen in this field were met with strong opposition. Helen wrote:

> Perhaps out of desperation, although he was never the virulent atheist I had become, Bill read a few books on what I had no hesitation in describing to Louis as "the nutty fringe of religion." When Bill made a mild reference to something he had read on reincarnation, I was convinced that he was really slipping....I refused to read the books he suggested, and tended to get uncomfortable and angry when he brought the subject up.

Helen thus remained

> firmly opposed to taking such strange things seriously, even though my position might seem somewhat inconsistent. I did not see it that way myself. Things were happening to me that were hard to explain, and that was all. It did not justify assuming any weird sort of extrasensory basis. The idea of reincarnation was particularly repugnant to me. I regarded it as nonsensical....I was also aware that it made me very anxious.

Again, we shall find a totally different Helen in her letters to Bill that date from this same period. The letters, uncensored by the later literary or social concerns that affected her account of these experiences, most definitely reflect her belief in reincarnation. These letters are the subject of the next chapter.

These "strange" and "nonsensical" events continued to occur, however, and the next series of picture images began with Helen observing

> a thin, frail girl in an opulent French drawing room. The time seemed to be about the middle of the 18th century, judging from her dress. It was all white, fitted to the waist and reaching to the floor, with many flounces, bows and lace edgings. She was playing a musical instrument resembling a harpsichord in a gathering of magnificently-dressed ladies and gentlemen, apparently guests at a lavish social event. The girl was eighteen at most, and obviously ill. "She's too frail," I said as I watched her. "She won't live another year. She can't do anything but just fade away. It's a mistake. She's never going to make it." A splendidly-dressed butler stepped forward and closed the drawing room doors, rather in the manner of someone closing the curtains on a scene in the theater. The girl was gone.
>
> Shortly afterwards there was an even vaguer picture of another girl, somewhat older than the first, lying on the straw-covered floor of an airless room in a prison. Her arms were bound tightly behind her with rope and her feet were chained to the floor. The time seemed to be somewhere around the 12th or 13th century, and the place was unknown. It might still have been France, but this was by no means definite. There was no conclusive story associated with the girl, although I had the frightening feeling that she was probably killed in the end. I have no idea why.

Subsequent pictures included a nun, appearing in different times and places, and not always Christian. The clearest of these took place in France, where the nun was an

> elderly, arthritic and bitter woman, worn thin and ill by a life of severe austerity, and emotionally warped and sterile. She was walking down the side aisle of a large and beautiful church strikingly reminiscent of the Cathedral of Notre Dame in Paris. The aisle was dim and the candle the nun held tightly in her

right hand helped hardly at all. As she walked, she ran her left hand slowly along the grey stone wall beside her as if searching for a door or perhaps more literally a way out. She did not find it. The grim lines on her face deepened as I watched her. "She doesn't know," I thought. "She's trying, but she doesn't know." I was repelled by her hard expression, but I felt a deep sympathy for her lost cause.

These three unhappy images, all of which took place in France, would certainly seem to be related to Helen's curious ambivalence about that country. She could speak French beautifully, and was able to sing by heart sections from Debussy's great opera, *Pelleas et Melisande,* and yet she hated to use this ability. In fact, I very rarely heard Helen speak French at all. Bill once told me how, when they were attending an international psychological conference in France, Helen refused to speak French at all, a refusal which placed these two Americans at a decided disadvantage. In fact, Bill once literally had to plead with Helen to use her French to help them out of a practical jam, in which the people they needed help from spoke no English at all. On the other hand, it was while in southern France that Helen had that wonderfully ecstatic experience of love that was discussed in Chapter 1.

The following image of the young girl, the last in this series, was unique. Her innocence finds practically no counterpart in any of Helen's experiences, with the exception of the priestess, and obviously reflected that Self that had practically no expression in her life.

In striking contrast to that grim figure [of the Notre Dame nun] was one that recurred at intervals and still crosses my mind every once in a while. This one was the only image that kept returning in completely unchanged form. This was a picture of a girl who resembled me in many ways, although she did not seem to be over sixteen. Her head was thrown slightly back in happy laughter and her arms were extended as if in universal welcome. She was wholly joyous; literally incapable of feeling grief or pain. She was standing on a bright green lawn [once again, note this symbol for the real world] and in her extraordinary happiness her bare feet hardly seemed to touch the ground. She was dressed in a loose blue dress that was not reminiscent of any particular time or place, although

117

there was something of a Greek feeling about it. However, nothing about her really suggested the past, nor did she seem to be at all concerned about the future. I do not really think she regarded time as we do.

As with the priestess, Helen recognized herself in the young innocent girl. Filled with "happy laughter," she was "wholly joyous" and knew nothing of grief or pain. Moreover, there was a timeless quality about her that suggested her not really being in the world at all, though appearing to be. Again, this was an image of the Self beyond "Heaven and Helen."

As these images continued, Helen was hard put to explain them, and finally had to concede that her logical mind and scientific background were of no help. This concession seemed to usher in a new level of psychic experiences, providing additional evidence for her that her scientific mind was severely limited in its explanatory power.

The new phase started one day when Bill and I were working on a research report and I was concentrating on the statistical treatment of the data. Suddenly and very unexpectedly I laid the papers down and said, with great urgency, "Quick, Bill! Joe, your friend in Chicago, is thinking about suicide. We must send him a message right away." Bill sat down next to me as I "sent" an earnest mental message to Joe. The words I used were: "The answer is life, not death." Afterwards, I said to Bill, "I bet there was nothing to it," but I was wrong. Bill called his friend that evening to ask him if he was all right. Joe was glad he had called; he had been very depressed, and had actually picked up a gun that afternoon, but something held him back. He put the gun down.

It was hard not to be impressed, particularly as surprising events continued to happen for a while. Bill had gone to an out-of-town meeting, and on his return I described the place where he had stayed in great detail even though I had never seen it. I also told him a number of things that had happened there before he had a chance to tell me about them, apparently with extraordinary accuracy. [In one of them] I had seen a clear picture of him at the top of a staircase, standing there hesitantly, turning, and then returning downstairs. Bill told me that he had in fact done that. He had not noticed where the bathroom was, and thought it might be upstairs. As he reached the top of the stairway, however, he saw there were

118

only unmarked and closed doors on the second floor, and suspecting that he must have missed the door downstairs, he hesitated to make sure, and then turned to go back. Later I gave him a very detailed description of a friend's house in the country where he stayed for a week-end, even to the colors of the walls and furniture. Still later, when he was away on vacation in the Virgin Islands I sent him a "mental message" in which I described a pin I would like him to bring me, a gold pin with a Florentine finish. I happened to notice that it was almost ten o'clock in the morning when the thought occurred to me. Bill handed me the pin on his return. He had been walking down a shopping street around ten o'clock after his arrival with a friend [Chip] who also knew me. They were passing a jewelry store. Bill did not want to go in, but his friend practically insisted. The friend also picked out a Florentine gold pin, urging Bill to buy it for me and telling him it was just what I wanted.

Helen had ambivalent reactions to these experiences. One part of her mind was proud of these abilities, even finding herself enjoying fantasies of power and prestige that this psychic ability might bring her. But another part of Helen's mind felt considerable fear, and desperately tried to explain away the episodes, going to "great and even preposterous lengths" to do so. This ambivalence of attraction and fear became stronger for a while, leading to nightmares she could not remember. Although Helen could not recall the dreams' content, she found it difficult to put associations of "witchcraft and evil" out of her mind.

Yet pride kept pace with anxiety, and though I felt an increasing sense of danger I also experienced a concomitant feeling of self-inflation.

It was while in what Helen termed her "magic phase," that something happened that involved a

strange mixture of fact and fantasy but which also pointed to a definite future direction. The episode began with evident magical overtones, continuing on a more religious note and ending with a simple, real-life situation.

This episode, as will be clear from Helen's account, was one of the most significant experiences she and Bill shared together.

Its "message" provided a very down-to-earth foreshadowing of the Course's message of joining by sharing another's interest. As the manual for teachers would later say of the teacher of God:

> His qualifications consist solely in this; somehow, somewhere he has made a deliberate choice in which he did not see his interests as apart from someone else's (manual, p. 3).

Helen's narrative continues:

> The hospital wanted to send Bill and myself to the Mayo Clinic to study their psychological assessment procedures. The evening [September 9, 1965] before we left, a picture crossed my mind that was so sharp I felt impelled to call Bill and describe it in writing: "We will go to Mayo on the 10th. We will see a grey stone church with a slightly darker grey center steeple which is very tall, and two much taller ones, one on each side. (I thought briefly that there were spheres on the small spires, but then I dismissed that as too obviously phallic. But maybe symbols aren't involved, if they're just there.) There is a small stone cross on top of the largest spire. On the corner to the left (as you face the church) is a wire trash can under the street light. At first I thought the church was Catholic, but it's probably Lutheran. The street behind the street light goes uphill sharply. It's a little crooked. There may be a parking lot or some sort of empty lot with grey stones on the corner across from the street light. There are little shops on both sides of the hill, but none on the sides of the church, or opposite it. I think there's just grass and bushes maybe."
>
> The details stood out with startling clarity. I seemed to be looking down on it from above, at an angle which suggested I might be seeing it from a low-flying plane. The picture was so clear that I abandoned caution and told Bill I was sure we would see the church when we landed in Minnesota the next day.
>
> I was disappointed and angry when we saw nothing of the sort. I had gone way out on a limb, and felt let down and embarrassed. In an attempt to restore my injured self-esteem, I tried to sound a lot more certain than I felt. I said, with great conviction, that we would find the church somewhere in the town of Rochester. It was late when we arrived, we were tired and we had an early appointment the next morning. At the hotel, I looked up a church directory, and found there were

quite a number of churches in different parts of the city, and I still thought the church I was looking for was Lutheran, I was no longer really too sure of anything about it. We went to our rooms for a short nap, planning to meet for dinner.

I could not sleep. I had to find that church. It had become outrageously important to me. We took a cab after dinner and tried to find my church. Before we started out I picked out several churches from the hotel directory that for one reason or another looked as though they might be likely candidates. They were not right. Then I described the church to the taxi driver and asked him if he knew of one reasonably like it. He did not sound hopeful, although he suggested a few more possibilities. [My memory of Helen and Bill's recounting the story was that, of the twenty-seven or twenty-eight churches in Rochester, Minnesota, they saw twenty-four.] At length Bill wisely insisted that they go back to the hotel and forget the whole thing. I hated to give up, but the driver was obviously getting worried about us, and wanted us out of his cab. Besides, it was getting very late and we were both quite tired by that time.

I dozed off from time to time, but kept waking up with a start, in the grip of a long series of bad dreams. When I met Bill the next morning we were both red-eyed and tired. We had barely slept. We got through our tightly-scheduled day somehow, and toward evening drove wearily out to the airport. Bill went to look at a newsstand while I sat down and closed my eyes. I was too tired to look at anything. I was just dozing off....

"And here's your church," said Bill, holding a picture from a guidebook in front of me [see p. P-6 for a picture of Helen's church].

"Oh, yes, that's it!" I said, now happily wide awake. "Where is it?"

"Nowhere," answered Bill. "Here. Read about it yourself."

Bill was right. The church was indeed nowhere. It had once occupied the site of the Mayo Clinic, but had been torn down when the hospital was built.

"So that's why I was looking down on it," I exclaimed, "It was because it's in the past. It had nothing to do with planes."

And then a chill went over me and I did not want to talk about the church any more. There wasn't too much to say, really. The episode had, however, a most unexpected and very real conclusion.

On the way home we had to change planes [in Chicago], and waited a good hour in a cold, almost empty airport. Huddled against a wall was a solitary young woman. I could feel waves and waves of misery going through her. I pointed her out to Bill, who was against my talking to her. We were both exhausted, it was very late, and he was not up to getting involved with strangers at that point. Besides, I might just be imagining her distress. She did not give any outward signs of anything but sleepiness. I could not, however, escape the feelings of pain I was receiving from her. Finally I told Bill I could not help myself, and went to talk to her.

Her name was Charlotte and she said she was scared stiff. She had never been in a plane before that day, and had already been several hours in the air during a very rough trip. She was severely shaken, and dreadfully afraid of going on to New York, for which she was headed. Would I sit with her and hold her hand? "Of course," I told her. "It's just that way at first. After a while you get so used to it that you don't mind it a bit."

I took Charlotte over to Bill, explained the situation, and suggested that she sit between us on the plane so she would have a friend on both sides. Bill was courteous, of course, but I could tell he was not pleased with me. He had not had a very happy trip, and it was the middle of the night. He felt, with some justice, that we could do with a peaceful trip home.

Charlotte shook badly as the plane took off, but I patted her hand and she calmed down quickly. Then she wanted to talk. Charlotte was nineteen, and was leaving home because her stepmother hated her, and her father, whom she loved had turned against her. She intended to get a job and never go home again. It turned out, however, that she had done remarkably little in the way of planning and had no idea where she would stay in New York, and it had not occurred to her that the airport might be some distance from the city. She was not worried, however, because she had three hundred dollars with her. Besides, she was a Lutheran, and she was sure that all she had to do was find a Lutheran church and they would be glad to take care of her. Bill and I exchanged glances. The message was not hard to grasp. "And this," said the Voice, "is really my church."

Bill may have objected to getting involved with Charlotte originally, but he certainly rallied now. When we reached the airport Charlotte went to the ladies room. Bill and I held an emergency conference while she was gone. It was obvious that she could not take care of herself in the city. Bill phoned a New York hotel for women [the Barbizon] and reserved a room for her. We took her to the hotel in our cab, and told her I would call her there the next day.

When I called, Charlotte sounded happy and excited. She was going sight-seeing and shopping. I gave her my address and phone number, and told her to get in touch with me if she needed anything. We had no trouble in keeping in touch with her. That afternoon Bill ran into her accidentally in a department store [Bloomingdale's] and the following evening she dropped in at my house for dinner. Louis and I were both friendly, so she came back the next evening. Her money was getting low, and she thought maybe we could find a less expensive place for her. There was a Lutheran church nearby, and after dinner I walked Charlotte over to it. It was crowded and there was a long waiting list [for a room], but they somehow made room for Charlotte. The place was clean, safe, and inexpensive. It seemed perfect. Charlotte usually ended up at my apartment around dinnertime.

Charlotte stayed in New York about ten days. She found a job, and announced that she was really settled at last. The next evening she called just before midnight. She sounded desperate and talked almost incoherently. She said that she had to go home immediately, because she had called her father and found that he had attempted suicide because she had left. She said she had been walking up and down in the street for several hours before she made her decision. She did not have much money left, but she still had enough for a cab to the airport, and she bought a return ticket with greater foresight than I would have credited her with.

Charlotte's story sounded odd, but there was no doubt that she was frantic. She said the plane was leaving shortly, and she had no time to arrange to have her luggage sent on. She gave me her home address, and asked if I could take care of it. I told her to forget about the luggage and go, since it was clear that she was going to do just that anyway. The next day I made the necessary arrangements, and dropped Charlotte a line to tell her the things were on their way. Shortly afterwards, I got a long letter from her. She said she wanted to tell me the truth, because her conscience was bothering her. She was, it seemed, quite a bit older than she had said. She was married and had three children, but they were "difficult," and she and her husband did not get along. She had been getting "terribly nervous," and had decided to go to New York and make a new life for herself. She said that New York was a wonderful place, and everyone was so nice to her that she knew the bad things people said about big cities weren't true. She hoped some day to come back for a visit.

Charlotte and I have corresponded for years now. She seems to have gotten herself fairly well straightened out, although she still has her ups and downs. I always enjoy hearing from her, especially as I am very grateful to her. I have an idea that I might never have found that scroll [*see below*] without her help. It might well be that magic had to end in the plain fact of Charlotte before I could make the final decision to abandon magic in exchange for something much more desirable.

Thus the experience concretized Helen's decision to abandon the temptation once and for all to misuse the power of her mind (magic), choosing instead to utilize it on behalf of Jesus' love (the miracle). As *A Course in Miracles* later said about psychic powers:

> The Holy Spirit needs these gifts, and those who offer them to Him and Him alone go with Christ's gratitude upon their hearts, and His holy sight not far behind (manual, p. 60).

Helen always spoke fondly of Charlotte, and I recall her receiving a call from Charlotte in my presence and their having a brief though warm conversation. For her part, Charlotte remained grateful to Helen and Bill for their loving and caring help. Incidentally, Charlotte ultimately left her husband, but reported to Helen that she was happy and peaceful.

Helen's "magic phase" came to a stunning end with one final "picture episode," in which she knew that she had made an "irrevocable choice," a choice to set aside any temptations to misuse the power of her mind. This was a choice she obviously, according to these summer experiences at least, had been most ambivalent about in the past.

> I saw myself entering a cave in a rock formation on a bleak, wind-swept seacoast.[27] The entrance to the cave was low, and

---

27. Some time afterwards Helen wrote: "When I went to Israel several years later, I was startled to see that same seacoast at Qumran, where the Dead Sea Scrolls were found." *See* pp. 356f.

the cave was quite deep. All I found in it was a very old and large parchment scroll. Its ends were rolled around heavy, gold-tipped poles, the two sides touching at the scroll's center and tied together by a strip of parchment that fell away as my fingers touched it. I untied the ends and opened the scroll just enough to expose the center panel, on which only two words were written; "God is," and nothing else. Then I slowly unrolled the scroll further, and tiny black letters began to appear on both side panels. The Voice explained the situation to me:

"If you look at the left panel you will be able to read about everything that happened in the past. And if you look at the right panel you will be able to read about everything that will happen in the future."

The little letters on the sides of the panel were becoming clearer, and for several minutes I was tempted to look at them. Then I made a decision. I rolled up the scroll to conceal everything except the center panel.

"I'm not interested in the past or the future," I said, with finality. "I'll just stop with this."

The Voice sounded both reassured and reassuring. I was astonished at the depth of gratitude that it somehow conveyed. "Thank you," it said. "You made it that time. Thank you."

And that, it seemed, was that.

As with the subway experience several years earlier, an aspect of the cave experience likewise found its way into the Course. The workbook states: "We say 'God is,' and then we cease to speak, for in that knowledge words are meaningless" (workbook, p. 315). What is of God and therefore remains beyond the world, remains also beyond the capabilities of words to express its truth. The manual for teachers states:

God does not understand words, for they were made by separated minds to keep them in the illusion of separation....Let us not forget...that words are but symbols of symbols. They are thus twice removed from reality (manual, p. 51).

Again, the cave experience, together with the Mayo Clinic episode, seemed to bring this period to a successful close, and marked the end of Helen's preparation for the scribing of *A Course in Miracles*. Whatever ego issues remained for her on a conscious level, she nonetheless on a far deeper level had decided irrevocably to allow her mind to be a clear instrument for the love of Jesus to pass through. As she wrote simply, again: "And that, it seemed, was that."

This unusual but wearying period from June to the end of the summer had now ended, and Bill suggested it might be a good idea to take a few days off and go to Virginia Beach to visit the Association for Research and Enlightenment, the organization founded by Edgar Cayce. As already mentioned, Bill had become most interested in Cayce and his work, and felt that a visit might be helpful to clarify the events of the past summer. Helen, as would be expected, felt different, though she reluctantly agreed to go.

> The idea did not appeal to me. That sort of thing still frightened me and I did not want it to be true. It was bad enough that I did not understand what was happening to me. I particularly did not want any exacerbation of my unfortunate "magical" efforts, which I was by now more than willing to abandon. Nevertheless, the idea of a short vacation sounded good, and my husband, knowing I was tired, encouraged me to go. It was a perfect time of the year for the trip, and he thought it would do me good. He and Bill had become friends, and although he felt Bill was developing some rather strange interests, my husband knew he would take care of me. I set out for Virginia Beach with some misgivings, but looking forward to the rest.
>
> As it turned out the trip was anything but restful for me. The people at the Association for Research and Enlightenment, then only a small group devoted to making the Cayce material available to the public, were intelligent, sincere and obviously sane. Nor was the massive documentation something one could easily brush aside. I was impressed but very uneasy. As Bill's interest deepened, my own anxiety grew. Bill read further on the subject that afternoon, and he also bought some books to take home. I rifled through a volume and put it down abruptly, in sufficient discomfort to border on panic. I was glad when the trip was over. Back home I glanced at several of the books Bill had bought, but I could not read them. To me they merely seemed to sound the "magic" note again.

Helen and Bill were to return to Virginia Beach shortly

after the Course began, and over the years developed a helpful friendship with Hugh Lynn Cayce, who was extremely suppor-tive of Helen. Helen and Bill made copies of the as-yet-incomplete manuscript for him, and he was obviously impressed with what he read. Helen and Bill later told me that Hugh Lynn felt that his father Edgar had something to do with the transmission of the Course. After one of their visits at the A.R.E., Cayce walked Helen to the door of his office saying: "You must be a very advanced soul, but you certainly don't look it!" Helen later wrote about her experiences at the A.R.E.:

> Fortunately, as my anxiety subsided and I became more famil-iar with the work of the A.R.E., this inaccurate picture of its activities and purposes was corrected. I have been a member for a number of years now, and have considerable respect for the group and its aims. I am particularly indebted to Hugh Lynn Cayce for giving so much time out of his very busy life to my manuscript, and also for his consistent friendship, patience and encouragement.

After the scribing was completed, Helen and Bill prepared a copy of the manuscript for Hugh Lynn. This, incidentally, was the manuscript I first saw, and which Helen, Bill, and I always referred to as the "Hugh Lynn version."[28]

There were some isolated experiences of that summer, all positive, that are worth quoting here as well. One set of experi-ences reflects the growing awareness in Helen of joining with others, and its obvious importance in the journey back to God. Incidentally, this kind of experience, with which Helen was becoming increasingly familiar, was markedly different from Helen's more usual and powerful feelings of separation.

> Several times that summer I felt something like the "sub-way experience" of years before, although with much less intensity. It generally took place in a crowd of people, for whom I would feel a brief but powerful affinity. One took place on a warm evening when Louis and I were walking along a crowded resort boardwalk [in Atlantic City—*see* her letter to

---

28. This appellation should not be taken to suggest that there were other ver-sions of the Course; it referred only to the latest typing of the manuscript.

Bill, p. 156]. *A sudden sense of deep emotional closeness to everyone there swept over me, with a clear and certain recognition that we were all making the same journey together to a common goal.* Another took place when Bill, Louis and I were sitting in a darkened theater. Sitting in the darkness, I was suddenly aware of an intense inner light that began in my chest, growing increasingly strong and encompassing until it seemed to radiate throughout the whole theater *and include everyone in it.* My awareness of the light and the peace and joy that accompanied it lasted for some ten minutes. It was so strong that I could hardly believe no one else noticed it [my italics].

A somewhat similar incident occurred later on in southern France, which I have already presented in Chapter 1.

A completely different set of images involved pictures of a chalice,

> sometimes gold and sometimes silver, but always with a bright light shining on it. At first these images frightened me because I associated them with sacrifice and loss, but I was silently but completely assured that they were really symbols of great joy. I did not actually experience much emotion related to them, however, but at least I ceased to be afraid of them.

In *A Course in Miracles*, the chalice is used as a symbol of the Atonement, the Course's term for the Holy Spirit's correction of the belief in the sin of separation. The term (and therefore its symbol of a chalice) is deliberately set against the traditional view of atonement, which is that God demands suffering and sacrifice as payment back for our sin against Him. The chalice at the Last Supper, and Jesus' supposed prayer during the "agony" in the Garden of Gethsemane—that his Father "remove this cup" (of his sacrificial death on the cross) from him (Luke 22:42)—thus have for two thousand years represented for Christians God's plan of suffering and sacrifice. This was the meaning of Helen's fear. Helen's interest in the chalice surfaced again during the summer of 1973, as will be discussed in Part III.

There was one time when Helen remembered asking specifically for an experience to cheer her up when she was feeling a bit low:

The answer came in the form of a picture of a plant nursery, with very young plants in neat rows, carefully labelled and apparently tended with great care. Next to the plants was a large watering can. There were no weeds or dead leaves there, and the plants were green and obviously healthy. The picture meant nothing to me and I found it mildly irritating.

"And much good that is," I grumbled. "What's so helpful about that?"

"Look where it's growing," said the Voice, patiently and gently.

"But what does it mean?" I asked, still indignant.

"Look—where—it's—growing," repeated the Voice, slowly and distinctly.

"Oh, all right," I said, somewhat sulkily. Then I looked at the picture more carefully. The plant nursery was completely surrounded by a bleak, lifeless desert. Only the little area in which the plants were growing was moist and green.

"And now that it's finally started," said the Voice, "you will go on watering it, won't you?"

I was quite overcome, but I promised I would try.

The symbol of deserts changing into gardens, again, is found in the Course, notably in the section "The Little Garden" (text, pp. 364-66), and in this beautiful passage from the workbook, borrowed in part from Portia's famous speech from *The Merchant of Venice*:

> Miracles fall like drops of healing rain from Heaven on a dry and dusty world, where starved and thirsty creatures come to die. Now they have water. Now the world is green. And everywhere the signs of life spring up, to show that what is born can never die, for what has life has immortality (workbook, p. 463).

Finally, there was an interesting and comforting experience about the insignificance of the world of time:

> There were also some brief periods during which shifts in time awareness took place. Perhaps the most compelling of these happened one evening while I was brushing my hair, deciding I needed a haircut and feeling anything but inspired. Suddenly I saw my life symbolized by a golden line stretching infinitely backward and infinitely forward. The time interval representing my present life seemed so incredibly tiny that it could easily have been overlooked entirely unless one looked very carefully

for it along the line. Then one could see a miniscule dip before the line continued. I clasped my hands in real delight.

"What can it possibly matter what happens in this little and meaningless eye-blink of time?" I asked myself, in happy amazement. "It seems so long and important while you're in it, but in less than an instant it's as if it never happened." I was certain of this for several minutes, during which it seemed as if a great weight had been lifted from my mind. The certainty had gone by the time I told Bill about it, although I still felt "I saw eternity the other night."

The notion that all of our experiences in the world are nothing more than a "miniscule dip" ("so incredibly tiny") in the line of eternity recurred in the Course with the phrase, "tiny tick of time" (text, p. 511). A parallel passage in the Course, which remained until Helen and I went through it together for the last time, was taken out by Helen under Jesus' instructions. I never fully understood why, nor did Helen, although she was quite clear about its coming out. It appeared in what is now Chapter Nineteen[29] in the text, in the section called "The Unreality of Sin." It fell between the words "And when correction is completed, time *is* eternity" and "The Holy Spirit can teach you how to look on time differently." Here it is in its entirety, as Helen took it down:

> Time is like a downward spiral, that seems to travel down from a long, unbroken line, along another plane, but which in no way *breaks* the line, or interferes with its smooth continuousness. Along the spiral, it *seems* as if the line *must* have been broken, but, at the *line*, its wholeness is apparent.
>
> Everything seen from the spiral is misperceived. But, as you approach the line, you realize that *it* was not affected by the drop into another plane at all. But, *from* this plane, the *line* seems discontinuous. And this is but an error in perception, which can be easily corrected *in the mind*, although the body's eyes will see no change. The eyes see many things the mind corrects, and *you* respond, *not* to the eyes' illusions, *but to the mind's corrections*. You *see* the line as broken, and as you shift

---

29. To ease possible confusion, I am writing out the numbers of chapter referred to in the text of the Course, while retaining the arabic numbers when refer to chapters in this book.

to different aspects of the spiral, the line looks different. Yet in your mind is One [the Holy Spirit] Who *knows* it is unbroken, and forever changeless.

Before we turn to the actual scribing of *A Course in Miracles*, we first examine, in the next chapter, the group of letters Helen wrote to Bill during the summer period.

Chapter 6

HELEN'S LETTERS TO BILL (SUMMER, 1965)

During the seven-and-a-half years that date from Bill's "There must be another way" speech to the end of the Course's scribing, there was a period when Helen and Bill's relationship seemed to change for the better. There survive a series of letters Helen wrote to Bill in the summer of 1965, and some journal notes that Bill kept in the late summer and early fall of 1966. From these letters and journal entries it is clear how hard Helen and Bill worked in applying the principles they were learning from Jesus. This learning included not only the lessons from *A Course in Miracles* itself, but from the more personal teachings they were receiving from Jesus—which began *prior* to the start of the Course—that encompassed their individual lives as well as their relationship with each other. There was a sense of hope that did not exist before or after, not to mention an openness to examine truthfully their own misperceptions of themselves and each other. In this chapter we examine Helen's letters, and leave Bill's journal for Chapter 10.

Almost all of the letters were written to Bill while Helen and Louis were vacationing in southern New Jersey, or when Bill was vacationing out of town. None of them was dated, and only a couple of the letters even noted the days of the week. Thus it is impossible to place them exactly, or to be sure of their proper sequence. However, from other evidence, it seems all but certain that they date from the summer of 1965. I cannot therefore vouch for their correct order, but have placed them as best I could based on the content of the letters themselves.

The reader will also find in much of these letters an authoritative, though gentle and defenseless tone. It obviously came from a "Wisdom that is not...[Helen's] own" (workbook, p. 246). In her analysis of her own and Bill's situations, not to mention the advice she gives, Helen sounds overall more like the Jesus of the dictation, whose words were to be so gently incisive and helpful. Similar to my practice in presenting material from the original dictation of the Course, as will be explained in Chapter 8, I have deleted overly personal material, as well as extraneous comments by Helen on her writing style, typing mistakes, etc. For ease of reading and reference, I have omitted ellipses to denote such omissions, and have numbered the nine letters.

One final note: these letters come within the context of the intense period, compressed into a few short weeks, that immediately preceded the Course's scribing. Helen's occasional quick shifts from one subject to another is better understood when seen within the context of this intense self-examination. Since we do not have access to the daily inner and outer events of this period, some of the material found in the letters can be difficult to understand. I have added commentary when needed in an attempt to explain the workings of Helen's mind.

Letter One

We begin with a document that is not really a letter to Bill, but Helen's reflections to herself about material she had not discussed with Bill in an earlier phone conversation. The "letter" is quite long, and at times borders on a stream of consciousness. After a while, the reflections shift to a direct communication to Bill. I include most of it here, as it provides some wonderful examples of Helen's openness regarding her relationship with Bill, Louis, and others. It is clear that during this period Helen was paying careful attention to almost every thought in her mind, faithful to Jesus' request to her and Bill, later stated this way in the Course:

> Watch carefully and see what it is you are really asking for. Be very honest with yourself in this, for we must hide nothing from each other (text, p. 56).

By the reference in the letter to Helen's birthday (July 14), we know that this was written in July. We can also date the year for certain as 1965, as that was when the pictures of Mars Helen refers to were sent back to earth.

Helen began by referring to a conversation she had with Bill, where she had changed a word related to Joan of Arc:

> I thought it was better to change the word before I said it. I was tempted to correct this several times, but dismissed it as unimportant.

This trait of altering some aspect of truth, however small, was an integral part of Helen's magical attempts to control her world and keep God out. The defense worked like this in Helen's system: if the truth is changed and discarded, it thus becomes false and non-existent; Helen's replacement for it is then made into truth by virtue of its acceptance as her reality. The new "truth" is now under her control, while God's truth has been replaced. We shall see other examples of this trait later on, particularly when we consider the editing of the Course, where it reduced Helen's anxiety to be able to make very minor changes (such as substituting "that" for "which," and vice versa), or to be in "charge" of punctuation and some capitalizations.

Helen then shifted to a discussion of a close friend of Bill, whom I identify here simply as S. As will be clear from Helen's statements, she did not like him at all, and believed that he exercised a negative influence on Bill. Helen also felt that Bill often used S as an indirect means of expressing hostility towards her. Bill's friend assumes an important role not only in this communication, but in other letters as well.

A painful symbol of the issues raised for Helen by S and his friendship with Bill was a house in Watermill, a beach suburb of New York City located on Long Island. It was a place to which Bill often went during summer weekends. He was half-owner of the house, the other half owned by some other friends of Bill, a married couple. Helen felt that Bill used the house in part as a way of avoiding her, and she resented it very much. She was able to persuade Bill and his friends to allow Louis and her to come out, which they did fairly often. But, as will be seen, this arrangement never really worked out, and seemed to be yet another wedge of guilt and attack in her and Bill's stormy relationship. Helen's comments on her relationship with S, which I have excerpted, point up both the extent of her ego's hostility, as well as her sincere attempts to be honest with herself and Bill, not to mention her efforts to undo such ego projections.

> When I mentioned [to Bill] S, whom I did not expect to discuss at all, the thought crossed my mind, "My God, you mean I have to love him too?" This annoyed me to an incredible extent, and I dismissed it as silly. I still think it's silly, and I wouldn't want to love S under any circumstances. In fact, I feel extremely negative toward him, and I insist that he's a bad influence on Bill (in some sense I do believe this), and I think he's a real menace to me. I remembered at the time that S has several times mentioned (he was drunk, I think), that I "make him nervous." He gave different reasons for this each time, and Bill told me it's not unusual; I "make a lot of people nervous." This is ridiculous, and is primarily a negative sentiment of Bill's toward me. Bill's attitude has not helped me to regard S more charitably; it has blinded Bill to his actual antagonism towards me; and has also given S a false sense of security because of Bill's unconscious backing. There's really a very good reason why I make S "very nervous." It's not to his credit, either.

This last comment is probably an allusion to a past life hateful mistreatment of women by S, in part sexual, and his fear of counterattack brought on by his guilt. Helen no doubt believed that S' homosexuality was chosen by him as a defense against women for his "sins" against them, sins for which Helen's ego clearly wished to hold him accountable. Helen returns to this later in the letter.

It is interesting to note here as well that during this period, contrary to her later accounts (*see above*, p. 99), Helen's thoughts about others frequently involved references to past lives, in part influenced by explanations Jesus had given her. Her receptivity to this kind of thinking was set up on one level by Bill's having introduced her to the writings of Edgar Cayce, which are replete with references to reincarnation. In addition, by now Helen most likely had had the series of visions described in Chapter 5, which clearly imply reincarnation.

We continue with additional comments bearing on Helen's unforgiveness of S:

> The following crossed my mind at various times throughout the next day, without any emotional concomitants at all. I

thought of S, and the remarks I had made the day before to the effect that he needs my forgiveness very badly, but he'll never get it. He does not know how to ask for it; I could tell him, but even if he asked right, I would still not give it to him. I meant that. Except for that, I forgot the whole matter at the time. Nothing relevant happened until Bill told me that he was driving out earlier [to Watermill] than he had intended "on an impulse." It occurred to me briefly that S, as always, was interfering at a time when I needed Bill very much. All I thought then was "Let him. It's just one more thing."

By the next morning, I was glad that Bill had gone, because I thought he was better off at Watermill, and I was feeling much better. In fact, I was genuinely gentle, and quite consciously relieved of an intense hatred of men. I was really constructive when I found he [Bill] had left a lot of messy things all over the kitchen. I did speak to him about it, but I was not angry. I talked of the matter entirely as a real problem of his, and one which I thought he would be better off working out. He agreed that this was so, and did not react with his usual antagonism when this sort of thing occurs.

During the morning, S occurred to me again. It seemed to me that he was very anxious to give me a present, and wanted particularly to do so on my birthday. (S actually did mention "Bastille day" when I spoke to him over the phone on Friday, but I could hardly hear what he said because there was a lot of noise going on at the time. I did not ask him to repeat it. I don't like talking to him.) This time, I thought that he has every reason to want to give me a present on that day, and especially something that goes around the neck. I remembered that when he asked me originally whether I liked jade, I told him that I don't, and also that I think it is a very unbecoming color to me. He had said that he had a jade necklace he liked, and had intended to give it to me from Bill. I answered that I'd prefer something else,—or better still nothing,—and repeated that I don't like jade. It struck me at the time that it was odd that he nevertheless did give me the necklace. While I thanked him, and assured him that I liked it very much, (largely on the grounds of courtesy),[30] I was struck by the fact that he seemed to have forgotten my repeated emphasis on my dislike of jade. That made it an odd present, I thought. I had the beads

---

30. Helen, incidentally, was almost always socially appropriate, despite her frequent feelings to the contrary.

restrung, but I have never worn them. At first, I tried to return them on various acceptable grounds, but S did not seem to hear.

S may yet try to give me something for the neck that really is beautiful. (This is not mysterious in itself; Bill told me that S wants to give me the chain.) When I first heard about this, my immediate response was "I couldn't take it," to which I added silently, "and besides I wouldn't." Now it occurred to me that this gift is really a rope, which S is impelled to give to me, and which he must see me wear. The picture of the rope which crossed my mind was very repellent to me, and I knew that if I should accept it from him it would represent a symbol that I have forgiven him, which he needs so much. My immediate reaction was one of a refusal to be bribed. I have, incidentally, lost my interest in jewelry rather suddenly. I have plenty, and hardly need any more. In fact, I guess I've bought plenty of just about everything. (When I went shopping on Saturday, I bought a sweater for Bill—Bill, I'll change it if you don't like it,—and some caps for Jonathan [Louis]. I didn't want to buy myself anything.)

Returning later to the rope, I thought, "but this time it's beautiful. Maybe that makes the difference." This seemed like a happy idea at the time, and I did not think of the matter again.

These comments would seem to refer to a past life when S had hanged Helen with a rope (or was a party to such a hanging). He was now asking for forgiveness by presenting Helen with a beautiful chain, which "makes the difference."

Helen continues:

The day was very pleasant, although I did not enjoy *The Gondoliers* [Helen loved Gilbert and Sullivan] very much, even though the performance was excellent in many ways. For some reason, I felt impelled to see a number of flaws in it.

I woke up suddenly around 5 this morning, experiencing such an intense hatred for S that I had to get up and have coffee and a few cigarettes. It was very hard for me to overcome this and get back to sleep. I even tried to pray (which I found very embarrassing, and hate to admit). (Jonathan told me that I really am religious and have always been so actually, and why fight it? It's a good question.)

Despite his detachment from much of Helen's life, Louis often demonstrated insightful observations about Helen, such as the above. Helen then returned to S:

> I also could not get away from the idea that he is bringing out the worst in Bill. (Don't be angry, Bill,—but to some extent I do think that imitating S, which you sometimes do, is not the best use of your relationship. S' "triviality" is something he will have to overcome. There are better ways of dealing with depression.)
>
> So eventually I went back to sleep and got over my hatred of S to some extent. It was breath-takingly intense while it lasted.

Helen then "tuned in" to a dream Bill was having, which she cleverly interpreted as a play on S' actual name, which meant that she and Bill would be able to get beyond the blockage in their relationship, symbolized by S. The letter then continues with an important observation about Helen's and Bill's ability to help each other, a point which will be returned to many times in these letters, as well as in the original dictation of the Course:

> Unintentionally, I omitted the thought that neither Jonathan [Louis] nor Chip [Bill's roommate] can help either Bill or me very much at the moment, but we can help both of them *very* much. It will not be reciprocal for some time, but eventually it will be. The two people who are ready to help each other now are Bill and me. But we have to get some things straightened out first.

Helen followed this with an oblique reference to the photographs of Mars, "which I believe are scheduled to be sent back to earth on July 14th." This portion of the letter then concludes:

> And now I think this is over. Which is just as well, because I have a lot of other things to do. I am very grateful that I do not really remember what I wrote, and would prefer not to read it.

There was probably a pause here in Helen's writing, but then the letter continues, now addressed directly to Bill:

> Bill, I'm really sorry I got you into this whole mess, even though I am nasty enough to say "you started it." Well, maybe it'll turn out for the best,—says who? Please regard this as the

effort of a lifetime, although I am really better at writing research designs, and certainly *much* safer.

It is my conviction that no man ever loved me, though a lot of them have wanted this or that from me. Since I am so giving, sweet, and generally lovable (hiss), they generally get very fond of me. Irresistible, that's me! Except that I am now a million years old, and this worries me.

I am very jealous of anybody who loves. I think they're supposed to love me. Being quite aware of this, I have been very careful not to hurt people, and I have actually done a great deal to be objective with the many people who have confided their love problems to me and asked me for help. Most of them, I am glad to say, have turned out rather well. Only I get mad every time. But that is a private matter, and I really don't let it interfere with what I either say or do.

We have already noted this aspect of Helen's ego personality, which believed that she must sacrifice her own happiness in the process of helping others. On a deeper level, her commitment to Jesus made it impossible for her *not* to help those in trouble. And so she continually found herself in conflict with her Self: unable not to extend the loving will of her Lord, and yet unable to accept that love for her personal self. We shall discuss this issue again in Part III.

The following comments on a dream, "from which I never recovered," are extremely interesting, and relate to a

green and red rubber ball, which showed up in so many dreams all by itself, until I finally tracked it down in a dream from which I never recovered. It was in the crib, at the foot, and my father came into the doorway and I was lying very happily thinking how pretty I was and how warm. He just stayed there and looked and didn't come in, and I was very little so I couldn't get up myself and go over. In the dream, I saw myself turn from a very pretty little girl into a very ugly one, and he just looked and then went away.

So I *did* turn into a very ugly girl. I was fat and horrible, and all the boys turned me down. My mother said I looked like an elephant, and she couldn't stand it.

Many years later Helen spoke with me about her father and the green and red ball, but said that it was a memory of an actual event, not a dream. This is interesting given that Helen

140

would have had to have been considerably less than a year old when the "event" occurred. In Helen's recalling this "event" to me, she described the cold objectivity of her father. At any rate, whether a memory or dream, the experience certainly reflects Helen's rather bitter perception of her father's aloofness from her. The letter then seemed to conclude:

> You just called. Since you know it from then on, I won't repeat it. Sleep well. Love—Helen.

There was a break here, but then another letter follows, also in page sequence. Evidently, Helen wrote these while Bill was away, and then either sent them to him all together, or, more likely, gave them to him when he returned. Thus these were more like Helen's own particular form of journal notes. The next entry begins:

> Dear Bill: I am so glad you called when you did. It's frightening how much can happen to me that I don't even notice. So I tried to pray, (really), and I think I did for just a very little while. I can't get over how hard it is for me. I asked him [Jesus] to get me back on the ladder, and meant it but it didn't last. I don't generally kneel, because I think it's a silly position and makes you look ridiculous. But I did try, and I started to cry (which I seem to be doing a lot of) but it wasn't bad. When I got up I rather unexpectedly said out loud, "And thank you very much for letting me try again after all." (I guess it should be a capital "Y.") I intended to say a prayer for my mother, as you suggested, and I started to, but it came out a bit different. What I think I said was, "Please don't let me ever hurt anybody living or dead." There was a slight break, and it ended "in the past or the present or in the future." I meant it.

The sincerity of Helen's feelings here are obvious. A part of her never wished to hurt anyone, and that was again expressed in her willingness to be of help to anyone who needed it, regardless of her negative feelings about the person, or her experience of imposition. The love of her priestess-Self was thus able to be released. Helen then reflects her acceptance of the joining that was the meaning of her and Bill's relationship, as well as her directly urging Bill to change his mind.

> Bill, I am happy about one thing; very happy, I think. It's nice to do things together, because we're supposed to be like

that. If you build up your faith (which was very lacking, by the way), you *must* come out of suspension. Maybe that's all you have to do. Because if you *start* with that, you won't have to go through all this mess to get it. I have always been character-ized by a marked tendency to start at the end and work my way back to the beginning, sometimes getting balled up around the middle. This is not the easy way, believe me, and probably never was necessary. But some of us don't appreciate the value of a straight line being the shortest distance between two points. But it is.

I have to stop smoking without a holder. I was surprised that for some reason I have been smoking without it for a long time now (2 weeks or so), and it didn't hurt my eyes a bit. (Really). But the idea was wrong. You're not supposed to use power that way. It's a misuse of what may be a better kind of immortality. Love—Helen.

This last comment, coming early in the summer of 1965, foreshadows Helen's cave vision, wherein she vowed not to misuse her mind's power. Helen, incidentally, was a chain smoker, averaging about four packs a day until she almost choked to death while on a trip sometime during the scribing of the Course. She gave up her habit right then and there, and never touched another cigarette. Note also Helen's reference to her concern for her eyes, an important theme we shall return to presently. Finally, this passage refers to what Jesus would later describe (text, p. 2) as the error of confusing the levels of the mind and body. Sickness comes from the level of the mind (though frequently manifest on the bodily level), and healing therefore can come only by changing one's mind. Altering one's physical level (as in Helen's using, or not using, a cigarette holder) in order to effect a symptom cure, constitutes magic: "You're not supposed to use power that way." This is not evil or sinful in and of itself (text, p. 20), but if taken seriously the magic can lead to the aforementioned confusion of levels, thus hindering the true healing that results only from forgiveness, the whole point of the Course.

Helen then added the following:

I would prefer not to add this, but I guess I should. I am saying this in a very small voice, really a whisper, in the hope that you can't hear it. (There seems to be a slight case of

synesthesia[31] here.) You're right, Bill. There's no sense in saying "God is on my side." You have to say, "I am on His."

This, of course, looks forward to that most important theme
in *A Course in Miracles* of bringing the darkness to the light,
not the light to the darkness; we must come to where God is by
changing our minds about Him, not demanding that He join us
in our deluded minds: we join *Him*.

Letter Two

The second letter contains a wisdom that integrates (as does
the Course) a sophisticated psychology with an advanced spiritual attitude. The specific context is Helen's difficulty with
the Watermill house, a major forgiveness lesson for her, as we
saw in the previous letter.

Dear Bill:
This seems very necessary to write before tomorrow. I hope
you will bear with it, because it may be important for both of
us. However, I will try to keep the responsibilities mine,
because I will have plenty. It begins with that saying I found
rather quaint but appealing from one of the books you gave me.
I am slightly changing it, because it has universal application
anyway, if it has any at all:

A child sees a house as a house.
An adult sees a house as many things.
A sage sees a house as a house.

I think I said, rather flippantly last week, that I was looking forward to Watermill because in a way it's always essential
to return to "the scene of the crime." I also said (I hope) a
number of much more positive things too, and I am sure it will
be more that way. However, maybe I had better clear up that
one before I come. It could be risky.

Frankly, I had not realized that Watermill will represent a
rather severe test. We have both seen it "as many things" and
it is wrong to invest a place with personal symbols because in a
way it violates the actual meaning or existence of the place in

---

31. The combination of two sensory modalities, as in "hearing" a color, or "seeing" a sound. This combination is not quite the case in Helen's letter, which is
why she uses the qualifier "slight."

itself. This results in a loss of the only kind of appreciation that is really safe, and also genuinely rewarding. I think I could guess your symbols in that connection reasonably well, but that is not my assignment now. If you ever care to go into this, (and you may want to), fine. I would probably have something to say, if only because I am more familiar than you, perhaps, in searching for the right thing in the wrong way and at the wrong time. Meanwhile, let me confine myself properly to my own problems, because I could have a lot of trouble unless I relearn this particular lesson. If I am really successful, I may be able to overlearn it and earn stable protection for the future.

I have hated Watermill probably above all places on the face of this earth. However much rationalization I may have applied to this most disastrous state of affairs, it remains my responsibility to undo a symbol of so much evil. A house is *not* many things, and it is not really a symbol at all. There is probably no part of it which I have not endowed with something that is not there, and which I am singularly likely to fall over or slip on. This is obviously merely because I have made it dangerous. A place is never dangerous, but people are sometimes, and then there is a lot of confusion. I am quite afraid of Watermill, because I think it's a real threat to me. Since I made it that way (or thought I did) I can surely undo all this, because the truth is that I did not make it at all. It's a house on a beach (and a very pretty one, too) and I had nothing to do with its creation or its setting, physical or human.

I interrupt Helen's letter to point out the wisdom of her comments, very similar to the point made much later in the manual for teachers, where Jesus explains:

> Perhaps it will be helpful to remember that no one can be angry at a fact. It is always an interpretation that gives rise to negative emotions, regardless of their seeming justification by what *appears* as facts (manual, p. 42).

As has already been commented on, and to which we shall return in Part III, there was a wisdom in Helen that most certainly predated A *Course in Miracles*, and which her experiences with Jesus reminded her of. This wisdom, belonging to the priestess-Self that existed beyond "Heaven and Helen," is reflected here in her comments to Bill that come from her awareness of the illusory nature of form, which is nothing more

144

than a neutral symbol onto which the mind projects either the sin of the ego, or the holiness of the Holy Spirit. As the later Lesson in the workbook teaches: "My body is a wholly neutral thing" (workbook, p. 435). Thus the Watermill house is neutral, and Helen here recognizes that her thoughts about it come from her, and are totally independent of the house itself. Therefore, since these are *her* thoughts, she can change them. As I will point out again later, it is clear from comments such as Helen makes here that she did not need *A Course in Miracles* to teach her its wisdom. It was already present in the unity that existed between her and Jesus, *predating* the beginning of the scribing.

The letter continues:

> I had hoped to get some rest there this time, and I may yet. I have really prayed that I will not misunderstand things, and see them wrong. I think it's especially important for me to remember that, if I ever get suddenly mad (and I'm afraid I may) that I have hardly been sinless in the matter, and am really lucky to have another chance to perceive it better. It's not technically necessary for me to go to Watermill to do this, of course, but there is a certain directness about "returning to the scene of the crime" provided you do so to remove the crime rather than reinforce it. (I am having a lot of typing trouble now, but I guess it's better to get this over with now, rather than later.)
>
> I hope that by the time I leave Watermill this time, I will do so with thanks and a sincere blessing for the house and everybody there. I don't know if I can really make this, but I hope, at least, I will make a very genuine effort. I could easily louse this up, but it would be a most unfortunate mistake, especially for me. I will also take whatever sins I cannot overcome there into every house I go into, including my own. I don't want to do this, and I think I can gain a lot if I use the chance right.

The closing of the letter was handwritten, as is explained:

> The typewriter is acting up so I'll stop. Help me, Bill, you may also be helping yourself.
>
> Happy vacation to all of us.

> Love,
>
> Helen

145

Unfortunately, Helen was not able to put into practice the goal of forgiveness she was able to write so movingly about in this letter. She did make the attempt, but years afterwards she was still unable to speak of Watermill without bitterness and anger towards Bill. Nonetheless, she was at least able to be clear about the principle to be learned, and clearly this letter demonstrates her willingness to learn the "other way" and to forgive. It also illustrates the split in her mind: one part clearly reflecting the wisdom of Jesus, the other just as clearly demonstrating the wrong-minded stubbornness of the ego.

Letter Three

This next letter contains a dream, which appears to symbolize Helen's ego being displaced by Jesus (the man), whose messengers do not oppose her. The lady in the dream would seem to symbolize the Holy Spirit; while the children—especially the dark-haired girl—could symbolize the innocence of Christ.

I am beginning this with the dream of Friday, because you said to write it down. I didn't do it at the time, but I think I remember it pretty well;—it's hard to say, because this will cover Saturday and a lot of other things.

The dream, which I thought came in 2 identical parts, seemed to begin just after I fell asleep, but I wasn't ready for it then although it had already started. Anyway, I think I actually thought "Later, not yet." It seemed to happen again just before I awoke. The doorbell rang, and when I answered it a lot of beautiful children came rushing into the hall and into all the rooms. They were led or supervised (I'm not sure of her actual role) by a lovely dark-haired lady whose black hair was parted in the middle, and whose beautiful very dark brown eyes looked either extremely serene or extremely blank. I seem to change my mind again and again about this. The lady handed me several sheets of paper, which, I felt, accounted for her coming with the children. (I had gotten back into bed, and she handed me the papers from the foot of the bed where she was standing.) Somehow I gathered from the papers (none of which I actually remember) that the children were to live in the apartment, (I think the lady was to be there, too, and sort of take over).

The idea was not at first at all objectionable or in any way dangerous. The danger element apparently came in much later, after the children had been running about rather happily, and the lady had stood quite still looking at me for a long time. Then it suddenly dawned on me that the whole situation was not what it appeared to be. In fact, I suddenly realized that I was going to be dispossessed, and this alien family was coming to find a home out of which they planned to drive me. I reached for the phone quite frantically and called you [Bill], asking you please to hold the wire because I was in a very dangerous situation and might need your help badly. You said you would hold on, and I kept the phone to my ear during the whole next part of the dream. The lady did not attempt to interfere with the call, and made no comment on it. She made no comment on anything. She also did not change her expression throughout.

I told her rather sharply that she and the children would have to get out, or I would call the police. I asked her how she dared come in looking so madonna-like, when she was actually in the service of "the man." Angels should not work for devils, I said. Nor had she any right to pervert the beautiful children to make them part of an evil story. The lady made no comment, but held out her hand for the papers, which I returned to her, immediately regretting having done so. I asked her to return one particular paper to me, so I could check on the name of "the man." She made no move to hand it back, so I said, with a confidence I did not feel:

"I'll get the police onto him, whether you give me the paper or not. I'll remember his name in time, and when I do I won't forget it. Hiding the paper won't save you, or him." The lady said nothing. She merely called the children, and herded them through the door and out into the hall. Just before the door closed, a little brown-eyed dark-haired girl, (who looked something like the lady herself, come to think of it), came back, and ran over to my bed with her arms out. She seemed very spontaneous and innocent, and I thought to myself, "I wish you were what you look like. But you've been trained to play your role, and the role is wicked. It's a real shame, because you're potentially so lovely. But you're not here for any good purpose, and they've already trained you thoroughly as to what you must do." The little girl turned and went back to the lady, who held the door open long enough for her to slip through, and then closed it after her.

Then I spoke into the phone, and said, "Thank you, Bill. It's all right now; they've gone and they won't come back. There's no danger now. But I can't think of the name of 'the man,' and even though I said I would, I can't. I guess you'll be the one to tell me."

As mentioned at the beginning, this dream appears to symbolize Helen's fear of Jesus ("the man") displacing her from her home in the ego; the innocence of the children would replace the guilt within her mind. Again, it is interesting to note the total non-defensiveness of the lady, who does not seek to impose her will, nor pressure Helen into accepting her and the children's presence. In this sense the dream is very similar to Helen's earlier one of "The Gentleman," presented in Chapter 3. The reader may recall the gentle defenseless way the Gentleman, representing Jesus, simply presents his "case" for a better, happier world to which Helen is invited.

Both dreams reflect an important theme in *A Course in Miracles*. This theme is especially evident in Lessons 182 and 160 in the workbook, where Jesus repeatedly impresses upon his students that in this world we (as Christ) are truly aliens:

This world you seem to live in is not home to you. And somewhere in your mind you know that this is true. A memory of home keeps haunting you, as if there were a place that called you to return.... Yet still you feel an alien here, from somewhere all unknown (workbook, p. 331).

In the dream Helen is fearful she will be displaced from her home by this alien presence of Christ's innocence. And yet in truth it is her ego that is the alien. As Lesson 160 states regarding fear, representing the ego self:

"I am at home. Fear is the stranger here."

Fear is a stranger to the ways of love. Identify with fear, and you will be a stranger to yourself. And thus you are unknown to you. What is your Self remains an alien to the part of you which thinks that it is real, but different from yourself.... There is a stranger [i.e., our egos' fear] in our midst, who comes from an idea so foreign to the truth he speaks a different language, looks upon a world truth does not know, and understands what truth regards as senseless. Stranger yet, he does not recognize to whom [his Self] he comes, and yet maintains his home belongs to him, while he [his Self] is alien now who is at home.... Who is the stranger? Is it fear or you that is unsuited to the home which God provided for His Son? (workbook, p. 295)

Thus Helen, in characteristic ego fashion, has turned reality upside down. The innocence of Christ, her Self, becomes the alien threatening to dispossess her, and is described as wicked. However, in reality it is the alien ego self that believes it has dispossessed God and His Son.

I might mention, too, that one of Helen's favorite books was Chesterton's *The Man Who Was Thursday*. For the better part of this novel readers are led to believe they are in the midst of a clever spy story, only to discover that the conspirators—each of whom is given a code name of the days of the week—are really in the service of Jesus: Sunday. The plan calls for them insidiously to "take over" the world.

Helen's letter now continues with another important theme:

> The thing I did not want to talk to you about yet was a lifelong fear of being deserted, first by my mother and later by Jonathan [Louis]. Jonathan is singularly unlikely to desert me (his constancy is among his many virtues, most of which I do not yet really appreciate), but I was always afraid he would die and leave me. I can't stand the idea of being alone, and always felt that I would commit suicide rather than face solitude. I am still very uncomfortable about the whole subject, I note. Anyway, I realized that this is one area in which "Thy will be done" does not hold for me. Here it's going to be my way, even if I have to kill myself.
>
> The strange, or perhaps "bad" thing is a better word, is that in his capacity as "company" for me, I never really considered Jonathan (and perhaps not my mother either) as a person in his own right. I have kidded about this by saying, "I have to protect my investment, which is merely the part of foresight and intelligence." The word "investment" which I really have used in this connection, is much more applicable to a thing than to a person, of course. And yet, that's somehow the way I feel about it. It's mine, and I insist on hanging on to it. I do not care if it's good for Jonathan or not; or even if it's really good for me. I need this, and I have devoted practically my whole life to protecting it. You'd be surprised how many weird things I did to protect my mother, (except to be nice to her, of course).

One could not ask for a more specific description of the terrible nature of special relationships, wherein we seek out in others only what is necessary for our own salvation, as we understand it to be. The other person is never really seen as he or she really is, as Christ, but only as a shadow drawn from our past, based upon *our* needs and expectations. One of Helen's most painful fears, dating back to her childhood, was of being alone and deserted, and so others—notably her mother, Louis, Bill, and I—served her ego only by being there *for her*.

Helen's discussion continues, focusing first on Louis (Jonathan), and then on an important visit to his mother:

> To return from the past to the recent bus ride. [I thought] that Jonathan was going to die. I thought he'd come as far as he could this time, and just wasn't going to make it, so he was ready to give up and go soon. Then I suddenly thought, "no," that's not right yet. He'll be very sick, but he won't die unless I want him to. I could yet save him if I really wanted to, and really help him become a self-directed person if I tried. And I suddenly wanted to try. So it seemed to me that he was very ill and in the hospital, and somehow I managed to pull him through. The way I did it was to love him. Then I looked at him (he was sleeping at the time, which is probably just as well).
>
> I also loved everybody in the bus for a little while, too. I looked at Jonathan, and thought he really can make it this time, and doesn't have to wait. It's late, but aren't we all. He's got real possibilities, and if I help him (and you too for rather surprising reasons which come next) he will develop determination and strength right here and now, and won't be lost any more. The "holy alliance" for this incarnation seems to be a shifting one, but it *is* holy in its way. When it first occurred to me (the funniest things come to me in meditation; it worries me a little, but I guess it's all right), that my purpose this time is to make a holy alliance, I thought first of one with you. But this time I thought maybe Jonathan must be included.
>
> The weather, by and large, was not good at Asbury [Asbury Park, New Jersey], so on Friday I suggested we go to Long Branch and see Jonathan's mother and get it over with. Jonathan was glad, because I have always been sort of rotten (by omission) to his mother, and this has upset him. He said I didn't have to go, and he would "cover up" for me, although he admitted she'd love to see me. She is ridiculously proud of me.

And I do know that my visiting her would represent something very important to her, even though I think her reasons are wrong. But why should I be concerned with more than giving an old woman some pleasure on whatever her terms may be? So I decided to go. And then I had a real fit. I went upstairs to get a tranquilizer (I'd have taken more than one, but I didn't have any more), and all the way there I was literally trembling. Jonathan was very nice and even quite sympathetic about it. He made things as easy for me as possible, and even asked the cab driver to wait, which is very unlike Jonathan. (As it happened, the driver didn't charge for waiting, but Jonathan gave him a big tip, which is also unlike Jonathan. He has a thing about tipping, even though he's very generous otherwise.)

When we got to mother's place, everything turned out very well. The lawn was lovely, and if the driver had not been waiting I would have been glad to stay a while. Mother introduced me proudly to a lot of people, but there was time just to sit in the sun, and it was very pretty and peaceful. I was glad to see mother, too. Even if her reasons are warped, there aren't many people left (if there ever were) who want to see me so much. You'd think I'd have been grateful for that before, wouldn't you? Especially me, with this intense need to be wanted. And there she was all the time, wanting me to come, and I wouldn't. A mistake. I'm glad I had a chance to make it up a little, and I wish I could with my own mother. I once didn't see her (or father) for about 2 years. Something to do with analysis, I think. I couldn't stay in the same room with her. But I did call her, and she came down [to visit] before she died. And I remember telling her that I really did love her, and I was glad she'd come.

Helen's visit to her mother-in-law and re-union with her own mother are examples of correcting old mistakes. It was a process, as was described by Helen in her autobiography, that Helen and Bill began, even before the scribing of *A Course in Miracles*. Such overt expressions of forgiveness were an integral early part of the mind-training program in which Jesus was instructing them.

Helen then continues with a discussion of her relationship with her mother, another good example of the special relationship later described in great detail in the Course:

When I thought Jonathan was going to be drafted, I asked mother if I could come and live with her again. They had an extra bedroom and bath, and besides they were the only other home I knew, so I never thought I wouldn't be welcome. I remember my mother's surprising answer. She said I could come, of course, (her accent was *so* English), but I would have to do things her way, because she was set in her ways now, and did not want to be interfered with. She reminded me that I had always been rather difficult, and she did not want to have any problems since her heart attack. I was terribly stunned at the time, but I guess she was right. Anyway, Jonathan didn't get drafted, and I'm glad I asked her back before she died.

This last statement was a reference to Helen's earlier comment on inviting her mother to her apartment after not having seen her for two years. I might mention here that Helen was always guilty over having left her mother's room in the hospital while she was critically ill, and was therefore not with her at the moment of her death.

The letter goes on:

The time sequence here is terrible, but I am really trying to write this as it occurs to me. You know, Bill, I have kept repeating that you can accomplish things symbolically, by a certain kind of willingness. Actual experiences are sometimes necessary, but if you can somehow learn the lesson that the experiences would have taught in a symbolic way, that has as much conviction as you would have gained from the real happening; you can avoid the actual experience of pain in many cases.

The Course student may be interested in a similar discussion in the text, where Jesus explains that it is not necessary for us literally to repeat his crucifixion.

...by being able to hear the Holy Spirit in others you can learn from their experiences, and can gain from them without experiencing them directly yourself....You are not asked to repeat my [Jesus'] experiences because the Holy Spirit, Whom we share, makes this unnecessary (text, pp. 86f).

Helen then returned to Louis (Jonathan):

I don't think Jonathan will be sick at all. I was sure of it then, and I was also sure he would live a long time, because he always said he doesn't mind getting old if he's well enough to enjoy it. He thinks there are lots of things to do, and he never could understand my own fear of aging. People don't die until they want to.

Again, the Course student will find of interest these comparable statements in both the text and workbook:

No one can die unless he chooses death (text, p. 388).

And no one dies without his own consent (workbook, p. 274).

We continue, the subject still being Louis:

It suddenly occurred to me that he would have no trouble in old age, and would really enjoy it a lot. I thought, "his hernia is gone now," and there I made a mistake, I think. It is not a gift of mine to see the future, except symbolically. *You*, Bill, are the one with the real gift of factual prediction. That's why I have to ask you about it. I realized afterwards—this may seem like hedging, and to an extent it is, but I really think that factual predictions are dangerous for me, because they might make me proud, and I have trouble in that line already. You, on the other hand, *need* it.

This passage is an important one in its emphasis on the danger in Helen's making factual predictions. We shall return to it in Part III when we discuss some of Helen's mistakes in hearing, outside her scribing of the Course. Her letter continues with the same theme:

Two years ago, I made some predictions out of the top of my head about you and me and Chip and [some others]. I didn't tell you about the one I made about Jonathan, because it scared me. I think I just said he'd be sick, and recover. I mentioned it at the Harkness Pavilion [part of the Columbia-Presbyterian Medical Center] the other day, and said, "Well, he does have a hernia." I tried, quite superstitiously, to tie in what I really had thought with the hernia, and cover up the other thing. I thought at the time that he would develop cancer, and then I thought it would be cancer of the prostate, and not very serious. But it worried me a lot. So I tried to settle for just the hernia. Symbolically, I think what the hernia stood for to me at the time *is* gone. And I will try to help Jonathan find his contented old age, because he will make terrifically good use of it.

In the bus coming back, there was a lot more about Jonathan's happy old age. I don't think he will be seriously sick at all. That's all over.

Jonathan has always had a secret wish to write an encyclopedia of New York, a city which he loves. At one time, he went so far as to make up a card file of all the references he came across, and kept this up for some time. Then he dropped it, because the idea of writing a book struck him as quite impossible for him. But I don't think it will remain impossible, somehow. I think when he gets old that is exactly what he will do. I have always been worried about providing for him, but we've taken care of that now, and Jonathan should be financially adequately though not elaborately provided for for life. Maybe you will see the book; I somehow don't think I will. But I'm very glad about it, anyway. I can't tell you how glad I am.

In point of fact, Louis has very much enjoyed his old age. As of this writing (1991) Louis is nearing his eighty-third birthday, and has survived Helen by over ten years. Largely because of Helen, he has been very well taken care of, and since her death, Louis has for the first time in his life felt financially secure. He is in good health and keeps very active, seeing friends and family constantly. In fact, the only consistent time I can reach him by phone is seven o'clock in the morning, after which he is out, beginning his busy day by having breakfast in a favorite local eating place. Incidentally, Louis has never been seriously ill. A number of years ago he did have surgery for his hernia, but with no complications. Helen refers again to Louis' book in a later letter, and so we shall discuss it further below.

Helen then returned to her discussion of symbols:

This has gone on forever, and I hate to be redundant after such a long bit. But you *can* do things symbolically, if you suddenly really understand the symbols. I never had much experience with life, but the one asset I always had (I don't think this is a matter of pride so much as a question of fact) is that I was always a very good learner when I tried to be. Perhaps it's not a matter of pride so much as a way of grace. When I was little, and not yet too concerned with pride (that came later, I think, after I got fat and unacceptable) I used to understand a lot of next steps without being taught. My uncle, (that's the mathematician) used to be quite surprised about me in mathematics, a subject that always frightened me so badly I wouldn't attend classes. However, it seems that I could give some very accurate answers provided the level was one which I could understand. Oddly enough, the level always seemed to be much higher than what I would have known if I had understood the teacher, which I usually didn't. The whole thing was quite trying, and was particularly upsetting in exams.

For much of her adult life Helen had a reading phobia, and hardly read a book, as I mentioned earlier, except perhaps for the Bible and some poetry. Her not only getting through graduate school, but at the top of her class no less, was therefore a tribute to her tremendous learning skill. Helen always had an extraordinary sense of logic (an ability utilized, for example, in the logical way that *A Course in Miracles* develops its argument). And so she was able to read a paragraph or two and deduce the basic argument of the book, or listen to a lecture and deduce the whole of the thought system of the course she was taking from just that small part. Similarly, as a psychologist, she could understand the totality of a person's ego system from just a few clues gleaned from a seemingly inconsequential statement. This makes sense when one considers that the ego's thought system follows a fierce though consistent logic. Thus, when one understands a piece of it, the rest inevitably follows if one is attuned to the underlying logic, as Helen certainly was.

Helen's letter concludes with a quotation from her favorite piece of literature, *Hamlet*:

> I think the quote is a remarkably accurate statement of symbolic experience, which in a way is the overall theme here. Shakespeare used it for death; maybe it's also true of life:
>
> > "If it be now, 'tis not to come;
> > if it be not to come, it will be now;
> > if it be not now, yet it will come;
> > the readiness is all."
>
> to which I humbly add, "and given readiness, you may not need to suffer the experience." Those, by the way, have always been my very favorite lines. I hate to touch them, but we have agreed that style is not the point. Especially since the lines conclude:
>
> > "Since no man has aught of what he leaves,
> > what is't to leave betimes? Let be."

And so I will. And yet, I think whatever it is I wrote, (I don't remember, really) is true.

The phrase "the readiness is all," incidentally, twice found its way into the important teaching in *A Course in Miracles*: readiness does not mean mastery (text, p. 29; manual, p. 14). One can be *ready* to forgive, for example, without one's having *mastered* the willingness to do so; a little willingness is all that is required.

> Added comments (put in Monday a.m.)
> I forgot the boardwalk bit. One evening we were walking and Jonathan pointed out a brain-injured boy (about 12 or so) who was being pushed by his parents in a carriage. There were other cripples[32] there, too. As we walked I suddenly (and briefly) got a sense of everyone walking happily and very much together on the same path. Like on the ladder. We can't all walk alone yet, but we'll all make it home eventually. Sometimes I love everybody very much.

Again, we find reference to Helen's recurring experience of all people joined as one, and the great happiness this realization brought her.

Letter Four

This next letter, a brief one, brings back the image of Helen's priestess, in content, if not necessarily in form.

> Dear Bill: I was not going to write you about this. It has occurred to me that some things that happen to me are just for me, but others are imperatively for both of us. I thought this was a private one, but it seems it isn't. The rule (for now) seems to be that anything that has to do with light, sight, or brightness is also for you. That is how I should tell the difference. I am unwilling to do this, but it definitely has to do with light, so I guess I should.
>
> Bill, I don't have visions, but sometimes pictures come to me. They used to be perfectly still, but they seem to include much more action now. Also, they have come to be much more

---

32. The British term for the retarded; Helen's fondness for England, obviously on one level based on her identification with her mother, often found itself reflected in her speech.

associated with me, instead of a kind of nameless person, or place, or thing suspended in motionlessness. This one crossed my mind while I was meditating,—a thing you very much want me to do. It annoyed me to death at first, but it's gotten to be very restful. I don't think it's silly any more, but I don't know what it is yet.

Anyway, this was one to be around the theme (I guess it's an admonition, is that the word? I'm not sure) of "Thy will be done." I don't pick these things in advance, but the idea of the right one seems to come just before I lie down. So I did it. The accompanying picture was quite clear and very bright (so again it belongs with both of us).

I did not see quite the beginning. I came in at the point where I was kneeling in an almost Japanese kowtow,—I think that's right, although it was Siamese in *The King and I*. Come to think of it, that last is a very good association. Perhaps this is the next chapter of Heaven and Helen. Anyway, I was kneeling, with my head and arms touching the ground, and a very bright light in front of me. It had no shape, and it did not quite touch me. In my hand was a laurel wreath, a symbol of victory to the Romans and most older cultures, I *think*. I am missing something here, but let it go. This one is short.

The idea seemed to be that the wreath should not be mine, but belongs to the light. I think it went into the light and burned up. There is a missing link here, because the transition is missing. Something happened, and the wreath disappeared.

I think the idea is that victory is not made by us, but it is made for us. It embarrasses me very much to have written this, but since it is also for you I thought I should, I am afraid you'll laugh, but remember I did try.

This "next chapter of Heaven and Helen" reflects Helen's attainment of the One-mindedness of the priestess— transcending both her wrong and right minds—that I have briefly introduced earlier in the book, to be returned to at its end. As Helen describes here, this stage of attainment is characterized by the total absence of a personal self: "the wreath should not be mine, but belongs to the light. I think it went into the light and burned up." It is not her and Bill's "victory," but the victory is given *to* them. As with the many other previous glimpses (and some later ones) into this transcending oneness, there was no apparent effect on Helen's everyday life.

Letter Five

The conflict between "Heaven and Helen" continued, as is seen in this next letter, which appears to have been written the following day. The reference to the "strange things" that were happening to Helen would seem to refer to the events of the summer of 1965, and so would also lend support to dating these letters in that time period.

Dear Bill, I was very happy last evening for a while, and feeling very restful. Things began to go wrong, but slowly. I have not yet recovered. I have had to be very careful today, and not do anything until I'm sure it's right. I do feel I should write this now, but what I wrote last night has to be torn up [this perhaps explains why the surviving letter—Letter Four—is so short]. The way it began is all right, but the rest isn't. So I will begin again the same way.

I thought, yes, I do see visions and always have. Briefly this seemed real, and though I thought it was a trifle dangerous for a second, I came round and thought, it's a very happy thing because it's a source of hope. There was a picture of the devil I caught sight of in a book, and I thought how very *un*frightening. What happened next is hard to describe, but it began when I thought it was really quite odd that, what with all the strange things happening to me, I don't really believe anything is happening. You do, but I don't. That's very peculiar. I bet if I asked people whether they thought it was noteworthy or not, chances are they'd say yes. Not me. You yes. Jonathan yes (though he doesn't know yet what's really happening). Me no.

I was struck by the similarity in what I read to you over the phone and what I had said before. And then, after a short period of conviction (that word I think should be noted), I thought, no, perhaps I glanced ahead and don't remember. People get fooled so easily. (Like the miracle at Lourdes.) I thought I was sure, but I wasn't. A rather savage doubting set in, and I suddenly realized I could probably account for a lot of the things that happened in other ways quite within normal chance variation, and how could I ever be so silly as to fall for all this?

The reader will find in these words the same doubts Helen expressed in her autobiographical account of this time period. And yet obviously, as will be seen, another part of Helen did believe, or at the very least, trusted enough in what was happening to allow the experiences to continue.

> So I said a prayer (like you said), and it occurred to me that I had better just let things wait. In fact, I thought it might even be dangerous not to. I tried to write out what I was thinking, but I knew it was wrong. I even think it was evil, and the only thing I think I should write here is a curious misspelling of "primaeval," which came out "prime evil." I didn't sleep very long, even though I was very tired, and I do hope I can take a nap soon, because we're going out in the evening.
>
> This morning, I promised myself that I would do only what I seemed to feel essential; be very accurate and keep close to honesty even in the most unessential details of what I say. I have tried to do this.
>
> A lot of horrible things crossed my mind, and most of what I wrote (and have torn up) was horrible. It was something about distorted miracles. I can forget that now.
>
> This morning, I kept saying, sort of without intention and it's gone now—"I am a channel," which seemed to mean something at the time. But the channel got clogged up, so it doesn't always work except when things get through the intervening mass. It's not open yet.

This last statement is a reference to the same idea expressed in the vision of the boat sequence, where Helen was not ready yet to use the "receiving and sending set." We therefore can see again Helen's honesty in observing both sides of her split mind: the channel as well as the interference.

Helen's next comments use terminology from her great love, statistics. The meaning, however, is clear even to the layperson, as Helen speaks of the importance of her relationship with Bill (a "cluster") in providing a much-needed balance for one another, thereby correcting each other's mistakes of specialness before they continue on their respective paths.

> Bill, what I think I am safe in writing now is only that I think people get together in little clusters of lights for a time,

while that cluster serves best in the syndrome analysis.[33] But the nodes[34] change, and their meaning changes as they do. Lots of times the clusters remain together for a long time, until the balance is stabilized and all the lights shine equally. Then another cluster becomes better for the members of the original one, and the pattern shifts.

I think you and I belong in the same cluster for quite some time. We have a special balance problem at the moment, which not only needs straightening out, but which is very crucial to the next balance problem, which I think we will again need each other for. The weighting system has been poor, and that has obscured the real meaning of the data. We have both done some very odd things in the attempt to correct this, but further adjustments are still necessary. We have already changed some of the names for the dimensions in the factor analysis,[35] and I think a very important change was a shift we made a while ago in changing the polarity passive-aggressive to passive-creative. That was the beginning of a much better understanding of the dimension, and all names assigned to clusters are arbitrary, based only on what you think the factors in them mean.

This discussion anticipates the explanation Jesus provides early in the Course's dictation of the differences between Helen's and Bill's egos. Here, Helen's explanation to Bill contrasts her ego's misuse of her very strong will (as in the evil priestess of her visions) with Bill's more consistent focus, which, however, had been severely weakened. This explanation continues now, utilizing the terms "creative" (substituted for "aggressive"), and "receptive" (substituted for "passive").

I think we need each other badly now to restore the balance on this dimension. I have misused the creative extreme, and you have misused the receptive one. We have neither of us neutralized these urges well, and so we do not understand that no position on the continuum is dangerous in itself. We have also lost the realization that the real control lies in a sense of proportion, because we are too out of balance to see it.

---

33. Study of characteristics or variables that go together.

34. The isolated or outstanding points of the cluster being observed and studied.

35. A complicated and sophisticated statistical form of analysis.

It is curious that, much against what either of us would probably have predicted some years back, we have each done much to encourage and help the other in the direction we would hardly have anticipated. At least, we would have anticipated it if we had been really honest at that time, which we weren't. I am trying very hard to bring you toward dominance, of which you are very much afraid. The reason for your fear is that you have defined the extremes inaccurately, and are therefore confused as to where hostility lies. It doesn't lie *anywhere* along the continuum. Your notion of receptivity has been equated with thievery, and your private definition of creativity is murder. While you believe that, you cannot either receive or create, even though you are really capable of either. But don't make any step yet. You're still too bound by your own definitions.

A substantial portion of the early dictation of the Course was devoted to Jesus' helping Bill with this very problem of confusing receptivity with thievery, and creativity with murder, as the problem manifested itself regarding a class he was to teach at Columbia University. As will be discussed below, Bill's fear of public speaking and professing (Jesus' pun on Bill's being a professor) a thought system stemmed from his former misuse of the power of his mind. Thus he equated creativity (or teaching) with murder. On the other hand, not sharing the love and truth that was contained in his mind produced guilt over selfish hoarding, i.e., having stolen this truth, keeping it for himself. All of this is a direct foreshadowing of the Course's later teachings on special relationships, which re-enact the original separation belief that we misused our minds to *murder* God and *steal* His power. These self-definitions of murderer and thief replace God's definition that we are, and always will be, His innocent and loving child.

Helen then shifts to herself, and to her self-accusations of pushing others away so as not to receive love from them, or to keep their love away by manipulating them—"using the hooks"—into becoming her slave.

I come into this with an opposite kind of distortion. I have been very much afraid of receptivity, and won't even listen to God with an open mind. Nobody can get very near me, because he might give me something, and since I want it very much I

161

might be tempted to take it and burn up. My notion of receptivity is death. And so I have closed the channels. Creativity, on the other hand, is more associated in my distortions with power and especially with a kind of spell-binding which is particularly vicious. I do not associate it as much with murder (I think that is more *your* error) as with enslaving people. I use magic to spin hooks and fishing sinkers, and poor fish get caught on the spikes. I don't really mean magic, so much as wits. I am in a peculiar dilemma, which is somewhat the opposite of yours, because I think that my choice is between death (and it's a violent death, too) and using the hooks. You cannot move because you think you must either steal or murder. We are both wrong.

Again, a student of *A Course in Miracles* will recognize here in Helen's words precursors of later discussions on special relationships. In these insane and vicious defenses against truth, the choice is always made between our own death, or preserving our seeming life through baiting others, thereby symbolically killing them. The body is the means for accomplishing the ego's goal, and of this the Course would later say:

> What would you save it [the body] *for*? For in that choice lie both its health and harm. Save it for show, as bait to catch another fish, to house your specialness in better style, or weave a frame of loveliness around your hate, and you condemn it to decay and death (text, p. 479).

Helen then continues, sounding like the voice of Jesus, imparting the same tone of gentle wisdom that is so characteristic of *A Course in Miracles*, and yet which once again predates the Course's scribing. We thus can see further evidence of the wisdom that was present in Helen, despite her successful attempts to conceal it. Specifically here, she addresses the need for her and Bill to change their self-concepts, and the important role their having joined together—"our recent Alliance"—plays in this re-definition.

> In our recent Alliance, you have done much to change your definitions, but you can't appreciate the magnitude of the shift because your definitions, though now open-ended, are still not right. I can't move too much yet, because I am still afraid to open the channel and redefine both extremes. Bill, this

dimension *has* to be straightened out. The lights in the cluster are all off-balance.

After some material which I have not included here, the letter continues:

(I remembered my brother threw me into the water—it was very deep because I think it was a lake and he was rowing; he said it was to teach me to swim. You know, Bill, it's curious about this life and defenses; Freud was right about them, except that when you find traumas to yourself, they are defenses too. It's not what other people did to you that accounts for things. If that's what you look for, you can analyze forever and nothing much will happen, even though it's probably true. And then if you decide to hate your brother *because* he threw you into the water, you miss the point twice.[36])

Helen's wise comments here are similar in form and content to the earlier ones, expressing the recognition that we are upset not because of what others have done to us in the past, but because we choose in the present to be upset: "It's not what other people did to you that accounts for things. If that's what you look for, you can analyze forever...." In Part III I return to this theme of Helen's wisdom by citing three examples from her pre-Course life that illustrate her intuitive understanding of how the external has no effect on her state of mind. Clearly, such insights represent the total opposite of Helen's ego thought system that blamed everyone and everything else for her own misery and unhappiness. These letters emphasize again Helen's incisive awareness of her split mind.

Letter Six

Another "letter" follows, which Helen wrote to Bill while at the Medical Center, waiting in her office for him to return to their private offices in another building:

It is my impression that this report is crucial. Not for the past, but for the future. The questions (and the vision) were for you

---

36. The first miss is hating someone else; the second is blaming that hatred on what was seemingly done *to* you.

through me. And since this begins from last night, you weren't there at the time.

The picture that came to me before I went to sleep was of a dark sky with only one star in it. The star was very bright, but also very distant. But in spite of its distance, there was one perfectly uninterrupted ray beaming out from it and reaching your forehead in the center. I did ask for an explanation [from Jesus] of this, and I believe we both need it. But explanations are not generally necessary, and should stop before we get bogged down in the past. Thus far, but no further.

The theme that is to run all the way thru here is the word "one."

The dark sky is the ego's world of fear and guilt (the self-definition), while the *one* star is the Christ that is the true definition of our Self. This Self seems to be "very distant," but access to it can be gained in an instant through that "uninterrupted ray" that represents the Holy Spirit, or the memory of God's Love in our minds. This ray thus unites us with our reality, even though we believe we are here in the world.

Helen's instructions to Bill continue:

The curious paradoxical thread in your life history is very striking. That is really because you were literally star-crossed. (At this point I said I don't believe in the influence of stars. I was right about this. But what happens is not that the stars themselves have influence, but a person chooses a particular star pattern because it shows him what the setting will be. He merely reads the signs, which show him the right setting. The influence comes from him, but the stars show him where the most appropriate influences will occur.)

The phrase "star-crossed" refers to Bill's experience of the conflict between his parents, from which he felt very victimized. Helen, however, is telling him that the conflict was internal, and was simply projected outward. Her comments about astrology are of note, for they support her position that we are not victimized by forces outside our minds. Helen is essentially saying that the constellations of stars do not have a *causative* influence on our lives, but rather a correlative one. In other words, the cause of our behavior lies in our minds, *beyond* this physical world entirely, and the same decision that determines our behavior also determines the configuration of the stars.

Understanding the setting of the stars (and planets) can help us to understand the choices we have made—"it shows him what the setting will be"—but the stars themselves should not be attributed any causal power.

Helen goes on, referring again to Bill's belief that he was the victim of his parents, and takes the discussion one step further:

> My question about "was your father left handed" was not irrelevant, and I should have followed it up, but with a more open mind. It crossed my mind then that there is something in your heredity that is crossed, or interfering with progress. One side seemed then to come from your mother and one side from your father. That interpretation of heredity, which was essentially genetic, was too literal. You may have chosen them for that reason, but the actual conflict is in karmic inheritance. There were two equally strong forces in your karmic inheritance, which were entirely contradictory, and which are in themselves irresolvable. At first I thought that one was evil and the other good, but I don't think so now. The thing is that they were *different*, and cannot be handled simultaneously. Taken together, they *must* induce paralysis or suspension. Taken one at a time, they will both lead to better unification.
>
> The first move out of the impasse had to come from you, by your making a real decision to stick with one and totally disregard the opposite pull. You did this when you suddenly decided to help me wholeheartedly. It's curious that what you saw in me was the one thing you were most afraid of. I was never star-crossed myself, but I was working under the influence of both sides of the same star.

Helen is thus describing the different forms in which her and Bill's conflict manifest: Helen's, within one star, representing the erratic though strong nature of her single-minded pull to God; Bill's, between two stars ("star-crossed"), the conflict which greatly weakens his attraction to God. The "karmic inheritance" of Helen's explanation can be more properly understood as the conflict buried deep within Bill's mind between his pull towards God, and his fear of aggressively seizing the divine power. Since time is ultimately non-linear, the so-called past is simply symbolic of a more repressed thought that is actually coexistent with the more conscious ones experienced as occurring in the present.

165

Note again, incidentally, the firmness of Helen's personal belief in reincarnation, clearly contradicting the much later anti-reincarnation statements in her autobiography. These statements supposedly reflect the beliefs she held from the same pre-Course period as do these letters. This discrepancy in Helen's writings points up once again the occasional unreliability of her reporting. The statements from her autobiography, written much later than the described events, dramatically contrast with her actual experiences at the time. These later statements thus serve to protect Helen's public image as a rational and scientific atheist, not to mention their serving a dramatic literary purpose as well.

The discussion continues:

> You couldn't stand the contradiction (which you know perhaps more about than I do, actually), and you felt an impelling need to resolve it. The result was that, in me, the star (the one star) came into the right perspective. But at the same time, you gave up the influence of the crossing star in yourself, and went sharply (and very correctly) in one direction.
>
> This is picked up this morning. I woke with a very clear but rather odd sentence, "Never underestimate the power of denial" on my mind.[37] I am sorry about this, but the one thing that saved the situation was that I meant it kindly. Unfortunately, it also leads to a curious ineffectualness in me, and a real loss of rapport between us. I would like to repair this. (I won't hurt anybody any more, but I *do* run the constant risk of not helping nearly as much as I should and must.)
>
> It is my own responsibility (and this was told me [by Jesus] very sternly, too) to see to it that you understand, realize, and fully accept the *fact* that you are not star-crossed any more. None of that matters now. The only reason why I was asked (and even urged) to write this is because you *must* learn that the past is helpful only as it contributes to the learning conditions in which you function in the present to create the future. And make no mistake—you *do* create it.

This latter point was an important one for Bill, as he felt clearly trapped by his unhappy past, and tended to blame it for

---

37. This later found its way into the Course in the form: "Do not underestimate the power of the ego's belief in it [the attack on God]" (text, p. 77).

his current conflicts. Helen here was trying to free him of this. We will see the same, though more detailed, attempts made by Jesus in the Course's dictation to help Bill with this issue. Note also Helen's clarity about her decision not to hurt anyone anymore, but note as well the remaining ambivalence about the helping of others that clearly would interfere with the loving help she could really offer.

Helen's counsel to Bill continues:

> Bill, you can put it any way you want; your house is ready; or the door is open; or there is only one star now. You *must* listen to me about this. You are perfectly free now. You weren't, but you are. It may take a little time before this is really accepted—oddly enough, something to do with the time it takes for starlight to reach the earth. There can be a real time discrepancy here, and sometimes we even see stars which are no longer there. Forget it; it's really gone. When it comes back, which will not be for some time, it too will be the only one.

Helen here insistingly tells Bill that he no longer is a prisoner of his past: "You are perfectly free now." Even though it still seems as if the past is a determining factor in Bill's life, the truth is that the past is undone. Astronomers teach that there is a time delay between the reality of the star's light and when we on earth actually perceive it. Similarly, we may perceive a star's light when, in reality, the star has already disappeared. Bill's "star-crossed" conflict is gone, despite his continued experience of it. In the world of illusion, some time must still elapse until this end of conflict is experienced by Bill, and his one Self is known: "it too will be the only one."

The letter concludes:

> The only thing that needs to be added here is another line from Wordsworth [the first line is not recorded here]. It too was with me when I woke up, or maybe just a little after. The line is, *(please* listen)—
>
> "Fair as a star when only *one* is shining in the sky." I always thought this is one of his better lines. The phone has just rung, and I said to Joan [Helen's secretary] "Yes, I want to speak to Dr. Thetford," because this is finished. Will be right over.

Helen is thus urging Bill finally to choose to give up his fear of uniting with the one pull to God—the one star—since on another level he has already given up all other stars but this one. In other words, he *is* ready.

Letter Seven

Two important letters follow, written from a hotel in Morristown, New Jersey where evidently Helen and Louis were spending the weekend. It is possible that Bill was vacationing at Watermill at the same time. This letter clearly reflects Helen's experiencing Jesus' authority as strong if not stern, and in clear opposition to her ego self. And yet there seems to be no question but that she will "obey."

Dear Bill,

I am not sure I want to write this, but I have an idea I am obeying an Order. These Orders are rather stern, and the main feeling I get is that I wouldn't dare to disobey them. This is the 2nd one, the 1st one being given on Thurs. morning when I was so convinced that I *must* be sure you know you are fully released and perfectly free. I seem to wake up with certain very definite Instructions from a compelling Authority who is definitely *not* fooling.

The heart of this Order is, briefly, that now that you are released, *you* are definitely in charge of anything that has to do with Timing. That goes for both of us. I do not know what I am doing in that respect, and have no judgment about it, either. You are *much* better balanced that way. You will have to get over your cautiousness eventually, but meanwhile I *must* follow your directions in that dimension.

Since Bill has been freed of his inner conflict, as was discussed in the previous letter, Helen states that he has been placed (presumably by Jesus, referred to in a later letter as the "Top Sergeant") in charge of the timing of certain decisions. Helen continues, reflecting a shift in her ego's position by saying that "disobeying" an Order does not lead to punishment, but simply to the loss of peace.

I am not to interfere with your sense of tempo at all and will lose a great deal if I do (this was originally going to be "will be very severely punished," but it seems that "lose a

168

great deal" is more appropriate now). The "punishment" emphasis is over, and we both have to realize this. But the choice of progress versus stasis seems to remain a problem. You will gain as you choose to go forward and I will gain as I choose to follow you right. You have to earn a right to lead, and I have to learn how to follow.

In general, I am not to tell you much about you unless *you* ask (I think I may get some further Orders about this from time to time. I am then to follow them, but never exceed them). I *think*, however, that maybe each time there will/may be a short addendum, which I am to write or tell you about. Last time I did *not* write it, as instructed, but after some hesitance and a very careful check with you (as you may remember) I told you about it.

I am undecided about this, and keep vacillating. But I think there is more yes than no about it. Also, I do *not* like the idea. I guess it depends on what I write it *for*.

The student of *A Course in Miracles* will recognize the later references that emphasize purpose as the criterion for evaluating the meaning of anything in our lives. See, for example:

"What for?" This is the question that *you* must learn to ask in connection with everything. What is the purpose? Whatever it is, it will direct your efforts automatically (text, p. 61).

In any situation in which you are uncertain, the first thing to consider, very simply, is "What do I want to come of this? What is it *for*?" (text, p. 341)

The test of everything on earth is simply this; "What is it *for*?" The answer makes it what it is for you. It has no meaning of itself, yet you can give reality to it, according to the purpose that you serve (text, p. 479).

The above excerpt continues Helen's counsel to Bill, as well as to herself: Bill is to learn more assertiveness and acceptance of a leadership role, while Helen is to do just the reverse: learn to become less assertive and more accepting of another's (Bill's) leadership.

The letter continues:

If I do it [give Bill advice] because I'm proud of how much I know, hell will undoubtedly break loose. If I do it because it may reassure you (and perhaps me too) about a better future,

I'll be all right and you will hear it. You seem to be safe in either case, though if I do it wrong, you may not gain. Actual danger is only to me. I am going to take a minute or so out and say a prayer about this (I did not like to write this, so I had better do it quick).

OK—this is still an Order, but the crucial question is the opening. I was going to begin with "I think all those things I told you about were true." This would have been a deadly error. (My eyes are hurting me suddenly, but I think it's all right. I'll wait, though. I really *must* learn patience.)

Things got a little gentler. It[38] says "Open your heart to the gift of God and *follow it*." I'll try, but I have *to be* careful. I think it's safe to go on. You are entitled to an explanation of course, the word "explanation" was impertinent of me. The word should have been "clarification," and it does *not* come from me. (It's not *for* me, either.)

This is an aside from the main but it's an *essential* diversion, maybe as safeguard for me. I thought yesterday that the internal consistency of all the strange things I said was astonishingly high. And then I thought (very imperatively, too) that internal consistency at that level is God's business, *not* mine. The reason is that inter-rater agreement is impossible to determine, because there is only one Rater. I gather, however, that One is enough.

These statistical references—"internal consistency" and "inter-rater agreement"—cleverly make the point that however consistent the ego might be, however often it is in agreement with itself, it might still be wrong for it is not God, the only true Rater.

(I paused here, because unfortunately it occurred to me that that last [the aforementioned reference to the "one Rater"] is kind of cute. Actually, even that is all right, *provided* that I recognize that I am referring to a gift—or maybe even a loan—which is genuine enough, but *must not* be misused. My eyes hurt again—I'll wait.)

It says "Go ahead, I *am* helping you." I guess it's all right, Bill (and Helen too). So—

It seems that I have spent many years vacillating between

---

38. Note Helen's use of the less-threatening "It" instead of "He"; we shall return later to this word-play defense against Jesus.

being an evil priestess with a sincerely religious streak, and a new or a real priestess of some kind with a persistent streak of evil.[39] Either way it never worked out, naturally. The dilemma has not been completely neutralized yet, either, but it will be. That's why I can't lead now. I'm too much attracted to danger, and cannot be depended on to ask for and give real help consistently.

I am to stop *immediately*.

This letter, as in many others, was repeatedly being interrupted by Helen herself. She made frequent asides to Bill about her writing style and typographical errors (all corrected by me). These reflected her anxiety and ambivalence in writing these letters to Bill, as she herself comments on. Helen's anxiety is clearly related to the degree of honesty she is exhibiting here with Bill, and her willingness to, as a workbook lesson would later say, "step back and let Him lead the way" (workbook, p. 284). Following Bill's lead thus would be Helen's symbol here for following Jesus or the Holy Spirit.

Letter Eight

In this next letter Helen also comments on following Jesus' "Orders." It is dated Sunday, presumably the day Helen and Louis were to return home, as seen by the reference to her own typewriter in the first paragraph.

Dear Bill,

This is *absolutely* the last thing I want to do now, but this has been a very strange weekend, and I guess this is part of it. I was trying to take an after-breakfast nap but I wasn't sleeping anyway and I suddenly became sharply aware of having work to do (namely this) and I had to do it. Rest is actually the peace of God. We look for it in sleep and vacations and things like that, and we are wise enough in doing so for the time being. But it's not the complete answer. Oddly enough, you have to work very hard for real rest. I keep saying if I could wait for my typewriter this evening it would take half the time or even less. Yes indeed, and that's the whole idea. It's *supposed* to take effort.

---

39. An obvious reference to the visions of Helen's past lives that belonged to the summer of 1965, presented in Chapter 5.

Once again we can observe Helen's gentle wisdom, this time regarding the world's view of rest versus the true rest of God, and the "work" involved in attaining His peace. Helen then continues with her comments on the growing role Jesus was assuming in her life.

> I am not used to being in the army (maybe it's really the army of the Lord) and I have had a rather rough time this weekend. A Top Sergeant (who says that's the right term to use, and don't abbreviate it, either, because TS has exactly the implications I am specifically to avoid) has literally been issuing orders which, though they have not been punitive, have been *very* stern. In the main, I have not resented this, but I *have* found them quite compelling. Writing this is one of them, and this is one of the very few I resent to some extent. I *will* try, though.

The Top Sergeant of course is Jesus, and it is important to note that Helen's experience of his "orders" as *very* stern reflects just that, her *experience*. Jesus obviously is not stern; yet, Helen's fear of his love colored, not to mention distorted, her experience of it. This is the same phenomenon reported by so many followers of Jesus (or the Holy Spirit) as well. I remember many years later Helen telling me that she knew when it was Jesus speaking to her, because he told her exactly the opposite of what she wanted to hear. Within the framework of the experience of her inner conflict—Heaven and Helen—Jesus' will and her own were always separate. And yet, as will be discussed in Part III, Jesus' love is abstract and not personal, and perfectly unified with our real Self. Love knows nothing of specifics, and so any perception of Jesus in personal terms—e.g., stern *or* gentle—reflects the projections of the individual. This accounts for why people experience Jesus in so many different ways.

Helen's letter goes on:

> I woke yesterday with the definite conviction that I was to step back and do everything Jonathan said until further notice. I tried and mostly succeeded, I think. The first reason which came to me for this order was its use for me. (I have *always* put me first—its been my big mistake.) At lunch I sort of filed a brief objection, asking if I really had to be quite this

"subservient." The answer was stern and quick, "Only until you're safe. I have use for you." (This Top Sergeant is *not* kidding.)

On and off during the day it occurred to me that I have never really cared for anyone else's well-being and that I don't really know how. Intellectually yes—emotionally no. Since I *have* been able to keep the intellectual area relatively humble and genuine, it has helped me keep out of major trouble, because intellectually I never would have held that nobody but me existed.

Bill—I know I'm writing mostly about me this time. That's part of the Order at this time, because of your tempo. But I think it won't end with that.

Emotional, not intellectual arrogance has been my persisting sin and its extent appalls me. (Aside—which I resent at this moment—"The Lord is my Shepherd," a phrase I am afraid of because I associate it with funerals. But I am safe doing this, because it's done in obedience. This makes an *enormous* difference, in terms of safety.)

Helen's almost stream of consciousness here reflects her willingness to be obedient to Jesus—"The Lord is my Shepherd"—even though the phrase itself has connotations of death for her. This obedience is what she has been choosing in relation to Bill and Louis (Jonathan). Her willingness to set aside her own self-will therefore provides the safety and protection, for it puts her under the divine protection within her mind.

The more basic point in this segment is Helen's awareness of the distinction between her intellectual understanding of truth, and her inability to accept it emotionally. She is correctly quoted near the end of her life as having said about the Course: "I know it's true. I just don't believe it." This statement has been very much misunderstood by Course students, however, to suggest that she did not *believe* in the Course. The situation was just the opposite. Helen did believe in the truth of the Course's teachings, not to mention in the existence of its author. However, she was not able *emotionally* to accept its truth into her own personal life. Note, too, the extension of the lesson from the previous letter of letting Bill have a leadership role; now it includes Louis (Jonathan) as well.

The letter continues, with Helen discussing the subject of intellectual understanding and its value:

> Intellectual will is a great asset as long as it's all you've got. Then you have to use it. It will never lead to love, but it can and does help you keep clean until you learn a better way.[40] It also leads to the better way quicker, because it's the human counterpart of another will which has the real Authority. The major difference is that human will, though strong in its way, is never fair, and so its direction can be right but is *always* limited.
>
> Last night I asked the Top Sergeant (rather timidly) if I couldn't please see a little light, maybe—I thought I'd obeyed pretty carefully. You're right, Bill—there are *no* bargains. He was still quite stern about this. I probably won't see very much light for a while—and it may be a long while, too, because when I see it again it has to be for good.

This was the truth, as it turned out. Helen did not *seem* to "see very much light" in the balance of her life, nor did she progress step by step, as is more usual in people's experience. Near the end of the manual for teachers, Jesus states:

> The curriculum is highly individualized, and all aspects are under the Holy Spirit's particular care and guidance (manual, p. 68).

And it did appear, as I discuss at the end of the book, as if Helen's clarity of vision did come all at once at the moment of her death. The decision that permits such vision to come occurs on the level of the mind, which exists outside time and space, an important teaching of the Course that I return to in Chapter 7. Helen's decision, as we have already seen, was reflected in her earlier dreams and visions, such as in the one involving the "God Is" scroll.

The letter concludes with some added comments about Louis (Jonathan), beginning with a reiteration of the importance of Helen's letting him assume more of a leadership role

---

40. This is an obvious reference to Bill's "There must be another way" speech. Helen and Bill, not to mention Jesus in the Course, frequently substituted the word "better" for "another" in their references to Bill's statement.

in their relationship. Helen also expresses the importance of her letting go of the need to control other people:

> Today I finally got an inkling of what Jonathan needs. I was really surprised at how naturally he slipped into the driver's seat when I got off it myself. (He also saved my life in the Morristown traffic, which is really wild.)
>
> Jonathan must learn to want his freedom, and I must learn to give it to him. (I *still* think this problem is essentially between you and me in the sense of karmic debt, but we can both run into trouble if we build up future debts to others.) As we work it out together (and we *have* come a long way from our initial head-on explosion, thanks to a combination of your guidance and my will, neither of which is sufficient now)—we *must* clean up our other relationships concomitantly.

The point here is that even though *A Course in Miracles* itself teaches that when we truly forgive one person, all people will be forgiven, it does not mean that we do not nonetheless work on healing all relationships at the same time. Helen and Bill clearly had the greatest difficulty in forgiving each other, yet they were urged by Jesus (and here by Helen herself) to forgive all their other relationships as well.

Helen continues to Bill, ending the letter abruptly:

> I *must* not speak for you here. But for myself. I will be able to love people to the extent to which I can make them free of me. This is particularly true of Jonathan. He has a book to write, and I am to help him get ready to write it. (I doubt if I'll be here when he does write it, but I think *you* will. Please help him. It's for both of you.) He needs my spirit with him for a while, and he said he'll dedicate the book, and every page he writes, to me. He was kidding, of course, but not really, though he doesn't know it yet.
>
> His book will be a very real step toward independence. God forgive me for having made him weaker rather than stronger (I'm crying a little now), and with His help I'll help him yet (I'm crying a *lot* now).

Louis never did get to writing his book, unfortunately, since it indeed would have given him a great deal of pleasure, and probably would have been a joy for New Yorkers. He always spoke of wanting to write a book about his beloved New York City, his only home. While it was difficult for Helen consistently to help Louis emotionally during her lifetime, she was able to do so symbolically after her death by amply providing for his material well-being, as noted above. Moreover, at the end of her life, as I will discuss in Chapter 18, she increasingly turned to him for help. In her final weeks she continually called out to him in an infantile dependent way, "Louis, Louis." While this period was a particularly trying one for him, Louis nonetheless felt gratified that Helen finally needed him, a feeling he had never really felt before.

Letter Nine

The final letter is dated Sunday, 11 A.M. The mention of Virginia Beach in the second paragraph is another reference point for dating these letters in the summer of 1965, as Helen and Bill went to see Hugh Lynn Cayce in September of that year. Among other things, Helen here gives Bill some sage advice concerning meditation, basically instructing him on the difference between form and content. As has already been seen in some of the previous letters, Bill was continually urging Helen to meditate. We also find here another reference to the importance for Helen of letting Bill make certain decisions for her.

Dear Bill:

This is the right time to do this. I have been waiting until it was. I was going to do it yesterday evening; we got home around 11 PM and I turned on the Jean Shepard show (which I like), and I would have done it then, but I decided I am very nice and am entitled to hear something I enjoy. In fact, sacrifice as such doesn't mean anything and does not purify. It can even be a sin. (The whole topic here is sin anyway.)

This starts off with an admonition for you. You are still in charge of this venture [of finding "another way"], and will probably remain so for some time. The whole Virginia Beach idea is entirely in your hands, and I do not think I will bring it up myself, although I'm not sure. Either way, all timing in this matter is up to you.

Anyway, I think you were wrong about when and where you can meditate. The answer *is* anywhere and anytime. Sin is a lack of perspective and proportion.[41] I have been guilty of being too unaware of externals, but you have been guilty of being too dependent on them. Please try to get used to the idea that when you feel it's a good time [to meditate], it is. It doesn't really depend on being in a familiar place (that's just a thing with you), and being quiet can happen anywhere. It's not the outside noise that counts. I think I was right in saying that I remembered that my own most religious experience happened in the subway, of which I was very much afraid at the time. I think that wherever you are afraid is probably your best chance of being quiet. It is a mistake to think that a stage setting is the play, just as I made a mistake in thinking that you don't need any setting at all.

The reason why you don't always need your own setting is that sometimes meditation can actually save you from disaster.

This last comment refers to the "disaster" that might be experienced by attempting to solve a problem or deal with an emergency situation by oneself, rather than with Jesus or the Holy Spirit. Interestingly enough, this instruction on the crucial difference between form and content—in the discussion of not needing externals to meditate—came *before* the scribing of *A Course in Miracles* began, in which this very important teaching is emphasized. The chief characteristic of special relationships, which can be understood as the ego's most important weapon in its war against God, is the confusion of form and content. Our dependence on the ritualistic forms of prayer— how? where? when? what?—mirroring our dependency in relationships—obscures the content of love that *is* the heart of prayer. Helen then continued:

Please bear with me now, because I will try to be very accurate, and wherever I am wrong now it will be corrected in time. I feel I should tell you that I will make some mistakes here, but I think the main ideas are true.

I want to thank you for saving my eyes, which I was going to lose. This was *not* because of retribution; I don't think the

41. *A Course in Miracles* would later teach that the "lack of perspective" lies in viewing sin as deserving punishment, as the ego would have us believe, rather than as a mistake to be corrected by the Holy Spirit.

retribution idea should be too much emphasized because it's never the main point.

Again, Helen's excessive concern for her eyes will be discussed in a number of different contexts later on. I do not know the exact context here of Helen's remarks about Bill's "saving" her eyes, but it is important to note her gratitude to Bill for his help. It is also interesting to see how Helen was moving away from the idea of punishment, which plays such a crucial role in the ego's insane thought system of sin.

The theme of Helen's eyesight is continued now, in the context of the following incident. We also find here further examples of Helen's desire to help others, as well as her continued attempts to be honest with Bill and herself about her own ego.

I got into that cab in a slightly mixed up mood, because I thought I was supposed to meditate from 5:45 [P.M.] to 6 [P.M.] and then call you. Afterwards I knew it didn't matter, because your train [from Watermill] would be late, and you couldn't get in by 6 anyway if the departure time was right.

Sam's wife held me up a while, and I really wanted to help her. She is a very nice woman and very pretty, but she has a lot of desperation about her and she really needed some reassurance. She was pathetically grateful, which she needn't have been. I think we worked out a more restful and optimistic approach, though. Then Charlotte wanted to drive to the [train] station with me, and she took forever (this is an exaggeration, but it almost seemed like that at the time; I do not like to have other people interfere with my plans, even though I am beginning to get the idea that plans help but they can't rule and neither can I).

The cab, which we did not get immediately, took forever (not really). When we got held up in traffic, I briefly got kind of wild. Then it occurred to me that you can't set the time and place for meditating always, and I was late because I had really tried to help Gale (Sam's wife), and waiting for Charlotte had been a nice thing, too. So doing nice things is the best preparation for meditation, and since it was almost 6, I thought why not right here. I am very glad I did.

So I shut off the noise, though I still heard it, and I thought about the things you told me too, about "Mine eyes have seen the glory," and all the rest, and I began to feel better, although the pain did not leave my eyes. I thought maybe I'd finish it

when I got home, but I kept thinking why wait? So I kept coming back to it. When we got out of the traffic snarl and onto
the driveway [the FDR Drive that wraps around the eastern
border of Manhattan], I closed my eyes and thought a lot.

Please listen, Bill—the next part is as important for you as
for me. This is really for both of us now. The first thing I
thought was "I have been blind." Then I thought of "eyes
have they but they see not." I thought It would (I don't
understand the capitalized It but I won't correct it) be nice to
see, because the world God made is beautiful, and part of my
legitimate inheritance. It was made for me and all of us, but I
have refused to see it. So I asked to be able to see it and join up
with it, so we could all go on together. It was a nice feeling, and
one I really enjoyed.

A Course in Miracles, of course, teaches that God did *not*
create the physical universe, but did create a world of spirit—
Heaven—which consists of Christ and Himself. The reflection
of Their unity and love within the dream that *is* this world, is
referred to in the Course as the aforementioned "real world,"
the split mind's state of total innocence that reflects the reality
of Heaven. This would be the world that Helen, even without
the benefit of Jesus' specific teachings in the Course, was referring to. And we see expression of Helen's joy in the idea that by
joining with what was originally perceived to be outside her
mind (*see* Lesson 30 in the workbook for an exercise that
exactly expresses this experience), we all are able to return to
God together.

The letter continues with Helen's cab journey home. The
cab developed some engine trouble not far from Helen's apartment, and so Helen got out and hailed another one. We pick up
the story here, with Helen still very concerned about her
eyesight.

Bill, dear, there would have been an accident if I had not
suddenly wanted to see [why this is so is not clear from Helen's
letter]. I would have been blinded. But it would not have been
out of retribution. It would have been merely because if I were
blind the thing I would have wanted most would have been
sight, which I have bitterly neglected. It has been a sin.

It's time to catch up on something that came before,
because it fits in here. When we were in your office and you

179

were trying to help me with the strain on my eyes, I thought briefly about blindness and breast cancer, and I thought would I be willing to have them if it was better that way. (I don't think smoking will hurt my eyes anymore.)

Then I thought briefly that I would be willing if it was necessary, because it was really kind. I felt better after that. But I think that being willing can be a real substitute for disaster, if you don't do it any more. I have not cleared up the breast cancer yet, but I don't think I will get it. Somehow, I seem to have escaped that too, and I thank you, but I am not clear yet how. It has something to do with misusing the body and being proud about the same thing.

As long as I really wanted to see, I don't have to be blinded. When I thought of being blind and also being willing, it occurred to me that the next time [i.e., the next lifetime; *see below*, Jesus' comment to Helen on pp. 500f] my vision will be perfect, and I will be able to use it properly. Maybe now it will get better this time.

In *A Course in Miracles*, sickness is understood, among other things, as being a decision the mind makes to atone for our sins against God. He is conceived by the ego as bloodthirsty in His need for vengeance, and so our suffering seeks to assuage His wrath by our taking the punishment into our own hands.

> Illness is a form of magic. It might be better to say that it is a form of magical solution. The ego believes that by punishing itself it will mitigate the punishment of God (text, p. 78).

Once our guilt is gone, however, through changing our minds and forgiving others and ourselves, the need for retribution is gone as well: "being willing can be a real substitute for disaster." Helen's concerns for her blindness, as well as her fears of developing breast cancer, are thus the inevitable effects of such guilt. These concerns also nicely serve the ego's purpose of distracting Helen from God and her life's purpose, both of which on one level were so frightening to her.

Helen then returned to a topic that was an important one for her, as it pointed up a particular characteristic that worked wonderfully well in maintaining conflict: not always telling the truth, although it appeared different. I mentioned this trait above, and here it is again:

In the evening, *please listen Bill*, I had a most uncomfortable idea. (I suddenly decided to call you here.) I remembered the small lies I told you; or the reinterpretations of truth with a slightly off-beat emphasis. I mentioned this to you yesterday, and you said you always knew it; I got defensive here, but I don't think it matters now. You also got briefly assaultive, but neither of us was intense enough to interfere seriously. I think what I told you was true. You did seem to stand there like an unassailable block, unwilling to move or give or join. So I tried to creep into your house by any open door, some of which were not nice. I thought I had to reach you, but I forgot that the end does not justify the means.

I realized then that from the level I was at at the time I was not being dishonest, except that the level of honesty was low. Besides this, I had misused reality to make it fit in with my own idea of how I wanted reality to be, which I did not know at the time. So I have to let it alone, and fit my ideas into it rather than the other way around. I don't have to pay for the past, but I must try not to do it any more. That will be enough.

Helen's discussion of this trait of hers contains a description of everyone's ego thought system. We all attempt to make reality into what *we* want, reminiscent of the core Course teaching on the beginning of the ego's existence: our original thought of separating from God in which we believed we could actually re-make reality. Helen then continues:

So all next day I tried to say everything as honestly as possible. I cut out a number of perfectly innocent but entirely unnecessary comments to the cab driver that evening, not because they were bad but because they would have been slightly inaccurate. Reality is not mine to describe or create. I should just look at it. I caught myself a number of times with Phil and Mary later [old friends of Helen and Louis], and I am astonished at how much of my life that must have been. It's hard to correct, *but at least I see it* [my italics].

And that, after all, was to be all *A Course in Miracles* would ask of us: the little willingness to be able to *see* in our minds what we have thought and done, without protecting it by unforgiveness. That vision of non-judgment suffices to allow the Holy Spirit's love to heal all sources of our pain and unhappiness. In an important statement made later in the dictation, Jesus says to Helen that all that you need to do to escape from suffering of any kind is to "look upon the problem as it is, and not the way that you have set it up" (text, p. 540); i.e., through projecting responsibility onto external agents.

Helen now moves to an account of a squabble she had with Louis (Jonathan), and demonstrates again her tremendous openness during this pre-Course period to shift her perceptions and accept responsibility for her own thoughts and feelings.

> In the late evening, I had a bad time (briefly) with Jonathan, but I *think* it came out all right. For reasons of his own, he had changed his socks, (he explained this rationally enough, but the explanation did not cover why he left the others on the table in the living room). I got absolutely wild when I saw them, and yelled at him (briefly again). He took them away immediately (though with what I thought was a humoring attitude).
>
> He also gave the most ridiculous reasons for being late coming home. I guess maybe there was some truth in it, but put it all together and it doesn't make sense. I did not get mad about it (which is rather unusual for me), but I thought he will have to undo his own rationalizations, which are not really any threat to me. If I keep on attacking him on the grounds that he won't change until he sees through them, I am not really helping him, but am emphasizing my own hatred, which is really irrelevant to the issue. Besides, the only outcome then will be greater defensiveness on his part, and I will set up a lot of reasons for justifying rather than seeing my own injustice in the future.

The argument continued, involving Louis' brushing of his teeth:

> Then he barged (this word is really unfair) into the bathroom where I had been washing my face, and began to wash his teeth. It was the longest routine of tooth-brushing I have ever seen. My impression was that it took about five years. Then he turned and asked me why I was just hanging around, and I burst out "You just came in and took over; didn't you even notice my things here?" Jonathan, (correctly, incidentally) answered that I was exercising when he came in, and had apparently interrupted my washing myself; how was he to know about it? This struck me as reasonable, so I just waited. Jonathan returned to the tooth-brushing bit (he does not brush

them more than once a day, which I think is a mistake, but when he does, I expect he's trying to make up for the omission). He said that's the way I should let him brush them, because that's how he wants to do it, and why should I get mad and look at him with such rage? I said I wasn't, which was not true. Still holding the toothbrush, which made me even madder, he said, if it wasn't rage it was hatred, then. I said, trying to get through this kindly, "You're wrong; I wasn't looking at you at all." He said, "Boy, if you can deceive yourself to that extent, what can I say?"

My answer, "I wasn't looking at you at all," began to worry me here. There is no doubt that I *was* looking at him, but I certainly wasn't seeing him right. So I corrected it by saying, "I was looking at you, and I am trying to see you more kindly. I am sorry about the hatred" (I meant that).

It's a sin not to look at people [correctly]. Not only don't you help them, but you cut them off. This is not the right way. We all need each other.

I would like to stop now, but I think I should just sum [up] one theme that seems to run through this. If you're willing, you don't have to pay. And it's much better and easier to be willing than to be crucified. Only what has to go ever needs to be crucified, anyway. Bill, my eyes feel wonderful now. There is no strain on them, and I am wondering what I will see. It will be wonderful.

Again, Helen is reflecting here the little willingness to look honestly at her own responsibility for her perceptions of others. This undoes the guilt that *is* the cause of the fear of punishment and the belief in the necessity of sacrifice to attain peace and God's Love: "If you're willing, you don't have to pay." Helen's discussion here thus illustrates very well again her choosing to look non-judgmentally at her "sins" of "looking" with her ego. By changing her mind about Louis (i.e., looking through Christ's vision, or the perception of the Holy Spirit), she could then *see* him as he was, in the innocence with which God created him. It is this vision that allows us to experience our oneness with all of God's creation. Thus it is not even that "we are all better off together," as she says below, but that we have never *not* been together. Her inner vision healed, Helen's eyes correspondingly were healed as well, and she can happily report that they "feel wonderful."

Their strain merely mirrored the inner strain of opposing Jesus and his message of true vision.

The letter concludes with a brief discussion of Helen's no longer wishing to exclude others from her life. As an expression of her ego's underlying need to be separate, Helen always needed to keep herself protected from people. She accomplished this either by actual isolation (she allowed very few to come to her apartment, for example), or by the subtle psychological means of carefully controlling the boundaries of her relationships. But obviously, this was preventing not only others from being with her, but Jesus as well. It is during this period that Helen was beginning to recognize the great price she was paying for this exclusion, and she expresses again that she no longer wishes to pay it.

> And Jonathan was right. I hate him because his living in my house interferes with me, as I planned the house. The plan was wrong. There's lots of room. There really are many mansions. I think that's all.
>
> I have never wanted to fit in, and I have shut out anything that didn't fit in with me. I hope all my very dear friends will come back, so I can fit in with them. We are all better off together.

This completes the series of Helen's letters to Bill. Chronologically we are now at the end of the summer of 1965, and near that October evening when the scribing of *A Course in Miracles* began, the subject of the next chapter.

Chapter 7

THE BEGINNING OF *A COURSE IN MIRACLES* (1965)

One day toward the autumn of 1965, Helen mentioned to Bill that she had the feeling she was "about to do something very unexpected," something obviously far more unexpected than what had already transpired: "I had no idea what it was, but I knew it was going to happen soon." Ever since the visit to Virginia Beach earlier in September, Helen had, on Bill's urging, been keeping "a sort of diary" of her various experiences, writing down her own thoughts, as well as messages from Jesus (or her internal Voice as she sometimes preferred to think of him).[42]

Bill now suggested that Helen write down anything that occurred to her in connection with the "unexpected something," feeling that perhaps this might help Helen identify what it was. Reflecting back on this writing, Helen later wrote that "nothing much came of my attempts at first," but her entries seem to belie this. The scribing of the Course actually began on the evening of October 21, but the entries for October 18, 19, 20, and the morning of the 21st are interesting indeed, particularly as they witness to Helen's experience of Jesus and trust in him, *prior* to *A Course in Miracles*. Some of these notes are similar to the tone and content of her earlier letters to Bill, being Helen's writing to herself, with some of the notes coming in a stream of consciousness. I reproduce excerpts here.

The first entry is actually undated and was found loose in Helen's notebook. However, from internal evidence it almost definitely can be placed before the notes of October 19 and 20, which were dated. The most compelling reason for predating

---

42. The notebook in which these thoughts and messages were contained unfortunately is gone, if indeed there even were a separate notebook. All that remains from this "pre-Course" period of writing are an entry that was written on three separate sheets of paper, and several pages written on the three days immediately prior to the beginning of the scribing. These pages are contained in the same notebook as the opening pages of the Course.

this to the 18th is the reference to the biblical quote, "In as much as you do this to the least of these..." which must antedate the reference to the confusion in wording that is found in the note of October 19. On the same page that these notes begin is a list of things for Helen to do, which is similar to the list heading the notes of the 19th, hence the rationale for assigning these entries to the 18th. One final comment: as in the early dictation of the Course itself, the speaker in these notes shifts back and forth between Jesus and Helen. This first entry begins with the voice of Jesus discussing God's non-involvement with the problems of His children.

> The reason why God does not interfere with man's free will is that [that] is the ultimate in respect, and God *does* respect His creations even though His creations don't. If He interfered with their will He would be enslaving them and God *does not* enslave.

The meaning underlying this explanation is expressed later in the text, with the non-interfering agent there being Jesus. It may be found in the fourth paragraph in "Fear and Conflict" (Chapter Two), and in the opening paragraph of the succeeding section, "Cause and Effect."

Incidentally, explanations such as the one given here were expressed in the form Helen could understand at the time, as I shall discuss in Part III. It is clear from the later dictation of *A Course in Miracles* that God's non-involvement truly comes because He does not even know about the world: being outside His Mind, which alone is reality, the entire world of separation must be illusory and therefore cannot exist. How then could God involve Himself in what is not there?

The notes then continue with Helen's commenting on a dream she had forgotten, but she is told by Jesus that the meaning of the dream is: "You mustn't neglect your responsibility *here*." Jesus' insistence to Helen on the importance of her remaining faithful to her worldly responsibilities (which would include both personal and professional ones) is consistent with his emphasis in the Course on paying attention to the forms of the classrooms we have chosen, within which we learn our lessons of forgiveness. Despite the Course's teachings on the illusory nature of the world and the body, we are nonetheless continually urged not to skip over the steps of our learning the Holy Spirit's lessons *here*, where we believe we are.

Jesus then continues with a punning message for Bill:

> Tell Bill if he can learn to substitute "teach strong" for "head strong" he will be all right.
>
> Helen: I claim this is a *very* bad pun, and also associate [it] with an order, which I did *not* follow, to look up "teach" as a word last night—all I remember is I thought of another word with "ea"—maybe head or learn. I did look it up this AM and among other things it means "impart or communicate knowledge."

Some information is obviously lacking here, but as will be explained in the next chapter, Jesus' punning was a means of expressing his love for Bill, who was a marvelous punster. Helen's rebelliousness of course was typical of her interactions with Jesus, and the equation of teaching with communicating knowledge would become clearer to her once the scribing of the Course began: teachers of God, through the Holy Spirit, become instruments for communicating (or reflecting) the knowledge of Heaven using the symbols of the world.

Jesus, in a manner with which Helen would become very familiar later, here continues by correcting a famous biblical statement:

> Correction: "in as much as you do this to the least of these
> (   ) you do it unto Me[43]" has been mistranslated.

The parentheses were put in by Helen who became confused about what belonged next—"my brothers" or "my children," or even nothing—and, as mentioned above, this was discussed the following day. Jesus now supplies his new meaning for the quotation:

> What it really said was "in so much as you give more to those who have less, you give it unto Me."
>
> Helen: I thought this was kind of cute, and He laughed and said, He was glad I liked it; He borrowed it from one of my own

---

43. Again, I shall comment later on Helen's use of capitalization for words and pronouns associated with Jesus.

fund raising talks [for the Shield Institute of Retarded Children]. "To him who hath shall be given." This seems unfair unless you look at it closer. It does *not* mean to him who hath least you should give still less. But if you think of it as an order to give *more* to those who have less, then it becomes a way of helping all men to become free and equal (which may yet be how things were created).

The next paragraph is a message for Bill, the theme of which will play an important part in a later segment of the scribing:

And tell Bill that his fear of teaching comes from his fear of controlling minds. He is mixed up about brain and soul, so he is afraid to interfere.

Helen: That's for both of us.

Jesus: The fallacy is if brain is mind (which it is not) don't *dare* touch it. Error obvious.

The point made here is a subtle one, but nonetheless important. Jesus is explaining to Bill that his fear of teaching comes from a made-up belief that he can really attack other minds. In line with Jesus' later explanations to Helen, this would come on one level from an earlier (past life) misuse of his mind. Nonetheless, no mind can attack another, *unless* that other mind has already chosen to be attacked. Once this error has been made real, and the mind equated with the brain (which appears to be capable of being taught by other brains), the obvious protection against making the mistake again is to refrain from teaching altogether. Bill's fear of public speaking, to which we shall also return later, results from the same erroneous thinking that inevitably leads to maladaptive defenses: protecting something that is not really there.

Incidentally, it is important to point out here that the equation of the mind with the brain is a very common one, made by almost all researchers, not to mention laypeople. It becomes an important part of the Course's theory that the mind is *not* in the body, though the brain most definitely is. Both brain and body remain projections of the illusory thought of separation that is contained in the separated mind. It is the mind, however, that is the decision maker; the brain merely carries out its directives.

Jesus now returns to Helen. The crown that is mentioned is symbolic of Helen's true Identity, which was symbolized in her earlier visions by the figure of the priestess:

> You *cannot* lose your crown: I may have to keep it for you *again*, but that will *always* be because you threw it away. Free will is terribly misunderstood, and people keep misunderstanding because of projection. They even blame themselves and each other for My crucifixtion [*sic*] which I assure you was done because of My perfectly free will.
>
> You are supposed to be perfect even as your Father in Heaven is perfect: He made you that way.

In *A Course in Miracles* itself, Jesus would have corrected the last statement to read: "He *created* you that way."

The final part of this October 18 note is a plea from Helen to her colleague David Diamond, who was in a coma and dying. I shall discuss Dave when we consider the notes of October 20. I simply present the passage now, in which Helen talks to Dave in her mind:

> Helen: Dave - Just remember *not* to be condemnatory in any way and *help* if you can. X and Dave couldn't work it out this time but they will.
>
> Jesus: Be grateful you and Bill are ready now. Amen.

We now move to the notes from October 19. Helen begins:

> I *think* there is an error about this not noticing and not remembering names, etc. I don't think it's only or even primarily projection. It *may* be more a fear of involvement or interaction due to an interpretation of interaction as one alone and the other subservient, or one getting by the other losing. You avoid this if you don't meet. Or even see.

See below, pp. 240f, for a fuller discussion of Helen's misuse of names; also, recall our earlier discussion, p. 102, of Helen's (and the ego's) principle of one or the other: one wins, another loses; one lives, another dies. This principle also nicely serves the aforementioned need on Helen's part of keeping herself isolated and protected from the perceived threat of others.

The notes continue, again with Helen as the speaker.

> Also, the idea of "who ever heard about me" syndrome
> *seems* to me more of a way of denying ability. While it *does*
> serve as a rationale for exploiting another, it *may* also be a
> denial of my own strength which, I fear, has been misused. I
> may even have suppressed a lot from misusing it (you too, Bill).

This syndrome is an example of the ego's arrogance
masquerading as humility that the Course would discuss later,
wherein we deny an ability that has come from God's Love,
believing that we know better than He does. Thus, the ego
would have us arrogantly believe that we have the power to
change what God created. This belief is the foundation of the
entire ego thought system of separation and usurpation. More
specifically, Helen and Bill would later be asked by Jesus not to
deny their ability to participate in the "collaborative venture"
of bringing the Course into the world. Helen's final comment
above refers to the ego's exploitation of apparent weakness as a
ploy to manipulate another through guilt and pity.

Helen now discusses an extremely important theme, similar
to Jesus' message to Bill in her note of the 18th regarding his
fear of teaching:

> The fallacy now is if I don't use anything of mine, I won't
> hurt anybody so I won't be hurt myself. The obvious answer is
> that paralysis won't get you anywhere, literally as well as
> figuratively....

The notes continue the following morning, October 20.

> I think under the projection and all that stuff is a hidden
> nostalgia for the soul. We want it back so we can identify with
> it, because that is what we *are* really, and somewhere we know
> it....

This reflects what would later become a fundamental tenet of
the Course's teaching; namely, that the entire ego thought
system—"projection and all that stuff"—is a defense against
our underlying yearning to return to God—"a hidden nostalgia
for the soul"—which we on some level know is there. As the
text would later state:

> Under the ego's dark foundation is the memory of
> God.... You realize that, by removing the dark cloud that
> obscures it, your love for your Father would impel you to

answer His call and leap into Heaven....For still deeper than the ego's foundation, and much stronger than it will ever be, is your intense and burning love of God, and His for you. This is what you really want to hide (text, pp. 225f).

The notes then continue, with the aforementioned reference to the biblical quote cited the previous day. Jesus urges Helen to say to Bill:

I think it's odd that I couldn't remember the correct quotation "in as much as you do this to the least of these My children/brother...." I first decided the quote probably stopped with "the least of these" and I was merely confused about an addition. I was sticking in but what was *not* really there.

This of course reflects the important characteristic of Helen's ego that was mentioned above, and repeatedly pointed out to her by Jesus, as well as by herself: the characteristic of always "sticking in" her own interpretations of situations that were "not really there." Helen continues:

Then I couldn't decide whether it was children or brother, and I was told to ask you [Bill]. It *is* odd that you apparently couldn't decide between the same two terms. The Order [i.e., from Jesus] is to be *sure* you know this is important for both of us.

Note: I am afraid of Cornell [a meeting to be held at the Cornell University Medical Center] today....If I can get my soul in place it will be all right, though.

I was really quite depressed this A.M. which is now *very* unusual (I used to be all the time[44]) but He says "Be of good cheer that I have overcome the world."

I was very glad you [Bill] called, even though I don't *think* I was upset beyond a brief moment. I went briefly and very inappropriately into shock when you said "Dotty is waiting and you can get into a cab alone, can't you?" There is *no competition* at all between Dotty and me, and I thought chances were she *did* need you more at the time. I *know* you'll never abandon me. So the cab was waiting at the corner.

---

44. This, the reader may recall, was one of the motivators for Helen's returning to school.

As in Helen's letters, we find here the same honesty in observing her ego in action, enabling her to move quickly beyond its interpretations of slight and hurt to the truth. Acknowledging the oneness of the Sonship and the safety of God's always-present Love prevents any thoughts of the ego from developing strength. This awareness was always very present in Helen. However, it was only during this period that she was able consistently to accept it. More often than not in her later years, she chose to deny this truth, the result being the anger and pain that was her usual experience.

Helen's openness to herself and to Jesus continued with these notes, which reflect her acceptance of the desire to be genuinely helpful to others, an important aspect of the new thought system *A Course in Miracles* would soon be advocating:

> A rather surprising thing happened while I was meditating after your [Bill's] call. I said just what you suggested: "I am quite distressed about something which is probably an error in perception of some past [experience] and would You [i.e., Jesus] please straighten me out."
>
> So He said "In dying you live. But be sure you understand what this means." I got terribly frightened because I thought I must be dying, and then I figured it's not a bad way to go, so just relax and enjoy it. So I just got resigned and very calm.

Helen, of course, misunderstood Jesus' message. In confusing form and content—the literal words with their meaning—she did not realize here that Jesus was referring to the death of her ego, not to the death of her physical self. A few weeks into the dictation of the Course, Jesus clarified this point for Helen in a passage currently found near the end of Chapter Three in the text:

> As you approach the Beginning, you feel the fear of the destruction of your thought system upon you as if it were the fear of death. There is no death, but there *is* a belief in death (text, p. 46).

Helen continues, still preoccupied with thoughts of her own physical death:

> And then it happened. I suddenly realized that this was terribly selfish, and then I decided . . . that if I just died off, you

[Bill] would be terribly shocked and your progress might even be arrested and after you had come so far too. Please let me stay and help him a while longer. And Jonathan would never get over it because he isn't ready yet, either....

So I prayed that I could stay as long as I could help, and wouldn't it be wonderful! I can only be all right then. I was very happy about this for a while, and then got frightened....

Dream: being very scared and tired and upset, I doped myself up and went to sleep early, but I did ask Him [Jesus] to pray while I knocked myself out for a short pause.

This A.M. it occurred to me that I had no right to waste anything—money, clothes, or my own life, because everything has to be used right. It all has a place in the Plan. And you must *not* throw gifts away. Life is a gift you receive to help you gain eternal life. It is the major way He can help you now.

Life insurance—and really what you *should* say is that you want to live as long as you are any use to Him, and then you will do just that. And *only* good can come of this to everybody—Amen.

So I decided to die soon [i.e., prior to Jesus' message], which I would have done. This was not a decision I should make because it *may* be a terrible waste which I would have to answer for. But you *can* change prophecies if you change your mind, so maybe I should say I'd rather leave it up to Him.

(Bill—I'm upset about this but I *know* it's right.)

A primary focus in these entries was David Diamond, Helen's aforementioned colleague. (In her notebook, incidentally, Helen almost always recorded a person's correct name, in distinction from her usual practice of forgetting or changing names.) Dave was dying, and Helen obviously felt it was an "assignment" to pray for him. She asked Dave to accept the help of Jesus (here most often called Christ), and to forgive another colleague, Harry Silver (my pseudonym), whom Dave had hurt. These entries are quite moving in their expression of Helen's fervent desire to be of help, typical of how she lived her life.

The cabdriver asked if I minded music and I thought maybe it would help me pray for Dave, so we started with a march and I thought "Come on Dave, join us and we can all go marching together," and then it was a ballet, and I thought "Come on, Dave, God has room for lighter moments too."

Dave don't give in—you have a real mission—don't lose your chance—miracles *are* the natural law. Then I asked Christ to help Dave know *He* was there and to see Him and know the truth so he could be free.... "If any two come together in My name"[45]—Dave, *you* must be that other—we need you—life heals, not death....

Maybe while Dave is sleeping our unconscious minds can reach Christ and He will unite us in prayer—"We can do it, Dave."

Dave once stood in Harry Silver's way and somehow interfered with his progress. Silver knows he must forgive him and do everything he can to release him. That's why Silver loved Dave on sight and has been patiently devoted to him. Silver is afraid to "let Dave die" because he knows this is his karmic debt. Dave is in no position now because of what he did to Harry and they're both in prison.

Dave, listen to me now and let Christ help you—leave it to Him and rest. *Don't* hurt Harry again by walking out on him. Harry needs a miracle to teach him that the brain is *not* the seat of life but God is. He can learn this if you are willing to stay and teach him. Help save us all, Dave. *Please* cooperate. You once denied the truth to Harry Silver—please release him and yourself now. You taught him wrong Dave, but remember how good you always were in teaching the emotionally disturbed, and teach him right now.

Dear Dave, show Harry that the spirit does *not* live in the brain. Turn your statement the right way, and *know* that spirit can heal the brain which it made. *It is not* the other way. Release the children this time, Dave—please for Christ's sake, Amen.

Dave—remember your little girl—she was unmarked even though she was conceived by accident in a uterus that was supposed to be sterile because it was so damaged by fibroid tumors. They said it had to be removed. But it was still a temporary home for a perfect child, against all odds according to human medicine. Please, Dave, don't identify with your brain. Know your own immortality and break the prison for Harry Silver. Listen please, Dave—you can destroy your enemies by making them your friends. You hurt Harry but he loves you. Thank God you can help him now—I am awed by your mission, and I

---

45. The actual biblical quotation is as follows: "For where two or three are gathered together in my name, there am I in the midst of them" (Mt 18:20).

194

pray I can help Christ to help you. Dave—sooner or later you will have to settle this, and you can save thousands of years right now. We *must* call the children back. Christ will give you the most now, if you will take it, because you have reduced yourself to the least. Take it for Him, who wants to give you all power in Heaven and Earth.

Dave, help Christ to reach your spirit and don't depend on your brain. Help us, Dave, and hear Him. . . . Dave, change your identity from Diamond to Pearl of Great Price, and claim your right to forgiveness *now*. Your spirit and mine *can* unite and then the two of us *have* come together in Christ's name. Jesus promised to be there, Dave. Your brain does not matter if you will understand life as Jesus did. When He said "Father, into Thy Hands I commend My Spirit" He was referring to His *resurrection, not* His death. Remember and understand that because it can save you now. The anoxia of His death did *not* hurt His brain [i.e., mind]. Please, Dave—hear Him say "I am the resurrection and the life, and whosoever believeth in Me *shall not perish.*"

Dave, it means something that your names are Diamond and Silver. Remember where your real treasures are. Silver has the whole Neurological Institute watching you. But they all think life is brain. Help them, Dave—you are a teacher. Dave, you can still hear the call "Come forth"—Lazarus was already dead; you're not.

This important entry expresses four themes that form the heart of the teachings of *A Course in Miracles* that were about to come forth:

1) *joining with another*: "Come on Dave, join us and we can all go marching together"; Helen's exhorting Dave to join with Harry, a joining that reflects the meaning of forgiveness.

2) *joining with Jesus*: Helen's asking Dave to let Christ (Jesus) help him: "If any two come together in My name"; pleading later with Dave, Helen wrote: "Your spirit and mind *can* unite and then the two of us *have* come together in Christ's name."

3) *the role of the miracle*: "miracles *are* the natural law"; interestingly enough, this was written two days before the dictation of the miracle principles began (*see* especially #6: "Miracles are natural. When they do not occur something has gone wrong" [text, p. 1]). As in the early pages of the text, the miracle appears to be associated here with the body, as in

Helen's asking Dave to live so that Harry can learn: "Harry needs a miracle to teach him that the brain is *not* the seat of life but God is. He can learn this if you are willing to stay and teach him." Later in the Course, however, Jesus makes it clear that miracles only involve a change in mind, and that the body is not involved with sickness *or* healing. The text teaches, for example:

> The miracle is useless if you learn but that the body can be healed, for this is not the lesson that it was sent to teach. The lesson is the *mind* was sick that thought the body could be sick; projecting out its guilt caused nothing, and had no effects (text, p. 553).

4) *the power of the mind (here called "spirit") over the brain*: Helen pleads with Dave to teach Harry that "the spirit does *not* live in the brain. Turn your statement the right way, and *know* that spirit [i.e., the mind] can heal the brain which it made. *It is not* the other way." And then: "Dave, help Christ to reach your spirit and don't depend on your brain." After a discussion of Jesus' resurrection, Helen asks Dave to teach "the whole Neurological Institute ... (who) think life is brain." Once again we can see that Helen was more than just a blank channel through whom Jesus dictated *A Course in Miracles*. In her own right, when identifying with her healed mind, she was the Voice of Wisdom.

The following entries seem also to have been written on October 20, and reflect Jesus' attempts to help Helen and Bill; more specifically here, it is Jesus and Helen seeking to help Bill overcome his resistance to Jesus and so get closer to him:

> If you do not get an answer it is always because you are amiss.
>
> Helen: I said He promised to come when He was called on, and Bill asks and does not recognize and has really tried to knock and it has not been opened to him. I think the door is ajar abit but I really wouldn't call it very open. Is it all right if I ask for him [Bill] since he wants me to?

This idea of Helen's asking help for Bill (and others) remained an important issue for her, and we shall return to it in Part III.

The notes continue now with Jesus in the role of the first person. The principal focus remains on Bill:

I can't answer where he [Bill] asks amiss. When he asks right I *have* answered. He has a tendency to get part of an answer and decide himself when to disconnect. He should ask if that's all. Since I don't know when he's going to ring off I have to be very short and even cryptic. It chops messages up too much.

There is also interference from three major areas.

1) He doesn't have much real confidence that I will get through. He never just claims his rights. He should begin with much more confidence. *I'll* keep my promises, but you [Helen] do not act as if you really expect him to. . . .

2) He has to learn better concentration. His mind flits about too much for good communication. Suggest a very short phrase like "Here I am Lord" and don't think of *anything* else.[46] Just pull in your mind slowly from everywhere else and center it on these words. This will also give him the realization that he [Bill] really *is* here. He's not too sure.

3) Tell him to be sure not to mistake your [Helen's] role. If he overreacts to or over evaluates you as a person, both of you will be in danger [i.e., from their own guilt].

Helen: He [Jesus] thinks it's time for some explanations which we are probably ready for. There are always risks in speed-ups. The whole thing was undertaken because things are getting behind schedule because so many people persistently lost more than they gained.[47]

This next entry appeared to be written in the morning of October 21, the day the Course actually began. It, too, centers on the theme of Helen's willingness to help others, as well as her resistance to such extensions of love.

Helen: A.M. It crossed my mind last night that something very wrong had happened. I got mad because I thought I shouldn't be asked to ask [Jesus] for you [Bill], and it was a form of exploitation [i.e., from Bill] that was *very* dangerous for me and represents an avoidance technique for you. I thought the whole thing was so dangerous that I had to tell you not to do it

---

46. At another time Jesus gave Bill a second phrase to help to focus his mind more on him: "Jesus, my brother, show me your love."

47. This later became part of the explanation that was given Helen regarding the recent inner events. *See below*, p. 200.

again. Briefly it crossed my mind (but with no emotional impact at all which is *always* suspicious)—that I might just resent asking for someone else because I prefer the "exclusive" idea.

Christ says I can tell something is wrong whenever I get a "snappy" answer.... The *tone* is wrong.

This morning it was very clear to me that in connection with you I have not been right since I asked you what *you* wanted so I could really be asking *for you*. This *was* essential...You have every right, in fact you *should* ask me to ask for you. This is *not* a selfish gift, and it *is* a real one. (This upsets me too.) It *has* to be used for others, and *particularly* you.

Jesus: Ask Bill please to help you get over being mean about it *fast*.

Helen: Note—At the moment I have serious doubts about everything. This is holding everything up.

While recording some of these thoughts on the evening of October 21, Helen heard the now "more or less familiar" inner Voice begin to give her definite instructions. While quite accustomed by this time to receiving messages, she certainly was not prepared for what the Voice said. Helen incidentally was well aware, again, that the Voice belonged to Jesus, but she often did her best to keep his identity in the background of her mind. With the beginning of the dictation of *A Course in Miracles*, however, she could no longer really do this. In her original autobiography, which Helen fully expected at the time would be made public (hence her careful editing), she wrote of him in this way, again attempting to deny Jesus' identity as the Voice. Who he was, however, was obviously apparent to her as seen in the notes of October 19 and 20, not to mention the series of letters we have already considered. Helen's words from now to the end of the chapter are thus taken from this edited autobiography. We begin with her observations of the inner Voice:

I [did not] understand the calm but impressive authority with which the Voice dictated. It is largely because of the strangely compelling nature of this authority that I immediately referred to the Voice with a capital "V." The particular combination of certainty, wisdom, gentleness, clarity and patience that characterized the Voice made that form of reference seem perfectly appropriate.

In Helen's and my editing of her autobiography years later, the issue of writing about Jesus made her so anxious that she chose to omit that paragraph entirely, as well as other references to the authorship. Thus, she left it to me, as I discussed in the Preface regarding one of the purposes of the book, to describe her relationship with the "Voice."

Jesus began the dictation of the Course this way:

> This is a course in miracles, please take notes.

Helen continued for about a page of notes before calling Bill in a fright. She explained to him what was happening, and her feeling that the Voice "seems to want to go on.... I'm sure there's more." Bill wisely suggested that Helen continue as best she could, and that they would meet at the office early in the morning to discuss this startling turn of inner events. For a while longer Helen continued. Before presenting what she scribed, an explanation need be given about the obvious differences between the material Helen originally took down and the published Course.

During the first month or so of the dictation, Helen's anxiety level was so high that the *form* (not the *content*) of the dictation was affected in the sense of the writing being ungraceful and sometimes overly terse. Several times Jesus would correct a mistaken word or phrase a day or two after it had been written, when Helen's mind was open to receive the correction. An analogy might be made to an unused faucet, which when it is first turned on runs rusty water. As the water runs for a while, the rust clears out and the water "returns" to its clear nature. The "rust" of interference, which would seem to result from a long period of not being used, was really due to Helen's fear of the power of her mind, and more specifically, her fear of the love of Jesus with which she was so truly identified.

Even more to the point of the difference between the original and published early pages, however, was that Helen's initial experience was of Jesus being with her as an elder brother to his sister, gently and lovingly speaking to her. At about what is now Chapter Five of the text, the tone of the writing begins to change and become increasingly flowing and more objective, reading more like a lecture than a dialogue. In the beginning, therefore, the actual teaching (what is essentially found in the published books) was interspersed with personal material designed to help Helen and Bill with their own relationship, other relationships in their lives, and with their own personal problems. In addition, there were comments given on certain professional issues to aid Helen and Bill bridge the gap between their understanding of psychology and that of the Course. On instructions from Jesus, Helen and Bill removed these passages that were outside the Course's specific teachings, as they were not meant for the general readership. I shall return to the original manuscript and to its subsequent editing in later chapters, where I shall present some of this deleted material by way of illustrating the intensely personal nature of Helen's contact with Jesus, and his loving concern for her and Bill.

As we have just seen, the explanation for the coming of *A Course in Miracles* began even before the start of the scribing. Later, in her autobiography, Helen expressed it this way:

> I was given a sort of mental "explanation"...in the form of a series of related thoughts that crossed my mind in rapid succession and made a reasonably coherent whole. According to this "information," the world situation was worsening at an alarming pace. People all over the world were being called back to help, and were developing what to them were highly unexpected talents, each making his individual contribution to an overall, prearranged plan. I had apparently agreed to take down a course in miracles which the Voice would dictate to me as part of the agreement, and my doing it was actually my reason for coming. It did not really involve unexpected abilities, since I would be using abilities I had developed very long ago, but which I was not yet ready to use again [symbolized by the "receiving and sending" set in the bottom of the boat in Helen's vision]. And that was why I would have so much trouble doing it. However, people had reached a point where they were losing more than they were gaining. Thus, because of the acute emergency, the usual slow, evolutionary process of spiritual development was being by-passed in what might be called a "celestial speed-up." I could sense the urgency that lay behind this explanation, whatever I might think of the content,

not to mention my not understanding it. The feeling was conveyed to me that time was running out.

I shall discuss this "explanation" in Part III, when I consider the various levels of Helen's relationship with Jesus.

Helen then continued:

> I was not satisfied. Even in the unlikely event that this were true, I did not regard myself as a good candidate for a scribal role. I stated my opposition silently but strongly.
>
> "Why me?" I asked. "I'm not even religious. I don't understand the things that have been happening to me and I don't even like them. Besides, they make me nervous. I'm just about as poor a choice as you could make."
>
> "On the contrary," I was quietly assured. "You are an excellent choice, and for a very simple reason. You will do it."
>
> I had no answer to this, and retired in defeat. The Voice was right. I knew I would do it. And so the writing of the "course" began.

This answer was typical of many that Helen received from Jesus. Their very practical and logical nature precluded any argument on her part. For example, Helen was already taking down the Course, and so she could not very well argue with Jesus' reasoning: "You will do it." In addition, of course, on another level Helen had already agreed to be the scribe for the Course, and so she could not go against what her mind had committed her to do.

The scribing was referred to by Helen as "internal dictation"; that is, she did not go into an altered state, a trance, or engage in automatic writing. She was always aware of what she was doing, even if she chose not to pay attention to it. Regardless of her attitude, the writing would continue.

> I would feel it coming on almost daily, and sometimes more than once a day. The timing never conflicted with work or social activities, starting when I was reasonably free to write without interference. I wrote in shorthand in a notebook that I soon began to carry around with me, just in case. I could and very often did refuse to cooperate, but I became so acutely uncomfortable that I soon learned I would have no peace until I did. Even so, I maintained my "right to refuse" throughout, and not infrequently acted on it for some time. Sometimes I

did not write for over a month, during which I merely became increasingly depressed. But there was never anything automatic about the writing. It always required my full conscious cooperation.

Evenings turned out to be a favored time for "taking dictation." I objected bitterly to this, and often went to bed defiantly without having written anything. But I could not sleep, and eventually, I got up in some disgust and wrote as directed as the lesser of two evils. Sometimes I was so tired that I went back to bed and fell asleep after taking down only a few paragraphs. [Those instances are witnessed to by the uneven quality of the lines of Helen's shorthand.] Then I would be impelled to continue before breakfast the next morning, perhaps finishing the section on my way to work or at odd moments between work pressures during the day. I never knew when I started a sentence how it would end, and the ideas came so rapidly that I had trouble keeping up with them even in the system of shorthand symbols and abbreviations I had developed during many years of taking class notes and recording therapy sessions.

Helen's *experience* of Jesus' dictation, especially after the beginning weeks, was similar to having a tape recorder in her mind that she could turn on and off at will, with no effect on the material itself. In Part III, incidentally, I discuss the difference between Helen's experience of Jesus, and the reality of her relationship with him. This, however, is how she described the process of the internal dictation:

> The writing was highly interruptable. At the office I could lay down the notebook to answer the telephone, talk to a patient, supervise a junior staff member, or attend to one of our numerous emergencies, returning to the writing without even checking back to see where I left off. At home I could talk to Louis, chat with a friend, answer the telephone, or take a nap, picking up afterwards without disturbing the smooth flow of words in the slightest. It did not even matter whether I had stopped in the middle of a sentence or at the end of a paragraph. It was as if the Voice merely waited until I came back and then started in again. I wrote with equal ease at home, in the office, on a park bench, or in a taxi, bus or subway. The presence of other people did not interfere at all. When the time for writing came, external circumstances appeared to be irrelevant. There could be interruptions of hours, days, and on occasion even weeks, without any loss in continuity.

The "highly interruptable" nature of the dictation becomes even more impressive when one considers the high quality of the more poetic sections, with their often complicated sentence structure coming in perfect iambic pentameter.

Helen was a "fierce" editor, who almost literally attacked a manuscript with the aim of purifying it of all irrelevant words, phrases, and punctuation. Her professional writing style was concise, crisp, and succinct, traits that were perfectly appropriate and respectable in scientific writing. With the poetic and metaphoric language of *A Course in Miracles*, however, Helen's style was totally inappropriate. I shall return to this aspect of Helen's writing and editing in more detail when I discuss our own detailed review of the manuscript in 1974. For now, however, here is her own descriptive experience of attempts to improve on Jesus' dictation:

> At the beginning, particularly, I was sometimes tempted to change a word here and there, in what I thought was the interest of consistency. Usually the urge to change it back to the original was so strong that I did so fairly soon. In fact, I was apt to feel uncomfortable until I did. Further, it quickly became apparent that the words were not chosen at random. Sometimes what seemed to be inconsistent at the time was to be explained later, and the original wording was necessary for subsequent clarity. At other times, specifically-worded ideas were to be mentioned later in contexts of which I was not yet aware, so that any changes I might make were likely to reduce consistency rather than enhance it.

During the seven years it took for the Course to be scribed, Helen's initially "acute terror" and anxiety lessened considerably. And though she "never really got used to it," the scribing did become an integral part of her life, so much so that she admittedly missed it when it stopped. This was the case despite her general perception that the writing was "a major and often infuriating interference in my life." During one of the aforementioned periods when she delayed the ongoing dictation of the text for about a month, she became depressed and sick. Helen's husband Louis, always supportive though deliberately uninvolved with what was happening, finally said to her: "Why don't you go back to what you were doing; you always seem to feel better when you do it." But the surprising thing to Helen throughout the process, as she would discuss with me afterwards, was that she never really thought of *not* doing it:

> Yet despite periods of open rebellion, it never seriously occurred to me to give it up....

And yet, even in the midst of this sense of imposition, Helen experienced moments when

> [I] felt curiously transported as I wrote. On these occasions the words almost seemed to sing, and I felt a deep sense of trust and joy, and even privilege. I noticed afterwards that these sections turned out to be the more poetic ones. But these were only brief though happy periods of respite.

Some of those transporting passages included the Course's version of the Lord's Prayer at the end of Chapter Sixteen in the text, the sections "Holy Week," "For They Have Come," and "Choose Once Again" (in text chapters Twenty, Twenty-Six, and Thirty-One, respectively), and the final paragraph of Lesson 157 in the workbook.

Far more difficult for Helen than the scribing itself, which though distressing, went relatively smoothly and easily, was reading the notes to Bill the next day. They had agreed that at the end of the day, or whenever they could find time in what was then a very busy work schedule, Helen would dictate to Bill what had been dictated to her the previous day. And Bill would type it, as he jokingly remarked later, "with one hand on Helen and the other on the typewriter."

> I hated to hear what I had taken down. I was sure it would be incoherent, foolish and meaningless. On the other hand, I was likely to be unexpectedly and deeply moved, and would suddenly burst into tears. I could never tell in advance when this would happen, and the uncertainty added to my already intense anxiety. Bill was extremely supportive, particularly during the earlier transcriptions, which were very difficult for both of us. It would take me a long time—sometimes even hours—to be able to read intelligibly. Getting a single page typed was a real achievement, and a very exhausting one. I could hardly read the notes aloud at all. I began to stutter, a problem I had neither before nor since. I also suffered acute coughing attacks or went on prolonged yawning jags, making it

all but impossible for me to speak long or clearly. Sometimes I lost my voice entirely.

Bill would then read back to Helen what he had just typed, and this served as a check against possible mistakes.

Bill's original typing was continuous except that he started each day's typing on a fresh page, which he dated. Later we both re-read the whole thing and agreed that this method seemed to break up the actual content and did not reflect the more natural breaks in the material, which seemed to fall into more natural patterns. We therefore noted down what seemed to be the more logical subdivisions, and still later inserted chapter titles and subheadings, which, like the material itself, came to me very quickly and easily once I had agreed to put them in. Then I retyped the manuscript myself [actually Helen typed the text twice], which was not too difficult for me. However, I could not read it afterwards without great discomfort, so Bill agreed to do the proofreading and we corrected my typographical errors together. The only actual changes we made in the original were to omit some highly personal references which had been originally included toward the beginning [as indicated above, Jesus had so instructed Helen and Bill]. Afterwards, the wording became more impersonal, and we felt that the material could be reproduced just as it had been taken down.

It was clear to Helen that though she was the one hearing Jesus' voice, the scribing was, in the words of the Course, a "collaborative venture." As Helen wrote later, "much of its significance, I am sure, lies in that." Indeed, the major theme of *A Course in Miracles* is forgiveness, one definition of which might be two people, formerly separated by their ego perceptions, joining together in a common interest. Helen and Bill's agreeing to help each other find the better way of relating symbolized this joining, and the Course represented Jesus' answer to their request. However, Helen and Bill not only shared their desire for the better way, but their anxiety over this way as well.

Bill and I had many discussions about the odd kind of double bind in which I found myself, nor was Bill without similar conflicts. He had to deal with his own problems of disbelief and my fairly constant panic states, surely a discouraging combination. To add to his difficulties, he recognized that I could not continue without his support and active encouragement, which were hard to offer consistently in the face of his own uncertainties. And yet it no more occurred to him to drop the whole matter than it seriously occurred to me. We seemed to be fulfilling a joint assignment which we both felt was important to continue, in spite of our wildly contradictory feelings.

Bill later referred to this joint assignment as a "sacred trust" that he and Helen felt had been given to them, and which they knew they would honor.

Helen continued, however, to find herself in a paradoxical situation. She still consciously clung to her avowed professional atheistic position, yet certainly could not deny *what* and *who* was involved with the scribing. Helen came to refer to *A Course in Miracles* as her life's work, yet disturbingly found herself in the impossible situation of professing not to believe in it, "a situation as ridiculous as it was painful." And yet as Bill once pointed out to Helen in regard to Jesus: "You must believe in him, if only because you are arguing with him so much."

> As for me, I could neither account for nor reconcile my obviously inconsistent attitudes. On the one hand I still regarded myself as officially an atheist, resented the material I was taking down, and was strongly impelled to attack it and prove it wrong. On the other hand I spent considerable time in taking it down and later in dictating it to Bill, so that it was apparent that I also took it quite seriously.

It is clear, however, from Helen's letters during this period, not to mention her notes *prior* to the Course, that her faith was very strong, and that her belief in Jesus was quite tangible. It was also clear that the conflict she was experiencing was totally internal.

> External circumstances were surprisingly favorable. The writing was apparently timed so as to cause minimal disruption, and in spite of his own conflicts Bill offered me consistent positive reactions and remarkably sustained support.

However, as psychologists, Helen and Bill could certainly explain Helen's most peculiar situation of fighting against what on another level she obviously believed in. They understood the dynamic of dissociation, wherein one splits apart the two parts of the self that are in seeming conflict, thereby allowing them to continue to coexist in the mind. The two selves of course are the parts of the mind containing the thoughts of the ego and the Holy Spirit. When brought together the ego must vanish, just as darkness disappears in the presence of light. Therefore, the ego's defensive system protects its thought of fear by dissociating the love that threatens its existence.

Interestingly enough, Columbia-Presbyterian did its part to aid the dictation as well. In 1963, Bill was surprisingly and unexpectedly appointed to the Research Planning Committee whose responsibility was to allocate space in a new research building that was being constructed. The building was to be named after William Black, the coffee magnate (Chock Full O' Nuts) and a major donor of the Medical Center. Thus Bill had the opportunity of designing a large enclosed and relatively secluded area that included offices for Helen and him, that opened into a larger secretarial space (later used by me when I joined them in 1973). These offices were totally separate from their regular psychology offices in the Neurological Institute (Helen) and Psychiatric Institute (Bill), and from their secretaries, who were housed in these two buildings across the street from the Black Building. Bill was also able to procure an elaborate telephone hook-up so that they could be in easy verbal communication with the rest of the department, and yet retain their physical privacy. The Black Building was completed in the summer of 1965, and Helen and Bill promptly moved into their offices. Only weeks later these would serve as the "manger" for the birth of Jesus' twentieth-century message of forgiveness.

In addition to the Medical Center's "cooperation" in the scribing, Louis' attitudes

> were unexpectedly positive and helpful. He could hardly fail to notice my frequent periods of writing, and he was entitled to an explanation. So, with considerable misgiving I decided to tell him what was happening, although I did not anticipate his approval in view of his own agnostic set [Helen also should have mentioned his strong Jewish identification]. Happily, he was more than tolerant; he was actively encouraging, although he preferred not to read what I had written. On the few

occasions when I showed him a few of the typed pages, he limited his comments to remarking on the clarity of the language and, in some cases, the poetry of the wording. It was apparent, however, that the whole thing made him extremely uncomfortable, and he tended to dismiss it as "just not his cup of tea." Once or twice it even seemed to make him angry, and so I stopped showing the material to him after a while. Yet despite his personal disinclinations about the material itself, he was actually enthusiastic about my writing it. He did not understand where it was coming from, but was apparently willing to overlook that question. Every once in a while he would remark that the thing was really quite surprising, and once he went so far as to say that he often thought about what an odd thing it was. He even recognized on occasion certain similarities between the bits I showed him and some mystical concepts he had read about somewhere. The writing process itself he quickly began to take more or less for granted, and did not seem to find it anxiety provoking.

Perhaps this is the place to intersperse a few words about Louis. At the time of Helen's death they had been married over forty-eight years, and in their own unique way, were an ideally matched couple. Though they were different on all levels, and in many ways lived separate lives, they remained totally devoted to each other. To the day she died, Louis stood in awe of Helen's intelligence, and this from a man who when Helen was practicing the administration of the Wechsler Adult Intelligent Scale (a standard IQ test) for graduate school, scored an almost unheard of perfect score on the verbal scale of the test.

Louis is a Jew, and very much identified as one. However, to this day he would maintain that he is an atheist. This has never prevented him, however, from frequently reading about religion and mysticism in general, and about Jewish religious thought in particular. When I questioned him about his atheism one day, he replied that he did not believe in God because he was afraid that He would punish him because he was so sinful. While Louis had his fair share of guilt, like everyone else, he nonetheless led a life characterized by a gentle benignity (except to himself), and a real concern for the welfare of others. In fact, I still joke with him that he is the most religious atheist I have ever met.

Louis' relationship to the Course was an interesting one. On the one hand, Helen's scribing of *A Course in Miracles*—its subject and especially its source—made him very anxious. On the other hand, he was, as we have just seen, supportive of Helen's taking it down. The reader may recall how during one period of the scribing when Helen went on strike, as it were, and resisted taking down any dictation for about a month, it was Louis who suggested she return to what she was doing. As Helen pointed out, Louis basically demonstrated no interest in seeing the manuscript, but was glad that Helen had Bill, whom Louis always liked and trusted, to support her more directly in this work. He was thus very grateful he could be left out of it.

In July 1975, if I may jump ahead of our story a bit, we were all going to California to present the Course (*see below*, Chapter 13). Some time before we left, Helen said to Louis one night that she thought that the least he could do was read the manuscript and have an open mind, especially as all these people we would be meeting were said to be so interested in it. Besides, Helen continued, she was his wife after all. Louis reluctantly agreed, as Helen's request had a reasonableness he could not really refute. And so, over an agonizing period of a few days, read the Course he did. At least his eyes went down every page. I occasionally observed Louis "reading." There he sat in his favorite chair after dinner, and, tight as a drum, he would turn each page of the voluminous manuscript with a rigid unyielding expression on his face.

One afternoon on this trip, we all sat in a room with a group of people obviously very interested and impressed with Helen and Bill's story. Louis almost never attended these sessions, but he was there this one afternoon. Finally, one person turned to him and asked what he thought about all of this, and he replied: "Well, my wife does some pretty unusual things." To this day he still refers to the Course as "my wife's book." Once, after Helen had died, my mother asked him whether he thought that Jesus (or God) had written *A Course in Miracles*, and he quickly replied: "Of course not, Helen did."

A few years ago an article on the Course appeared in the *New York Times*. It was a relatively brief one that sketched the origins of the Course and the growing interest in it. The article was not the best, but it was positive in attitude and did have some of the facts correct. The *Times* was Louis' Bible, and so he was impressed with the fact that it would print something about "his wife's book." Later that day he called to tell me about the article, and when I asked him if he liked it, he replied in characteristic fashion how he did not read it. After all, he said, I knew how hearing or even reading about Helen and the Course made him uncomfortable. In point of fact, it was his cousin Dave who had called to tell him about it. And then he said, "But Ken, I have to ask you a question. Dave told me that the article said that the Course had been dictated to Helen from Jesus. That's not true, is it? Helen never told me that." I explained to Louis that I was afraid that it was true, but I was sure he remembered how uncomfortable all of this made Helen, and that was why she never spoke about it. "That's right," Louis said, "she never liked to talk about it." And there the matter rested.

However, to this day, Louis remains fascinated about "Helen's book," and its phenomenal history from a publishing point of view. And he never fails to be touched by the countless stories he hears from people about how the Course has helped them. Moreover, he has always been very insistent that I make sure that people know that *A Course in Miracles* is a religious book. He has repeatedly expressed concern to me about people presenting the Course in a non-religious and purely psychological manner, since he knew that Helen was a religious person and that the purpose of "her book" was to lead people closer to God. He moreover once acknowledged to me that he knew that if Christianity had taught the principles of the Course, there never would have been 2,000 years of anti-Semitism. And all this, of course, from a man who never studied it, and still does not speak of it to his family and close friends. It has become his guilty secret, just as it had been his wife's.

In returning now to Helen's reactions to the scribing, we note that it was clear to her, despite her strong ambivalence about Jesus, that she was not the source of the writing. On that she was unequivocal. It was also clear to her that Jesus had made use of her "educational background, interests and experience, but that was in matters of style rather than content." I defer further discussion of this important issue of the Course's "style (form) and content" until Part III, when I shall consider, again, Helen's relationship with Jesus: its differing levels of form and content, illusion and reality.

In her autobiographical account, Helen noted that she was totally unaware of the mystical traditions of the East and West, all of which are important themes in the Course's material. When Bill pointed out the Course's parallels with traditional mystical thought, Helen became quite disturbed.

> The fact that my writing [i.e., scribing] was in apparent agreement with material about which I knew nothing was extremely disconcerting. The oblique and at times even quite direct explanations which turned up from time to time in the writing itself was even more distressing to me. It seemed most unlikely that Jesus or the Holy Spirit could or would use me as a vehicle for communication. Besides, I was by no means sure I believed in them.
>
> For a few brief periods I did believe in the truth of what I was writing, and they were happy times of respite. I remember once getting into a cab and saying to myself unexpectedly, "Of course I believe in healing! Why fight it?" and the whole cab seemed to light up with happiness. But for the most part, I was bleakly unbelieving, suspicious and afraid.

The reader is asked to recall again the discrepancy between Helen's actual words that were written during this period in her letters to Bill and the pre-Course notes, and what she later retrospectively wrote, years afterwards, in her autobiography. In the former, Helen's belief in Jesus was consistently and clearly, if not emotionally, stated; while in the latter, Helen's fear led her to adopt a posture of disbelief which was clearly superimposed, *after the fact*, upon her actual experience.

To summarize, we may say that Helen's taking down *A Course in Miracles* inevitably aroused tremendous anxiety in her, and we can identify two major sources of this discomfort: the identification of Jesus as the inner Voice, and the Course's presentation of a thought system that was totally antithetical to her conscious beliefs and the way she lived her life. Let us briefly examine each of these in turn, beginning with Helen's relationship with God and Jesus.

Though, again, much has been made in *A Course in Miracles* circles of Helen's once having written that she was an atheist, this statement was given in the same spirit of retroactively protecting the guilty secret of her inner life that we have been discussing. Helen adopted a "persona" as an atheistic New York psychologist to mask her underlying love of God. Closer to the truth would have been the phrase "militant (or angry) atheism" that Helen occasionally used to describe her religious outlook. And clearly one does not need to be a trained psychologist to recognize that one cannot be militantly opposed to something (or someone) that is not believed in. I have already spoken of Helen's lifelong inner conflict as reflecting what the Course refers to, from the ego's point of view, as the battle between God and the ego. Once *A Course in Miracles* began, the dynamics of this conflict centered firmly on the figure of Jesus, the problem she believed she had successfully resolved through a process of dismissal and inattention.

The second source of anxiety associated with Helen's scribing *A Course in Miracles*, and closely connected to the first, was the ego-threatening nature of the Course's teachings themselves. Helen's "war against God" was strengthened by her 1) ongoing preoccupation with sickness; 2) a continual self-identification as a victim, justified in making angry judgments of almost anyone and anything; and above all, 3) the firm conviction that she was in control of her life, certain that she knew her own best interests. And yet here she was devotedly taking down, at a considerable personal cost of time and energy, her "life's work" that taught exactly the opposite: namely, 1) sickness was a defense against the truth, a decision made in the mind and then projected onto the body; 2) attack and judgment of others were never justified, but were simply a projection onto others of our own responsibility for feeling separated; and 3) we do not know our own best interests, and should rather leave all decisions to the loving guidance of the Holy Spirit or Jesus.

Helen intuited that consciously to allow God into her life meant the end of her own ego system, and any control she would exercise over her life. *A Course in Miracles* states:

You have built your whole insane belief system because you think you would be helpless in God's Presence, and you would save yourself from His Love because you think it would crush you into nothingness.... You think you have made a world God would destroy; and by loving Him, which you do, you would throw this world away, which you *would* (text, p. 226).

And so from her ego's point of view, Helen was quite correct in maintaining her defensive system.

Confronted now with this perceived double onslaught—Jesus and the Course—to the existence of her own set of beliefs, Helen's ego responded. Her initial defense was simply to ignore as best she could the person of Jesus, referring to *him* as an "it," or as the Voice, not to mention her refusing to pay attention to the thought system he was dictating to her. As we shall see below, Helen chose to concentrate only on *how A Course in Miracles* presented itself, not *what* it presented. As she said to Bill: "You pay attention to the content; I'll pay attention to the form."

However, another part of Helen's mind sincerely attempted to "pay attention," and to practice the Course's principles of forgiveness. Both Helen and Bill, in the early years of the transmission, and even prior to it, worked on healing other relationships in their lives, trying to undo their past mistakes of judgment and separation. They experienced various levels of success, but their attempts in their own relationship did not lead to such clear-cut results. At first, Helen and Bill strove to change their misperceptions of each other, and apparently had moderate success. We shall see later, however, that they could not long sustain this forgiveness, for soon after these advances they retreated to their old patterns of recrimination, almost with a vengeance. By the time that I met them, in late fall of 1972 right after the Course was completed, their relationship was at an all-time low, and it only seemed to worsen from there. It was almost as if Helen were determined to prove that Jesus' Course was ineffective at best, and deleterious at worst, enabling her to feel even more justifiably bitter about her life.

We shall return in later chapters to Helen and Bill's relationship. We now begin to examine the actual scribed material, with the following chapter describing the early weeks of the dictation.

Entrance to Presbyterian Hospital

Stone sign on the Black Building, site
of Helen's and Bill's private offices.

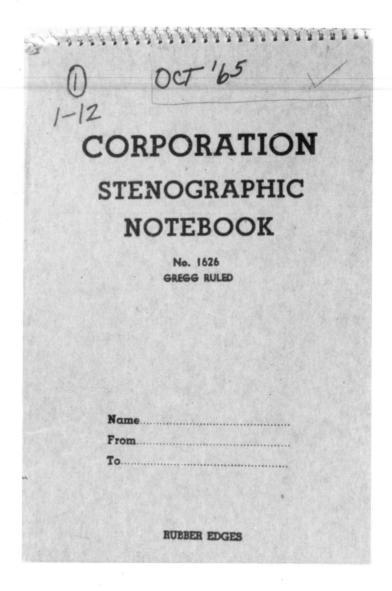

CORPORATION

STENOGRAPHIC

NOTEBOOK

No. 1626
~~GREGG~~ RULED

Name.......................................
From.......................................
To...

RUBBER EDGES

Cover of Helen's first notebook, which contains the beginning scribings of *A Course in Miracles*. (The writing on the cover is mine.)

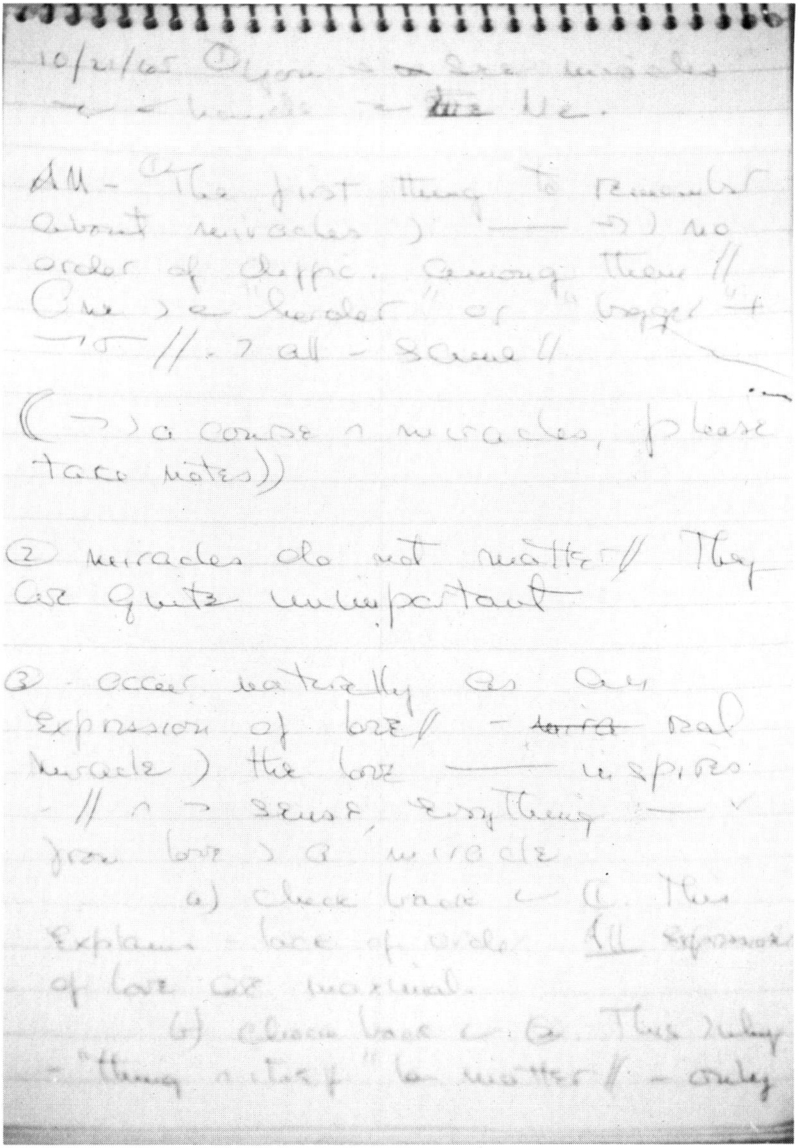

The page on which Helen's scribing of the Course began.

William Thetford

Helen Schucman, at a New Year's Eve party.

The picture from Bill's guidebook, with "Helen's church"—the present site of the Mayo Clinic—in the lower right corner.

Helen, Bill, and I in the cave at Lavra Netofa, Israel, 1973

Helen, Bill, and I on the Mount of Olives, Israel, 1973

Qumran

One of the Qumran caves that Helen identified as the cave in her "GOD IS" vision; view towards the Dead Sea.

"God Is" scroll which I had made to Helen's specifications.

Helen
(Face "blemish" from light reflection in original photograph)

Statue of Our Lady of Latroun
Abbey of Latroun, Israel

Bill, Helen, Judy, and I, ca. 1975

Louis, ca. 1975

Helen, Bill, and I, ca. 1975

Elohim altar in my apartment, 1976

Helen and I, ca. 1975

Helen and I, ca. 1975

A COURSE IN MIRACLES

Chapter 8

THE SCRIBING OF *A COURSE IN MIRACLES*—A
(1965)

The Early Weeks: The Miracle Principles

While Helen unfortunately was not able to leave us an altogether accurate, reliable, or complete account of her life, particularly regarding her experiences with Jesus and the scribing of *A Course in Miracles*, we nonetheless are fortunate that her original scribal notes are extant. These portray, as her later recollections would not, the scope of her personal relationship with Jesus, the intimate connection between this relationship and the Course, and the extent to which Jesus was attempting to be of help to her and Bill as friend and teacher. In this and the following two chapters, I present extensive excerpts from these early notes—deleted from the published Course—as illustrative of this relationship. These notes, more than anything else, I feel, should set to rest the misunderstandings surrounding Helen's personal experience, not to mention her own religious stance.

As mentioned previously, the beginning chapters of the text were not dictated as they appear now in the printed Course. The content certainly remains the same, but the form is markedly different from what the student of the Course is accustomed to seeing. The reader is asked again to keep in mind that these early notes were given to Helen informally, interspersed with personal material designed to help her overcome her tremendous anxiety. As will be seen presently, for example, some obvious errors in "hearing," leading to awkward phrasing, were subsequently corrected by Jesus one or two days later.

Clearly emerging from this personal material is the specific mind training that is inherent in the thought system of *A Course in Miracles* itself. We have already seen the beginnings of this training even prior to the start of the scribing. However, in these notes, readers will be able to see for themselves how

Jesus was training Helen and Bill to think along the lines the Course sets forth. Specifically, he was teaching them to recognize that the cause of all their distress did not lie in external events, situations, or with each other, but rather in the manner with which they were *perceiving* these circumstances and each other. Intrinsic to this training was Jesus' repeated urgings that Helen and Bill (and thus of course all of us) call upon him for help, for only through him would they be able to set their egos aside. As he dictated several months later:

> When you unite with me you are uniting without the ego, because I have renounced the ego in myself and therefore cannot unite with yours. Our union is therefore the way to renounce the ego in you ["yourselves" in the original] (text, pp. 136f).

While these crucial themes are found in the Course itself, the deleted dictated material illustrates just how personal this instruction originally was. I shall present several examples of this instruction as the teaching proceeded over the first few months.

The actual dictation, then, began with the words: "This is a course in miracles, please take notes." It went on with the first of the miracle principles. The published introduction, incidentally, except for the two sentences that come shortly, was added somewhere between Bill's original typing and Helen's first re-typing. In that version, the introduction actually came in two parts, though in Helen's second re-typing they were combined as they are now. Helen later told me that she had complained to Jesus that the text needed a better introduction than "This is a course in miracles." And so Jesus obliged, although the notes for this are not extant. It is quite possible that Helen simply typed the current introduction without first taking it down in shorthand. One final comment before beginning: whenever Helen felt that a word or phrase was emphasized in her mind, she underlined it. Not all of these words were kept, however; those that were, of course, appear in italics. Here then is the first principle of miracles:

> 1. The first thing to remember about miracles is that there is no order of difficulty among them. One is not "harder" or "bigger" than another. They are all the same.

2. Miracles do not matter. They are quite unimportant.
3. They occur naturally as an expression of love. The real miracle is the love that inspires them. In this sense, everything that comes from love is a miracle.

    a) Check back with 1. This explains the lack of order. *All* expressions of love are maximal.

    b) Check back with 2. This is why the "thing in itself" does not matter. The only thing that matters is the Source and this is far beyond human evaluation.

In obvious response to Helen's attempt to minimize what she was experiencing, Jesus then said to her as an aside:

> You are braking [*sic*] communication by thinking it's cute. You are not wrong but it diverts your attention.

Helen: That's true.

Jesus: Of course it's true, and I'm really glad you got the idea. I am *not angry* when this kind of thing happens, but the lesson deteriorates under lack of focus.

    Please read these three points (with corollaries) as often as you can today, because there may be a quiz this evening. This is merely to introduce structure, if it is needed. It is *not* to frighten you.

This reference to the quiz was obviously a joke, but Jesus' emphasis on Helen's and Bill's reading the notes carefully was serious, and was repeated frequently during the early part of the dictation.

Helen: Well, would You regard this [communication] as a kind of miracle, maybe?

Jesus: You better reread this now. There is nothing special or surprising about this at all. The *one* thing that happened was the Universal Miracle which was the experience of intense love you have felt. (Don't get embarrassed—things that are true are *not* embarrassing. Embarrassment is only a form of fear, and actually a particularly dangerous form because it reflects egocentricity.)

    (No, don't think of how Bill will find this fascinating, either. I told you to re-read them and you did not.)

Helen: I am now.

Jesus: Do not feel guilty about the fact that you are doubting this. Just re-read them, and their truth will come to you. I love you. And I am *not* afraid or embarrassed or doubtful. *My* strength will support you, so don't worry and leave the rest to Me.

Do not run to Bill to tell him. There will be time, but don't disrupt things. I'll arrange the schedule. You have a lot to do today. Get dressed or you will be late. [Obviously, this paragraph at least was dictated the following morning.]

But when you *do* see Bill, be *sure* to tell him how much he helped you through by giving you the right message. (And don't bother with worrying about how you received it. That doesn't matter, either. You were just afraid.)

While riding in the taxi taking her to the Medical Center, Helen was obviously fearful about a communication from Jesus that related Dave Diamond's healing and Louis' hernia. Her fear reflected the "one or the other" principle, under which she lived. Thus, if Dave lived, then Louis would have to die. But then Helen was able to correct this mis-thought, and wrote down:

No, it's wrong to think maybe Dave will be healed (with great fear here, because I want to separate the next thought from Dave who *is* dying in human terms) and Louis' hernia will be cured.

Jesus: Remember point 1, and re-read *now*.

Helen also wrote down two other points during the first evening's dictation: "You will see miracles through your hands through Me." And: "Help me [Helen] perform whatever miracles you want of me today."

Although Helen and Bill supplied the dates of each day's scribing activities, they did not begin this until slightly later in the process. And so we can only approximate the dates of these early notes. We continue, with what later became the fourth miracle principle. Originally, the statement was unnumbered:

All miracles mean Life, and God is the Giver of Life. He will direct you *very* specifically. *Plan ahead* is good advice in the world, where you should and must control and direct where you have accepted responsibility. But the Universal Plan is in more appropriate hands. You will know all you need to know.

Make *no* attempts to plan ahead in this respect....

Helen's notebook at this point contains some notes relating to work, and then continues with the next miracle principle:

4. Miracles are habits and should be involuntary. Otherwise they may become undemocratic. Selective miracles are dangerous, and may destroy the talent.

This principle was subsequently corrected by Jesus in Helen's handwriting in the original typed manuscript (nicknamed by us the "Urtext," meaning original text): the second sentence was removed and replaced by: "They should not be under conscious control"; and the third sentence was amended to read: "Consciously selected miracles are usually misguided, and this will make the talent useless." Still later this last sentence was changed to its current form.

The next five principles (6–10) were virtually dictated straight through, as they are found in the published Course. The current ninth principle originally came as two separate ones, however. Helen then wrote:

Helen: I don't think Bill wants this course, and I'm not sure I do, either. He is *very* snappy.

Jesus: I think this is *slightly* true because something *is* bothering him, but he is certainly not *very* snappy. So why not try to help him instead of blowing it up into an obstruction? He helps you all the time.

Helen: I resent this. He is *supposed* to help *me*. *Note*: I do not always feel this way. It's a danger signal now, and just means something's wrong.
   Anyway, presumably this course is an elective.

Jesus then responded, in what was then typed in as the introduction to the text, albeit in a more simplified form. Later, this introduction was added to, as explained above. What follows is the earlier version, beginning with Jesus' answer to Helen's presumption:

No it isn't. It's a definite *requirement*. Only the time you take it is voluntary. Free will does *not* mean you establish the curriculum. It only means you elect what to take *when*.
   It is just because you are not ready to do what you should that time exists at all.

Helen then amended the opening lines, per instructions from Jesus that were not written down.

From time to time Helen would dictate to Bill "without notes," simply speaking the words she was "hearing" internally. The following line was the first example of this.

> It is crucial to say first that this is a required course.

The next entries are from October 24, and contain Helen's dreams from the previous night. Interspersed in these was the following aside from Jesus regarding the Course:

> Yes indeed, the *way* the course is given you is quite unusual, but as Bill says you are *not* the average American woman, which is merely a fact. Your experience in your life has been atypical....

Helen now recalls in her notes an earlier dream, and then this one from the night of October 23:

> There is also one in which three animals, little ones, were in the same room, and I knew that I had to keep them apart because they hated each other. Being so busy, this was a great additional strain on me. One of them was pregnant, and the other two wanted to kill her, but the other two hated each other too. Oddly enough, I was quite sorry for all of them because they were all three mixed up, but in different ways. I felt I had to get the pregnant one out first, though, because of the child.
>
> (I thought this is an improvement over the recurrent dream I had for years about animals starving to death, and me sometimes grieving, sometimes trying desperately to help them—at times also realizing I had starved them and feeling very guilty—but *never* saving them.)

Indeed, this does seem like an important dream, for it reflects Helen's inner commitment to letting Jesus' loving help extend through her. In this respect, the dream pictures the same inner decision reflected in the cave sequence with Helen choosing *not* to use her mind's power for personal gain. Her promise to continue to water the plants growing in the desert reflects the same decision; on one level the plant-watering symbolizes Helen's nourishing her decision to return to her function, yet on another level it can also be understood to symbolize the nourishing of the people who believe they inhabit the material world which *is* the desert. A later symbolic experience of Helen's helping a wounded starfish, reported in Part III, also reflects this decision to help.

There was one more dream this same evening, expressing the theme of Helen's helping concern for others:

> The last dream was about a child on the CDP program [a child research unit Helen was consultant to]. It seemed that I saw the child's protocols, and suspected some sort of rather obscure diagnosis or problem. I was unwilling to go on record, because it was a medical thing and I thought Gates [the psychiatrist heading up the project] would disapprove.
>
> But I felt an obligation to the child and called her M.D. about it. I got a letter in return, saying the physician was very grateful, and that the child's life was saved and the information was badly needed.

Jesus then continued:

> [When you say] "If you want me to I will," please add "and if you *don't* want me to I won't." This is the *right* use of inhibition. There has to be *some* control over learning for channelizing purposes. Remember retroactive inhibition [a learning theory term], which should be easy enough for you. Sometimes the new learning is the more important, and *has* to inhibit the old. It's a form of correction.

This last sentence is the first of many instances of Jesus' teaching Helen through examples drawn from her psychological background, which included both experimental (learning theory, statistics, etc.) and clinical (psychoanalysis, personality theory, etc.) psychologies.

The miracle principles then continued to come, interspersed with personal comments to Helen. I include some of these here:

> Jesus: The one more thing is Bill's fear of punishment for what is done *now*. Everybody makes mistakes. Those errors are completely trivial. Tell him that where the past has been forgiven, those minor infractions are very easily altered. . . .
>
> Helen: Last night I was planning to type up the Course for you [Bill], and was strictly ordered [by Jesus] not to go back to it

before I got over S [Bill's aforementioned friend whom Helen
still had not forgiven].

It seems that the Course has a lot of answers, and carries
very high point credits, but as you always say, you have to
know the questions first.

This morning I did ask for help with S. The answer seems
to be in points 6 and 7. That's why He gave me the chalice for
S. It belongs to him but he cannot find it.

I discuss the important symbolism of the chalice in Chapter 9.
Jesus then gave Helen special instructions:

Jesus: Notes on this course have to be taken only under good
learning conditions, and should be reviewed.

Helen: I was going to write "refused."

Jesus: The same goes for review periods. I'll tell you when, but
remember to ask.

Regarding miracle point 16, that it is as blessed to give as to
receive, Jesus urged:

Be very careful in interpreting this.

Then followed some extensive personal messages. The first of
these contrasts Helen's and Bill's ego dynamics, one of many
such messages. The second message discusses the first miracle
principle about no order of difficulty, within the context of
Helen's concern that her ego's darkness was too strong for the
light of love. We are still, incidentally, within the first week of
dictation.

You [Helen and Bill] both have an identity problem, which
makes you unstable but in different ways. He [Bill] lacks
confidence in his identity, and needs to strengthen it. You
vacillate in your identity and need better control. Both of you
needn't worry.

In response to Helen's feeling fearful that God would abandon her, and justly so, Jesus said:

I told you I forgave you and that meant all hurt and hate you
have ever expressed is cancelled. I need the children of light
now and I am calling you to be what you once were and must
be again. The interval has vanished without a trace anywhere.
You who live so close to God must not give way to guilt. The

Karmic law demands abandonment for abandoning, but you have received mercy, not justice.

Help the children because you love them and love God.

Remember a miracle is a spark of Life. It shines through the darkness and brings in the light. You must begin to forget and remember.

This is a private point, just for you. It is not part of the course. A miracle is love—you always wanted presents, and a closed package was intolerable. *Please* open this one. You act like it's a time bomb. When I said "a miracle abolishes time," you might look back and review the point in parentheses. ["Time is a teaching device, and a means to an end. It will cease when it is no longer useful for facilitating learning."] You're afraid there won't be *enough* time for you. Forget it and remember that there is no *real* difference between an instant and eternity....

Remember that there is no order in miracles because they are always *maximal* expressions of love. You *did* make a maximum effort for Chip and the *only* reason you did it was because you loved Bill. You might tell him to think about that sometimes because he *does* need signs of love. But he doesn't always recognize them because he does not have enough confidence. You practically gave up your life for him quite voluntarily, but you do not know that what you were *really* giving up was death. This is what "dying to live" really means. And I said Myself that greater love no man hath.

This, by the way, was the first of many examples where in the dictation Jesus refers to statements attributed to him in the Bible: "And I said..." These should not be taken to mean that the historical Jesus actually said those words. However, since Helen basically believed that Jesus did make these statements, the biblical quotations became a convenient point of reference to reinforce or illustrate something Jesus was currently teaching her.

Jesus then returns to his exhortation to Helen that she study the dictated material:

Review your note from yesterday that your identification is strong but erratic, and that is why you have so much will power but use it wrong at times. Bill was right about the misuse of it when you were sick and it *was* a sign of superhuman will totally misdirected. Your body does not need it, but your spirit [i.e., mind] does. And I need it too.

The purpose of this course is integration. I told you that you will not be able to use it right until you have taken it. As long as your identification vacillates, (and Bill's is weak) you cannot accept the gift that belongs to you. You are still vacillating between recognizing the gift and throwing it away. Bill regards himself as too weak to accept it. You do not yet know its healing power. After you have passed the course, you will accept it and keep it and use it. That is the final exam, which you will have no trouble in passing. Midterm marks are not entered on the permanent record.

This last statement should be an encouragement for all students of the Course (or any spiritual path for that matter). We need only do the best we can now; in the end—and the "outcome is as certain as God," as we shall see presently—the mistakes along the journey will simply disappear.

The next recorded date for the notes is October 28, and principles 17 and 18 were given, followed by this allusion to Helen's beloved mathematics:

This is why you cannot keep that thing about S. If you do, your own value can be estimated at X, or infinity minus that. This is meaningless mathematically, and is therefore inestimable only in the literal sense. (I threw that in specially for Bill, because he *does* need special signs of love. He does not really, but he *does* think so.)

I have deleted some of the personal material for Helen and Bill, after which this message followed from Jesus for Bill:

...and be *sure* to tell him I *did* kiss him on the forehead and am kissing him again now. He is doing *very* well, and I am deeply grateful for his efforts. I *do* need help with this course.

Jesus always made it a point to let Bill know how much he loved him. As will be discussed again later, the numerous puns were one expression of that love.

This is not the place for a detailed examination of Helen's notebooks. However, I state again that to illustrate the intimately personal nature of Helen's relationship with Jesus, not to mention his loving concern and attentiveness to her and Bill, I present these excerpts from some of the personal material. I also quote from some of the corrections that Jesus had given to Helen, clarifying some points that her initial anxiety clouded over. This will also illustrate the informal, conversational tone of the early dictation, whose purpose was not only to present the basic material of *A Course in Miracles* itself, but to be of direct help to Helen and Bill.

Often in the beginning of the dictation, as I mentioned above, Helen's anxiety was such that her "hearing" was affected, not in the content or meaning of what was being given to her, but in the form or style of it. A clear example is in the current miracle principles 19 and 20. They read:

> 19. Miracles make minds one in God. They depend on cooperation because the Sonship is the sum of all that God created. Miracles therefore reflect the laws of eternity, not of time.
>
> 20. Miracles reawaken the awareness that the spirit, not the body, is the altar of truth. This is the recognition that leads to the healing power of the miracle (text, p. 2).

But when Helen originally took these principles down, they read quite differently. Here is the sequence, beginning with Helen's notes and then Jesus' corrections:

> 19. Miracles rest on the law and order of eternity. Not of time.
>
> 20. Miracles are an industrial necessity. Industry depends on cooperation, and cooperation depends on miracles.

Then followed a long instruction, never recorded from Helen's notebook. I reproduce excerpts from this now as evidence, again, of the personal level of teaching that occurred in the early weeks of the dictation, not to mention Helen's love for Jesus.

> Jesus: Miracles rest on flat feet. They have no arches. (Bill will be better with this than you.)
>
> Helen: He'd better be because I don't get it at all, and I am becoming very suspicious of it too. Bill—did communication break down, or does this mean something?
>
> Jesus: Clue—it has something to do with "here I am, Lord." Bill knows [This is a reference to the short prayer Jesus had given Bill to say; *see* p. 197].

The idea is that I don't want to emphasize your specific language too much.

Helen: My own associations here are very bad; a Rorschach response of "footprints" to the top red on 2.[48]

Jesus: No—it's all right: it's the arch of time. There isn't any. So it means "miracles rest on eternity."

Helen: I must say this is the hard way, and I'm *sure* this could have been done more directly. I don't see why I should get a message in a way that makes me miss the point and that I have to go into a mental coma to get it.

Jesus: You've been doing that all along. You have not even bothered to *look* at the others that are *very* clearly stated. I just thought I'd give you this one in a way you *couldn't* overlook it. It's an example of shock effect sometimes useful in teaching students who won't listen. It compels attention....

And remember to thank Bill from Me for his all-out support. I *need* it, because you won't listen to *anything*. But don't worry, the three of us will make it. We're nowhere near the final. By the way, you are an example of the point on cooperation. And don't underestimate your cooperation either. You don't listen, and you would save yourself a lot of pain if you did. But you did get Chip over his misperceptions of S with very creditable integrity.

Helen: So I said, suddenly a little timid and *very* surprised, "You mean you think I'm *nice*?" And burst into tears. And He[49] said He must think so, really, because He keeps giving me everything, and He's not angry because I keep on rejecting Him. But He's sorry because I suffer so much for no reason. He was really very nice about it. I told him I really do love Him, but I have trouble about it (though I *did* mean it for a little while anyway, before I got embarrassed), and He said he understood very well, and would keep on trying.

---

48. This is a reference to the ten inkblots created by the Swiss psychiatrist Hermann Rorschach as a psychological tool to help understand how people perceive their world. The second of these consists, in part, of two red blots at the top of the card.

49. Helen regularly capitalized the pronouns relating to Jesus until he instructed her much later to use the lower case. Jesus' point in that was to emphasize his inherent equality with us. As he wrote: "Equals should not be in awe of one another because awe implies inequality. It is therefore an inappropriate reaction to me" (text, p. 5).

The dictation then continued:

21. Miracles are cobwebs of iron. They unite human frailty to the strength of God.

Helen considered changing "iron" to "steel," but was told:

No. "Steel" would *not* be a better word. Steel is very useful but it does have to be tempered by fire. Iron is the raw material. The point of miracles is that they replace fire, thus making it unnecessary.

The principle is corrected a little bit later.

Another portion from the notebooks—omitted from the published text—followed, and is given here:

Don't worry about your autism.[50] It's just a misused talent, which you really need. You have to tune out this world to see another. This ability is a gift, and when it comes under involuntary control rather than involuntary *lack* of control, it will be very useful.

The dictation went on with current principles 21 and 22, along with "Explanatory Instructions," part of which became the first paragraph on page 8 of "The Escape from Darkness" in Chapter One of the published text. Then followed the corrections for the earlier miracle points. The exact order of the next few pages is problematic, as the order of the notebooks does not coincide with the typed manuscript. I have pieced together the different dictations as best I could.

Correct the point [now 20] about "cobwebs of iron." This is upside down as stated. The part about "uniting human frailty with the strength of God" is all right, but the explanation stops too soon. If iron is the raw material, cobwebs can't become the iron. That is only the way it seems, because cobwebs are associated with frailty and iron with strength. If you look carefully at the phrasing, you will see it is reversed (one point already tells you that miracles reverse the physical or lower order laws).

The raw material, or iron, is heavy but crude, and stands for the body, which is a crude creation. The cobweb concept is

---

50. A clinical term for the psychotic state wherein one blocks out the external world.

closer to how the body *should* be regarded, i.e., as an airy and very temporary home, which can just be blown away with a slight breeze.

Helen: Corrected as per instructions.

Jesus: The point should read "A miracle reawakens the awareness that the spirit, and not the body, is the altar of Truth. This is the recognition that leads to the healing power of the miracle."

Miracle principle 23 then was dictated, followed by further explanation of the scribal error:

Jesus: Tell Bill about the idea...

Helen: still dim to me

Jesus:...that the reason is not that you (plural) doubt, or distantiate,[51] or cannot believe. It is more of a reaction formation[52] against a pull which you both recognize is so intense that you are afraid that you will be uprooted. But remember that a cobweb is really stronger than the iron, if you see it properly. This fear is why you couldn't get the point straight, too.

Jesus continues here with word-play that was fairly typical of him during these early weeks of the dictation:

By the way, it is not true that you are both *"just scribes."* You might remember that the Scribes were very wise and holy men and are even spelled sometimes with a capital S. If you want to go further, you could even shift "just" from "merely" to "honest," a term used in the Bible in association with "might." Tell Bill you couldn't make that pun if the original phrasing had been singular.

[Helen made an aside about liking an earlier pun more, referring to a "special" pun for Bill.]

Jesus: He [Bill] is still under the impression that he needs special signs of love. Note also that the special language here is a combination of both yours *and* his. You two came together in

---

51. A psychological defense characterized by "standing away" from thoughts judged as harmful.

52. A psychological defense characterized by reacting in a way opposite to what is truly being felt unconsciously. This dynamic was particularly prominent in Helen, as Jesus explains.

My name. Answer: It was cuter, but this one *means* more. The *real* reason you don't like it is because it refers to you in a *very* lofty position. This makes you nervous.

And don't lose sight of the emphasis on cooperation, or the *not singular*. That point about "industrial necessity" should read "corporate," referring to the body of Christ, which is a way of referring to the Church. But the Church of God is only the sum of the souls He created, which *is* the corporate body of Christ. Correct to read: "A miracle makes souls one in God." Leave in the next part about cooperation, though.

Jesus then continued:

Remind Bill to get another notebook. [Helen was then using a smaller one, and needed the regular size.] I don't give up as easily as *he* does. If I could get *you* to listen, I can get him to register. Getting you to listen was a miracle in itself, and he should appreciate this more than anyone else, having had some trouble with this problem himself.

"Lord heal me" is the only legitimate prayer. This also means "Lord atone for me," because the only thing man should pray for is forgiveness. He *has* everything else.

Now take this personally, and listen to Divine logic: If, when you have been forgiven, you have everything else, and *if you have been forgiven,* then you *have* everything else.

This happens to be the simplest of all propositions.

If P then Q.
P.
Therefore, Q.

The real question is, is P true? If you will review the evidence, I think you will find this inescapable. I went on very personal record to this effect, and I am the only completely True Witness for God. You have every right to examine *my* credentials —in fact, I urge you to do so. You haven't read the Bible in years.

The foregoing syllogism is among the most basic propositions in logic, a form with which Helen was more than familiar, and which recurs in the Course. Incidentally, Jesus' urging Helen to read the Bible should be understood in the context of her having used the avoidance of the Bible as a symbolic means of avoiding Jesus. Reading it again now would thus be symbolic of turning back towards him.

At this point Helen took down notes on the Atonement, which were subsequently placed in the later miracle principles and latter portions of the first chapter of the text. In the context of principle 27, Jesus stated that the Atonement is the "natural profession of the children of God, because they have professed me." He then used this as a punning way of making a point to Helen and Bill. The puns, as commented on earlier, were meant by Jesus to be special gifts to Bill, who again was an excellent punster.

> Tell Bill that that is what "Professor" really means. As an Associate Professor, he must become associated with My strength. As an Assistant Professor, you must assist both him *and* Me. The children need both strength and help. You cannot help until you are strong. The Everlasting Arms are your strength, and the Wisdom of God is your help.

The subject turned to revelation, the material of which is largely contained in the beginning of the section in Chapter One called "Revelation, Time and Miracles." It was interrupted in the notebooks by this passage, omitted from the published text, which seems to describe an intense experience of Helen's:

> Helen [to Jesus]: Lord, I will leave my desire to help him [Bill] in Your Hands. If You will tell me what to do, I will to do it.

> Jesus: And that ... *is* the answer.

> Helen: The impact of this was incredibly intense, like a great burst of unexpected clarity. It was briefly so compelling that it seemed as though there was nothing else at all. The whole world just disappeared. When it faded out there was no after effect, except a dim sense of wonder that also faded out, though a trifle slower.

> I was told to "write nothing else that evening," but we'd pick up the Course again in the morning. It was also explained that that kind of experience was at the Revelation level, which is different but not by any means out of accord.

The notes then continued with a discussion of the difference between revelations and miracles, part of which is found in Chapter One. As an aside, Jesus said:

Tell Bill that miracles *do not* depend on Revelation. They *induce* it. He is quite capable of miracles already, but he is still too fearful for Revelations. Note that *your* [Helen] Revelation occurred specifically after you had engaged at the visionary level in a process of *denying fear*.... Tell Bill that your propensity for Revelations, which is very great, is the result of a high level of past communion. Its transitory nature comes from the descent into fear, which has not yet been overcome. His own "suspended" state mitigates against both extremes. This has been very apparent in the course of both of your recent developmental patterns.

Miracles are the essential course of *action* for both of you. They will strengthen him and stabilize you.

Note that the much more personal than usual notes you are taking today reflect the Revelatory experience. This does *not* produce the more generalizable quality which this course is aimed at. They may, nevertheless, be of great help to Bill personally, since you asked for something that *would* help him personally. It depends on how he listens, and how well he understands the *cooperative* nature of your joint experience. You can help only by reading this note *first*. Ask him later if this should be included in the written part of the course at all, or whether you should keep this note separately. He is in charge of these decisions.

This latter point is consistent with what we noted in Helen's letters from a month or so earlier, where she recognized the importance of leaving certain decisions to Bill.

The following morning, after some additional dictation (including several miracle principles) not included here, Helen awoke with fear, thinking of the Biblical phrase, "God is not mocked," anticipating punishment. Jesus explained that the quotation was

intended as reassurance. You are afraid that what you wrote last night was contradictory, conflicting with some earlier points, especially because you were writing while all doped up [Helen took a strong sleeping pill each night]. Remember, "God is not mocked" under any circumstances.

Contradictions in *My* words mean lack of understanding, or scribal failures, which I make every effort to correct. But they are still *not crucial*. The Bible has the same problem, I assure you, and it's *still* being edited. Consider the power of My Word,

> in that it has withstood all the attacks of error, and is the
> Source of Truth.
>
> Tell Bill that there are certain advantages in being a
> psychologist. A major one is the understanding of projection,
> and the extent of its results.

The statements here about the Bible should not be taken as
literally true. I have already pointed out, and will return to
this in Part III, that the form of the Course was directly
influenced by Helen (though certainly not its content), and that
Helen knew the Bible well, believing certain statements in the
gospels were the words of Jesus. Therefore, the content of
Jesus' message here came in consonance with this belief system. In our later discussion I shall also point out the
unreliability of Helen's hearing when it related to specifics.

After some more material on projection, Jesus cautioned all
who attempt to be helpful, i.e., to be miracle workers:

> One of the major problems with miracle workers is that they
> are so sure that what they are doing is right, because they
> *know* it stems from love, that they do not pause to let Me estab-
> lish *My* limits.

Later in the dictation, Jesus commented to Helen about a
famous healer who also did not always ask when he should
"perform a particular miracle," and consequently caused himself "unnecessary strain." This then led to the following
comment:

> Anyone who is unable to leave the requests of others
> unanswered has not entirely transcended egocentricity. I
> never "gave of Myself" in this inappropriate way....

Jesus thus requested that Helen ask him first, before seeking to
help others; this request is now found in the second paragraph
on page 7 of the printed text. Again, we shall return in Part III
to this issue of being certain one is right about hearing the
voice of Jesus or the Holy Spirit.

Several encouraging asides to Bill followed, and then Jesus
gave Helen the message ("special revelation"), quoted earlier
on page 19. This was followed by:

> This Revelation was permitted because you did *not* project onto
> Bill the blame for your omission to *ask Me* if you should

transcribe the notes. The fact that *he* should have done so does not exempt you from your own omission.

Thanks for blessing him with a miracle instead of cursing him with projection.

We find here the same openness to looking at the ego that Helen demonstrated in her letters to Bill.

Some notes regarding Louis followed (omitted here), and then:

> Jesus: Blessed are you with Mary as the mother of the children.

> Helen: I asked for forgiveness for having thrown away all the money [a reference to the omitted notes on Louis], but He [Jesus] said "It's all right. You lived in scarcity then, but now you are forgiven. So you live in abundance. There is no longer any need to throw anything away, or to want for anything either."

What followed next is unclear from Helen's notes, but there appeared to have been some experience of Jesus as an infant, which led to Helen's stating:

> Helen: Behold the handmaid of the Lord; be it done unto me according to Thy Will.

> Jesus: Egocentric is right! I do not need another physical mother, and she [Mary] was the only one that conceived without any lack of love....

In Part III I shall discuss the connection between Helen and Mary, the biblical mother of Jesus.

The dictation then continues with Jesus' words of encouragement to Helen and Bill. Then he asks Helen not to be ashamed of him, another important theme to which we shall return later when I discuss Helen's relationship with Jesus.

> Tell Bill that as soon as both of you have completely entered the second phase you will be not only willing to enter into communion, but will also understand peace and joy.

> Your commitment is not yet total. That is why you still have more to learn than to teach. When your equilibrium stabilizes, you can teach *as much* as you learn. This will give you the proper sense of balance.

Meanwhile, remember that *no effort is wasted*. Unless you remember this, you cannot avail yourself of *My* efforts, which are limitless.

Have a good day. Since only eternity is real, why not use the illusion of time constructively? You might remember that underneath are the Everlasting Arms.... *Note*: The Biblical quotation "If you are ashamed of Me I will be ashamed of you" is interpreted as a threat *only* as long as you remain in the first step [i.e., one does not recognize that there is nothing that one would *want* to hide, even if it were possible to do so].

What it [the quotation] *really* means is that if you are ashamed of Me (or embarrassed by love), you will project and make it impossible for Me to reach you.

Make every effort you can *not* to do this. I'll help you as much as you will let Me.

Some notes followed regarding a friend of Bill, and then the miracle points continued with what became principle 24, and an additional correction:

Miracles make time and tide wait for all men. They can heal the sick and raise the dead, because man himself made death and taxes, and can abolish both. *Note*: "tax" also means "strain." Look up "miracles"—I think the third definition is best: "that which or one who is of surpassing excellence or merit."

That's right—*You* are a miracle. God creates only "that which or one who is of surpassing excellence or merit." Man is capable of this kind of creation too, being in the image and likeness of his own Creator. Anything else is only his own nightmare, and does not exist. Only the creations of light are real.

By the way, about the flat feet. This is a slang term for "policemen," or the guardians of law and order. This was used first, *before* the "it has no arches" bit. Correct to read: Miracles rest on the law and order of eternity. [This was even further corrected later to read, as quoted earlier: "Miracles therefore reflect the laws of eternity, not of time"—part of principle 19.]

As long as you take accurate notes, every word is meaningful. But I can't always get through. Whenever possible, I will correct retroactively. *Be sure* to note all later corrections. This means that you are more receptive than you were when I tried before.

Dictation of principle 25 followed, which Jesus then illustrated by an incident involving a friend and colleague of Helen. Portions of this illustration were later used in Chapter One as they specifically referred to Jesus' ability to cancel out errors, being "in charge of the process of Atonement."

Helen then asked if there were any corrections that Jesus wanted her to make on the notes. He answered:

> Yes, to change the word "sin" to "absence of love." Sin is a man-made word with threat connotations he made up himself. No *real* threat is involved anywhere. Just because "nature abhors a vacuum," which is true enough, it does *not* follow that a vacuum is filled with hellfire. Nothing is gained by frightening yourself, and it's very destructive. Miracles need freedom from fear. Part of their Atonement value involves just that. The word "atone" really means "undo."

This next portion from Helen's notebook was never transcribed, although later dictations covered the same idea of turning to Jesus for help, allowing him to be our guide in all things, large or small:

> The reason I direct everything that is unimportant is because it is no way to waste *your* free will. If you insist on doing the trivial your way, you waste too much time and will on it. Will cannot be free if it is tied up in trivia. It never gets out.
>
> I will tell you *exactly* what to do in connection with everything that does not matter. That is not an area where choice should be invested. There is better use of time.
>
> You have to remember to ask Me to take charge of all minutiae, and they will be taken care of so well and so quickly that you cannot bog down in it.
>
> The only remaining problem is that you will be unwilling to ask because you are afraid *not* to be bogged down. Do not let this hold us back. If you will ask, *I* can arrange these things even if *you* are not too enthusiastic.
>
> Prayer can be very specific in little matters. If you need a coat, ask me where to find one. I know your taste well, and I also know where the coat is that you would eventually buy anyway.
>
> If you do not like the coat afterwards, that is what would have happened anyway. I did *not* pick out the coat for you. You said you wanted something warm, inexpensive, and

capable of taking rough wear. I told you you could get a Borgana, but I let you get a better one because the furrier needed you.

This reference is to a coat that Helen had recently bought, on Jesus' recommendation, at Klein's department store. Helen was accustomed to shopping at some of the City's finer stores, such as Lord and Taylor or B. Altman. Klein's, which was a five-minute walk from Helen's apartment, was known as a real bargain store, and hardly one in which a woman with Helen's taste would have bought a winter coat. Yet Jesus had instructed Helen to go there. Not only did Helen find exactly the coat she wanted, but the salesman who waited on her needed Helen's help very badly. He had a retarded child and was at a loss at what to do, and Helen was able to be extremely helpful to him. The point Jesus was trying to make to Helen here was that by consulting his "Higher Shopping Service" (*see below*) she would not only receive what she believed she needed, but that he would be able to help others through her as well. It was ultimately then, a lesson in how the miracle saves time. His explanation continues:

Note, however, that it is better in terms of the criteria *you* established. I could do this because *you* saw the coat more that way than in terms of a particular material. You thought of Klein's yourself a few days ago, and then you decided against it because Borgana is price-fixed. Then you remembered a coat Grace [Louis' sister] once got there that was much cheaper, and seemed pretty much the same, and asked yourself whether it was really right to be sold on a particular trade name through advertising. That opened your mind.

I cannot save you more time than you will let Me, but if you are willing to try the Higher Shopping Service, which also covers all lower-order necessities and even quite a number of whims within reason, I have very good use for the time we could save.

Remember, the specific answer you get depends on the specific question you ask. The fewer limits you impose, the better the answer you'll get. Ex: You could ask where do I find a Borgana coat? or where is the coat I want? or where is the coat I should get? and so on. The form of the thought determines the level of creation.

Helen could never really incorporate this principle into her relationship with Jesus, especially regarding her letting go of the limitations she placed on him by asking for specific help. See Chapter 17 in this book for the elaboration of this idea that came many years later, when obviously Helen was more open to the full teaching.

The notes continue now with the same theme of saving time by choosing the miracle and the help of Jesus, Helen being urged to curb her need to control.

> Miracles depend on timing, which is why you shouldn't waste time. I told you awhile back that time would cease when it was no longer useful as a learning aid. There is a way of speeding you up. And that is by leaving more and more time for Me. So you can devote it to miracles.
>
> The *first part* of what you wrote last night is right. Check this now. (Corrected under advice.) The second part[53] was put in by you, because you didn't like the first. It was an attempt to re-establish your own control over time. Remember, you cannot stand not knowing what time it is.
>
> I am *not intruding* on your will, but I *am* trying to free it. I told you the next part of the course will place increasing emphasis on Atonement, and I defined this as "undoing." You know very well that changing learning patterns requires undoing the old ones. The real meaning of retroactive inhibition is simply that when two kinds of learning coexist, they interfere with each other.

This next brief note provides a fine example of how Jesus again uses Helen's formal interests (here statistics and experimental psychology) to reinforce the content of his teaching, specifically the message of the Atonement: minimizing and eventually undoing the effect of the ego on the Holy Spirit's Presence.

Jesus: You were wise in setting up William Rockford[54] to allow

---

53. I cannot ascertain for sure what these two parts refer to.

54. This refers to William Rockwell, one of Helen's major professors at New York University, mentioned before. Helen's proclivity for forgetting or changing names is discussed at length by Jesus below. Incidentally, Helen related to me that once while in Professor Rockwell's class, she addressed him as Dr. Rockhead.

measuring both the old and new learnings, thus permitting *ratio measurement.* Actually, I helped you with this one....

Helen [interrupting]: I am mad about this.

Jesus:...because most studies just measure learning decrement [loss] caused by new learning with the old. But the emphasis *should* be on how to minimize the effect of the old on the new. This is a much more helpful area to work in....

The dictation then returns to the specific teaching of the meaning of the Atonement and the willingness to learn it.

Do *not* get bogged down in those dreams of last night. They are reflections of old learning patterns. They arose because you did not like what I said about leaving minutiae to Me. They merely illustrate your willingness to get bogged down because you are afraid of the course. So don't use them that way. If you are tempted to do this, ask Bill to stop you. This course is about willingness, *not* unwillingness. Unwillingness has to be replaced by willingness, because willingness is part of readiness, without which learning cannot occur.

Go and look up Atonement, and then get dressed. To save time, wear *exactly* what I tell you and go.

Helen then wrote down what she found in the dictionary, followed by Jesus' comments:

Atonement - obsolete - short for "set at one" and "reconcile," "to agree." Obviously, before reconciliation or agreement is possible, the discordant or out of accord must be undone. It may seem as if darkness must be dispelled *before* light can come in, but the truth is that darkness is dispelled *by* light.

Dictation of more miracle principles followed (we are back to notes that were typed by Bill), current numbers 35–39, and where "Holy Spirit" is now found, the term "Spiritual Eye" was originally used by Helen, another example of how her fear interfered with her hearing clearly on the form level. This was changed afterwards to its proper term.

What is now miracle principle 40, was followed by:

Tell Bill that this is the true "strawberry mark" of brotherhood. This is just a sign of special concern for him, because he keeps worrying about this.

The reference to the "strawberry mark" comes from Mozart's opera *The Marriage of Figaro,* a favorite of Bill's. In the third act, Figaro escapes a difficult situation by suddenly discovering his long-lost mother by the strawberry mark on his arm, which she had placed there. The reference is thus but another example of Jesus' personal gifts to Bill, wherein he attempted to help Bill release his resistance to love through holding to his own sense of unworthiness. These "special" gifts (which, again, included the Course's plethora of puns) were meant by Jesus as symbolic of his love for Bill.

It is interesting at this point to contrast Helen's and Bill's quite different primary defenses—projection for Helen and denial for Bill—in terms of Jesus, fearing his love for them, and theirs for him. Helen basically fought with Jesus, projecting onto him her own failures, seeking to make him responsible for her feelings of unhappiness. Bill, on the other hand, continually attempted to deny the person of Jesus, finding it difficult even to say his name, preferring J.C. in place of the name "Jesus." In his later years, Bill would publicly as well as privately state his belief that the source of the Course was the Christ Mind or Christ Consciousness, thereby continuing to avoid the personal presence and love of the one to whose Course he so faithfully dedicated his life. This denial was a particularly important defense for him.[55]

Jesus continued, and the reader familiar with *A Course in Miracles* will notice again how much of the personal material meant for Helen and Bill found its way into the Course itself.

> You might add that his [Bill's] false idea about his own exclusion from universal love is fallacious in your terms, and arrogant in his. *His* real specialness does *not* stem from exclusion, but from inclusion. *All* My brothers are special. He should stop interpreting this as "all except Bill." This is ridiculous!

---

55. On one level, as I shall discuss in Part III, one can say that Bill was correct in describing *A Course in Miracles* as coming from the abstract "Christ Mind." However, the specific motivation behind his speaking this way appeared to be Bill's denial of his own personal relationship with Jesus *as* Bill. It was thus the voice of fear speaking, not wisdom. Jesus' frequent attempts during this period to help Bill develop his relationship with him were aimed at reducing this fear.

Tell him that the implied lack of love that his version contains is *way* off the mark [another pun], and misses the level of right thinking entirely. He *must* heal his perception in this respect. He must work a miracle on behalf of himself here.... Tell Bill that fifty million Frenchmen *can* be wrong, because the notion is too fragmented. What *can't* be wrong is the universal Sonship of which he is part.

Additional notes followed, including those on the Golder Rule, now found in Chapter One. Jesus then turned to a prominent if not sometimes humorous defense of Helen's: her penchant for forgetting names, or seeking to change them. The most significant of these changes was in using the name Jonathan for her husband Louis, as we have already seen. She also, at the moment of giving her name on the baptismal certificate at the age of thirteen, "inadvertently" gave her mother's maiden name instead of her own last name. Jesus explained this defensive phenomenon to her in this way:

I emphasize again that your tendency to forget names is not hostility, but a fear of involvement or *recognition*. You had misinterpreted human encounters as opportunities for magic, rather than for miracles, and so you tried to *protect the name*. This is a very ancient and primitive way of trying to protect a person.

Note the very old Jewish practice of changing the name of a person who is very ill, so that when the list is given to the Angel of Death, the person with that name will not be found.

This is a good example of the curiously literal regression which can occur in very bright people when they become afraid. You and Bill both do it. Actually, it is a device closely related to the phobia, in the sense that they both narrow fear to a simple aspect of a much larger problem in order to enable them to avoid it.

A similar mechanism works when you get furious about a comparatively minor infraction by someone to whom you are ambivalent. A good example of this is your response to Jonathan [i.e., Louis], who *does* leave things around in very strange ways. Actually, he does this because he thinks that by minor areas of disorganization he can protect his stability. I remind you that you have done this yourself for years, and should understand it very well. This should be met with great charity, rather than with great fury. The fury comes from your awareness that you do not love Jonathan as you should, and you narrow your lack of love by centering your hate on trivial behavior in an attempt to protect him from it [i.e., the hatred]. You also call him Jonathan for the same reason.

Note that a name is a human symbol that "stands for" a person. Superstitions about names are very common for just that reason. That is also why people sometimes respond with anger when their names are spelled or pronounced incorrectly. Actually, the Jewish superstition about changing names was a distortion of a Revelation about how to alter or avert death. What the Revelation's proper content was, was that those "who change their mind" (*not* name) about destruction (or hate) do not need to die. Death is a human affirmation of a belief in hate. That is why the Bible says "There is no death," and that is why I demonstrated that death does not exist. Remember that I came to *fulfill* the law by *reinterpreting* it. The law itself, if properly understood, offers only protection to man. Those who have not yet "changed their minds" have entered the "hellfire" concept into it.

A little later, Jesus re-emphasizes the point about asking his advice and help:

> The reason you have been late recently [for work] because you were taking dictation is merely because you didn't remember to ask Me when to stop. This is an example of the "indiscriminate or uncontrolled" miracle-working we already spoke of. It is well-meant but ill-advised.... Note also that you closed the book and put it aside *without* consulting Me. Ask "is this all?"... Scribes *must* learn Christ-control, to replace their former habits, which *did* produce scarcity in place of abundance. From errors of this kind, the sense of deprivation *is* inevitable, but very easily corrected.

Among other topics, there followed an extensive discussion of reliability, validity, and other statistical concepts that were meaningful to Helen. In the midst of this discussion, the following was said, related to Helen's earlier experiences of a desert, a symbol also found later in the Course itself, as indicated before:

> A desert is a desert is a desert. You can do anything you want in it, but you *cannot* change it from what it *is*. It still lacks

241

water. This is why it *is* a desert. The thing to do with a desert is to *leave*.

While Helen was taking down notes (near the beginning of notebook 4), a friend called to tell her that Dave Diamond had died. The exact date is unclear, but is sometime in early November 1965. Helen then observed that maybe that was a way of leaving the desert. She wrote down the following notes, none of which were transcribed, as they were *Helen's* reflections on Dave's last days and her visits to him. I include some of them here as illustrative of Helen's state of mind, and her sincere attempts to join with another in Jesus' name, asking his help that she might be truly helpful. Helen was also able to generalize this lesson to Louis.

> Helen: I went into the [hospital] room (under instructions) and spoke to Dave, who was very groggy. Everytime he opened his eyes I said, "We all love you, so don't be afraid." I prayed that he would be able to love everybody in return (this too was under instructions) [Helen had previously referred to some unforgiven relationships in his life], having been told (I *think* on Great Authority), that his only real danger came from lacks in *this* connection.
>
> I did not visit him on Friday, but I am sure this was right, because I was *very* careful to ask. I was going over, too, after the lecture, and was told not to. Perhaps there was no "need to know" involved.
>
> I am upset about it, and am leaving my notes for a while. I think I'd rather pray right now.
>
> Esther [a mutual friend] said Terry [presumably Dave's wife] was talking about giving away the baby [presumably an adopted child]. I jumped to the conclusion that I was supposed to take her, but that may easily be an indiscriminate miracle impulse. I think I'd better just stop now.
>
> I prayed for Dave, and said that whatever miracles I could do for him even now, or any of his family, I would will to do [*see below* p. 244 for an explanation]. I also asked Jesus to help Dave with the course. Then I was told to go in and visit with Jonathan, and pray for him, particularly if he was asleep, which he was. It was the only time so far I prayed *intensely* for him. When that happens, I am *strongly* aware that I am not praying alone. We [i.e., Helen *and* Jesus] told Jonathan that he should forget about [his past sins] . . . and all the rest, because it

does not matter. He showed a lot of love this time, and should claim his forgiveness. He does *not* need to hurt himself, and *must* stop those symptoms of disequilibrium and establish his freedom. He woke up, and said he was feeling better but hungry.

I was going to wash my hair after fixing his dinner, but I was told to visit his mother. Am not too enthusiastic about this, but am going now.[56] It occurred to me while waiting for the elevator that I was glad I was going, because it was a way of atoning to Jonathan for my being so nasty to her (he was *always* happy to have me visit his mother), and in a way of atoning for Dave, too. The *impersonal* nature of miracles is because Atonement itself is *one*. By being one it unites all creations with their Creator.

These last two sentences were probably dictated by Jesus, for they led into the continuation of the dictation of the miracle principles, as well as material which was placed after the principles, yet still in the first chapter of the text. Much of these were comments on the need to have Jesus control the expression of the miracles, which Helen obviously had been able to do, as seen in these comments by Jesus to her:

> You did surprisingly well today, after a rather bad start. Actually, Dave helped you, but this will *not* be explained. (I got very frightened about this.) It's just an example of how no miracle is ever lost, and *always* blesses the doer. This has *nothing* to do with magic. The Golden Rule is the law of justice, *not* spells. We've been over that already.

Somewhat later Helen wrote, echoing her decision not to abuse her mind's power: "I *don't* want scribal errors to enter too much within the course. Though I guess they'll be corrected when they do." Jesus then commented that scribes

> have a particular role in the Plan of Atonement, because they have the ability to *experience* Revelations themselves, and also to put into words enough of the experience to serve as a basis for miracles.

---

56. The reader may recall Helen's account in one of her letters to Bill of visiting Louis' mother at the New Jersey shore. Her mother-in-law's place of permanent residence, however, was New York City.

This refers back to Helen's experience, described on p. 230, after which she had written: "If You will tell me what to do, I will to do it." She had not known that the word "to" was inserted, and had merely intended to write "I will do it." This recognition, as Helen mentioned, had a terrific impact, for it reflected an active decision on her part to do the will of Jesus, who then said to her regarding this experience:

> This is why you *experienced* that Revelation about "I will to do" *very* personally, but also *wrote* it. What you wrote *can* be useful to miracle workers other than yourself. We [the first appearance of the editorial "we"] said before that prayer is the medium of miracles. The miracle prayer *is* what you wrote, i.e., "If You will tell me what to do, I will to do it."*
>
> This prayer is the door that leads out of the desert forever. [A reference to the earlier statement about leaving deserts.]
>
> *Helen: Correction next day.
>
> Jesus: This is not a complete statement, because it does not exclude the negative. We have already told you to add "and *not* to do what you would not have me do" in connection with miracles. The distinction has also been made here between "miracle-mindedness" as a *state*, and "miracle-doing" as its expression.
>
> The former needs *your* careful protection, because it is a state of miracle-*readiness*. This is what the Bible means in the many references to "Hold yourself ready" and other similar injunctions. Readiness here means keep your perception right side up (or valid), so you will *always* be ready, willing, and able. These are the essentials for "listen, learn, and do." You must be *ready* to listen, *willing* to learn, and *able* to do. Only the last is involuntary, because it is the *application* of miracles which must be Christ-controlled. But the other two, which are the voluntary aspects of miracle-mindedness, *are* up to you.
>
> To channelize [mentioned earlier] *does* have a "narrowing down" connotation, though *not* in the sense of lack. The underlying state of mind, or Grace, is a total commitment. Only the *doing* aspect involves the channel at all. This is because doing is always specific.
>
> As Jack [Jack Cohen: A New York University statistical psychologist] said, "A reliable instrument must measure something," but a channel is also valid. It must learn to do *only* what it is supposed to do. Change the prayer to read: If you will tell me what to do, *only that* I will to do.

Helen: I object to the doggerel sound of this, and regard it as very inferior poetry.

Jesus: It's hard to forget, though.

The notes continued with material found in Chapter One on revelation, the miracle, the role of Jesus, and principles 46–48, after which Jesus returned to Helen and Bill's relationship.

> Tell Bill he is right in providing you with the consistent strength you need to get, and he needs to offer. Your instability and his weakness have resulted from bad karmic choices, and your relationship *now* is crucial for the future. You must both exert every effort to restore it to what it once was. Both of you are correcting where you have failed before. This has already enabled you to fulfill a very unexpected role in your joint salvation, and the salvation of many other children I will entrust increasingly to you. These are by no means chosen at random. Bill should know that his preparation is not only in terms of sharing in the results of your better application of some rather unusual talents. His own role, which he will understand after his preparation is complete, will be equally surprising. He will need your help then, as you need his strength now.

Helen and Bill, and later the three of us, spent considerable time ruminating about Bill's later "surprising" role. But it never materialized, neither did what certainly seemed to be Jesus' expectations about Helen's and Bill's additional functioning besides the scribal one. I shall discuss this issue in more detail in Part III. Jesus' dictation on Helen and Bill's relationship continues now:

> Note that you [Helen] *do not* need his [Bill] help as a scribe, because you developed this ability by your own efforts, and finally placed them at *My* disposal. By lending you his strength, he strengthens himself. When he gains this through his own efforts, he will need your help in a very unexpected way. But this is just another example of the reciprocal nature of miracles....
> You and Bill *do* have special talents which are needed for the Celestial Speed-up at this time. But note that the term speed-up is not one which relates to the *transcending* of time. When time is abolished, and all the Sons of God have come home, no special agents will be necessary. But do not

underestimate the power of special agents now, or the great need there is for them. I do not claim to be more than that Myself. No one in his right mind (a term which should be specially noted), ever wants either more or less than that. Those who are called on to witness for Me *now* are witnessing for all men, as I am.

The role of the Priestess was once to experience Revelations and to work miracles. The purpose was to bring those not yet available for direct Revelations into proper focus for them. Heightened perception was always the essential Priestess attribute.

After *A Course in Miracles* became public, and Helen's identity as the scribe who heard the voice of Jesus became known, she was frequently approached by people to ask Jesus for advice for them. With the wisdom of the priestess, Helen would tell them that she would be happy to pray *with* them, and help to facilitate *their* hearing the answer for themselves. Frequently I heard Helen tell others that there was nothing special about what she did; they could hear for themselves. Needless to say, this was the attitude Jesus fostered in the Course. As he said: "All My brothers are special" (previously quoted, *see* p. 239).

Helen then wrote down this important note, which obviously made it possible for Jesus to make his next statement to her:

Helen: This morning was the first time I ever said that I would be honored if there were any notes He wanted me to take. He said He did.

Jesus: I told you you were now restored to your former role in the Plan of Atonement. But you must still choose freely to devote your heritage to the greater Restoration. As long as a single slave remains to walk the earth, your release is not complete. Complete restoration of the Sonship is the only true goal of the miracle-minded....

Your earlier acute problem in writing things down came from a *much* earlier misuse of very great scribal abilities. These were turned to secret rather than shared advantage, depriving them of their miraculous potential, and diverting it into possession.

Helen then wrote down in her notebook a special revelation

which was not transcribed by Bill. It refers back to one in the series of "flashbacks" with Bill, where she was once again an ancient priestess, to whom Bill brought people in need. Bill's role now, however, was taken over by Jesus, who said to Helen: "Priestess, a brother has knelt at your shrine. Heal him through Me." Helen then wrote, from herself:

> Helen: I have an idea that the "shrine" merely referred to the "altar within," which the Priestess served. I imagine that the communication was direct, and the "brother" always nameless. I think the Priestess responded automatically by praying directly to God, standing with upraised arms to draw down a blessing on her brother, who knelt outside. Her response was completely automatic and impersonal. She never even thought of checking the outcome, because there *was* no doubt. .I imagine there is *still* no doubt, really. Except that the Priestess can no longer ask alone. It was originally "sister," not "Priestess" [ostensibly referring to Jesus' salutation].

This description is remarkably similar to Helen's priestess experience earlier that summer with Bill, which I presented in Chapter 5.

Helen then asked Jesus a question regarding past memories, and he answered:

> As long as you remember *always* that you never suffered anything because of anything anyone *else* did, this is not dangerous. Remember that you who want peace can find it only by complete forgiveness. You never really *wanted* peace before, so there was no point in knowing how to get it. This is an example of the "need to know" principle, which was established by the Plan of Atonement long before the CIA.

In addition to the cute allusion to the Central Intelligence Agency and its "need to know" principle, we can see here a succinct summary of the Course's teaching that our one *need* is forgiveness or the acceptance of the Atonement, which allows us to *know* (or remember) the truth that has always been within us, but which we have forgotten.

The notes continued with material now found near the end of Chapter One, as well as the last two miracle principles. The dating here is imprecise, but we are somewhere in the beginning of November.

247

Chapter 9

THE SCRIBING OF *A COURSE IN MIRACLES*—B
(1965)

Specific Teachings

We begin the chapter with an early November 1965 reference to Helen and Bill. Jesus explains that their differing but complementary ego dynamics present an ideal classroom for both to be healed, with the unspoken proviso that they gratefully accept the learning opportunity. In her letters to Bill, Helen also commented on their ego differences, as well as these differences serving a useful purpose in their minds' healing. We have already seen evidence of the important emphasis Jesus places on this theme, as it directly reflects the Course's principal message of forgiveness. We shall now consider it in more depth below.

Jesus' discussions on Helen's and Bill's ego defenses basically focus on two related points: 1) Helen's use of projection, and Bill's of denial; and 2) Helen's very strong though occasionally misguided will, and Bill's weaker though more consistent will. Characteristically, as we have already observed, Helen was the much stronger personality: volatile and easily aroused to anger. Bill, on the other hand, tended to handle his anger in more passive and subtle ways, and often was unaware of the true nature of his feelings. Thus, Helen was always much more out in the open about her emotions relating to God and Jesus, projecting her own thoughts of rejection onto Them, feeling justifiably angered by Their seeming lack of response; while Bill very often denied his emotions altogether, and was thus not in touch with them. It was his ego's defense mechanism of denial that resulted in Bill's weak, though steady identification with his function. Thus Bill remained faithful to this function, although his denial did not allow him to experience its relationship to Jesus. Helen's projecting, on the other hand, correlated with her strong will, though her volatility resulted in great inconsistency. It was nonetheless always clear to Helen that her work was done in close relationship with Jesus, the "Top Sergeant" of her letters.

The situation of complementary ego dynamics of projection and denial, when not accepted as a classroom for learning forgiveness, unfortunately turns into a stormy battleground in which the ego lesson of "one or the other" reigns supreme. As the years wore on, it was the battleground that became the reality for Helen and Bill. But for now, the honeymoon was still in session. We turn now to a brief comment from Jesus. Still later in this chapter, as well as in the next one, this important theme will return.

> *You* [Helen] are both more miracle-minded, and less able to recognize fear because of your stronger, but split, identification. Bill, also characteristically, is less miracle-minded, but better able to recognize fear, because his identification is more consistently right but weaker. Together, the conditions needed for consistent miracle-mindedness, the state in which fear has been abolished, can be particularly well worked out. In fact, it *was* already well worked out before.

In the midst of a discussion on the Atonement (what is now in the beginning sections of Chapter Two), Jesus responded to Helen's obvious discomfort:

> The reason this is upsetting you is because the Atonement is *total* commitment. You still think this is associated with loss. This is the same mistake *all* the separated ones make, in one way or another. They cannot believe that a defense which *cannot* attack also *is* the best defense. Except for this misperception, the angels *could* have helped them. What do you think "the meek shall inherit the earth" *means*? They will literally take it over because of their strength. A two-way defense is inherently weak; precisely *because* it has two edges it can turn against the self very unexpectedly. This tendency *cannot* be controlled *except* by miracles.
>
> The miracle turns the defense of Atonement to the protection of the inner self, which, as it becomes more and more secure, assumes its natural talent of protecting others. The inner self knows itself as both a brother and a son.

The above notes were taken down with great difficulty by

Helen and constituted the only series thus far that was written very slowly. When Helen asked Jesus about this, she was told:

> Don't worry about the notes. They are right, but *you* are not sufficiently Right-Minded yet to write about the Atonement with comfort. You will write about it yet with joy.

In other words, the ego thought system, with which Helen was so identified, found the Atonement principle—the separation never truly happened—too threatening to its own existence. The "loss" Jesus refers to is the loss of the ego. It is only when one's identity shifts to the Holy Spirit's thought system (right-minded thinking) that the Atonement can be accepted with joy, rather than terror.

Helen then continued with an interesting experience that pointed up her ambivalent feelings towards Jesus. Helen herself is the speaker:

> Last night I felt briefly but intensely depressed, temporarily under the impression that I was abandoned. I tried, but couldn't get through at all. After a while, I decided to give up for the time being, and He said "don't worry. I will never leave you or forsake you." I did feel a little better, and decided I was really not sick, so I could return to my exercises. While I was exercising, I had some part-vision experiences which I found only mildly frightening at times, and quite reassuring at others.
>
> I am not too sure of the sequence, but it began with a very clear assurance of love, and an equally clear emphasis on my own great value, beauty, and purity. Things got a little confusing after that. First, the idea of "Bride of Christ" occurred to me with vaguely inappropriate "undertones." Then there was a repetition of the "wave of Love," and a restatement of an earlier experience, now as if it were *from* Him *to* me: "Behold the Handmaid of the Lord; be it done unto you according to His Word." (This threw me into panic before, but at that time, it was stated in the more accurate Biblical phrasing: "Be it done unto me according to His Word.") This time I was a bit uneasy, but remembered I had misperceived it last time, and probably was still not seeing it right. Actually, it is really just a statement of allegiance to the Divine Service, which can hardly be dangerous.

There then followed a "strange sequence" that involved Jesus and some confused sexual thoughts, and then this statement from Helen:

> Helen: I *almost* thought briefly that He [Jesus] turned into a devil. I got just a *little* scared, but I thought it so silly, that there is no point in taking it seriously....[57]
>
> This morning we reviewed the whole episode. He [Jesus] said he was *very* pleased at the *comparative* lack of fear, and also the concomitant awareness that it [the devil fantasy] *was* a misperception. This showed much greater strength, and a much increased right-mindedness. This is because defenses are now being used much better, on behalf of truth *more* than error, though not completely so.
>
> The weaker use of mis-projection [i.e., projection] is shown by my recognition that it [the devil fantasy] can't *really* be that way, which became possible as soon as denial was applied against error, *not* truth. This permitted a much greater awareness of alternative interpretations. It was also explained (the shift to the passive form instead of "*He* also explained" should be noted. This is an expression of fear.)...

This shift, incidentally, was an ongoing pattern for Helen, who as we have already seen, continually sought to place distance between herself and the personal presence of Jesus by this unconscious defense of describing his voice in the passive mode, or as an "it." During our years together I would frequently kid her about this tendency to say "It said" rather than "Jesus said." However, it was a "habit" she could not easily release.

Helen's above experience of Jesus powerfully expresses the intensity of her love, as well as his assurance that his love would always be present for her. Her fear, also present, took the form of confusing the experience of love with sexual and devil fantasies. Earlier in the dictation, in a passage later edited and now found near the end of the first chapter of the text, Jesus explained to Helen:

> The confusion of miracle impulses with sexual impulses is a major source of perceptual distortion, because it *induces* rather

---

57. An important theme of *A Course in Miracles* is the fear of God's Love that characterizes the ego's thought system, causing us to turn love into its opposite: fear, hate, or evil; in this case, Jesus becomes the devil.

than straightens out the basic level-confusion which underlies all those who seek happiness with the instruments of the world.

Thus, it was Helen's fear of her love for Jesus (the miracle impulse) that led to her defense via the sexual thoughts. Incidentally, the shift from "sexual impulses" to "physical impulses," as it reads now in the text, was made by Helen and me in our later editing, with Jesus' approval. It is another example of how a phrase which was originally meant specifically for Helen was changed to fit the more generalized teaching of the Course: *all* impulses of the body are designed by the ego to distort and hide the miracle impulses of the Holy Spirit. Both "impulses" are found within the split mind, as is our capacity to choose between them.

After a brief section, omitted here, we continue with the dictation:

> You have perceived it [Atonement] largely as *external* thus far, and that is why your *experience* of it has been minimal. You have been *shown* the Chalice many times, but have not accepted it *for yourself.* Your major improper use of defenses is now largely limited to externalization. Do not fail to appreciate your own remarkable progress in this respect. You perceived it first as a vessel of some sort whose purpose was uncertain. You *did* notice, however, that the *inside* was gold, while the *outside*, though shiny, was silver. This was a recognition of the fact that the *inner* part is more precious than the outer side, even though both are resplendent, though with different value.

The reader may recall Helen's mention of the chalice in a letter to Bill regarding S, Bill's friend whom she experienced so much difficulty in forgiving. The chalice of Atonement remained for her an important personal symbol of forgiveness. In *A Course in Miracles*, "the chalice," though used only once in the published edition, is yet another example of Jesus' aforementioned correction of the traditional Christian association of Atonement (and thus the chalice or cup from which Jesus drank) with suffering and sacrifice. Its single occurrence in the published Course comes in an important passage written shortly before Easter, and thus its message of forgiveness is couched in the Easter symbolism:

> Beside each of you [i.e., Helen and Bill] is one who offers you the chalice of Atonement, for the Holy Spirit is in him. Would you hold his sins against him, or accept his gift to you? Is this giver of salvation your friend or your enemy? Choose which he is, remembering that you will receive of him according to your choice (text, p. 394).

Jesus continued with the dictation, with words that can be found in edited form in the published Course:

> The reinterpretation of defenses is essential to break open the *inner* light. Since the Separation, man's defenses have been used almost entirely to defend themselves *against* the Atonement, and thus maintain their Separation. They generally see this as a need to protect the body from external intrusion (or intruding).... The main error in both is the belief that the body can be used as a means for attaining Atonement.
>
> Perceiving the body as the Temple is only the first step in correcting this kind of distortion.
>
> Helen: Here I scalded my hand. There was no butter in the refrigerator, but it occurred to me that the Atonement was the remedy for the error.

The burn appeared to be minimal, and caused Helen little discomfort. Thus this ego defense of attacking her hand in a rather transparent attempt to prevent the scribing was quickly undone by Helen's turning to the Atonement as a defense. This provided her with a very clear example of how the defense of Atonement can undo the ego's defense of attack the instant it is chosen.

In response to Helen's request for a special message for Bill, Jesus said:

> Tell Bill his delaying tactics are holding him back. He does not really understand detachment, distantiation and withdrawal. He is interpreting them as "holding himself aloof" from the Atonement.

Jesus' reference here was to his previous discussion of the *proper* use of defenses—"detachment, distantiation and withdrawal"; namely, to separate oneself from the ego, rather than from the Atonement. When one does separate from the Atonement, increased guilt must be the result. Regarding the

Atonement and healing, Jesus pointed out the reciprocal nature of healing to Helen in this important passage:

> You don't understand healing because of your own fear. I have been hinting throughout (and once stated very directly, because you were unfearful at the time) that you *must* heal others. The reason is that their healing merely witnesses to yours.

Still later, this passage on healing and how it is temporarily interfered with by Helen's and Bill's fear:

> The healer who relies on his own readiness is endangering his understanding. He is perfectly safe as long as he is completely unconcerned about *his* readiness, but maintains a consistent trust in *Mine*. (Errors of this kind produce some very erratic behavior, which usually point up an underlying unwillingness to cooperate. Note that by inserting the carbon backwards, Bill created a situation in which two copies did not exist. This reflected two levels of confidence lack, one in My readiness to heal, and the other in his own willingness to give.) These errors inevitably introduce inefficiency into the miracle worker's behavior, and temporarily disrupt his miracle-mindedness. We might also make very similar comments about your own hesitation about dictating at all. This is a larger error only because it results in greater inefficiency. If you don't say anything, nobody can use it, including Me. We have established that for all corrective processes, the first step is know that this is fear. Unless fear had entered, the corrective procedure would never have become necessary. If your miracle working propensities are not working, it is always because fear has intruded on your Right-Mindedness, and has literally upset it (i.e., turned it upside down).

As has been readily apparent, Helen's anxiety level was quite high during this period, and her ego's fear of the undoing of its thought system extreme. One of her defenses, as Jesus already noted, was to attempt to undermine his authority. This merely intensified the split in her mind, since obviously another part of her mind accepted his authority and his love. In the following passage, written down on November 15, 1965, we find one of Helen's more ingenious attempts to catch Jesus in an error, specifically a grammatical one. Her attempt was to prove to her fearful mind that if Jesus were indeed shown to be mistaken, then he could not be who he said he was: the Course would thus be invalidated and her ego safe once again. The specific error was in the agreement of a singular subject with a plural verb, wherein the singular "Neither" was apparently paired with the plural "have."

> Jesus: Everyone experiences fear, and nobody enjoys it. Yet, it would take very little right-thinking to know why it occurs. Neither you nor Bill *have* thought about it very much, either [my italics].

> Helen: I object to the use of a plural verb with a properly singular subject, and remember that last time in a very similar sentence, He said it correctly and I noted it with real pleasure. This real grammatical error makes me suspicious of the genuineness of these notes.

> Jesus: What it really shows is that *you* are not very receptive. The reason it came out that way, is because you are projecting (in the inappropriate way) your own anger, which has nothing to do with these notes. *You* made the error, because you are not feeling loving, so you want me to sound silly, so you won't have to pay attention. Actually, I am trying to get through against considerable opposition, because you are not very happy, and I wish you were. I thought I'd take a chance, even though you are so resistant, because I *might* be able to make you feel better. You may be unable not to attack at all, but do try to listen a little, too....

You and Bill have been afraid of God, of Me, of yourselves, and of practically everyone you know at one time or another. This can only be because you have miscreated all of us, and believe in what you have created. (We spent a lot of time on this before, but it did not help very much.) You would never have done this if you were not afraid of your own thoughts. The vulnerable are essentially miscreators, because they misperceive Creation.

You and Bill are willing to accept primarily what does *not* change your minds too much, and leaves you free to leave them quite unguarded most of the time. You persist in believing that when you do not consciously watch your mind, it is unmindful. It is time to consider the whole world of the unconscious, or unwatched mind. This will frighten you because it is the source of fright. You may look at it as a new theory of basic conflict, if you wish, which will not be entirely an intellectual approach, because I doubt if the truth will escape you entirely. The unwatched mind is responsible for the whole content of the unconscious, which lies above the miracle-level. All psychoanalytic theorists have made some contribution to the truth in this connection, but none of them *has* [my italics] seen it in its true entirety. (The correct grammar here is a sign of your better cooperation. Thank you).

The "basic conflict" mentioned above refers to this important theme in the body of psychoanalytic theory, wherein each theorist had his or her own understanding of what this conflict was. While in graduate school, Helen wrote a term paper on the topic, as I mentioned in Chapter 4. Jesus' point—his "new theory of basic conflict"—is that the ego believes it is at war with God, and that this conflict occurs only within the dream world of the split mind.

In a further discussion of psychoanalytic theory, designed to help Helen and Bill look at Freud's (and his followers') contributions in a different light, Jesus stated:

> The structure of the psyche, as you [Helen] very correctly noted yourself [in the graduate school papers], follows along the lines of the particular libido [basic energy] concept the theorist employs.

Helen then objected, believing the facts to be the other way around. Jesus then countered, exposing Helen's underlying purpose of distracting him and the dictation from the purpose at hand: changing her mind. He said:

> This confusion arises out of the fact that you *did* change the order—several times in fact. Actually, it didn't matter, because the two concepts *do* flow from each other. It was a *terrific* waste of time, and one in which I hardly care to become engaged myself. *Please!*

More notes on Freud and psychoanalysis followed, and then a whole section on fear and conflict, and the Last Judgment, which was dictated directly to Helen from Jesus without written notes (she spoke the words to Bill who typed them out). Almost all of this material is currently in Chapter Two of the text.

The final two paragraphs currently at the end of the first

chapter, dealing with the need to study the Course to accomplish its goal of mind-training, originally appeared in the midst of a discussion that came at this point in the dictation. Jesus was again specifically urging Helen and Bill to study the scribal notes, just as teachers would urge their students to study the material given to them in class.

All learning involves attention and study at some level. This course is a *mind-training* course. Good students assign study periods for themselves. However, since this obvious step has not occurred to *you*, and since we are cooperating in this, I will make the obvious assignment now.

Bill is better at understanding the need to study the notes than you are, but neither of you realizes that many of the problems you keep being faced with may *already* have been solved there. *You* do not think of the notes in this way at all. Bill *does* from time to time, but he generally says, "It's probably in the notes," and *doesn't* look it up. He believes that, although he reads them over, they cannot *really* help him until they are complete.

First of all, he cannot be sure of this unless he tries. Second, they would *be* completed if both of you so willed.

You vaguely know that the course is intended for some sort of preparation. I can only say that you are not prepared.

I was amused when you reminded Bill that he, too, was being prepared for something quite unexpected, and he said, he was not at all curious about what it was. This disinterest is very characteristic of him when he is afraid. Interest and fear do *not* go together, as your respective behavior clearly shows.

Then followed a brief discussion of mental retardation (Helen's particular field of professional interest), including the use of it as a "maladaptive defense," wherein an intelligent person unconsciously "pretends" not to understand. As Jesus points out, Helen and Bill were expert at this particular form of defense. We pick up with this reference, after which Jesus returns to his exhortation to Helen and Bill to study this material.

This produces the "pseudo-retardation syndrome" which is justly classified as a psychiatric (or disturbed-level) symptom. Both of you do this all the time. Bill acts as if he does not understand even his *own* special language, let alone Mine, and you cannot read at all. This represents a joint attack on both yourselves *and* Me, because it renders *your* mind weak, and Mine incompetent. Remember, this puts you in a truly fearful position. If you cannot understand either your own mind *or* Mine, you do not *know* what is really willed. It is thus *impossible* to avoid conflict, as defined before, because even if you act *according to* will, you wouldn't know it.

The next part of this course rests too heavily on the earlier part not to *require* its study. Without this, you will become much too fearful when the unexpected *does* occur to make constructive use of it. However, as you study the notes, you will see some of the obvious implications, unless you still persist in misusing the defense of mental retardation. Please remember that its constructive use is hardly a *real* part of your own *real* equipment. It is a *particularly* inappropriate defense as you use it, and I can only urge you to avoid it.

The reason why a solid foundation is necessary at this point is because of the highly likely confusion of "fearful" and "awesome," which most people do make. You will remember that we said once before that awe is inappropriate in connection with the Sons of God, because you should not experience awe in the presence of your own equals. But it *was* emphasized that awe *is* the proper reaction of the Soul in the presence of its Creator. So far, this course has had only indirect recourse to God, and rarely even refers to Him directly. I have repeatedly emphasized that awe is not appropriate in connection with Me, *because* of our inherent equality. I have been careful to clarify My own role in the Atonement, without either over or understating it. I have tried to do exactly the same things in connection with yours.

The next step, however, *does* involve the direct approach to God Himself. It would be most unwise to start on this step at all without very careful preparation, or awe will surely be confused with fear, and the experience will be more traumatic than beatific.

Healing is of God in the end. The means are carefully explained in the notes. Revelation has occasionally *shown* you the end, but to reach it the means are needed.

These important words should be read and reread by students of *A Course in Miracles* as reminders of the need for willingness, diligence, and above all patience in working with and studying this material.

259

Helen then dictated the first paragraph of the following passage to Bill without any notes. The rest of this section was taken down by Helen and dictated to Bill in the usual way. It is a remarkable message, insofar as it is the only place in the dictation where Jesus systematically taught Helen and Bill from their own recent behavior, using it to illustrate the principles he was teaching them in the Course. The introduction is even more specific in this regard, and I present the entire passage without interruption.

The following is the only detailed description which need be written down as to how error interferes with preparation. The events specifically referred to here could be any events, nor does their particular influence matter. It is the process which is to be noted here, and not its results. The kind of beliefs, and the fallacious premises involved in misthought are as well exemplified here as elsewhere. There is nothing of special interest about the events described below, *except* their typical nature. If this is a true course in mind-training, then the whole value of this section rests *only* in showing you what *not* to do. The more constructive emphasis is, of course, on the positive approach. Mind-watching would have prevented any of this from occurring, and will do so any time you permit it to.

Tell Bill that the reason why he was so strained yesterday is because he allowed himself a number of fear-producing attitudes. They were fleeting enough to be more will-of-the-wisps than serious will-errors, but unless he watches this kind of thing, he *will* find the notes fearful, and, knowing him well, will mis-distantiate [i.e., detach from them]. His unprovoked irritation was pardonable [interestingly enough, Helen wrote this as *un*pardonable, unconsciously revealing her own unforgiveness of Bill] *except* by himself, and he did not choose to pardon it. *You* did, but I am afraid you were under some strain in doing so. This was unfortunate, and weakened your own ability to behave healingly toward Bill at the time, and later also toward Louis, both of whom *did* act "stupidly."[58] But one "stupidity" at a time is usually enough. You are getting too close to the misuse of mental retardation when "stupidity" sets in all around.

---

58. Here, as elsewhere in this section, Jesus' use of the word "stupid" reflects Helen's own judgmental use of it in her attack thoughts.

Bill, having already weakened himself, was very un-miracle-minded, first by not asking D if she wanted a lift in the cab, which was going her way. Even if she didn't want it, she would have been able to use the thought well. There is probably no human error that is more fear-producing (in the will/behavior conflict sense[59]) than countering any form of error with error. The result can be highly inflammable. By reacting to D's "stupidity"[60] with his own, all of the elements which are virtually certain to engender fear have been provided.

Bill should note that this is one of the few times that he had to wait for a cab. He thought he took care of it by holding the door of a cab which did come for that lady, but he was mis-guided in this belief. (Beliefs are *thoughts* and thus come under Christ-guidance, *not* control.) Actually, by giving this cab to her, he was very unkind to you. It was quite apparent that you were extremely cold, and also very late. The idea that giving her the cab would atone for his previous errors was singularly out of place, and well calculated to lead to further error. If, instead of attempting to atone on his own, he had asked for guidance, there would have been no difficulty what-ever in the cab situation. It was not necessary that anyone wait at all.

Bill's original slight to D, because of his own need to get home as he perceived it, stopped him from benefiting from the time-saving device of the miracle. He would have gotten home *much* quicker if he had taken time to use time properly.

You were still suffering from strain (see above), and got quite irritated at the girl who stood next to the door on the side which blocked its opening.[61] Her presence there made it neces-sary each time the door was opened to hold it for a much longer time than was necessary, and you were angry because this made you cold. Actually, the girl was taking care of the younger child who was standing outside, and both of them were really mentally retarded. If you will remember, the older

---

59. This is a reference to an earlier discussion of this conflict, omitted here because it is found in Chapter Two in the published text, the section entitled "Fear and Conflict," fifth paragraph. The conflict was corrected from "will/behavior" to "mind/behavior," since the will can never be in conflict. The essential point is that fear results when what we do conflicts with what we truly want. This reinforces our sense of separation, first from ourselves, and ultimately from the Holy Spirit and God.

60. It is unclear from Helen's account what D's "stupidity" was.

61. This is a reference to one of the exits from the Medical Center.

girl asked you very uncertainly about the bus, and you were well aware at the time of her extreme uncertainty. It would have been much wiser had you built up her confidence, instead of associating with her "stupidity." This reduced your own efficiency, and the only thing that saved you then was that you *did* remember, in the cab, to ask me about the notes, instead of assuming that you were necessarily to arrange to meet the next day and go over them. Bill had already become so misguided that it did not occur to him that his own will [i.e., his mind's decision-making] (which he justified by the contents of the recent notes,—a misuse of truth only seemingly on its own behalf) might be questionable. (You took poor notes yourself here, because you got mad at him on remembering this. While you did try to will right in the cab, you did not quite succeed. The error is showing up now.)

Bill thus placed himself in a condition to experience a fear rather than a love reaction. [Helen noted that she was going to write "an excellent position" instead of "a condition" but did not do so.] (You were right about the misuse of "excellent" here, and please do cross it out. You are *still* angry. An excellent position for miscreation is not a meaningful approach to the problem.) It was indeed discourteous ("indeed" is *not* necessary; it was your *own* error here; I am *not* saying this with any harsh overtones at all. I am just trying to create better learning conditions for the study periods. We want as little interference as possible, for *very* good reasons.).

Now, to go back to Bill; he *was* discourteous when he told you that *he* wanted to keep the original copy of the notes, having decided to have them Xeroxed on his *own* will, and then justifying it by a very slight misinterpretation of what *I* said about "useful for others." In fact, if he will re-read the actual quote, he will see that it *really* means "useful for *him*." *You* had interpreted it that way, and frankly this was pretty clear to Me at the time. But this sort of thing happens all the time. It should be noted, however, that the result was not only considerable and totally unnecessary planning on Bill's part, but also a failure to utilize what *was* intended for him as a help for *himself.* And before *you* get too self-satisfied, I would remind you that you do it all the time, too.

Bill acted inappropriately toward *you*, by saying that he wanted to be *sure* that the original was not lost or dirty. It is noticeable that, having already decided what *he* wanted to do, it never occurred to him that it *is* possible that *he* might lose or dirty them himself, especially as he had not entrusted them to Me. This is a form of arrogance that he would be much happier without. He should also note that this would probably not have occurred had he not been *already* literally "off the beam." Be *sure* to tell him that this pun is to reassure him that I am not angry.[62] If he does not get it, or does not like it, I *know* it is not *very* good. The reason is that *he* put Me in a position where I can really give him very little at the moment.

But I want him to know that I am *very* well aware of the exceedingly few times he now makes errors of this kind. He has come a *very* long way in this respect. It seems a shame that he should allow himself even this much discomfort from it.

I suggest to *you* that we pray[63] for him, and *I* pray for your full cooperation in this. This will correct *your* errors, and help him react better to the work on the bookcase, which may otherwise lend itself for misuse by mis-projection. There would have been no problem at all about the bookcase, and perhaps even no bookcase, if the solution of the storage problem had been left to Me. I have promised to guide you *out* of problems, and will certainly not create them for you. But this means that you do not undertake to solve them yourselves. A storage problem is hardly more difficult for Me to solve than a space problem (see comments under special principles for miracle workers).

You started well in your attempt to pray with me for Bill, but ended badly. This is because you had already made a number of earlier errors. You were wrong to be pleased with WG's criticism of T, and should not have enjoyed WG's description of J's caricaturing of her. You could have laughed *with* Bill, but *not at* T. Real courtesy *never* does this. You should know that all God's children are fully worthy of *complete* courtesy. You should *never* join with one at the *expense* of another.

When you called Bill about joining you, G & A at lunch, *you* should have waited to ask *Me*. In fact, you should not even have told A that you would call. Then you could have asked Bill *first* if *he* would want to come, and called A back. It is true that it was better that he came, but this has nothing to do with the real issue. There are ways of treating others in which *only* consistent courtesy, even in little things, is offered. This is a *very healing* habit to acquire.

---

62. The meaning of this pun is unknown to me.

63. "Pray" here, as in the Course, does not have the connotation of imploring God for a desired outcome, but rather of joining in forgiveness and love.

Bill's answer to your call was a clear statement of his own sadly conflicted state. He said, "I don't want to join you, but that's ungracious, so I'll go." Whenever *any* invitation to join others in a gracious way is offered, it should *always* be met with respect, although it need not always be accepted. However, if it is *met* ungraciously the resulting feeling may well be one of coercion. This is *always* a split-will reaction.[64]

Bill did not solve this by *acting* graciously. The lunch need not have entailed either mental or physical strain for him, and no "need to escape" should have arisen. This was a regression of the unprofitable kind. Bill will continue to experience this need from time to time, until he is willing to realize that there is nothing he needs or wants to escape from.

It is very hard to get out of the chain of miscreation which can arise out of even the simplest mis-thought. To borrow one of your own phrases, "This kind of human tragedy is far easier to avert than to undo."

You must both learn not to let this kind of chain reaction *start*. You will *not* be able to control it once it has started, because everything and everyone will be pulled into the mis-projection, and misinterpreted accordingly. *Nothing* is lovely to the unloving. This is because they are *creating* ugliness.

You, Helen, were definitely not acting right-mindedly by writing these notes right in front of Jonathan. (Note that you wrote his name as "Jonathan" this time, although previously in these same notes you referred to him as "Louis," *intentionally* using his real name. Actually, of course, it does not matter what you call him, but *note* that you *felt free* at that time to *choose* the name *you* preferred to use. This time, you were *forced* to call him "Jonathan" because you were *attacking* him when you took the notes in front of him, and are now falling back on the magical device of "protecting his name.")

Helen: I had been considering calling Bill rather ambivalently, and had gotten up to do so, but remembered to ask. The answer [from Jesus] was to call him at 8:30.

Jesus: It would be better if *he* called, but he may decide *not* to do so. If he does not, you [Helen] should try to get through, and if he has decided *not* to be there, just leave a message that it is not important. This is still a kindly gesture, and the message should be put in a gentle way. [Bill did call Helen.]

---

64. This is a reference to a conflict between what later is called the right and wrong minds.

Without going into further elaboration, and we could devote many hours to this, let's consider all the time that we had to waste today. *And* all the notes that could have been devoted to a better purpose than undoing the waste, and thus creating further waste. There *is* a better use for time, too. I would have liked to have spent some time on corrections of the past notes, as an important step before reviewing them. A major point of clarification is necessary in connection with the phrase "replacing hatred (or fear) with love."

(No, Helen, do *not* check this against the prayer that Bill very kindly typed for you on the card. That *was* a gracious offering on his part, and *you* also accepted it with grace at the time. Why should you deprive yourself of the value of the offering by referring this correction first to *him?*)

Jesus then commented on Helen's difficulty in hearing clearly:

These notes did not continue at this time, due to the obvious fact that Helen was still clearly not in her right mind. However, Bill later suggested that "correct" or "correct for" should be used instead of "replace." At the time, he was quite sure about this, and he was perfectly right. The reason why it was essential that *he* make this correction was that the word "replace" was his choice originally, and reflected a temporary misunderstanding of his own. It was, however, both courteous and necessary that he change this himself, both as a sign of his own better understanding, and of an avoidance of correction by someone else, which would have been discourteous.

The foregoing notes, probably more than any other, illustrate the very personal tutoring Helen and Bill received from Jesus. This continued for approximately one more month, the personal teaching being interspersed with the actual dictation of the Course. However, Jesus' loving attention to them never diminished. As we find throughout the Course, a firm authoritative voice was combined here with a loving gentleness, always patient and kind. One may recall Jesus' later words in the Course about taking him as our model for learning (text, pp. 71,84). While originally meant in terms of his defenseless attitude in the face of attack, taking Jesus as our model may also apply to our behavior towards each other. His gentle

265

admonitions regarding Helen's and Bill's ungraciousness and lack of courtesy speak to this same point.

On November 16, 1965, Helen took down a special message in the form of a prayer that Bill might say to Jesus:

> I [Bill] would like to pray that my will be united with Thine [Jesus'], recognizing that Thy perfect love will suffice (or correct) for my imperfect love. I pray that I may accept the Atonement with conviction, recognizing its inevitable worth, and my own divine worth as part of this identification with Thee. I pray that my fear be replaced by an active sense of Thy love, and Thy continual willingness to help me overcome the split, or divided will, which is responsible for my difficulty with this. I accept the divinity of the messages we have received, and affirm my will in both accepting and acting upon the Atonement principle.
>
> Here I am, Lord.

Jesus then extended the content of the above prayer in a message to both Helen and Bill, emphasizing again the importance of turning to him for help, and identifying with his goal rather than with the ego's.

> The major problem that both of you have is the continuing split will [i.e, mind], which naturally interferes with your true identification. To the extent that you hold onto this split, it will take longer to get through and will *markedly* interfere with your own integration efforts. Reliance has to be placed on Me, which is sufficient once you do this without distantiation or division in loyalties.[65] This will be strengthened through a continual affirmation of the goal you both want to achieve, and an awareness of its inevitability. In this way, you will both perceive and *know* your true worth, and the importance of maintaining a *complete* identification.

In an undated message, identified only as coming early in the dictation, Jesus again gave Bill words to say in prayer:

> I [Bill] have been unwilling to recognize that this quest is one of joy. Instead of reacting with anguish at times, and a feeling of frustration and futility, I will to see myself only as I

---

65. Jesus thus is urging Helen and Bill not to withdraw any further from him, nor to split their allegiance between him and their egos.

truly am. Nothing else can matter *but* this. The Kingdom is entirely filled with peace and joy, and I am an essential part of it. Therefore, I must be unwilling to recognize what is already obvious, even in my conflicted state.

I will only for God and His Kingdom. This is the only message that is meaningful, because it is my reality. All else is illusion. I will be helpful as I offer help to others. I will know myself as I recognize my only true relationship with all my brothers.

The "Special Principles for Miracle Workers" followed next, and these are now found in Chapter Two in the text. These were dictated on November 20. What is now Chapter Three began on November 22. I might mention that for a while Helen *and* Bill consistently misspelled "crucifixion" as "crucifiction," or variants thereof.

On November 24, Helen had "a sudden flash of illumination" and very much wanted to offer a prayer for Bill, which she did as follows: "Lord Jesus, help me see Bill as he really is, and thus release both him and me." She later thought: "Everytime there is anything unlovable that crosses one's mind...you should immediately recognize that you do not want to hurt your brother." Jesus then commented:

> You had a lot of trouble afterwards with the words (which are essentially irrelevant) partly because you were dissatisfied with yourself at the time, but also because you *are* confused about the difference between perception and cognition. You will note that we have said very little about cognition [later corrected to "knowledge"] as yet. (Aside: One of the exceptions is in the correction formula for fear, which begins with *know* first.) The reason is because you must get your perceptions straightened out before you can *know* anything.

This again underscores the basic process of healing that *A Course in Miracles* sets forth: we are not to focus on the truth (i.e., knowledge), but rather on the undoing of illusions by correcting our misthoughts or misperceptions. That was why, for example, Jesus spent so much time in helping Helen and Bill understand their mistakes. Once understood for what they were, these errors could then be corrected by Jesus as Helen and Bill would turn to him for help.

The notes for Chapter Three continue, and then Jesus inter-jects the following regarding Bill and Helen:

> Perception, miracles, and doing are closely related. Knowledge is a result of Revelation, and induces only thought.[66] Perception involves the body even in its most spiritualized form. Knowledge comes from the altar within, and is timeless because it is certain. To perceive the truth is not the same as *knowing* it. This is why Bill is having so much trouble in what he calls "integrating" the notes. His tentative perception is too uncertain for knowledge, because knowledge is *sure*. Your [Helen] perception is so variable that you swing from sudden but real knowledge to complete cognitive disorganization. This is why Bill is more prone to irritation, while you are more vulnerable to rage. He is consistently *below* his potential, while you achieve it at times and then swing very wide of the mark.
>
> Actually, these differences do not matter. But I thought you might be glad to learn that you are much better off with *different* perceptual problems than you would be if you suffered from similar ones. This enables each of you to *recognize* (and this is the right word here) that the misperceptions of the other are unnecessary. It is because you do not *know* what to do about it that Bill reacts to yours with irritation, and you respond to his with fury.

We observe again Jesus' emphasis on the great learning potential found in Helen and Bill's relationship.

Regarding Bill's punning ability, Jesus had these loving words to say:

> What man perceives as its [knowledge] attack is his own recognition of the fact that it can always be *remembered*, because it has never been destroyed. This is not a literal remembering as much as a real re-membering. (That is largely for Bill. I wish he would decide to use that talent of his constructively. He has no idea of how powerful it could be. Actually, it does come from the unconscious, and is really a distorted form of miraculous perception which he has reduced to word twisting. Although this can be quite funny, it is still a real waste. Maybe he'd care to let me control it, and still use it humorously himself. He doesn't have to decide it is one *or* the other.)

---

66. This was later changed to "experience," since knowledge *is* thought.

Bill's Class

Next followed an extensive discussion, primarily aimed at Bill, regarding a class in abnormal psychology he was scheduled to teach at the undergraduate campus of Columbia University. Bill always had a morbid fear of public speaking (although he was indeed an excellent speaker), and he was panic-stricken at the thought of this upcoming class. Jesus attempted to help him with this problem, and many of these notes were later kept in the text itself (primarily in Chapter Four). Bill subsequently was not able to teach the course himself, but Helen accompanied him and they taught together. Much of this extensive dictation is included here in order to show, as in the previous notes, Jesus' persistent and loving teaching in the early weeks of the scribing. This part of the dictation, incidentally, appears to have been taken down without shorthand notes, dictated by Helen directly to Bill; at least the notes do not survive, if there were any. This was written on December 7, 1965, and began with a discussion of Bill's relationship with his parents.

> As you [Helen] have so often said, no one has adopted *all* of his parents' attitudes as his own. In every case, there has been a long process of choice, in which the individual has escaped from those he himself vetoed, while retaining those he voted *for*. Bill has not retained his parents' political beliefs, in spite of the particular kind of newspapers that constituted their own reading matter in this area. The reason why he could do this was because he believed he was free in this area.
>
> There must be some acute problem *of his own* that would make him so eager to accept their misperception of his own worth. This tendency can *always* be regarded as punitive. It cannot be justified by the inequality of the strengths of parents and children. This is never more than temporary, and is largely a matter of maturational and thus physical difference. It does not last unless it is held onto.

This is an extremely important point: the past is not to be seen as determining present problems. This is a crucial theme in the Course's later teachings aimed at freeing us from the chains of the past. Thus the mind's power to choose in the present is given great emphasis. As indicated in the first sentence, this was a principle used by Helen in her therapy to aid patients in understanding that they need not be prisoners of their past. Since they have been the ones who selectively (though unconsciously) chose which of their parents' attitudes to be bound by, they are the ones who can now choose again.

The notion of choosing in the present to be bound by the past is elaborated on now by Jesus in the context of Bill's relationship with his father.

> When Bill's father came to his new office and "destroyed" it, it is quite apparent that Bill *must* have been willing to let it be destroyed. The many times that he has commented on this event alone would suggest the extreme importance of this misperception in his own distorted thinking. Why should anyone accord an obvious misperception so much power? There cannot be any real justification for it, because even Bill himself recognized the real problem by saying "How could he do this to me?" The answer is *he* didn't.

> Bill has a very serious question to ask himself in this connection. We said before that the purpose of the Resurrection was to "demonstrate that no amount of misperception has any influence at all on a Son of God."

This statement goes to the heart of the Course's teachings on forgiveness; namely, that no one has the power to take away the peace of God from us, regardless of what they do or think. Later Jesus would teach, regarding his crucifixion: "The Prince of Peace was born to re-establish the condition of love by teaching that communication remains unbroken even if the body is destroyed..." (text, p. 305).

The message for Bill continues:

> This demonstration *exonerates* those who misperceive, by establishing beyond doubt that they have *not* hurt anyone. Bill's question, which he must ask himself very honestly, is whether he is willing to demonstrate that his parents have *not* hurt him. Unless he is willing to do this, he has *not* forgiven them.

> The essential goal of therapy is the same as that of knowledge. No one can survive independently as long as he is willing to see himself through the eyes of others. This will always put him in a position where he *must* see himself in different lights. Parents do not create the image of their

children,[67] though they may perceive images which they do create. However, as we have already said, you are not an image. If you *side with* image-makers, you are merely being idolatrous.

Bill has no justification whatever for perpetuating *any* image of himself at all. He is *not* an image. Whatever is true of him is wholly benign. It is essential that he *know* this about himself, but he cannot know it while he chooses to interpret himself as vulnerable enough to *be* hurt. This is a peculiar kind of arrogance, whose narcissistic component is perfectly obvious. It endows the perceiver with sufficient unreal strength to make him over, and then acknowledges the perceiver's miscreation. There are times when this strange lack of real courtesy appears to be a form of humility. Actually, it is never more than simple spite.

What is meant here is that the ego first arrogantly believes it can make over what God created, substituting its image for the Self, and then "humbly" denigrates the shabby self it has made, believing it to be real.

Jesus now continues, addressing Bill directly through Helen:

Bill, your parents did misperceive you in many ways, but their ability to perceive was quite warped, and their misperceptions stood in the way of their own knowledge. There is no reason why it should stand in the way of yours. It is still true that you believe they *did* something to you. This belief is extremely dangerous to your perception, and wholly destructive of your knowledge. This is not only true of your attitudes toward your parents, but also of your misuse of your friends. You still think that you *must* respond to their errors *as if* they were true. By reacting self-destructively, you are *giving* them approval for their misperceptions.

In other words, in giving the attack thoughts of others power over our minds by virtue of our being hurt by them, we demonstrate that their perceptions were correct. We could not *feel* vulnerable and hurt unless we first believed that our sins deserved such punishment. Thus we are giving approval to the

---

67. In other words, we alone are the determiners of our self-image; others may reinforce it, but the responsibility nonetheless rests only with us.

attacking perceptions of others. This inevitably reinforces their own guilt over harboring such thoughts in the first place. The lesson continues:

> No one has the right to change himself according to different circumstances.[68] Only his actions are capable of appropriate variation. His belief in himself is a constant, unless it rests on perceptual acuity rather than knowledge of what he is.
>
> It is your *duty* to establish beyond doubt that you are totally unwilling to side with (identify with) anyone's misperceptions of you, including your own.

This important discussion about Bill and his parents is obviously applicable to all people. Its implications for psychotherapy, especially those forms that focus on the past, are equally important. Once again, problems are *never* caused by events of the past, but rather by a decision made in the *present* to hold on to the past. This is not to say that people's bodies may not hurt other bodies; as Jesus would say later in the Course: "Are thoughts, then, dangerous? To bodies, yes!" (text, p. 433). The point rather is that our true nature as Christ is totally invulnerable to the seeming attacks of others. Teaching us this of course was the purpose of Jesus' crucifixion (*see* text, pp. 84-88), as we indicated above. This principle then becomes the foundation for the Course's understanding of forgiveness; namely, that we forgive each other for what has *not* been done to us, not for what has. And this is the teaching implicit in Jesus' message to Bill here.

Jesus now shifts the focus to Bill's class, using it as another example to illustrate the meaning of forgiveness, helping him (and Helen too) to understand that the true purpose of all situations and relationships is to teach us the fundamental equality of *all* members of the Sonship. Differences certainly do exist in the world of form between parents and children, teachers and pupils, and we are not asked to disregard these.

---

68. The use of the word "right" can be confusing here. What is meant is that it is not possible to have our self-image be changed because of external circumstances, such as parental approval or disapproval. We are free to believe that it can, but that does not make it so in reality.

However, at the same time we are asked not to give these differences power to determine our self-worth or to affect our self-image.

> If you become concerned with totally irrelevant factors, such as the physical condition of a classroom, the number of students, the hour of the course, and the many elements which you may choose to select for emphasis as a basis for misperception, you have lost the knowledge of what *any* interpersonal relationship is for. It is *not* true that the difference between pupil and teacher is lasting. They meet *in order* to abolish the difference. At the beginning, since we are still in time, they come together on the basis of inequality of ability and experience. The aim of the teacher is to give them more of what is temporarily his. This process has all of the miracle conditions we referred to at the beginning. The teacher (or miracle worker) gives more to those who have less, bringing them closer to equality with him, at the same time gaining for himself.
>
> The confusion here is only because they do not gain the same things, because they do not *need* the same things. If they did, their respective, though temporary roles would not be conducive to mutual profit. Freedom from fear can be achieved by *both* teacher and pupil *only* if they do not compare either their needs or their positions in regard to each other in terms of higher and lower.

This last statement points out that the *form*—the differences between teacher and pupil—should not be allowed to obscure the underlying *content*—the unity among all the children of God.

> Presumably, children must learn from parents.[69] What parents learn from children is merely of a different order. Ultimately, there is no difference in order, but this involves only knowledge. Neither parents nor children can be said to *have* knowledge, or their relationships would not exist *as if* they were on different levels. The same is true of the teacher and the pupil. Children have an authority problem *only* if they believe that their image is influenced *by* the authority. This is an act of will on their part, because they are electing to misperceive the authority and *give* him this power.

---

69. In our world of illusion, this of course is true.

A *teacher* with an authority problem is merely a pupil who refuses to teach others. He wants to maintain *himself* in a position where he can be misused and misperceived. This makes him resentful of teaching, because of what he insists it has done to him.

The *only* way out of this particular aspect of the desert is still to leave. The way this is left is to release *everyone* involved, by *absolutely refusing* to engage in any form of honoring error. Neither teacher nor pupil is imprisoned by learning unless he uses it as an attack. If he does this, he will be imprisoned whether he actually teaches or learns, or refuses to engage in the process at all.

The role of a teacher, properly conceived, is one of leading himself and others out of the desert. The value of this role can hardly be underestimated, if only because it was one to which I very gladly dedicated My own life. I have repeatedly asked *My* pupils to follow Me. This means that, to be effective teachers, they *must* interpret teaching as I do. I have made *every* effort to teach you *entirely* without fear. If you do not listen, you will be unable to avoid the *very* obvious error of perceiving teaching as a threat.

It is hardly necessary to say that teaching is a process whose purpose is to produce learning. The ultimate purpose of *all* learning is to abolish fear. This is necessary so that knowledge can happen. The role of the teacher is *not* the role of God. This confusion is all too frequently made, by parents, teachers, therapists, and the clergy. It is a real misunderstanding of both God and His miracles. Any teacher who believes that teaching is fearful *cannot* learn because he is paralyzed. He also cannot really teach.

Bill was quite right in maintaining that this course is a prerequisite for his. However, he was really saying much more than that. The purpose of this course *is* to prepare you for knowledge. So is the only real purpose of *any* legitimate course. All that is required of you as a teacher is to follow Me.

Whenever anyone decides that he can function only in *some* roles but not in others, he cannot *but* be attempting to make a compromise which will not work. If Bill is under the misbelief that he is coping with the fear problem by functioning as an administrator and as a teacher of interns, but *not* as a teacher of students, he is merely deceiving himself. He owes himself greater respect. There is nothing as tragic as the attempt to deceive one's self, because it implies that you perceive yourself as so unworthy that deception is more fitting for you than truth. Either you can function in all of the roles you have properly undertaken to fill, or you cannot function effectively in any of them. This *is* an all or none decision. You *cannot* make inappropriate level distinctions within this choice. You are either capable or not. This does not mean that you can *do* everything, but it *does* mean that you are either totally miracle-minded or not. This decision is open to *no* compromise whatsoever. When Bill says that he cannot teach, he is making the same mistake that we spoke of before, when he acted as if universal laws [of love, happiness, peace] applied to everyone except him. This is not only arrogant, but patently untrue. Universal laws *must* apply to him, unless he does not exist. We will not bother to argue about this.

Descartes engaged in a very interesting teaching procedure, and one from which he himself learned a great deal. He began with doubting the existence of everything, except himself. He insisted that his own existence was not open to doubt, and rebuilt his entire thought system on the one premise "I think, therefore I am." It is noteworthy that he arrived at accepting the entire system he originally doubted, solely on the basis of this *one* piece of knowledge. There was, however, a distinct shift in his own perception. He no longer really questioned the reality of what he perceived, because he *knew* he was there.

We mentioned before that Bill is not too sure of this, and that is why we suggested that he concentrate on "Lord, here I am." A teacher is unlikely to be effective unless he begins with *being there*. Bill, this is not really open to question. You will lose all your fear of teaching and relating in any form once you know who you are. There is no point whatever in remaining in the prison of believing that this is up to you. You do *not* exist in different lights. It is this belief which has confused you about your own reality. Why would you want to remain so obscure to yourself?

This important message for Bill (though obviously for everyone) emphasizes the all-or-nothing nature of the Course's teachings, whose principles apply to *all* people in *all* situations, without exception. It is this all-inclusive nature of forgiveness that makes it so threatening a principle to the ego thought system that always attempts to separate out and make exceptions.

The dictation then continued (though still apparently without shorthand notes) with the material on the Last

Judgment and the authority problem currently found near the end of Chapter Three. And then this personal note:

> It is *essential* that the whole authority problem be voluntarily dismissed once and for all before his [Bill's] course. Neither of you understands how important this is for your sanity. You are both quite insane on this point. (This is not a judgment; it is merely a fact. No, Helen, you *should* use the word "fact" here. This is just as much a fact as God is. A fact is literally a "making" or a starting point. You *do* start from this point, and all your thinking is inverted because of it.)

The flow of dictation picked up again with the section that currently concludes Chapter Four. What is now at the end of the first paragraph of this section was originally written like this:

> *Nothing* made by a Child of God is without power. It is absolutely essential that you realize this, because otherwise you will not understand why you have so much trouble with this course, and will be unable to escape from the prisons you have created for yourselves. (This *was* an error. You should have said "made.")

This last comment reflects the important distinction Jesus establishes in the Course between the words "make" and "create": the ego makes, projecting its own illusions, while spirit—our true reality—can only create, extending the truth that is itself.

A little bit later, Jesus commented on Helen's and Bill's authority problem.

> You and Bill still believe you are images of your own creation. You are split with your own Souls [i.e., minds] on this point, and there is *no* resolution, because you believe the one thing that is literally *inconceivable.* That is why you *cannot* create, and are afraid to make or produce. You, Helen, are *constantly* arguing about the authorship of this course. This is *not* humility; it is a *real* authority problem.... You, Bill, really believe that by teaching you are assuming a dominant or father role, and that the "father figure" will kill you. This is not humility either.

Returning to Bill's class at Columbia, Jesus dictated the following lengthy passage, later incorporated into Chapter Three, and then Chapter Four in the discussion on teaching and learning. The message explains for Bill what is behind his fears of teaching or professing, and teaches him that he is free to make another choice: changing from identifying with his ego's thought system of separation and loss. Therefore, the purpose of Bill's class, which Jesus emphasizes was "very carefully chosen" for him and is an "assignment,"[70] was to provide an opportunity for him to change his mind and accept his true function of becoming what the teacher's manual would later call a "teacher of God," a teacher of forgiveness. In the passages that follow, I have omitted the dictated material that was substantially unchanged and appears as is in the published Course.

> Every symptom which the ego has made involves a contradiction in terms. This is because the mind is split between the ego and the Soul, so that *whatever* the ego makes is incomplete and contradictory. Consider what a "speechless professor" means as a concept. It literally means a "nonprofessing professor," or a "nonspeaking speaker." Untenable positions such as this are the result of the authority problem, which, because it accepts the one inconceivable thought as its premise, can only produce ideas which are inconceivable. Bill may claim (and has certainly done so in the past) that the *professorship* was thrust upon him. This is not true. He wanted it very much, and also worked hard to get it. He would not have had to work so hard either, if he had not misunderstood it.[71]
>
> The term "profess" is used quite frequently in the Bible, but in a somewhat different context. To profess is to identify with an idea and offer the idea to others to be *their* own. The idea does *not* lessen; it becomes *stronger*. The teacher clarifies his own ideas and strengthens them *by* teaching them. Teacher and pupil, therapist and patient, are all alike in the learning process. They are in the *same* order of learning, and unless they *share* their lessons they will lack conviction. If a

---

70. In reality, of course, Jesus (or the Holy Spirit) does not choose for us or make assignments. Our minds do the choosing and assigning, either with the ego or the Holy Spirit as our guide. However, since our experience is often that the Holy Spirit is *outside* us, Jesus frequently spoke like that to Helen and Bill, and to all of us in the Course.

71. *See above,* page 87, for Bill's quite different interpretation of the circumstances of his acquiring his professorship.

salesman must believe in the product he sells, how much more must a teacher believe in the ideas which he professes. But he needs another condition; he must also believe in the students to whom he offers his ideas.

Bill could not be afraid to teach unless he still believes that interaction means loss, and that learning means separation. He stands guard over his own ideas, because he wants to protect his thought-system as it is, and learning *means* change. Change is always fearful to the separated, because they cannot conceive of it as a change toward *healing* the separation. They *always* perceive it as a change for further separation, because separation *was* their first experience of change.

Bill, your whole fear of teaching is nothing but an example of your own intense separation anxiety, which you have handled with the usual series of mixed defenses in the combined pattern of attack on truth and defense of error, which characterizes *all* ego-thinking. You insist that if you allow no change to enter into your *ego*, your *Soul* will find peace. This profound confusion is possible only if one maintains that the *same* thought-system can stand on two foundations....

My lesson was like yours, and because I learned it I can teach it. I never attack your egos (in spite of Helen's strange beliefs to the contrary), but I *do* try to teach them how their thought-systems have arisen. When I remind you of your *true* Creation, your egos cannot *but* respond with fear.

Bill, teaching and learning are your greatest strengths now, because you *must* change your mind and help others change theirs. It is pointless to refuse to tolerate change or changing because you believe that you can demonstrate by doing so that the Separation never occurred. The dreamer who doubts the reality of his dream while he is still dreaming is not really healing the level-split....

All separation anxiety is a symptom of a continuing will to remain separated. This cannot be repeated too often because you have *not* learned it. Bill, you are afraid to teach *only* because you are afraid of the impression your image of yourself will make *on other images*. You believe that their *approval* of your image will exalt it, but also that your separation anxiety will be increased. You also believe that their *disapproval* of it will lessen the separation anxiety, but at the cost of depression....

Bill, if you will to be a devoted teacher rather than an ego-centric one, you will not be afraid. The teaching situation *is* fearful if it is misused as an ego involvement. If you become afraid, it is *because* you are using it this way. But the devoted teacher perceives the situation *as it is* and *not* as *he* wills it. He does not see it as dangerous because *he* is not exploiting it....

I need devoted teachers [i.e., Bill] as much as I need devoted priestesses [i.e., Helen]. They both heal the mind, and that is always My own aim. The Soul [i.e., spirit][72] is far beyond the need of your protection *or* Mine. The Biblical quotation should read "In this world you need *not* have tribulation *because* I have overcome the world." *That* is why you should "be of good cheer."

Bill's course was very carefully chosen, because "abnormal psychology" *is* ego psychology. This is precisely the kind of content which should never be taught *from* the ego whose abnormality should be lessened by teaching, not increased. You [Bill] are particularly well suited to perceive this difference, and can therefore teach this course as it should be taught. Most teachers have an unfortunate tendency to teach the *course* abnormally, and many of the students are apt to suffer considerable perceptual distortion because of their own authority problems.

In using the phrase "to teach the course abnormally," Jesus is referring to teachers making the ego's error real: teaching the abnormal psychology of separation through seeing themselves as separate from their students. This then reinforces the students' own beliefs in the reality of their separation from each other, their professors, and from God. Jesus is thus asking Bill to teach his students differently, so that he may learn a different lesson for himself.

Your teaching assignment (and I assure you it *is* an assignment) will be to present perceptual distortions without either engaging in them yourself, or encouraging your students to do so. This interpretation of your role and theirs is too charitable to induce fear. If you adhere to this role, you will both engender and experience hope, and you will inspire rather than dispirit the future teachers and therapists I am entrusting to you. I promise to attend Myself, and you should at least credit Me with some dependability in keeping My own promises. I

---

72. Helen was later told to change the word "soul" to spirit, to avoid any theological confusion about its meaning (*see* manual, p. 75).

never make them lightly, because I know the need My brothers have for trust.

There seemed to be a pause in the dictation at this point, which ended the discussion of Bill's class.

More Specific Teachings

We are now in a new section (text, p. 51), and Jesus begins by commenting on a question asked by Bill, the same question asked at one time or another by almost every student of *A Course in Miracles.*

Bill has asked lately how the mind could ever have made the ego. This is a perfectly reasonable question; in fact, the best question either of you could ask. There is no point in giving an historical answer, because the past does not matter in human terms,[73] and history would not exist if the same errors were not being repeated in the present. Bill has often told you [Helen] that your thinking is too abstract at times, and he is right. Abstraction *does* apply to knowledge, because knowledge is completely impersonal, and examples are irrelevant to its understanding. Perception, however, is always specific, and therefore quite concrete....

Your own [Helen] present state is the best concrete example Bill could have of how the mind could have made the ego. You *do* have real knowledge at times, but when you throw it away it is as if you never had it. This willfullness is so apparent that Bill need only perceive it to see that it *does* happen. If it can occur that way in the present, why should he be surprised that it occurred that way in the past? All psychology rests on the principle of continuity of behavior. Surprise is a reasonable response to the unfamiliar, but hardly to something that has occurred with such persistence.[74]

Jesus then shifts to comparing and contrasting Helen and Bill again. This is a typical discussion during this phase of the scribing, where Jesus presents Helen and Bill as examples of the dynamics of the ego thought system he is teaching them.

---

73. In other words, the past only *seems* to have an effect on people's lives.

74. For further discussion of this issue, with an answer given on a different level, *see* manual, pp. 73,77.

He also makes reference to Helen's eyesight, a discussion which will become even more meaningful for us in Part III, when I discuss how Helen's visual problems symbolize her defense against Jesus and his message in the Course.

> An extreme example is a good teaching aid, not because it is typical, but because it is clear. The more complex the material, the clearer the examples should be for teaching purposes. (Bill, remember that for your own course, and do not avoid the dramatic. It holds the student's interest precisely because it is so apparent that it *can* be readily perceived.) But, as we have said before, all teaching devices in the hands of good teachers are aimed at rendering themselves unnecessary. I would therefore like to use your [Helen's] present state as an example of how the mind can work, provided you both fully recognize that it need not work that way. I *never* forget this Myself, and a good teacher shares his own ideas, in which he himself believes. Otherwise, he cannot really "profess" them, as we used the term before.

> With full recognition of its transitory nature, (a recognition which I hope you both share), Helen offers a very good teaching example of alternations between Soul [spirit] and ego, with concomitant variations between peace and frenzy. In answer to Bill's question, it is perfectly apparent that when she is ego-dominated, she *does not know* her Soul. Her abstract ability, which is perfectly genuine and does stem from knowledge, cannot help her because she has turned to the concrete which she cannot handle abstractly. Being incapable of appropriate concreteness perceptually, because her ego is not her natural home, she suffers from its intrusions, but *not* from complete lack of knowledge.

> The result is a kind of "double vision," which would have produced an actual dyplopia,[75] if she had not settled for nearsightedness. This was an attempt to see the concrete more clearly through the ego's eyes, without the "interference" of the longer range. Her virtual lack of astigmatism[76] is due to her real efforts at objectivity and fairness. She has not attained them, or she would not be nearsighted. But she *has* tried to be fair with what she permitted herself to see....

This last discussion relates Helen's physical vision to her inner

---

75. An eye disorder wherein objects are seen twice.

76. An eye disorder wherein objects are seen indistinctly.

vision, wherein the interferences her mind introduced are reflected by her visual interferences. Her nearsightedness thus represents a compromise attempt to see things clearly and fairly, yet without the benefit of the "long-range" or spiritual perspective that would come from her inner wisdom. Jesus then continues to develop the analogy between inner and outer perception as he contrasts Helen's and Bill's vision.

> Belief that there *is* another way is the loftiest idea of which ego-thinking is capable. This is because it contains a hint of recognition that the ego is *not* the Self. Helen always had this idea, but it merely confused her. Bill, you were more capable of a long-range view, and that is why your eyesight is good. But you were willing to see because you utilized judgment against what you saw. This gave you clearer perception than Helen's, but cut off the cognitive level [i.e., the level of knowledge or God] more deeply. That is why you believe that you never had knowledge. Repression *has* been a stronger mechanism in your own ego defense, and that is why you find her shifts so hard to tolerate. Willfulness is more characteristic of her, and that is why she has less sense than you do.
>
> It is extremely fortunate, temporarily, that the particular strengths you will both ultimately develop and use are precisely those which the other must supply now. You [Bill] who will be the strength of God, are quite weak, and you [Helen] who will be God's help, are clearly in need of help yourself. What better plan could have been devised to prevent the intrusion of the ego's arrogance on the outcome?

Once again, Jesus emphasizes the complementarity of Helen's and Bill's egos, which ideally lends itself to the healing of their minds when they join together, a point with which he now continues:

> Undermining the foundation of an ego's thought-system *must* be perceived as painful, even though this is anything but true. Babies scream in rage if you take away a knife or a scissors, even though they may well harm themselves if you do not. The speed-up has placed you both in the same position.
>
> You are *not* by any means prepared, and in this sense you *are* babies. You have no sense of real self-preservation and are very likely to decide that you need precisely what would hurt you most. Whether you know it now or not, however, you both *have* willed to cooperate in a concerted and very commendable

effort to become both harm*less* and help*ful*, two attributes which *must* go together. Your attitudes, even toward this, are necessarily conflicted, because *all* attitudes are ego-based.

This will not last. Be patient a while, and remember what we said once before: The outcome is as certain as God!

After a considerable amount of material, most of which is in the published Course, Jesus continued:

You, Helen, have been more honest than Bill in really trying to see whom your ego has hurt, and also in trying to change your mind about them.

Helen here interrupted to express doubt whether this last statement was scribally accurate, as it was written at a time when she was very angry. Jesus then continued:

Jesus: I am not unmindful of your efforts, but you still have much too much energy invested in your ego. *This need not be.* Watch your minds for the temptations of the ego, and do not be deceived by it. *Know* it offers you nothing.

You, Bill, have not made consistent efforts to change your mind except through applying old habit patterns to new ideas. But you have learned, and learned it better than Helen, that your mind gains control over *itself* when you direct it genuinely toward perceiving someone *else* truly.

Helen again expressed doubts about her scribal accuracy. Her concern here, as well as in the above paragraph, that her anger was interfering with her "scribal accuracy" reflects Helen's conscious attempts to be ego-free in her scribing. However, in view of Jesus' similar remarks elsewhere in the dictation regarding Bill's greater tendency to deny than Helen, it is unlikely that her anger here had contaminated her hearing. These last two paragraphs do not seem unkind in their tone, and therefore would seem to be yet another example of how Helen was able to set aside her ego feelings in the service of being faithful to her "assignment" to scribe the Course.

Jesus' remarks to Bill continue:

Your lack of vitality is due to your former marked effort at solving your needless depression and anxiety through disinterest. Because your ego *was* protected by this unfortunate negative attribute, you are afraid to abandon it.

A little further on, Jesus once again encourages Helen and Bill:

> I was not mistaken. Your minds *will* elect to join with Mine, and together we are invincible. You two will yet come together in My name and your sanity will be restored.

As with other similar comments by Jesus, this last one must be understood within the context of the mind's existence outside time and space. There, the joining of Helen and Bill with Jesus has *already* occurred, and merely waits its acceptance. The reader may recall Helen's discussion with Bill in her letter from the previous summer, where she compared the seeming delay in Bill's healing with the time it takes for a star's light to be recognized on earth.

In the context of the ego's obliteration of the mind's attempt to ask meaningful questions (text, p. 60), Jesus makes reference now to Helen's dream "The Recorder," presented above in Chapter 3. He continues here to contrast Helen and Bill, specifically in terms of Helen's chaotic attempts to defend against learning the Course, whereas Bill demonstrates a more consistent willingness. Yet both are nonetheless weak in their overall desire to identify with the goal of learning. The students' motivation to learn remains the primary ingredient for effective teaching, and Helen's and Bill's forgiveness of themselves and of each other remained the primary means of undoing the blocks to their learning.

> If you remember your dream about the recorder, this was remarkably accurate in some ways because it came partly from ego-repressed knowledge; the real problem was correctly stated as "What is the question?", because as you very well knew, the answer *could* be found if the question were recognized. If you remember, there were a number of solutions you attempted, all ego-based, not because you thought they would really work, but because the question *itself* was obscure.
>
> When the Bible says "Seek and ye shall find," it does *not* mean that you should seek blindly and desperately for something you wouldn't recognize. Meaningful seeking is consciously undertaken, consciously organized, and consciously directed. Bill's chief contribution to your joint venture is his insistence that the goal be formulated clearly, and *kept in mind*.

You, Helen, are not good at doing this. You still search for many goals simultaneously, and this goal confusion, given a very strong will, *must* produce chaotic behavior. Bill's behavior is not chaotic, because he is not so much goal-divided as not goal-*oriented*. Where Helen has overinvested in many goals, Bill has underinvested in *all* goals. He has the advantage of *potentially* greater freedom from distractability, but he does not always care enough to use it. Helen has the advantage of exerting great effort, but she keeps losing sight of the goal.

Bill has very intelligently suggested that you both should set yourself the goal of really studying for this course. There can be no doubt of the wisdom of this decision, for any student who wants to pass it. But, knowing your individual weaknesses as learners and being a teacher with some experience, I must remind you that learning and wanting to learn are inseparable....

When I told Bill to concentrate on the phrase "Here I am, Lord," I did not mean "in this world" by "here." I wanted him to think of himself as a separate consciousness [i.e., being], capable of direct communication with the Creator of that consciousness. He, too, *must* begin to think of himself as a very powerful "receiving and sending channel," a description I once gave you very clearly, though symbolically. Remember that *he* understood it before you did, because you are more dissociative [i.e., split off] and less repressed.

Your great debt to each other is something you should never forget. It is exactly the same debt that you owe to Me.

A little bit later in the dictation, Jesus reinforces his previous words of encouragement to Helen and Bill, reminding them of their important roles, not to mention his own. The student of *A Course in Miracles* can see here the original personal nature of this important passage that is found in the printed text near the end of Chapter Four. As was previously explained, Jesus' statements of trust in "choosing" Helen and Bill should be understood as his speaking to them in a language they could accept and understand. I return to this point in Chapter 17.

My trust in you is greater than yours in Me at the moment, but it will not always be that way. Your mission is very simple. You have been chosen to live so as to demonstrate that *you* are *not* an ego. I repeat that I do not choose God's channels wrongly. The Holy One shares My trust and always approves My Atonement decisions, because My will is never out of accord with His.

I have told you several times that I am in charge of the whole Atonement. This is *only* because I completed My part in it as a man, and can now complete it through other men. My chosen receiving and sending channels [Helen and Bill] cannot fail, because I will lend them *My* strength as long as theirs is wanting. I will go with you to the Holy One, and through *My* perception *He* can bridge the little gap. Your gratitude to each *other* is the only gift I want. I will bring it to God for you, knowing that to know your brother is to know God.

Shortly afterwards, Jesus returned to specifically addressing Helen and Bill, and once again compared and contrasted their ego's defensive systems. Near the end of this passage Jesus returns to his attempts at correcting Bill's marked tendency to withdraw from others (distantiation), a similar theme to the one found in his discussion of Bill's class at Columbia.

Because you are all the Kingdom of God, I can lead you back to your own creations, which you do not yet know. God has kept them very safe in *His* knowing while your attention has wandered. Bill gave you [Helen] a very important idea when he told you that what has been dissociated *is still there.*

In other words, the Love of God which has been split off has not disappeared from the mind; it merely has been hidden by the ego's fear of it. Earlier, Jesus had told Helen these encouraging words:

You have not usurped the power of God, but you have *lost* it. Fortunately, to lose something does not mean that it is gone. It merely means that you do not remember where it is. Its existence does not depend on your ability to identify it, or even to place it (text, pp. 43f).

Jesus continues by thanking Bill for reminding Helen of that helpful idea:

I am grateful to him for that, and I hope he will not decide that it is true only for you. Even though dissociation is much more apparent in you, and repression is much more evident in him, each of you utilizes both.

Wisdom always dictates that a therapist work through *weaker* defenses first. That is why I suggested to Bill that he persuade you to deal with *repression* first. We have only just about reached the point where dissociation means much to you, because it is so important to your misbeliefs. Bill might do well—and you could help him here—to concentrate more on *his* dissociative tendencies and not try to deal with repression yet. I hinted at this when I remarked on his habit of disengaging himself, and when I spoke to him about distantiation and detachment. These are all forms of dissociation, and these weaker forms were always more evident in him than in you. That is because dissociation was so extreme in your case that you did not have to hide it because you were not aware that it was there. Bill, on the other hand, *does* dissociate more than he thinks, and that is why he cannot listen. He does not need to go through the same course in repression that you did, because he will give up his major misdefense *after* he has rid himself of the lesser ones.

Do not disturb yourself about repression, Bill, but *do* train yourself to be alert to any tendency to withdraw from your brothers. Withdrawal is frightening, and you do not recognize all the forms it takes in you. Helen is right that she will experience things that will cut across all her perceptions because of their stunning knowledge. You were right that this will occur when she learns to recognize what she *already* knows and has dissociated.

You, Bill, will learn somewhat differently, because you are afraid of all complete involvements, and believe that they lessen *you*. You have learned to be so much more clear-sighted about this that you should be ready to oppose it in yourself *relatively* easily. As you come closer to a brother, you *do* approach me, and as you withdraw from him I become distant to you.

Your giant step forward was to *insist* on a collaborative venture. This does not go against the true spirit of meditation at all. It is inherent *in* it. Meditation is a collaborative venture with God. It *cannot* be undertaken successfully by those who disengage themselves from the Sonship, because [by doing so] they are disengaging themselves from Me.

Around this time Helen took down a long message for her and Bill that was never typed. Once again we find an illustration of the personal nature of Helen's relationship with Jesus, as well as the specific ways he was attempting to help her and Bill. The major focus of this message was Jesus' urging Helen and Bill to consult with him more in their daily decisions. To make his point, he provides them with specific examples of how they failed to ask his help, and therefore how the unhappy consequences were inevitable. The full message now follows:

> The reason for the fear reaction is quite apparent. You have not yet been able to *suspend* judgment, and have merely succeeded in weakening your *control* over it. Since you have an unfortunate tendency to be self-punishing, you believe that control of judgment is a self-*preserving* function, and therefore require it as a *necessary* defense of your self. Weakening this defense delivery is thus perceived as dangerous vulnerability, which frightens you.

This rather sophisticated explanation refers to Helen's attempts to control her judgments *herself* ("weakening" the control), rather than allowing Jesus to control them for her (to "suspend" judgment). In this manner, Helen's ego "allows" her to appear to do away with her judgments by controlling them externally, all the while the judgmental thoughts remain hidden in her mind, thus preserving her ego-self. Without judgment as a defense, the ego's inherent vulnerability becomes more available, and fear is exacerbated. Jesus' message continues:

> Bill was right that you should ask before attempting it again.[77] It would be very unwise to try it before *we can do it together*, as I told you last night. I assure you I will be vigilant in identifying the right time, and as I told you very clearly next time we will do it *together*. I did *not* tell you when that will be because I do not know. *You* will tell Me that, but may not recognize that you have done so. That is why you need Me to relay your own message back to you. When you are *both* ready, it will not be fearful.
>
> In answer to Bill's question as to why he has so much difficulty in communication, you were right in what you said in the cab and Bill could not listen. However, he seems to be able to listen quite carefully to these notes. Ask him please to listen *very* carefully to these.

---

77. I do not know the meaning of this reference.

If you ask Me for guidance, you *have* signified your willingness to give over your own control, at least to some extent. Your frequent failure to ask at all indicates that at such times you are not willing to go even that far. But when you at least ask, you are acting on a cooperative *thought*, even though you may not lack ambivalence. You are therefore entitled to a specific answer, but unless you follow it without judging it, you will become defensive about the next steps that you will take.

The specifics of what follows are not clear, but the general idea was that Helen had asked Jesus for help—as she was urged by him to do—as to what time she should be picked up by her taxi driver. Bill reacted unkindly. Helen then reciprocated, and their egos were off and running. Here is Jesus' commentary:

You asked merely what you should do now. The answer was to tell Jack [Helen's taxi driver] to pick you up at 3. Bill's reaction to this was unfortunate, and yours was much more constructive, making it particularly unfortunate that Bill accepted your very correct response to his reactions with irritation. But this was inevitable because he had *already* given way to fear. Then *you* reacted to *his* mistake with irritation, and we lost our communication for a time. Let us try to re-establish our communication now.

Bill was unwise in deciding on his own that unless you went to his apartment, Jack would be in trouble. This association meant that he saw only *one* alternative, and was unable to keep an open mind. Certainly he should be confident that any guidance which comes from *Me* will not jeopardize anyone.

It should also be noted that he projected his misperception onto *you*, assuming that you were counting on magic to get Jack to take you home in spite of the traffic, and not realizing the situation as it is. I would like to tell him for you that this was a misperception of his, and although you have done this at times in the past [i.e., misperceived], you were *not* doing it then.

As you very correctly stated, but Bill could not listen at the time, you were merely reporting a message for which you had asked, and were not judging the outcome. Bill *was*. If you can continue not to evaluate My messages and merely follow them, they will lead to good for everyone. Since this is the same area of difficulty which is causing both of you trouble in meditation, practice in this is *essential*.

I do not yet know what decisions those who are involved in [what is] happening later today will make, but I assure you with a confidence I urge you to share that *whatever* things may be can be utilized for good if you will let them be. Why not unburden yourselves of this kind of responsibility which you *cannot* meet, and devote yourselves in peace to the many others which you can discharge *without* strain? It *is* your responsibility to recognize the difference. Any confusion in this respect is arrogance. Note also that I specifically told you in answer to your own question of this morning, that miracles should be offered both to Art [a colleague] and to your brother [Helen's brother Adolph]. They are urgently needed for *you* [Helen and Bill], although this is not the spirit in which you must undertake them. You have hurt yourselves and need healing. It does not matter whether the people you *think* have hurt you have really thought hurtfully. You have. We must undo this, and your attempts will surely be blessed.

Since both of you have asked Me to point up errors in perceiving, I would suggest that Bill review carefully his reactions to your suggestion that you go over the case at Neuro [Neurological Institute]. Even though you did not ask, which was a mistake, Bill immediately evaluated the suggestion in terms of his own convenience, which was another mistake. Your reactions were not uncharitable, even though your failure to ask for guidance was a sign of fear. You thought that Art would be able to understand Bill's going to the hospital, while he [Bill] could *not* understand your presence at P.I. [Psychiatric Institute].

Bill's reaction did not take alternate possibilities into account, which is one of his major problems. He should also train himself to learn that alternate possibilities are better not *left up to him. Whenever* he reacts as though they *are, he will* have trouble.

If *you* had asked where to go, and Bill had been willing to forgo control of the decision, *whatever* you had done would have been *only* benign. Could we continue the day in that spirit? If you will to help Bill overcome his irritation, which is totally unjustified in spite of his misperception, you will not only help him, but enable both of us [Jesus and Bill] to help you. This will institute the chain of helpfulness and harmlessness which always leads to the Atonement and becomes a powerful part of its beneficence.

I offer far more than partial guidance, although you do not

ask for more. The uneven quality of your skill in both asking and following My direction is due to the alterations you experience between ego- and the miracle-oriented perception. This *is* a strain, but fortunately one which can be overcome along with the rest. There will never be a time when I do not will to try again. You might be gladdened by remembering that.

We thus read again Jesus' pleas to Helen and Bill to avail themselves of the full extent of his love, *for their sakes.* They would feel much better asking for and accepting his loving guidance, than by acting on their own. In words that would come much later in the text, and to which I have already referred, Jesus is in effect asking them here: "Do you prefer that you be right or happy?" (text, p. 573). Let me be right for you, Jesus urges, and I guarantee that you will be happy.

Chapter 10

THE SCRIBING OF *A COURSE IN MIRACLES*—C
(1965–1972)

Special Messages

On December 14, 1965 Helen and Bill were told in an important message to ask the Holy Spirit for specific assistance to help a friend. In Part III I shall return to the issue of asking for specifics, and its place in the Atonement path. Picking up with the teachings from the end of the last chapter, the essential theme here is that Helen and Bill not withhold anything from the Holy Spirit. In addition, Jesus is emphasizing the necessity of Helen and Bill asking for help *together*. Incidentally, the message begins with another statement of Jesus' wish that all personal material be removed from the published Course.

Nothing that relates to a *specific* relationship belongs in the notes. But you *have* been told that if you ask the Holy Spirit for *specific* guidance in a *specific* situation, He will give it to you very specifically. When you and Bill are ready to ask Him *together* what you can do for M [one of Bill's friends], He will tell you, if you make *no* attempt to give the answer *for* Him. Prejudge His answer not, for if you do, you will *not hear it*. But be sure of this:

The Holy Spirit will *never* teach you to *disrupt* communication, but be wholly willing to let Him *maintain* it in *His* way. M is unhappy and afraid, because he thinks communication *through the body* can be sought and *found*. It is no harder for the Holy Spirit to teach him that communication is of the mind, and *not* the body than it is for Him to teach it to you. The Holy Spirit will have no difficulty, and much joy, if you *allow* Him to teach M this *through* you. But be sure that you are willing to learn it *with* him, or you will *inevitably* interfere with what the Holy Spirit would have him learn with *you*.

There is one extensive set of notes that were written on separate sheets and inserted into Helen's notebooks (at this point I do not know into which one they were originally placed), and which were not transcribed. While the exact date of their scribing is unknown, these notes can almost definitely be placed in this general time period. They would seem to have been written at one sitting, even though they deal with different topics.

The message begins with Jesus commenting on Helen's scribing, specifically with noting the lack of effect Helen's ego had on what was dictated. This is a witness both to the part of Helen's split mind that identified with her ego, and the part that identified with a deeper commitment to her function.

> You will note that a lot of terms are used in the beginning that are later clarified. This is because the beginning was written by an unwilling Scribe whose ego was in strong dominance, and whose Soul was dissociated most of the time. You may not realize what a strong testimony to truth these notes are without remembering that.
>
> The sharp ascent upward in thought which the development of the notes shows, and it is astonishing in human terms how steadily they evolve toward unity, is due to only one sign of assent. I asked her [Helen] to take notes, and she did.
>
> There have been very few real errors, and perhaps I can suggest that the first [note]book be gone over again from her notes, not all of which she read correctly. Some of the changes will be seen immediately, and she will probably remember most of the others. Don't bother now—a lot has been omitted anyway.

This last is a reference to the personal notes that were already taken out, as per Jesus' instructions. Helen and Bill incidentally did go over the scribed material very carefully in checking for possible mistakes, and evidently caught the errors. I have also checked the early notebooks against the typed urtext and found no "real errors." By this time in the dictation (we are already well into the third month and in the current fifth chapter of the text), any personal information given was not so woven into the teaching material of the Course itself, as I have already discussed. This, coupled with the diminution in Helen's anxiety, greatly minimized the possibility of scribal errors.

The message continues with a discussion of karma, a topic that was of great interest to Helen and Bill during this time period, its inclusion showing the influence of the work of Edgar Cayce on Helen.

> About the question of karma—most theories of reincarnation are essentially magical, and the whole question is not really necessary to religion at all. The chief value of the concept lies in its helpfulness in counteracting the idea of hell, a belief that is hard for the ego to relinquish. As the symbol of separation, the ego cannot escape guilt-feelings, and fear of punishment is inevitable. Do not dwell on these fearful thoughts.
>
> One of the main dangers of karmic theories is the tendency it induces to engage in the genetic fallacy, overlooking the *truly* religious fact that now is the only time.

We have already discussed Helen's interest in the subject of reincarnation, despite her later protests to the contrary. Here Jesus is cautioning against throwing out the baby with the bathwater. Even though the concept is inherently illusory, belief in reincarnation can serve a helpful purpose for some people. In the end, however, a belief in the reality of karma or reincarnation as viable concepts must be discarded, as they are still obviously linked to a linear view of time, which is one of the ego's magic tricks to obscure the reality of eternity. The "genetic fallacy," a belief the ego eagerly sponsors, reduces all current behavior and feelings to the past, whether attributable to former lives, genetic make-up, or early developmental experiences. The truth of course is that everything we do, think, or feel comes only from a decision made by the mind in the present: "now is the only time."

Jesus now returns to the accuracy of Helen's note-taking, here referring to the letters and notes that preceded the scribing of the Course, and which we discussed in Chapters 6 and 7.

> In answer to what Bill mentioned, some of the things Helen said before the notes started are true, some of them fact, and others symbolic. On occasion she was projecting, and several times she was merely being manipulative, though this was very rare and never attempted consciously. She also really tried to be honest about this, even though it made her ego very fearful of "being abandoned."

This last statement refers to the fear of Helen's ego that if she

exposed her manipulations, which always served to keep the
special person bound to her, Bill would leave her.

Jesus then reassures Helen that the Course is perfectly safe:

> I told you I would edit the notes with you when it was
> helpful to do so. At present, it is not needed, but when we are
> sure what we should do with things, we can consider it again.
> [The complete consideration of the editing awaited my coming
> on the scene, as we shall discuss in Part III.] I have already
> told you in connection with [Edgar] Casey [*sic*] that out of
> respect for his great efforts on My behalf I would not let his
> life-work lead to anything but truth in the end. [The notes on
> Cayce, which I have deleted, were scribed in late November
> 1965.] These notes are part of *your* life-work, and I will treat
> them with equal respect.

Jesus now returns to the "genetic fallacy," a concept intrinsic to the Freudian (and neo-Freudian) psychology that both
Helen and Bill subscribed to and identified with. Here, as elsewhere in the notes, Jesus is instructing them in his new
psychology.

> It is true that this will lead to something quite different
> because they [the notes] point only to the future. They lead to
> a future that *you* will know. There *was* a past, but it does not
> matter. It *does not* explain the present or account for the
> future. You both went over your childhoods in some detail and
> at considerable expense, and it merely encouraged your egos to
> become more tolerable to you. I would hardly want you to
> repeat that same error.

This is an allusion to Helen's and Bill's earlier experiences as
psychoanalytic patients. Later, in a section entitled "The
Unhealed Healer," which can be found in Chapter Nine in the
text, Jesus specifically exposes the fallacies inherent in the
traditional psychotherapeutic approaches. Helen's graduate
school papers, incidentally, reveal an occasional sympathy for
the non-traditional non-reductionistic position.

The message now moves to one of the key teachings of the
Course: remembrance of God (knowledge) can be acquired only
by learning that we have no interests that are separate from
another person's. This learning, which is the meaning of
forgiveness, undoes the ego's cornerstone of separation and

exclusion, and paves the way for the return to awareness of our fundamental unity with all people as God's one Son. Jesus thus makes an important point here. We do not *need* other people to return home, but certainly we need our forgiveness of them to remove the interferences impeding our homecoming. As we are frequently reminded by Jesus, this is not a Course on love, but on the miracles that remove "the blocks to the awareness of love's presence" (text, intro). By no longer seeing Bill as her enemy, but one she is to help, Helen "re-acquires" her function. Recall Helen's inner response on first seeing Bill: "And there he is. He's the one I'm supposed to help"; and then again a few days later: "Of course I'll go, Father. He's stuck and needs help."

> Knowledge is not won through curiosity, which is an ego attribute. Knowledge can be found only if it is sought to *give it to someone else.* This means that you are ready to appreciate its real value, and have *already* accepted its worth for yourself. That is what I meant when I told you you can not go to God with Bill, but you *can* go *for* him and bring knowledge back *to* him.

The last sentence is a reference to Helen's true Self as the priestess, who stands so close to God that she can bridge the gap for others.

Jesus then comments further on the emptiness of studying the past:

> If this is in the future [Helen's going to God], why would you care at all about the past, except to the extent that your ego objects to your rightful destiny? Are you interested in healing insanity, or in studying its past? That is of concern only if you believe that something that could remedy it happened in the past. Even *My* personal history is of no value to you *except* as it teaches you that I can help you *now*. But no history of irreconcilable viewpoints is helpful in establishing truth. The Soul [i.e., spirit] has no history, being the same yesterday, today and always. The history of a split mind is not a constructive focus for those who are being trained in an integrated and true concept of themselves.
>
> I am quite willing to take your question up again when it no longer is of any interest to your egos, and if it is of help to

someone else.[78] Otherwise, it would be much better to devote yourselves to knowing God. I once told you that the Atonement will not be complete until all the Children of God have come home. We do not care about where they have been or what they have done. We would not want to *evaluate* their past any more than we want to evaluate *them.*

In other words, the past is totally irrelevant—where people "have been or what they have done"—to the healing power of the Atonement. Jesus continues in this vein, referring to Edgar Cayce:

> It is almost impossible for the mind to look at some of Casey's [sic] records of the past totally without judgment of *any* kind. That is why he himself usually related the past to a bodily condition even though he knew that mind was the builder. His emphasis on gains and losses is not to be yours. These terms are evaluative, and are therefore in variance with the goals of your course.

Incidentally, as I will discuss in Part III, this important statement about avoiding discussion of "gains and losses" helps us to understand better the context in which the earlier "explanation" relating to the "celestial speed-up" was given to Helen. Since it deals specifically with people gaining and losing, it should not be taken too seriously as a true explanation.

The message concludes with Jesus stressing again the importance of letting go of the past as a prerequisite for learning this Course. Our skill of making judgments is to be used *only* for judging the ego's system as false, and the Holy Spirit's as true.

> We have discussed the Separation in some detail, as we have also done with its healing. The interim is of no importance. Your judgment is a real defense [i.e., that of the Holy Spirit], without any attack on truth, only when it evaluates the Separation and its symbols as what they are, and enjoins the withdrawal of your belief in them. I would indeed be a poor teacher if I allowed any interference in the development of a skill which you have by no means mastered.

---

78. This refers to the question about the past; *see* the notes presented above on p. 280.

In January 1966, Bill was asked by the administration of the Medical Center to attend a conference on the basic principles of rehabilitation at Princeton, New Jersey, sponsored by the New York Academy of Sciences. He did not wish to go, but felt that he was supposed to, which is corroborated in the following dictation which was designed to help Bill accept this "assignment." The message was not meant for *A Course in Miracles* itself, but the final prayer, which summarizes the theme of the message, was clearly supposed to be included. It has actually proven to be one of the more popular passages in the material, and is currently found, slightly changed, in Chapter Two in the text closing the section on "Special Principles of Miracle Workers." Here is the message in its entirety:

The truly helpful are God's miracle-workers, whom I direct until we are all united in the joy of the kingdom. I will direct you to wherever you can be truly helpful, and to whoever can follow My guidance through you. I arranged[79] for Bill to attend the rehabilitation meetings for very good reasons, and I want him to know them so we can share our goal there.

Properly speaking, every mind which is split needs rehabilitation. The medical orientation emphasizes the body, and the vocational orientation stresses the ego. The team approach generally leads more to confusion than anything else, because it is too often misused as an expedient for sharing the ego's dominion with other egos, rather than as a real experiment in cooperation of minds.

The reason why Bill needs this experience is because he needs rehabilitation himself. How often have I answered "help him" when you asked Me to help you? He, too, has asked for help, and he has been helped whenever he was truly helpful to you. He has also gained to whatever extent he could give. He will help *you* more truly by going, if he can remember all the time he is there that his *only* reason for being there is to *represent Me*.

Rehabilitation, as a movement, has been an improvement over overt neglect, but it is often little more than a painful attempt on the part of the halt to lead the blind. Bill, you will

---

79. *See* page 277, footnote 70, for an explanation of the meaning of terms like "choosing," "making assignments," or "arranged" in connection with Jesus or the Holy Spirit.

see this at every meeting. But this is not why you were chosen to go. You have a fear of broken bodies, because your ego cannot tolerate them. Your ego cannot tolerate ego-weakness, either, without ambivalence, because it is afraid of its own weakness and the weakness of its chosen home.

That is really why you recoil from the demands of the dependent, and from the sight of a broken body. Your ego is threatened, and blocks your natural impulse to help, placing you under the strain of divided will. You withdraw to allow your ego to recover, and to regain enough strength to be helpful again on a basis limited enough *not* to threaten your ego, but also too limited to give *you* joy.

Those with broken bodies are often looked down on by the ego, because of its belief that nothing but a perfect body is worthy as its *own* temple. A mind that recoils from a hurt body is in great need of rehabilitation itself. A damaged brain is also hardly a danger. *All* symptoms of hurt need true helpfulness, and whenever they are met with this, the mind that so meets them heals *itself*.

People recoiling from another's injury are reflecting their own need of healing, since they are, in the later words of the Course, making the error real. Sickness is only of the mind, and is its defense against the reality of Christ's perfection as God's Son. It thus is illusory, as the workbook later says:

> Pain is but witness to the Son's mistakes in what he thinks he is.... Pain is a sign illusions reign in place of truth.... If God is real, there is no pain. If pain is real, there is no God (workbook, p. 351).

Looking past illusions to the truth is the only truly helpful response to another, healing both the mind that believes it is sick, and the mind that perceives another as sick. As separation is the only cause of sickness, its healing can only come through joining.

The message to Bill continues:

> Rehabilitation is an attitude of praising God as He Himself knows praise.[80] He offers praise to you, and you must offer it to

---

80. The use of the word "praise" here does not of course reflect its general meaning. Rather, it is used as an expression of the Love of God, which unites us with Him in spirit, transcending all thoughts of bodies—sick and well.

others. The real limitations on clinical psychology, as it is evaluated by its followers at present, are not reflected by the attitudes of psychiatrists, or medical boards, or hospital administrators, even though most of them are sadly in need of rehabilitation themselves. The real handicaps of the clinicians lie in their attitudes to those whom their egos perceive as weakened and damaged. By these evaluations, they have weakened and damaged their own helpfulness, and have thus set their own rehabilitation back. Rehabilitation is *not* concerned with the ego's fight for control, nor the ego's need to avoid and withdraw.

Bill, you can do much on behalf of your own rehabilitation *and* Helen's, and much more universally as well, if you think of the Princeton meetings in this way:

I am here *only* to be truly helpful.
I am here to represent Christ, who sent me.
I do not have to worry about what to say or what to do,
   because the One who sent me will direct me.
I am content to be wherever He wishes, knowing He
   goes there with me.
I will be healed as I let Him teach me to heal.

"The Guide to Salvation" in Chapter Five was in part originally meant for Bill. It read like this in the original notebooks:

Bill, who has made a number of vital contributions to our joint venture, made a major one a while ago, which he himself did not appreciate or even understand. If we recognize its value together, we will be able to use it together, because it was an *idea*, and must therefore be shared to be held.

When Bill said that he was determined "*not* to see you that way," he was speaking negatively. If he will state the same idea *positively*, he will see the *power* of what he said. He had realized that there were two ways of seeing you, and also that they were diametrically opposed to one another. These two ways must be in *his* mind, because he was referring to *himself* as the perceiver. They must also be in *yourself*, because he was perceiving *you*.

Whereas sickness symbolizes our separation from God by rooting us in our bodies, rehabilitation (healing) reflects the change of mind that ultimately rejoins us with Him: "praising God as He Himself knows praise."

Within the world of separation, every person's mind contains both ways of seeing: the ego's guilt and attack, and the Holy Spirit's forgiveness and unity. Also, within this illusory world, Bill's perception of Helen ensures that she is there as well. On the metaphysical level, on the other hand, *A Course in Miracles* teaches that no one is outside our minds at all.

> What he was really saying was that he would *not* look at you through *his* ego, or perceive *your* ego in you. Stated positively, he would see you through the Holy Spirit in *his* mind, and perceive it in *yours*. What you acknowledge in your brother, you *are* acknowledging in yourself. What you share you *strengthen*. The Voice of the Holy Spirit *is* weak in you. That is why you *must* share it, because it must be *increased* in strength before *you* can hear it. It is impossible to hear it in yourself while it is so weak in your *own* mind. It is *not* weak in itself; but it *is* limited by your unwillingness to hear it.
>
> Will itself is an idea, and is therefore strengthened by being shared. You have made the mistake of looking for the Holy Spirit in *yourself*, and that is why your meditations have frightened you. By adopting the ego's viewpoint, you undertook an ego-alien journey *with the ego as guide*. This was *bound* to produce fear. Bill's better idea needs to be strengthened in *both* of you. Since it was *his*, he can increase it by giving it to you.
>
> I suggest that *he* might care to talk to you about it, and perhaps even let you take notes for him. He has much to teach through the Holy Spirit, and this might be a very good way to begin.

Slightly later, this about Helen in a passage we shall return to in Part III when we consider her in more detail, in particular her need to keep herself separate from others:

> You must have noticed how often I have used your own ideas to help *you*. Bill is right in saying that you have learned to be a loving, wise, and very understanding therapist, except for yourself. That exception has given you more than perception for others because of what you saw in them, but less than knowledge of your real relationships *to* them because you did *not* make them part *of* you. Understanding *is* beyond perception, because it introduces meaning. But it is below knowledge, even though it can grow *towards* it. It is possible, with great effort, to understand someone else and to be helpful to him, but

the effort is misdirected. The misdirection is quite apparent. It is directed *away* from you.

This does *not* mean that it is lost to you, but it *does* mean that you are not aware of it. I have saved all of your kindnesses and every loving thought you have had, and I assure you you have had many. I have purified them of errors which hid their light, and have kept them for you in their own perfect radiance. They are beyond destruction and beyond guilt. They came from the Holy Spirit within *you*, and we know that what God creates is eternal.

Most of this last paragraph was later joined with another message meant for Helen, and placed together in what is now a very moving passage that comes at the end of the section "Teaching and Healing" in Chapter Five.

Jesus now returns to his psychological contrast of Helen and Bill. This obviously was a form of teaching that they, both astute clinical psychologists, could relate to with a minimal amount of resistance.

Bill once spoke of the Kingdom in this way, because he yearns for what he has repressed. You are much more afraid of it, because dissociation is more fearful. Bill's better contact has allowed him the strength to retain the fear in awareness, and to resort to displacement, which he is learning to overcome with *your* help. That is because you do not perceive *him* as dissociated, and *can* help him with his repression, which does *not* frighten you. He, on the other hand, has no difficulty in seeing *you* dissociate, and *does not* have to deal with repression in you, which *would* produce fear in him.

Joining the Atonement, which I have repeatedly asked you to do, is *always* a way *out* of fear. This does not mean that you can safely fail to acknowledge anything that is true, but the Holy Spirit will not fail to help you reinterpret *everything* that you perceive as fearful, and teach you *only* what is loving *is* true. It is beyond your ability to destroy, but entirely within your grasp. It *belongs* to you because *you* created it. It is yours because it is part of you, just as you are part of God because He created you.

And later, a passage for Bill, again urging him to join; this time with *himself,* as well as with Helen, this being the way of his joining with Jesus. Thus Bill (and all of us) is being taught that it is not possible to join with one without the other, since in reality we are all part of the one Christ. Separating from one aspect of the Sonship, separates from all; likewise, truly joining with one, *without illusions*, joins with all. In truth we are, as we shall see below, both totally unified within our Self, as well as unified with all of Christ: "both *one* and *at one*."

> There is time for delay, but there need not be. God weeps at the sacrifice of His children who believe they are lost to Him. The "one more thing" that Bill must learn is merely that he is *not* the one more. He is both *one* and *at one*. If he will learn this *now*, he will be willing in accord with the last judgment, which is really only the Biblical reminder of the inevitability of self-*inclusion*. This is what "Physician, heal thyself" really means. Bill has frequently observed for *himself* that this is hard to do. He has, however, been perfectly aware of *just* what *you* should do about it.
>
> You might ask him for Me whether he does not think he might be dissociating *himself* from his own awareness, since he is so clear about the remedy for *you*. You might also remind him that to whatever extent he separates himself from you, he is separating himself from *Me*. This is a collaborative venture. Let Me therefore return his own ideas to him, so that you can share them and thus help each other to help Me.

Shortly afterwards, Helen wrote about herself, along with Jesus' correction:

> Helen: I...asked the Holy Spirit in me to listen in case our brother [Jesus] wanted to share some of His thoughts with me, and I would be honored if He wanted to. The answer was that that was not a good beginning because He *always* wants to share His.

In other words, Jesus' love does not come and go. His loving thoughts are always present in our minds, patiently awaiting our welcoming of them. We are the ones who leave him, thereby making his love appear inconsistent, a projection of our own inconsistent love. Our separation from these thoughts is therefore our responsibility, and so we are the ones who need to return to their constant presence.

In a message for Helen and Bill—in the context of what is now in the introduction to Chapter Six in the text—Jesus explains how he can use on behalf of the Atonement, the mind's power that had once been directed towards the ego.

> You have been chosen to teach the Atonement precisely *because* you have been extreme examples of allegiance to your thought systems, and therefore have developed the capacity *for* allegiance. It has indeed been misplaced. Bill had become an outstanding example of allegiance to apathy, and you have become a startling example of fidelity to variability. But this *is* a form of faith, which you yourselves had grown willing to redirect. You cannot doubt the *strength* of your devotion when you consider how faithfully you observed it. It was quite evident that you had *already* developed the ability to follow a better model, if you could *accept* it.

And for Bill who believed that teaching was martyrdom, Jesus comments a bit later in the spirit of his earlier teaching on Bill's class:

> Bill is an outstanding example of this confusion, and has literally believed for years that teaching *is* martyrdom. This is because he thought, and still thinks at times, that teaching leads to crucifixion rather than to re-awakening. The upside-down nature of this association is so obvious that he could only have made it *because* he felt guilty.

Later, in the context of the lessons of the Holy Spirit now at the end of Chapter Six, Jesus commented again on the difference between Helen and Bill. After the first of the three steps was described—"To Have, Give All to All"—Jesus stated:

> You, Helen, *had* taken this [first] step, and because you believed in it, you taught it to Bill, who still believed in the solution of sleep [i.e., withdrawal and passivity]. You were not consistent in teaching it, but you did so often enough to enable him to learn it. Once *he* learned it, he could teach *you* how to become more consistently awake, and thus begin to waken *himself*. This placed him, too, in command of the journey. His recognition of the direction it must take was perfectly stated when he *insisted on collaboration*. You, Helen, had taken a giant step *into* conflict, but Bill turned you both *toward the way out*. The more he teaches this, the more he will learn it.

In the midst of the discussion of the second step, Jesus made the following comments:

Meanwhile, the increasing clarity of the Holy Spirit's Voice makes it impossible for the learner *not to listen*. For a time, then, he *is* receiving conflicting messages *and accepting both*. This is the classic "double bind" in communication, which you wrote about yourselves quite recently, and with good examples, too. It is interesting that Helen claimed at the time that she never heard of it and did not understand it. I thought it might help both of you if you were called on to write about it together. You might remember our brother's [Bill's] insistence on its inclusion. You thought he had become quite demanding on this point, but it was quite strongly reinforced in *his* mind, and so he wanted to teach it in his text. This, of course, was a very good way for *you* to learn it.

A bit later in the dictation, in the midst of material that is currently in Chapter Seven in the text, Jesus interspersed specific comments about Helen to illustrate the general principle he was teaching about the Holy Spirit's use of abilities originally made to serve the ego's purposes. We thus can see here another example of the personal nature of Jesus' teaching during the beginning stages of the scribing. Incidentally, I shall return to this passage again in Part III, when I discuss Helen's scribing of the Course.

The Holy Spirit teaches *you* to use what the ego has made to *teach* the opposite of what ego has *learned*. The *kind* of learning is as irrelevant as is the particular ability which was applied *to* the learning.

You could not have a better example of the Holy Spirit's unified purpose than this course. The Holy Spirit has taken very diversified areas of *your* past learning, and has applied them to a *unified* curriculum. The fact that this was *not* the ego's reason for learning is totally irrelevant. *You* made the effort to learn, and the Holy Spirit has a unified goal for *all* effort. He *adapts* the ego's potentials for excelling to potentials for *equalizing*. This makes them *useless* for the ego's purpose, but *very* useful for His.

If different abilities are applied long enough to one *goal*, the abilities *themselves* become unified. This is because they are channelized in one direction, or in one *way*. Ultimately, then, they all contribute to *one result*, and by so doing their *similarity* rather than their differences is emphasized. You can *excel* in many *different* ways, but you can *equalize* in one *way only.* Equality is *not* a variable state by definition. That is why we once said that papers will be easy to write when you have learned *this* course. To the ego there appears to be no connection, because the *ego* is discontinuous. But the Holy Spirit teaches one lesson and applies it to *all* individuals in *all* situations. Being conflict free, He maximizes *all* efforts and *all* results. By teaching the power of the Kingdom of God Himself, He teaches you that *all power is yours.* Its application does not matter. It is *always* maximal. Your vigilance does *not* establish it *as* yours, but it *does* enable you to use it *always* and in *all ways.*

Regarding the dictation of the Course itself, the writing down was easy as we have seen: Helen and Bill truly joined with Jesus in scribing this "better way." With all other writing "assignments," however, Helen and Bill's experience was quite different. The great difficulty they experienced in collaborating on professional manuscripts reflected their difficulties with each other. One of my first experiences with this difficulty came during the summer I spent with Helen and Bill in 1973, and I shall relate this in Chapter 11.

On June 13 and 14, 1966, Helen wrote down on loose sheets two short messages that were never transcribed. These, incidentally, came while Helen was taking down the notes that would later come either at the end of Chapter Eight in the text, or the beginning of Chapter Nine (the dating was imprecise here). The first message deals with Bill and his tendency, as we have already seen, to exclude himself from the Sonship, specifically denoted here by its total invulnerability. Jesus' reference to the first principle of miracles underscores again its importance in the Course's thought system:

> Bill does not know his wholeness. He believes that there is a central core of himself which *is* invulnerable, but he does not include *all of himself* in it. His is a peculiar self-concept now, because he is shifting his belief about himself, but has not yet done so completely. As a result, he believes in *degrees of invulnerability*, a concept which does not really *mean* anything.
>   Invulnerability is the opposite of vulnerability, and is total. He once thought he was totally vulnerable. He now thinks he

is partly *in*vulnerable and partly vulnerable. This has *limited* his anxiety greatly, but has not yet gotten rid of it.

This is ultimately because of his persistent belief that there *is* an order of difficulty in miracles. He finds this easier to say than to believe, but when he *believes* there is no order of difficulty in following *everything* I teach, he will include *all* of himself in My teaching.

The next message is brief and focuses on Helen, spoken of here in the third person. Helen had evidently been upset, which upset Bill, a frequent occurrence as will be discussed in the next section. The solution, Jesus instructs Helen and Bill, is to focus only on what can be done about the situation in the present, and to let go of attempts to analyze the past. Jesus again exposes Helen's use of projection—her main line of defense—whereby an internal split is seen to exist outside of her mind, characteristically seen between her and Bill.

There is something *very* wrong with Helen, to which Bill is reacting badly *because it bothers him too*. The something is really nothing, and I would not dwell on what it is as much as how to get over it.

There has been a sharp rise in competition, which is really only an attempt to project one side of the internal conflict on practically any external situation she [Helen] sees. This is regressive, because it is a return to an earlier form of solving the problem.

Still later in the dictation, Jesus responded to Helen's complaints about the Course not helping her. An abridged version of this is found near the end of Chapter Eleven of the text in "The Problem and the Answer." The original read:

You complain that this course is not sufficiently specific for you to understand it *and use it*. Yet it has been *very* specific, and *you have not done what it specifically advocates*. This is not a course in the *play* of ideas, but in their *practical application*. Nothing could be more specific than to be told, very clearly, that if you ask you *will* receive.

On September 13 and 14, 1966, Jesus commented very specifically to Helen and Bill about the hatred in their relationship, and its role in hiding the love that was truly there. This came during the period when they were still both very sincerely willing to look at their relationship with openness and honesty. It was this small willingness on their part that obviously allowed Helen to hear these two short messages:

You have no idea of the intensity of your wish to get rid of each other. This does *not* mean that you are not strongly impelled *toward* each other, but it *does* mean that *love is not the only emotion*. Because your love has become more in awareness, the conflict can no longer be "settled" by your previous attempts to *minimize* the fear. The love makes attack untenable, *but you still feel the fear*. Instead of trying to resolve it directly, you have a strong tendency to *try to escape from the love*. Yet this is the *last* thing you would want to *escape* from. And even if you did, you can escape from everything *else*, but not from this. Be glad indeed that there *is* no escape from salvation.

You do not realize how much you hate each other. You will not get rid of this until you *do* realize it, for *until* then, you will think you want to get rid of *each other* and *keep the hatred*. Yet if you are each other's salvation, what can this mean except that you *prefer* attack to salvation? Be glad that neither your reality nor your salvation is a matter of your preference, for you *have* much cause for joy. But that the cause is *not* of your making is surely obvious. You *do* hate and fear each other, and your love, which is very real, is *totally* obscured by it. How can you know the meaning of love *unless* it is total?

This will be a very difficult period for you, but it will not be so for long. You are in danger, but you *will* be helped, and nothing will happen. But you cannot remain in darkness, and this will *be* the way out. Look as calmly as you can upon hatred, for if we are to deny the denial of truth, we must first *recognize* what we are denying. Remember that knowledge *precedes* denial, and that the separation was a descent from magnitude to littleness. And so the way back is to retrace the way to magnitude.

Your hatred is not real, but it *is* real to you. *It hides what you really want*. Surely you are willing to look upon what you do *not* want without fear, *even if it frightens you*, if you can thereby get rid of it? For you *cannot* escape salvation, and you *will* not escape fear until you *want* salvation. Be not afraid of this journey into fear, for it is not your destination. And we will walk through it in safety, for peace is not far, and you will be led in its light.

This message is obviously a very important one, and meant not only for Helen and Bill. It strikes at the very heart of Jesus' message in *A Course in Miracles* to all of us: that we be willing to look *with him* at our ego thoughts—without guilt and without fear. Only in that way can their darkness be brought to his light, and thus dispelled forever. Since we have made these thoughts of hate real, and then denied them, we must first be able to look at what we have hidden before we can realize their fundamental *lack* of reality and thereby accept the love that alone is real. As with all serious students of the Course, this was extremely difficult for Helen and Bill to do. And their inability truly to bring what the Course would later call their "hidden hates" and "secret sins" to Jesus resulted in their not consciously experiencing any real peace or healing with each other. I return to this in Part III.

On September 16, in response to Helen's question, Jesus dictated this special message for Bill, similar to his earlier messages about Bill's need to accept who he really is as a Son of God:

Question: Why is Bill more depressed than usual?

Answer: He is in a very deep sleep and much more resistant to waking than you are. The major problem with him is that his is a *passive* resistance, which implies a giving over of will. This always induces a state of resignation and therefore depression. Tell him that no one can resign from the Sonship, since membership is not optional. He has been looking for someone to *take his will away*, because he thought *it* was the cause of his trouble. Since the course has placed such persistent emphasis *on* will, and *since he agrees with the emphasis*, his past adjustment is threatened. *That is why he could not sleep.* His past came to "haunt" him *because* he is giving up the belief in ghosts.

Tell him again not to be afraid of ghosts, and remind him that he *has* no past. The return of his will is what he *wants*. No one can accept it but himself.

Two months later, on November 15, Helen took down the following note from Jesus for herself. It helped her to understand that her attacks on Bill could not be kept separate from others. Her belief that they could be, nicely served the ego's purpose of believing that hatred can be justified in certain instances and therefore limited. As we have already observed, to hate one part of the Sonship is to hate all parts, including oneself.

> Bill was right in not regarding this as a separate problem: the savage problem of personal rejection. There is no fear in perfect love. You do not want him to feel guiltless, but rejected. This area is the only one in which you want to retain this, but you will not be able to limit it. You will not see his purity until you give up rejection as a weapon against him *or* against everyone else. You think these are the only alternatives. Be sure to consider why you want to maintain this position. Bill will help you with this.

As was mentioned at the beginning of Chapter 6, Bill kept a personal journal during the almost two-month period spanning parts of August and September 1966. The journal entries fall into the chronological sequence we have been following so far in this chapter, and illustrate, again, the commitment Helen and Bill had made to work together to find the better way of relating. I thus interrupt the narrative of Helen's scribing of the Course to present this journal.

Bill's Journal

Bill's journal notes range from August 11 through September 28, 1966. I am reasonably sure he shared these with Helen, as it would have been most atypical of him not to have done so, but I cannot be absolutely certain. The entries clearly reflect, as do Helen's letters of the previous year, an unusual willingness and openness to look at the ego without projecting any responsibility for it. In addition, they point up the great importance Bill placed upon Helen's reactions. This need on Bill's part to have Helen be different from her ego never really left him, and became Bill's principal rationale for why their relationship could never truly be healed, nor his own mind for that matter.

Helen always felt that Bill did not really understand certain aspects of the Course, and his insistence on Helen's shift being a prerequisite for his own would suggest one aspect of this misunderstanding. One can see in these notes, therefore, Bill's continual references to Helen's state of mind, and use of "we" and "us" to denote their joint progress or lack of it. He clearly saw their respective salvation paths as being not only intertwined but interdependent. He thus believed that their salvation depended on the *other's* change of mind. To cite but one example from the journal, Bill wrote this note on September 11 regarding his own response to Helen's great variability in shifting back and forth between the ego's goals of guilt and illusion and the Course's goals of forgiveness and truth:

> [I] Know that Helen is trying, but find it difficult not to respond to my perception of fluctuations re[garding] goal direction.

As will also be seen, therefore, Bill was always concerned with other people's progress, experiencing it as somehow crucial to his own. Yet forgiveness, *A Course in Miracles'* central teaching, can occur only in one's individual mind, although this process of healing inevitably occurs in the *context* of a relationship with another. The guilt in Helen's and Bill's individual minds was due to decisions each made to hold on to it. This decision for guilt and separation was thus not accepted by them as a personal responsibility, but projected onto each other. Therefore, for genuine healing to occur, the projection would have to be undone and responsibility for their misery returned to themselves. To her credit, Helen always understood this intellectually, although she was never able consciously to apply this principle to herself.

Here is Bill's first entry:

August 11, 1966
Recall of events from Aug. 10.

When I saw Helen about 1:30 (for the first time that day) she appeared particularly radiant. It is startling how much her appearance changes when she is "with it." This radiance continued throughout the afternoon, although there was a relatively brief period in which she "fogged over," displaying a marked fear reaction, which briefly altered her appearance. However, she got back very quickly. The problem was in relation to meditation and "asking," which followed writing a letter re Chip's mother. I was aware of being somewhat upset while we were doing this, although also pleased to have an opportunity to share in this "miracle." The changes in Chip's mother are miraculous, and demonstrate very powerfully the effects of love. However, I seemed to be responding inappropriately to what I perceived as Helen's ambivalence about doing the letter. I suggested adding a statement at the end concerning her [Chip's mother] wishes at present to stay in the hospital, which she still regards as her home [*see* my comments below].

During meditation, I asked why I was having a conflict reaction, and received the answer. "You are afraid of release from imprisonment, which is what you were describing in the letter about Mrs. P [Chip's mother]." This makes good sense, and there is no question that I am afraid of release, although consciously it frequently seems otherwise. It is apparent that I still think the ego has something to offer.

Helen emphasized the importance of doing all those things which we have put off, but are still lurking about in our minds. List to be compiled in more detail later, and then *action*.

Helen called in evening and mentioned a correction in notes typed earlier in day. I was looking at exactly the page where the correction from "proof" to "truth" was indicated. As a matter of fact, I was just about to read that paragraph when Helen called, and stated that she thought I was reading these pages. She was right.

Bill, incidentally, was always extremely impressed by psychic ability, his own as well as others. And as we have seen, Helen was usually able to offer numerous examples of such paranormal phenomena. The section on the use (and misuse) of psychic abilities in the manual for teachers (pp. 59f) may in part have been dictated for Bill. The point of this section was that while such abilities can be helpful to the Holy Spirit regarding the demonstration of the lack of limits in communication, these same abilities can be temptations if seen as "powerful," capable of making certain people special. Helen's irrevocable decision in the symbolic cave not to exploit such ability, but rather to be concerned only with the *living* God, became the perfect example of turning away from such temptation. Bill's comment that he still thinks the "ego has something to offer," while not specifically aimed at that temptation, nonetheless would certainly encompass it.

As mentioned in the introduction to these journal notes, Bill's preoccupation with Helen's progress (or regressions) can be seen in this first entry. The "release from imprisonment," which was Bill's answer in meditation, would have come in the instant that he was able to release Helen from her role as savior, which gave her the power to affect his own spiritual progress and either save or imprison him.

The importance for Bill of people's positive changes was also seen in this note in terms of Chip's mother. Chip and his mother had been separated for many years, and he had no knowledge of her whereabouts. Helen was finally able to locate her in a state mental hospital outside New York City. It was a heartwarming story, and Chip, Helen's patient, was forever grateful to her for the loving efforts she made on his behalf.

We also find in this entry evidence of Bill's honesty in making efforts to look at himself and recognize *his* responsibility for his negative reactions to Helen ("I seemed to be responding inappropriately...").

Bill's journal continues, with additional notes reflecting his reliance on other people's progress, along with his openness to observe his "self imposed limitations on peace." In addition, we may note the importance for Helen and Bill of having their "hearing" confirmed by each other. This need never really left them, and I shall consider its implications in Chapter 17.

Recollections of Aug. 11.

Considerable slippage today, with the usual conflicts and self imposed limitations on peace. Was very favorably impressed with C's [a friend of Bill] ability to resolve overnight his weekend conflicts. Also [I] had been helping R [another friend] whose faith in his ministry was badly shaken. As usual, a convincing demonstration that peace and rest do not come from sleeping, but from waking.

This last comment is based on an earlier teaching from Jesus, currently found near the end of Chapter Nine in the text:

"Rest in peace" is a blessing for the living, not the dead, because rest comes from waking, not from sleeping (text, p. 146).

Bill's journal notes continue:

Was aware that Helen was having trouble, but did not respond in most helpful way to this. Rather, fell back on ego oriented perceptions. This always produces the same results, just as the opposite approach works invariably in accordance with our shared goals. All the usual material about deprivation, sacrifice in helping people, confusion about practically everything, difficulty in both asking and listening, fatigue, incoherence and illogical statements about problems were shared by both Helen *and* me.

Helen very upset about not having relayed message to me re JL [Bill's Chicago friend; *see above*, p. 118] preceding night, at about 11, when she was aware that I should call him. I also had rather dimly thought about this at the same time (11 P.M.), but had not paid any attention. Resolution to call him in the evening of the 11th. We both got the same time to place call: 9:30 P.M. [A reference to Helen's and Bill's asking Jesus or the Holy Spirit when they should call. *See* Chapter 17, again, for a full discussion of the subject of "asking."] When I talked to him (on schedule, of course), I asked him if he had been upset around 10:00 Chicago time the preceding evening, and whether he had wanted to talk to me at that time. Answer was yes to both of these questions. Although he did not feel free to say too much during our conversation, it was the same type of problem, and he felt better as we were talking. I emphasized importance to him of silent meditation, making his mind as blank as possible at the same time every day. He has promised to do this, and we will follow up next week.

Then, I called Helen and reported the above, which seemed to provoke the same kind of astonishment which she frequently shows when there has been a confirmation of our listening. She was very pleased, and agreed to start freshly today.

The next entry is not for another month, and is a review of the weekend of September 10–11.

Sunday, Sept. 11

Saturday A.M. went to meeting of International Parapsychological Association with Helen. Content of meetings seemed rather disappointing, but did talk to GM [identity unknown to me] re possible article for Journal.[81] Felt uneasy and

---

81. During this period Bill was Associate Editor of the prestigious journal of

strange in this setting, which doesn't seem to bear any real relationship to goals of [the] course. However, an interest in this area might open up more relevant implications as opposed to current mechanistic models in Psychology. Helen very disturbed about attending session. Had fallen and bruised knees. Considerable indications of environmental distraction, etc. Walked thru [Central] Park and back to apartment where we talked until about 4. Some improvement in general state after this. Know that Helen is trying, but find it difficult not to respond to my perception of fluctuations re goal direction.

Bill was always hoping to establish links between professional/academic psychology and the Course, as well as attempting to help Helen personally to bridge the gap between her experiences and the world, most notably the so-called New Age or parapsychological community. The latter attempts especially never seemed to take, as Helen always felt alienated from the psychics and healers she believed did not truly understand the profound nature of *A Course in Miracles*, which, she believed, was for only very few, and certainly not the masses. This issue will come up again in various discussions in Part III.

Bill's entry for that date continues, and makes reference to Cal (Hatcher). Cal was a hospital administrator with whom Helen and Bill shared the Course right from the beginning. Their relationship had an interesting beginning. About a year before the scribing began, Cal approached Bill to ask if he might speak with him about some religious experiences he had been having (these included visions of light, which Cal found rather frightening[82]). Bill replied that he was not the right person, as he had no knowledge of, nor interest in anything religious. However, shortly after the scribing began (and perhaps even earlier), Bill went back to Cal and changed his answer. Cal was immediately interested, and frequently would meet Bill in his office early in the morning to go over the latest scribal notes.

We now return to the journal, and another instance where Bill's mood changed as a result of someone else's progress:

---

the American Psychological Association, the *Journal of Abnormal and Social Psychology*. Helen assisted him in this position.

82. The reference in Lesson 15 (workbook, p. 25) to "light episodes" was put in by Jesus to alleviate Cal's anxiety: "Do not be afraid of them."

General state of mild depression, which lifted considerably during evening. Cal came before 7 and left after 11. During this time I was extremely impressed with how much he has learned by directly applying the course. There have been literally hundreds of episodes in his life where he has had immediate and startling results. Relationship with J [one of Cal's friends] has changed almost totally from past. As a witness, Cal is convincing in every respect. Went to bed around 12 feeling much more with it than I have been for some time.

Sunday A.M. got up around 7, and tried to devote attention to notes until 1 when Helen arrived. During this time, I felt extreme importance of mastering material, but still with a peculiar sense of unreality about it at times. The ego is hard to see for what it is.

Was aware when Helen arrived of her great effort to help me by demonstrating a dramatic shift from Saturday. She appeared radiant at times, but with a slight undercurrent of depression and strain. But her effort to be helpful was impressive, and I felt better in some respects. Still, however, an awareness of not being totally committed.

In evening, felt depressed. Conversation with Helen in which she again made every effort to be helpful. Aware that it is only my responsibility for what and how I perceive. But still have trouble with this. However, Helen's motivation, if sustained, must be very encouraging for both of us.

Assignment to keep daily record, and list of incompleted tasks:

A list of nine items then followed (not included here), of which five involved people. Helen and Bill frequently spoke of others they were to help as "assignments," and were usually faithful to being of whatever help they could be, despite the essentially negative reaction both their egos had to the seeming imposition. Occasionally in Bill's typing of the original manuscript from Helen's dictation he would type "you and your bother" instead of "you and your brother." This humorous "Freudian slip" reflected well Helen's and Bill's ego thoughts, though not of course the other part of their minds that remained faithful to their promise to be helpful.

The next entry repeats some of the same themes we have already seen.

Tues. Sept. 13

Great difficulty in getting up, feeling of generalized fatigue, etc., as continuation of previous depression. Found difficulty in changing this mood state, but improved as day continued. Discussed problem with Helen, who was obviously having a strong phobic reaction, but [I] was also impressed with her very genuine attempts to look at this problem as it is, and to give up belief in fantasy gratification as meaningful [i.e., the various forms of specialness]. Very marked steps toward goals of course. If she could also give up belief in attacking herself as an attempted solution to conflict situations, I know that she would feel immensely better....

Tried to focus in P.M. on Journal papers [the aforementioned *Journal of Abnormal and Social Psychology*]. Have felt somewhat depressed about getting correspondence out. But did write letters and dispose of about 12 papers in afternoon. This is certainly a record for me in handling this type of problem. Then, spent 1/2 hour at apartment with Helen re attempts to help us get in focus. We went through the usual bit about being too tired, too late, etc., but Helen did respond very well to this relatively brief time, and [I] left her feeling we had made real progress.

Spent about 1 hour in phone conversation with BN [another of Bill's friends]. (Should I try to see him this Wednesday P.M.?) He is in an extremely difficult situation, but did feel that talking with him helped both of us. If I really believed that there was no order of difficulty, etc. [reference to the very important first miracle principle: There is no order of difficulty in miracles], I would feel much more optimistic about J's [BN's wife] being able to change her mind. She is obviously terribly frightened, but is engaging in almost every possible distortion to avoid awareness of this fear. It must be important for me to make a direct contribution here.

Talked with Helen twice in P.M. Asked her to call me back after first conversation which she did. Improvement notable second time. Discouraged obviously self-destructive wish for exercises, etc., which she accepted (but without initial enthusiasm). We are making progress, but our vacillations are so great that it is sometimes hard to see this clearly.

I mention again, because of its importance in the painful final years of Helen and Bill's relationship which I shall return to in Part III, that Bill's ego was unfortunately setting him up for failure. By placing the means for his salvation onto Helen, he was reinforcing the special relationship dynamic of dependency, wherein one's happiness becomes directly connected to another's choices. Helen's eventual inability to demonstrate any consistent change marked the end of any hopes Bill had to "pass" the Course. His "failure" then became attributed to Helen's "failure," thereby justifying his anger at her. To digress for a moment, my coming on the scene in 1973 at such a low point in the relationship, and developing a close friendship with Helen, meant for Bill on one level that his failure was now permanent.

The next two days were covered in the following entry made on September 15, which is filled with optimism as to the progress that had been made in Helen's and Bill's personal and professional lives:

Notes covering Sept. 13 & 14

These have been turbulent days, and crucial ones, in terms of course application. In many respects, they have not been different from most of the days in the last few months or years, but as of now I *do* feel that we have made some very significant progress. Since we have made it, the worst that could happen would be temporary vacillation and dissociation of what has become *compellingly* real.

Tuesday and Wednesday afternoons were spent exclusively on attempts to face and understand fear and mutual hostility. Helen was in a great panic about this and found *everything* associated with our collaboration fraught with fear and danger. However, the main change has been the very clear-cut recognition expressed by her to me last night via phone that she *no longer saw anything fearful about the most recent notes*. It is apparent to both of us that an explicit statement of a problem, namely our ambivalent attitudes toward each other, can only lead to a constructive resolution of this long-standing conflict. Helen saw with great clarity last night that the glow of love entirely dispels fear, and felt quite radiant when she called. She also recognized something else which I regard of great importance, because its obviousness cannot be denied. Namely, that her physical appearance is entirely changed when she is out of conflict and believes only in the reality of love. This has been *very* apparent to everyone who has seen her during the past year. Her *own* recognition of this obvious fact should be very reinforcing for both of us.

As usual, Helen's predictions re me were quite accurate. I did go home and sleep very soundly before seeing WC [I do not know the identity of this person]. This is the first time that I have napped this week [Bill's lack of energy usually necessitated an afternoon nap]. While still somewhat groggy when I awakened, I did feel more with it, and was greatly relieved by the above mentioned conversation (phone) [with Helen]. I did not sleep particularly soundly during the night; a vague awareness from time to time that a great deal of unconscious material was being stirred up. Perhaps this deals with the beginning release of repression.

Other events of importance on the 14th: During the afternoon, I received a call from P [the usually hostile psychiatrist to whose child development research project Helen and Bill consulted], the sole purpose of which was to indicate some very positive attitudes about Psychology, based on a medical confirmation of a psychological prediction re a visual problem in a child two years ago. P very graciously emphasized that she wanted to indicate her ability to make a call which was not a complaint, but rather a compliment. It should be very striking to both of us [Helen and Bill] that her attitudes have changed completely, as our own perceptions shifted toward reality. A good example that "there is no order of difficulty."

Also, my attitudes toward DF [secretary] and replacement for N [Psychology staff member] are noteworthy. As long as I persisted in denying the truth in DF's mind we were having trouble with this decision. In the course of two conversations with her in the afternoon, there was a marked shift. During the first conversation, I made a real effort not to get angry, but nevertheless was somewhat judgmental and impatient about hiring someone because of personal charm, etc., rather than with an emphasis on typing skills. I strongly urged D to call references for the woman applicant whom we had seen on Tuesday. D then called me back shortly before 4 to indicate the extensively glowing recommendation she had received re this applicant, and that she would have her come in on Monday to meet HH [the department chairman].

Importance of above is that between these two calls, I did try again to look with greater awareness of reality on DF, and that the change reflected in her later attitudes *must* be related to the change in my own perceptions.

When will we stop denying the fact that the above examples are typical of what happens to us every time we are willing to look for truth and not error? It is really quite startling, but I am aware of my real difficulty in keeping this in mind without doubt or equivocation. *When I no longer deny the reality of my experience, all of these problems will evanesce....*

It was because the expectation for real change was so high during this period, that the later disappointment—that seemed to develop gradually—proved to be so painful. Again, Bill's error, despite his quite sincere efforts to practice the Course's principles, was in subtly falling into the ego's web of confusing form with content, expecting change to be external, and looking for such change as validation for the inner shift that *is* the Course's emphasis and goal. Once again, Bill's almost euphoric optimism based upon positive external events, without the corresponding internal shift, ended up to be an ego trap, into which he unwittingly walked.

The next entry, almost two weeks later, is the last one that survives, if there were indeed any others. I doubt, however, that there were; as mentioned above, keeping a journal was not an activity that Bill would usually pursue. And I suspect that as disappointment in his relationship with Helen began to become the rule, his motivation for continuing would have diminished. In addition, the early fall, when Bill seemingly stopped his entries, meant the return of his busy period at the Medical Center, which typically left Bill exhausted at the end of the day.

This entry, like the previous one, is quite optimistic about the future, and Helen's and Bill's ability to learn the Course. It begins with Bill's mention, again, of the importance for him of learning the Course with Cal Hatcher in their early morning meetings.

Sept. 28, '66

Considerable interruption in daily record, partly because most propitious time for doing this (as I see it now) is early in the morning. Have been meeting regularly with Cal Hatcher from 8–9 each morning since last week. This morning he did not show, which is in accordance with our agreement. Namely, no coercion about this. For my own learning, I think it is advantageous if I am here at 8 regardless of Cal. However, [I] did experience slight sense of disappointment when he did not arrive. The mutual interaction in trying to learn the material is facilitating for me, but attempted to review notes alone. This is helpful, but not quite as much as when done together, either with Helen or Cal.

Yesterday was noteworthy in that both Helen and I are making more of a concerted effort to look at the problem we are having, and experiencing more success in doing so. The manifest illogic of our position in vacillating all the time becomes increasingly apparent and, hopefully, increasingly unacceptable. Whenever we vacillate we are denying the reality of our experiences when we are in our right minds. That which always works when we are thinking in accordance with it can hardly be vacillating. Only our own perceptions, decisions, and willingness to learn that there is *only one thing we want to learn* is the problem. Everything else that we impose as learning blocks are quite evidently reactions of fear, resting on the belief that truth and love are destructive. This is *absurd*. While I still have difficulty keeping this in mind consistently, the logic or illogic of the situation, depending on which teacher we choose, is difficult to miss.

Was pleased that Helen and I gave a presentation which I believe was quite successful yesterday with the Neuro [Neurological Institute] residents. We were both anxious about this, despite the fact that Helen had very carefully prepared the appropriate illustrative material for this occasion. I felt that it was somehow necessary on this occasion to demonstrate that we did not need the tight structure which is frequently thought essential in *any* presentation. Although I experienced considerable anticipatory anxiety, I tried to keep in mind that the one who sent me would tell me what to do and what to say. [This of course was a reference to the message to Bill relating to the Princeton conference, *see above*, page 301, which concluded with the prayer, "I am here only to be truly helpful...."] *For the first time in my experience with this kind of professional talk*, I decided that it was not necessary to have notes, or an outline, and that I would simply try to follow what it says. From the standpoint of conviction, this should be very compelling to me, because I spoke for 20 or 25 minutes without any difficulty, and I believe with reasonable coherence, covering the essential orientation points which were necessary. It would probably be very difficult for me to reconstruct what I actually said, but I could gauge from audience reaction that it seemed in the right direction.

When I turned the session over to Helen at a time which seemed appropriate, she also presented the material very clearly and very well. If we could get it through our heads that everything can be handled easily, in a similar way, this should be enormously relieving and convincing for both of us.

I feel very encouraged that we are making considerable progress now, and much more than either one of us recognizes. Helen is beginning to see that there are really only two emotions, love and fear. This is perfectly apparent to me as I see her every day. When she is trying to deny love, she does become afraid and anticipates disaster. The current cold episode is highly illustrative of this. Yet, the opposite of this has been amply demonstrated many times, and she *is* at peace, happy, radiant and free from fear *when she recognizes that there is only one thing which is real, and only one thing which she wants.*

As we continue to see this clearly and with conviction, we should have no problems with the course, which is very explicit on this point.

This concludes Bill's journal. From later discussions with Helen and Bill, it was clear that this period of sincere attempts at forgiveness and reconciliation, not to mention the personal honesty that they openly shared with each other, was somewhat short-lived. At some point, they both fell back onto their ego selves, and reverted to their pre-Course states of projection and denial, and mutual attacks on each other. The recurring animosity and manifest failure of their relationship from the perspective of the Course now became the sole responsibility of the other: "If only you were different, I would be different and much happier."

Moreover, Helen and Bill both seemed to feel that *A Course in Miracles* had failed them, and obviously on another level, that they had failed the Course. Helen's fear of letting go of the conflict in her relationship with Jesus merely reinforced Bill's own ambivalence. As I have already indicated, Helen's apparent lack of growth in the Course allowed Bill to feel justified in his own holding back. His anger at Helen merely strengthened her own defensive posture with him, and so both ended up trapped in this vicious cycle of guilt and recrimination. And so by the time I would meet them in the fall of 1972, as I have already noted, their relationship was in their own words at an "all-time low." It did not manifestly improve from that point; if anything, it deteriorated still further, though my presence appeared to soften the direct expressions of the bitterness that existed. More of that in Part III; we return now to the Course's scribing.

Continuation and Conclusion of the Course

The end of Chapter Fifteen was written at Christmas time, 1966, and provides an interesting example of how Jesus could weave an external theme into his presentation of the course curriculum, in this case special relationships, sacrifice, and the holy instant. The chapter even closed with a lovely New Year's message. On December 30, Jesus dictated a special message on true versus false empathy. It was placed in the text exactly where it came in the dictation, and evidently was dictated by Helen to Bill without any notes. The message is reproduced almost word for word at the beginning of Chapter Sixteen, in the section called "True Empathy."

Helen's anxiety about the Course continued throughout, and every once in a while it would flare up with a vengeance. One such occurrence had a stunning climax to it. Here is Helen's description, taken from her autobiography:

> Until almost the very end of the text I continued to anticipate serious slips would come to light in my notes when I read them to Bill. He often reminded me that I was expecting a wild incoherence that I never found, but I seemed to be virtually unreassurable on the point. One rather striking episode took place that did succeed in impressing me for a while, although its kindly impact did not remain to give me permanent comfort. One evening I started late, and was writing with considerable resentment. As I wrote, I was aware of a sudden shift in style and tense, and I was sure that the incoherence I had feared for so long had finally happened. I hesitated to go on.

"Just write it as it occurs to you," said the silent Voice, very distinctly. [Note once again Helen's avoidance in this autobiographic reflection of the use of Jesus' name.] "You will recognize it later."

"But it's gone crazy," I protested. "I always knew it would, sooner or later, and now it has."

"Just write it down," said the Voice soothingly. "You're doing very well. And you will recognize it later."

I wrote on until the section finished, and then called Bill in real agitation.

"It's happened!" I announced, dramatically. "It's gone haywire. It doesn't make any sense at all."

"I doubt it," said Bill, who had been through this many times before. "But as long as you're so upset about it, try to forget about it now and we'll go over it first thing in the morning."

The next morning I arrived early, notebook in hand and sure of disaster. I read the notes to Bill, becoming more and more anxious as I got nearer the part where I had been aware of the shift. As I started to read it I paused an instant, and then burst into tears. The Voice had been right. I did recognize it. It was a version of the Lord's Prayer. It took me some time to regain my composure sufficiently to get to work.

Here "it" is, the cause of Helen's tears, as it is found at the end of Chapter Sixteen of the text. It was dictated on January 10, 1967:

Forgive us our illusions, Father, and help us to accept our true relationship with You, in which there are no illusions, and where none can ever enter. Our holiness is Yours. What can there be in us that needs forgiveness when Yours is perfect? The sleep of forgetfulness is only the unwillingness to remember Your forgiveness and Your Love. Let us not wander into temptation, for the temptation of the Son of God is not Your Will. And let us receive only what You have given, and accept but this into the minds which You created and which You love. Amen.

On May 31, 1967, Helen was in the midst of another crisis, and Jesus' answer to her was a special message, which is also not in the notebooks at all. Thus either Helen dictated it to Bill directly from her own inner hearing, or else she took it down on a separate sheet of paper that no longer exists. It was originally placed in its proper temporal sequence in the section now known as "Weakness and Defensiveness," between the words "And all uncertainty is doubt about yourself" and "How weak is fear." It was later put in Chapter Eighteen as the section "I Need Do Nothing," where the message is reproduced almost word for word.

Helen's crisis, which on an external level was literally a non-event, revolved around a threatened union strike that would have involved the elevator operators in Helen's building. She and Louis lived on the 16th floor, and Helen's fear was that the strike would begin at a time when she and Louis would be separated, one of them in the apartment and the other down below. Since in Helen's mind walking up or down the sixteen flights of stairs meant instant cardiac arrest, for either her or Louis, she was beside herself at the imminent threat of separation. Having thus defined the problem, her solution was obvious and logical: she and Louis would move to a near-by hotel. They did, where they remained for a week, never knowing that the strike was called off even before it had begun.

Jesus' message was in part an attempt to help Helen realize that she need do nothing about any perceived problem, since in truth there is no real problem "out there." The only problem that exists is our belief that we are separate from God, and this basic misperception must inevitably result in the misperception of everyone and everything. (This does not mean, incidentally, that one should do nothing behaviorally, but rather that we should not act on our own without the Holy Spirit's help.) In this particular case, there was also no real problem externally, since the elevators had continued to run normally.

The message also contained helpful information about the relationship between *A Course in Miracles* and other spiritual paths, which the interested reader may choose to consult in the text. Part of the message contained this important statement to Helen about avoiding judgment of other spiritualities, at the same time pursuing the path that was hers: "You are not making use of the course if you insist on using means which have served others well, neglecting what was made for *you*" (text, p. 363). That message would be given to Helen again years later in another form, as we shall see in Part III.

On March 11, 1968 Helen wrote down another special message, whose circumstances are unknown to me. It originally was placed in the midst of the section entitled "The Alternate to Dreams of Fear," between the words "must be a dream and cannot be the truth" and "You have conceived a little gap." It was later put in Chapter Twenty-Two, as the first two paragraphs at the beginning of "The Branching of the Road." It is virtually in the printed text as it was given to Helen.

On June 19, 1968, shortly before the text was completed, Helen wrote down this message for herself about the importance of not judging within the context of her functioning as a psychologist:

> As you see him you will see yourself. Whether this be through the use of psychological tests, or by making judgment in some other way, the effect is still the same. Whenever you have judged anyone, it is impossible for you not to make this judgment on yourself. If you see one of your brothers, who happens to be a patient, as exhibiting signs of a thought disorder, then you will experience this same disorder in your own perception. For whatever your thought may be about *anyone* determines how you will respond and react to yourself and everyone about you. Take heed then when you are called upon to fulfill your function as teachers that you teach the truth about God's Son. The only way that you can experience any peace while this unfortunate necessity for interpreting illusions remains is to recognize that you are *discussing only illusions*, and that this has no real meaning at all. Try to say a prayer for your brother while doing this and you will call forth and experience a miracle instead.

This certainly does not mean, incidentally, that psychologists should stop their worldly functioning, but rather that they should continue their work without taking their professional forms seriously. Jesus thus was not telling Helen and Bill to cease their work, but simply to be aware that they were "discussing only illusions." Thus they should use the illusion of psychological theory as the vehicle for teaching the content of truth. In other words, Jesus is telling all of us that it is our *thoughts* about our work that must shift, not necessarily the work itself. As the workbook would later advise us about bringing the light of truth into the world of darkness:

> And then step back to darkness [from the light], not because you think it real, but only to proclaim its unreality in terms which still have meaning in the world that darkness rules (workbook, p. 337).

Therefore, we do not stop making whatever personal and professional judgments are relevant to our functioning in the world. We but carry them out without condemnation and attack. Borrowing from the words of the gospel, frequently alluded to by Jesus in the Course, we are being taught how to be *in* the world, yet always remembering that we are not *of* it.

As the dictation of *A Course in Miracles* went on, Helen began to wonder when (or perhaps even if) it would ever end. Here is her account from the autobiography:

> Several times before the end I told Bill I thought things were winding up, but I was wrong. Then I began to wonder how I would know when it was really finished. I was given the answer. I would know when it used the word "amen." I still felt it was over before the word was actually used [I recall Helen's telling me that one such time was at the beginning of what would be the final section of the text, at the words: "For He *has* come, and He *is* asking this"], but it was not until the paragraph that begins "And now we say 'Amen'" that I knew the text was ended.

The text took almost three years to complete, concluding on October 10, 1968. The final paragraph, among the most inspirational passages in the material, if not in all spiritual literature, is as follows:

> And now we say "Amen." For Christ has come to dwell in the abode You set for Him before time was, in calm eternity. The journey closes, ending at the place where it began. No trace of it remains. Not one illusion is accorded faith, and not one spot of darkness still remains to hide the face of Christ from anyone. Thy Will is done, complete and perfectly, and all creation recognizes You, and knows You as the only Source it has. Clear in Your likeness does the Light shine forth from everything that lives and moves in You. For we have reached

where all of us are one, and we are home, where You would have us be (text, p. 622).

At that point, of course, nothing was said to Helen about there being any more to the Course, and so she and Bill had no idea that two more volumes were to follow. It would be a while until the workbook would begin.

And now, left with this massive tome, they set about trying to put the text into some kind of order. As noted earlier, Helen herself retyped the manuscript twice, and gradually she and Bill broke the material of the text into sections and chapters, supplying names as they went along. Most of the time the section divisions fell naturally, as dictation often stopped for the day after one of these natural breaks. In her autobiography, Helen described the initial editing period in this way:

> Then began the long and tedious job of checking for typographical errors and retyping. In order to get through this with the minimum of emotional disruption, I assumed the attitude of an editor whose role is to consider only form and disregard content as much as possible. We picked up a number of typing mistakes, which I marked in correct editorial style and indicated by page on my errata sheets. Bill was adamant in opposing any changes at all, except for deleting the too personal early references and correcting actual typing errors. I wanted to change just about everything, but I knew that Bill was right. Any changes I made were always wrong in the long run, and had to be put back. The strictly editorial attitude not only helped me get through a long and difficult job, but also proved to be the most helpful, as far as the actual material was concerned. It had a way of knowing what it was doing, and was much better left exactly as it was.
>
> When the typing was finally over, I put the cover over the machine, sighed with relief, and said to myself, happily, "And the sound of the typewriter is heard no more." I enjoyed my "release" for just about a week. Then I began to feel curiously purposeless. There was lots of work to do, but somehow it did not fill the void in my life that became increasingly large and oppressive. Some six months later, I was depressed in spirit and physically sick a great deal of the time. It crossed my mind, almost subliminally, that there might be something else I was supposed to do. I once mentioned this possibility to Bill, and hastily changed the subject. Actually, it was my husband who finally came out with it.

"Maybe you're not finished writing," he said, quite calmly and with evident sincerity.

"Don't say it," I answered angrily. "That's all I need."

"But maybe it's true," he continued. I did not answer. Several weeks later, however, I mentioned to Bill with an effort at casualness that I had an idea a workbook was supposed to go with the text. He said that that seemed like a very good idea. I did not bring the subject up again for some six weeks, during which I felt worse and worse. It seemed a workbook was indeed intended, and in due course I began to write it down. It was not so hard to write as the text had been. In the first place, I liked the general format even though I found the first few "lessons" rather trivial. [Incidentally, this was an opinion Helen never really lost, and their apparent simple-mindedness always made her somewhat uncomfortable. She was never able to move beyond the *form* of these early lessons to their profound underlying *content*.] Nevertheless, I thought it swung rather quickly into good style and very acceptable blank verse [by lesson 99], a realization which helped me a good deal. Also, the process of writing itself was no longer particularly strange to me. And finally, I approved of the precision of the arrangement of the workbook. It said at the outset exactly what it was going to do, and then proceeded to do it. Even its end was predetermined. It stated at the outset that there would be one lesson a day for a period of one year, and that was exactly the way it turned out.

Regarding the workbook and her preoccupation with form or style, Helen later told me that she had insisted to Jesus that the one-sentence introduction to all of the individual review lessons be different from each other (e.g., the introductions to Lessons 51 and 52 read: "The review for today covers the following ideas:" and "Today's review covers these ideas:"). The same "demand" on Jesus held for the second review as well.

The scribing of the workbook for students and manual for teachers proceeded relatively smoothly without incident. The workbook was taken down from May 26, 1969 through February 18, 1971; the manual began well over a year later on April 12, 1972, and ended towards the middle of September 1972 (the exact date is unknown). I might mention, that as in the text, the Christmas and Easter seasons inspired certain passages in the workbook (*see* pages 249, 273, 441).

PART III

THE YEARS FOLLOWING
A COURSE IN MIRACLES

INTRODUCTION TO PART III

We return now to my meeting Helen and Bill in the late fall of 1972, and the beginnings of my association with them. As I indicated in the Introduction to the book, that fateful November evening I certainly had no way of knowing the situation into which I was actually walking. Although there had been some improvement in Helen and Bill's relationship during the early months of the dictation, as I discussed near the end of Part II, their interpersonal situation, according to their own reports to me, had worsened considerably. The early seeming successes of applying the Course's principles to their relationship did not last long, and the initial attempts to overlook error—seeing only expressions of love or calls for love in each other—soon gave way to the old patterns of blame and self-blame. Helen and Bill were each firmly convinced that the other—now more than ever—was the cause of all problems and failures: past, present, and future. This did not become truly apparent to me for many months, however. First came the honeymoon period.

Part III begins with a chapter on the development of my relationship with Helen and Bill, and continues on with our editing of the Course, reflections on Helen and Bill's deteriorating relationship with each other and correspondingly with *A Course in Miracles* as well, additional scribings, an in-depth discussion of Helen's relationship with Jesus, and finally Helen's final months and death.

Chapter 11

SUMMER, 1973: THE CAVE

To reiterate briefly what I mentioned in the book's Introduction, after that first late-fall evening at Bill's apartment, I went off as scheduled to Israel, where I unexpectedly remained for about five months, in two monasteries. During this time I occasionally thought of "Helen's Book," and one of my purposes for returning to the States in May 1973 was to visit Helen and Bill and look at this book. I did, of course, and relatively soon after that—as I began reading the manuscript and spending time with my two new friends—realized I was to remain in New York: I had found my life's purpose and work.

I spent ten weeks in the States (as I will explain below, I did return to Israel for a brief period), a good part of this time being spent with Helen and Bill, recounting to them in great detail my own life's journey, in which they seemed interested. I also spent considerable time with each of them alone. My specific memory of this time is somewhat vague, although I do not think I consciously recognized any real difficulties in the situation. In part, I was too caught up with the aura of *A Course in Miracles*, and with these two very remarkable people, not to mention the changes rapidly occurring in my own life. And not the least of these changes, a mild understatement to be sure, was my sudden awareness of the presence of Jesus in my life. A few words need be inserted here regarding my relationship with Jesus.

I was, as Helen had pointed out to me, a very funny Christian. Baptized a Roman Catholic the previous September (though, as I mentioned earlier, without any identification with the Church or its teachings), and very much attracted to life as a Trappist monk, I was nonetheless curiously uninvolved with Jesus. This was all the more remarkable considering that during this Israeli period, when I was not in monasteries, I spent almost all of my time in the places associated with Jesus, having very strong experiences of God's presence while there. I even had had a very powerful dream of Jesus coming to me the

night before I went to Jerusalem for the first time. And yet all
the while, I never once consciously thought of the figure associated with these places, not to mention his central place in the
monastic life to which I was aspiring. While back in the States
this summer of 1973, I made plans to visit the Abbey of Gethsemani, the Trappist monastery I had originally thought to
enter, and many of whose monks I had become friendly with. I
also had promised one of the monks at Lavra Netofa in Israel to
visit his family in St. Louis, not too far from the Kentucky
Trappists.

I planned to take a bus from New York to the monastery, but
at the last minute Helen urged me to fly, saying she felt I
should save time. I trusted Helen's advice, and as I was about
to leave for the airport, Bill gave me an index card with one of
the workbook lessons typed on it. I arrived in Louisville late
that evening, and reached the monastery the next morning,
Ascension Thursday (the Catholic holy day commemorating
Jesus' ascension to his Father, forty days after the Easter
resurrection), in time to attend the end of the Abbatial Blessing
inaugurating Father Timothy Kelly as the new Abbot. Helen
was right—it was good that I had "saved time" and decided to
fly.

I ended up spending a week at the monastery, during which
time Jesus finally "showed up" for me. It occurred very early
Sunday morning. I was up about an hour before the monks'
first prayer service, which was to begin at 3:00 A.M., and was
continuing my first-time reading of the Course manuscript.
That morning I was reading the closing pages of the text. As I
began the paragraphs beginning with the words "Deny me not
the little gift I ask," it suddenly dawned on the conscious, non-
intellectual part of my mind, *who* the first person of the Course
truly was. I had known, of course, but not really. And now
suddenly I did know. Tears welled up inside me as I made my
way down to the Church for Matins.

The Abbot had given me a stall midst the monks to allow me
to participate directly with them during prayer, and at the
close of the service I remained in the dark and silent church
while the monks filed out for their period of private prayer. It
would be about two more hours until the next service would

begin, and I looked forward to being alone in the church. After a time I began to hear what was now becoming a familiar inner voice, which I always identified with God. But now, all at once, it occurred to me in a moment I shall never forget, that the voice was more personal than I had ever before experienced, and that the person was Jesus, the same Jesus whose gentle, loving, and authoritative voice was the source of *A Course in Miracles*. I could not contain the tears that streamed down my face, nor the inner joy I felt. It clearly had been, and still has remained, the central experience of my existence here on earth.

I remained at the monastery a few more days, basking in the warm glow of this new friendship with my ancient friend, whose name I have known for all time. The day I was to leave the monastery I stood in the visitor's lounge, awaiting the monk who was to drive me to the airport. I stuck my hand in my jacket pocket and discovered the index card Bill had given me. I could scarcely believe what I read, from Lesson 303, originally written for Christmas 1970:

The holy Christ is born in me today.

Watch with me, angels, watch with me today. Let all God's holy Thoughts surround me, and be still with me while Heaven's Son is born. Let earthly sounds be quiet, and the sights to which I am accustomed disappear. Let Christ be welcomed where He is at home. And let Him hear the sounds He understands, and see but sights that show His Father's Love. Let Him no longer be a stranger here, for He is born again in me today.

As I continued the second part of the lesson, I knew that in my heart of hearts I had finally welcomed the Son of God known as Jesus, as well as my true Self: two selves here, yet one Self in reality.

"Your Son is welcome, Father. He has come to save me from the evil self I made. He is the Self That You have given me. He is but what I really am in truth. He is the Son You love above all things; He is my Self as You created me. It is not Christ That can be crucified. Safe in Your Arms let me receive Your Son."

I completed the rest of my mid-Western "assignment," and

could not wait to return to New York to share with Helen and Bill all that happened. Helen especially seemed more than pleased with my "report," almost as if she had been waiting for this inner event to occur. I then began to spend more and more time at the Medical Center when not traveling around visiting with different people, and increasingly more time with Helen; we were obviously drawing closer to each other.

A major project that concerned Helen and Bill at this time was the completion of a chapter on "Other Psychological Personality Theories" for the second edition of the *Comprehensive Textbook of Psychiatry*, a prestigious publication. This was not an easy assignment. It called for Helen and Bill to collaborate closely together (professionally), an experience that in the past, as indicated earlier, was marked by very strong mutual antagonism, although the finished product was always very fine.

Although this was not clear to me at the beginning, in retrospect I understood how Helen and Bill could hardly do anything together (aside from the Course) without all of their grievances surfacing with a vengeance (literally!). And this article was certainly no exception. Bill would write, and then Helen would edit, and back and forth they would go. The tension was so thick you could cut it with a knife. I attempted to mediate somewhat, as I was familiar with the material they were covering, and had some writing and editing ability as well. My efforts to help were not harmful, but they did little to diffuse the battleground atmosphere of the office.

However, the tension always dissipated during those times when Helen and Bill listened attentively to my story, or when we spoke together about the Course. It was a most strange period for me, to say the very least. Here I was on the one hand becoming closer and closer to the two people responsible for the most remarkable book I had ever seen. On the other hand I was observing these two people caught in a horrific relationship that was clearly far, far beneath the spiritual stature present in both of them. From an objective point of view it made no sense, and this was probably my first introduction to the literally non-sensical circumstances I was now making my home, and very happily if not bewilderingly so.

For the most part I think I dismissed some of the

incongruity of the two scribes fighting together like children. Or at least I set the incongruity aside in light of the clear holiness of both of them. As the weeks went by, as I shall relate below, the incongruity became more focused for me, and I soon grew to accept both aspects of their relationship—its special and holy characteristics[83]—as fact.

On another level, one of the items that was increasingly to occupy all of us was a cave that existed at the top of the Israeli mountain (Mt. Netofa, I think it was called) that was the site of the Lower Galilean monastery to which I had thought to return after my "three or four weeks" visit to the States.

It was a cave that had been dug out by the community— joined by me in the last two months of the work—and which was to be used as their chapel. In fact, just before I left Israel, the bishop came to say Mass and consecrate the chapel. In what was most uncharacteristic of me (who am almost never attracted to places), I felt a curious connection to the cave from the moment I first laid eyes on it. And this attraction continued during the two months of work—splitting and moving heavy rocks, hauling dirt, etc.—in preparing for the bishop's visit. I spent many peaceful solitary hours sitting quietly in the cave's interior, and was especially drawn to the lower left-hand corner of the cave, made inaccessible by heavy stone.

Early in my conversations with Helen and Bill I mentioned this cave in passing. Immediately Helen "tuned in," and began to describe in remarkably accurate detail the physical characteristics of the cave. She also, before I had a chance to say anything, stated that she felt there was something of great value in that left-hand corner. This topic grew to become almost an obsession, especially as Helen felt that the "something" could very well have been the chalice of the Last Supper. Although Bill was a little more hesitant, especially at first, he too got caught up in this "speleological mischagass" (as we grew to think of this episode later; incidentally, "speleology" refers to the exploration or study of caves, while "mischagass" is a Yiddish word that means exactly what it sounds like). He

---

83. For a brief description of the Course's understanding of special and holy relationships, the reader may consult the Appendix.

thought perhaps there was an important scroll to be found there, buried in a cylinder.

I later learned that it was believed by some historians that this general area (Lower Galilee) was a hiding place for the new Christians who were fleeing the authorities and seeking secret places in which to meet after Jesus' death. It was conceivable therefore, we thought, that some of the followers of Jesus may have come to this very cave.

And finally there was Freddie, a young x-ray technician friendly with Helen and Bill, who was also the hospital "psychic." He too believed there was something of great value to be found in the cave. As for me, I did not have any real thoughts about what was there, yet did feel that there was something uniquely special about this cave site. And so we decided that I should do some exploring of the interior cave upon my return.

Even though it was now clear to me that I was to remain permanently with Helen and Bill in New York, for a number of reasons I nonetheless felt I should return temporarily to the monastery: staying in the community was a troubled young man whom I had promised to help; I wished to tell the monks personally I would not be entering their community; and now there was this cave to explore. Thus plans were made for me to return to Israel in the middle of July, with Helen, Louis, Bill, and Chip to come over at the end of the summer to see the cave, and tour Israel with me. We then would all return to New York together. At least *I* seemed clear about Helen and Bill's coming over. It took a while, as we shall see presently, for them to accept and complete the plans.

Incidentally, it was basically Bill who insisted on the trip. Helen hated to travel, and I think was somewhat apprehensive on one level about a trip to the Middle East, not the least reason being the Mediterranean summer heat. On another level, though, I feel she was really apprehensive because of the associations with Jesus. Louis, however, had always wanted to visit Israel. It was his desire, coupled with Bill's insistence that it was the least they could do, given their part in encouraging me in the cave enterprise, that convinced Helen at last to consent to the trip.

And basically the trip worked out as planned, although not without a great deal of time, energy, correspondence, and telephone calls expended on the speleological enterprise. While the full details of this should perhaps await another book, I shall briefly summarize my experience with the cave. Interestingly enough, the cave and its supposed contents began to assume the same importance for Helen as did the Mayo Clinic experience eight years earlier, with somewhat similar parallels as we shall see.

There was an interior entrance within the cave itself, that led, so we hoped, to the buried resting place of this unknown object. The abbot planned on sealing this entrance, which would then become the tabernacle and home of the Blessed Sacrament. I persuaded him, however, to delay this sealing for a couple of weeks, to allow me to do some exploring. He graciously consented, and so I began a four-day "dig" (August 9–12). Throughout the preparations for the fateful day— Thursday—that I was to begin, there was an almost daily correspondence between New York and Israel (I quote from this correspondence below). And for a more immediate report on my progress, I made weekly telephone calls to Helen and Bill as well.

But I found nothing after three days except some old coins and pottery shards, hardly unusual finds in that part of the country. The lower left-hand side of the cave, which was where we all thought there was something important, was totally inaccessible. There was no way to crawl down into it without literally blasting through rock, which would have certainly knocked down the cave walls and destroyed the chapel. Nonetheless, the process itself was an extremely meaningful one for me; my awareness of Jesus' presence deepened as I dug deeper into the inner recesses of the cave, obviously a personal symbol of going deeper into my mind.

I decided on Saturday, the third day of digging, that Sunday would be my final attempt, regardless of what was found or not found. And then, as we had arranged previously, I would call Helen and Bill on Monday. I awoke early Sunday morning from a very happy dream in which a little girl—the niece of one of the monks who was currently staying in the monastery with her mother—was happily jumping on my chest, and together we were singing the Walt Disney song, "Zippity Doo Da," climaxing with the words: "Everything is satisfactial." I then walked up the small hill on the way to the cave. The sun was just rising, and in its pristine brightness I could almost see the risen Jesus, and felt the rising joy of his resurrected life in me. I *knew* this morning would bring something.

I entered the interior of the cave for the last time, and not too long afterwards, while digging in an area I had already been through, found a stone-carved ring. It had etchings on it that I could neither decipher nor recognize, though it seemed ancient indeed. I felt a great joy, even though this was clearly *not* what Helen or Bill envisioned. But I felt then that the ring symbolized a gift from Jesus to me, symbolic of a wedding between our two selves. For me it was the culmination of the entire summer, beginning with my Gethsemani experience. I left the cave shortly afterwards, overflowing with gratitude for my wonderful gift.

I called Helen and Bill the following day, and although Helen especially seemed disappointed, I think on another level she was relieved that nothing had come out of this brief sojourn into the realm of magic. I also think my enthusiasm for the experience, regardless of the "negative" outcome, helped to buoy her spirits. We then began to complete the plans for their coming over. But before I continue this narrative, let me discuss the aforementioned correspondence between me and Helen and Bill. Among other things, Helen's letters illustrate her sense of humor and her ongoing struggles with faith in a Jesus whom she, despite her protestations to the contrary, obviously believed in and loved. It was also clear that she had accepted choices she had already made on another level, but which made no sense to her rational, logical mind. I cite some excerpts from Helen's letters to me, and from some of Bill's as well, although he was not the correspondent Helen was.

July 17

Ken dear—

....Needless to say, I am very uncomfortable about the whole thing [with the cave] and would much rather skip it, especially being the nervous type. I also *strongly* suggest that you check it with Him,[84] because I wouldn't want things to get out of hand, meaning His. As for me, all this seems kind of nutty.

Ken, dear, it was lovely having you with us, although I am quite confused at the moment. I hope all this works out somehow, and I suppose I don't have to know how. Your certainty was a great relief to Bill and me, and I sure miss it. Well—maybe you'll find something, even if it's only Truth.

July 20

Ken dear,

. . . .

We had a wonderful time together [the ten weeks prior to my return to Israel]. Didn't we? I can't help wondering where we go from here. I think I read something about trust some-where, but I'm not too good at it yet. We're doing our lessons, though, and I think they help. I particularly like the 11:15 one with you [Helen, Bill, and I had agreed to meditate on the daily workbook lesson every day at 11:15 A.M., New York time]. The feeling of joining is very heartening, and I'm so glad our group finally got started [*see below*, the letter of July 31].

July 23

Ken dear,

It was kind of wonderful talking with you this morning, and it came through clearer than a local call, too. We're very anxi-ous to get some letters, because we gather that some happy things have been happening. I got largely bogged down after you left, and Bill and I miss your cheery enthusiasm which, I'm afraid, does not really characterize either of us. Poe's raven, maybe, surrounded by Gestalt psychology [a reference to the chapter on personality theories Helen and Bill were writing]. I don't think we'll ever finish the chapter, and if we ever do I won't like it.

I'm so hoping that there really is something in the cave. It would be hard to overlook that, I should think, although Bill says I probably could. Jonathan [Louis] says, very pleasantly though, that we're all crazy. He does like you, and even spe-cially asks me to send his best. . . . It does seem odd that Freddie

---

84. *See above*, page 226, footnote 49, for an explanation of Helen's use of capital letters for pronouns related to Jesus.

[the hospital x-ray technician I mentioned above] was so specific, and seems to have seen very much the same thing that we did. I wish I knew if it's a real thing or a symbol, or maybe both. Waiting is very hard for me, especially on something like this. I suppose there's an off chance that Jonathan is right, after all. Still, perhaps not.

It was nice about the boat, though. I suddenly recognized it, and I'm surprised now that I didn't do it sooner. Even the angle at which I look at it is just the same as it was the first time I saw it with the anchor stuck deep in the mud. It changed its form several times in the long sequence of adventures that came its way, and this is the only time it looks just the way it did at the outset. But this time the water is very quiet and the anchor is quite secure. I doubt if it could be pulled up again. In fact, I have been assured [by Jesus] that it won't be. After all, there is a side of me that believes all this. Confusing, isn't it?

This was, of course, a reference to the boat in Helen's visionary sequence that culminated in her discovering the black book in the treasure chest. Helen is here referring to her having seen it with a flag in the mast, containing a ring of stars. She had seen this flag on two occasions; in one it contained six stars, in the other ten. The "six" came from Helen's belief that there would be a core inner group of five or six people who would truly understand *A Course in Miracles* (*see below*), and would provide its central focus in the world. The "ten" was more obscure, and we hypothesized that it might be a reference to the ten lost tribes of Israel, symbolically relating to our "being found," coming together now once again. Bill and I occasionally kidded Helen about the ten, saying that she had increased the "magic number" from six.

July 25
Dear Ken—

. . . .

I met Freddie in the hallway at lunch—all of a sudden I seem to meet him every day, not having run into him for months. I don't like to mention this, but he wants me to be *sure* to tell you not to throw away any bones you may find. He's sure they would have special historical value—Biblical, in fact. Me—I'm satisfied if you just find *something*. And maybe even what we thought. It would be wonderful, wouldn't it? I'm afraid it's hard enough for me to believe, even when I've seen. After all, as I keep telling myself, the course is *quite* visible.

I continually reminded Helen of this last statement in the years to come, as I shall discuss below.

July 28

Ken dear—

....And I do specially thank you for praying at the shrine of Mary Magdalene for me. I sure could use it.

Helen had a special attraction to Mary Magdalene, just as she had with Mary, Jesus' mother. I had written Helen that I remembered her while standing in front of the altar to Magdalene at the Church of the Holy Sepulchre in Jerusalem. The letter continues:

Bill and I had lunch and sat in the park a bit, and then I got a yen to go to church. So I heard Mass at St. Francis Xavier's. Frankly, nothing much, if that.

I'm afraid I've got very uneasy about going to Israel and the whole chalice bit. Seems I won't be happy pretty much whatever comes of that. And faith seems to be largely a secondary effect. I guess the idea is you follow Guidance and faith in it comes because you did. That's roughly what you do, isn't it?

Anyway, I'm *so* glad He [Jesus] keeps His eye on you. He'll probably get around to all of us in time. Meanwhile, we think of you a lot and do look forward to your letters. There's so much hope in them a little bit even rubs off on my fingers.

Love again—Helen

July 30

Dear Ken,

....

There is something I'd like to tell you about the cave. Bill thought I could wait, but I guess that's because I had a real fit when it happened. It seems (I note I'm still having a fit, but a relatively minor one) that Freddie told me last week that he thought Mary Magdalene is buried there. Now, don't faint. I've done that already. I swear I never mentioned the name, and didn't even hint at anything you and I said about her. Besides, as you well know, the whole thing makes me so nervous I am hardly likely to bring it up needlessly. He just said it, and that was that. He also said that the Thing in the cave will somehow explain what happened to her. I don't get that part. In fact, I don't get the whole thing. But I do think it's only fair to mention it. By the way, Bill says it could be merely an example of mental telepathy, which he thinks is more "mere" than I do. He says Freddie is adept at picking things up from people, and that may have been where he got it. That's an explanation? By the way, Freddie did tell me that you would go into the cave next Thursday [this was correct]. On that I gather he may have a point.

All I can say is that this used to be a very respectable Psychology Department, and nothing funny ever happened. It may have been a little dull, but nothing unexpected was likely to come by and shake people up very badly. I just about conked out with that Freddie bit, but Bill seems to think it's among the more ordinary of the more recent events. What do you think?

....I don't know what anything means, though, and that is hardly my preferred life style. I'm trying to get used to it, but I find it tough going. Bill wants to add a note, and I don't want to cramp him out [Helen was near the bottom of the page], so—love—Helen

Dear Ken—It was so good to talk to you today, and later receive 3 letters from you at my office....If I only had the extent of your conviction about guidance at all times! Speleology will never be the same! Love —Bill

The following letter is an important one, as Helen comments on the crucial difference between content and form ("fact and allegory"), and the parallels that Bill pointed out between the cave and their earlier experiences surrounding the visit to the Mayo Clinic.

July 31

Ken dear,

This is a letter I feel just has to be written, and written as soon as possible. It has to do with fact and allegory and the somewhat uncertain borderline between them. We have been thinking of the chalice and the cave and all that in very literal terms, and I think it was right to do so. Of course I don't know how it will turn out, and perhaps the more literal aspects are really there. Freddie does not understand symbolism; the dear boy can't even understand how a thing can stand for something else. Bill went over this with him, and all he could grasp was if you see something it's there. It's not that he's stupid, Heaven knows, but he just can't seem to get beyond facts, so he can be mistaken just because of that.

I want to give you the rest of his message first, before I get to my own concerns. He dropped in today, and asked me to be sure to tell you that the first and the second and even the third time you try will probably not be enough. He thinks the chalice (if such it be) is rather deeply covered up by time. We differ on that, if you remember. He also wants me to tell you that he thinks it's something rather small, and is afraid you may miss it because you're thinking of something bigger. He doesn't know you're asking what to do of Someone else, and I still would go more by Him than by this sort of thing, which can slip off all too easily. The other One can't.

This evening I called Bill and asked him what we were supposed to do if there's nothing in the cave; or at least if you don't find anything there. He gave an answer that maybe we should both think of. It even soothed me a bit, which takes some doing. He says perhaps we should remember the Mayo Clinic caper—that church wasn't there any more, either, but there was no question that the image and the place all meant something even more important. I guess the idea is not to allow the luxury of disappointment to come in. I'm sure that we can always ask what the lesson is, and there has to be an answer whatever comes out in fact. If you get the idea that I am writing more to myself than to you, you may be right.

Things have been fairly dismal, except that the chapter is almost finished. Just a day or so now. Come to think of it, there was one bright spot; I suddenly felt extremely joyous and said to myself, "We're all coming together again at last. And what wonderful things we'll do in Your Name!"

In what we later realized was a simultaneous experience, I was reading the Course one afternoon at the monastery when I set aside the pages in front of me and turned instead to "For They Have Come," Helen's and my mutually favorite section. I wept profusely as I read its "other-worldly" words, thinking specifically of Helen, Bill, and me, and of our having come together.

Helen's letter continues:

I got very excited about this, not disturbed by the fact that I had no idea what it meant. It didn't last, though. I don't seem to have your persistence in matters of this kind. In fact, as you see, I hardly remembered the whole episode. Well, its meaning will probably turn up, time being what it is. So now I've said what I think I was supposed to and will go to bed. I *wish* this cave thing were settled one way or another.

Love, Helen

P.S. Bill *always* sends his love, too.

August 2

Dear Ken,

....

As for your other assignment, the course will probably grow on you, and it does seem right that you get to know it rather well. It's quite compressed in writing style, and sometimes says an amazing amount in a sentence or so. Since you seem to be doing better with it than we are, your enthusiasm, which I hope is still there, may yet be a light to us.

August 3 (from Bill)

Dear Ken,

Your letters continue to be the most compelling testimony for the Course, its Source, and its applicability to the myriad seeming problems we encounter daily. I wish that after these many years of partial effort I experienced the extent of conviction which pervades all areas of your life. But partial efforts can only bring partial results, and I know that your help is an essential part of the plan for all of us. We do indeed seem to be approaching, more quickly than I thought possible, some resolution of many issues. At times it seems both exciting and baffling, since on some days Ariadne can unravel very rapidly.[85] But the new pattern, however it may be woven, is one which we all seek and must surely find, where stability and peace will replace these rapid shifts between two worlds.

....As for speleology and its special problems, we seem to be surrounded with expert guidance on all the specifics. If at least

---

85. A reference to the Greek myth of Ariadne's supplying Theseus with a thread enabling him to escape from the labyrinth.

one of Plato's prisoners found his way out of the cave, I'm certain that you will find the right way in. Incidentally, some major archaeological discoveries have been made by "amateurs," and I doubt that many of them came equipped with a near-gallon of rubber cement!

One of Freddie's recommendations was that I bring along some rubber cement in order to take an impression of the object I would find. I did attempt to use it for the ring I found, but the cement did not hold the impression.

Bill's letter concludes:

The travel folder on Israel is most helpful and fascinating. But most important of all is our daily awareness of your continually expanding venture in faith, and your eagerness to share it with us.

Peace,
and Love, Bill

On August 5, Helen wrote:

Dear Ken,

.... By the way, it sort of came to me it might be a scroll. And Bill had once thought it might be, too. Can't say, really. I am at the point where I'd settle for pretty much anything.

We got some guide books to Israel, just in case. I really do hate this uncertainty. In a sudden rush of religion to the head I went down to St. John's [a Capuchin church opposite Pennsylvania Station in New York City]...and heard Mass there. I thought the idea was for Bill to go too, which he did. It didn't send me, but it did send Bill—in fact, right out of the church. I doubt if we'll find it [the answer] there. Bill said it's all right if you think you get Brownie points for it, but he somehow didn't see it that way. No more did I. Sad, isn't it? It would be so easy that way....

I really was disappointed about...[the] church. Somehow, I keep hoping that sort of thing will turn out differently, but it just doesn't seem to. Nor do I have your happy way of looking at things as lessons, even though we have been assured that they are,—repeatedly, too. What do you think is wrong? I know it's not anything external, but couldn't it be that something internal got set off somehow? Never seems to work. Perhaps you can come up with a better idea....

Helen's last comments refer to the ego's magical hope that the outer determines the inner, so that faith in God could be brought on by externals, such as attendance at Mass. The letter then concludes:

> This is due to be the Big Week [of my entering the cave], I expect. Here's hoping, but I don't know for what. Things at least seemed to be better when I thought I knew what I was doing. And you?
>
> Love—Helen

The next day Helen wrote again:

August 6 or 7

Dear Ken:

> As is obvious, I am not quite sure what date it is. What I *do* know, though, is that it's getting into Cave Week, which I still find very unsettling. Bill thinks I have the speleological jitters, which I gather is very serious indeed, and there's no cure for it as yet. This is because it's very rare, and not much research has been done on it yet. In fact, practically nobody has it. As you can see, even my typing is adversely affected....
>
> It's still uncomfortable being half poised for flight. You can't walk steadily with one foot off the ground, and it's really difficult to know what to do about the other one at this point. So far there has been only dead silence from Above, or perhaps I should say Within. Perhaps the wires are crossed at the moment. It may be partly because I have been very reluctant to go back to the sound thing [*see* Chapter 14], not quite having recovered from the chapter. Perhaps the way to recover from the chapter *is* to go back to the sound thing, but I can't see it that way yet. You don't seem to have the trouble with assignments that I do.
>
> We are still meeting Freddie just about every day, even though he used to be quite rare on our horizons. It's getting so that we even know when he'll turn up, and where, too. I don't get just what his part is in all this (I didn't say all this mess, you'll note, but it obviously crossed my mind), but he seems to have something to do with it. Perhaps I should mention again that he was so anxious that you remember it may be quite a number of attempts before you find the ... the ...[86] who knows what.

---

86. Helen's ellipses.

I am beginning to look back with nostalgia on the good old days, when I was just depressed and anxious, but had a general feeling that I knew what I was doing. Things were much better then. Bill says they weren't, though. I expect it's that last step that's holding things up. It's a hard one to take for most of us. How did you ever manage?

Just think! By now you've been in the cave and all. I'm holding my breath. And meanwhile, Bill wants to say hello. So love—Helen

Dear Ken—Freddie and Angel [his friend] are stopping by my apartment on Thursday for a visit. Perhaps they will "tune in" on your progress today. Somehow I think today may have been important for you, but we shall soon know. . . . As always, your daily letters are a source of great cheer.

Love—Bill

In this next letter, after a brief reference to the cave, Helen mentions my parents, who were quite upset with their son's rather strange (to them) behavior of becoming Catholic and planning to enter a monastery.

August 9

Dear Ken,

. . . . This is C-day, about which I am quite apprehensive. Not that I think you will have trouble, but I don't know what or if, or even if. . . .[87]

It's too bad about your not hearing from your parents, and I more than understand your concern. It occurred to me briefly that I might be able to help [Helen did; *see below*, Chapter 16], but I wouldn't do anything about it unless you agreed. And maybe you've heard from them by now, and know that everything is all right. I know it's hard on you to handle this, particularly your mother, who does seem to have a self-destructive life style. Unfortunately, she may still think it will work.

You have the happiest knack of leaving things to the Driver, so I guess you know better than I what to do about your folks. I suppose the same applies to whatever happens in the cave (or out of it, for that matter). . . . Do you think something definite will turn up? Perhaps the cave is merely a little part of a larger something, as you wisely suggest.

---

87. Helen's ellipsis.

We are doing a particularly fortunate lesson for today, along with you ["The light has come."]. It seems especially good for cave-day, whatever may come of it....And I am grateful that you sure don't discourage easily. That's a prerequisite for everything.... [I] send my love again. Helen

Helen's letter of August 10, my second day in the cave, contains a reference to the "troubled young man" I mentioned above, whom I was helping to work through a psychotic break. I had been discussing him with Helen and Bill in my letters. I forget now the specific parallel Helen alludes to in her comments.

August 10

Dear Ken—

Now, it's after Cave Day I, and I do wish we could hear something. I more than understand the telephone problem you describe, which Bill anticipated. And maybe there's nothing to tell us. But perhaps in time.

You seem to be having quite a celestial adventure up there on the hill. I doubt if it's really place-related, though. In fact, I think there is even Biblical evidence to the contrary. And I gather there is indeed some very active practical help you are called on for even there. It may be that there really are no peaceful secluded hilltops any more, if there ever were.

It is interesting that you've run into a young man whose problem seems so much like those in the family [i.e., Helen and Bill] here. Perhaps that is a special thing for you. Who knows where we will all end up, or what we will be doing there? I'm sure we can be a big help to each other in doing it, though.

I'm really trying to be patient about cave news, but I'm afraid I'm rather deficient in that respect. I don't even rate A for effort. "Yet it sufficeth that the day will end," which is at least a pretty line. And so, love for today again—Helen

August 11

Dear Ken—

And so we are still waiting for news. It's so very nice to get your letters anyway—I'm by no means complaining about that. I suppose if I had your lovely happy outlook, I'd say it's so wonderful hearing from you, and getting such spiritually

352

uplifting messages that it's positively ungrateful to need more.
I'm practicing doing it, but you know I'm not the type (yet).
Your letters are still very welcome to both of us, I assure you. I
guess the cave just waits.

We are going to the Israeli Travel Bureau on Monday, just
to be ready in case. The whole thing seems quite dream-like to
me. Bill is more realistic. Like you, he says "You just go."
Me—I see problems. More practicing indicated.

I do hope you've heard from your parents by now and been
reassured about them. Long-distance worrying is particularly
painful. Your Friend might help—but I'm sure you've asked
Him. Your friendship seems to be growing, doesn't it?...Love
for now—Helen

On Monday, the day I would call Helen and Bill, Bill wrote
me a letter, largely about our mutual friend, Father Michael.
These portions are omitted.

August 13

Dear Ken,

While sitting at my desk early this morning I was thinking
of you, and of the possibility that we might receive an
unscheduled call. When I think of all the difficulties involved
in your making a call (even though your way is smoothed), I'm
not sure that this would be the best use of your time. But
perhaps this can serve as part of our attempts to improve the
frequency of correspondence. This time, I thought maybe
Helen would like to add something at the end, since she has
been representing us both so faithfully....

This afternoon, Helen and I are planning to stop by the
Israeli Tourist Office to pick up whatever relevant information
there may be. But, now it's time for Helen to tell you the rest -
Love, Bill

Ken dear—There's not much space [at the end of the page] for
the rest, but there isn't any, really. We're just sort of
suspended, and it feels a little funny. It would be nice to hear
something definitive—maybe soon. You're surely getting
letters from us now [the mail had been erratic]. We're writing
lots—Much love—Helen

Helen's last two letters were written after my telephone call to report on the cave, and consisted mainly of the upcoming trip, which Helen and Bill were finally able to make definite.

August 16

Dear Ken—

It's funny to go over all this, because by the time you get this letter you will know all about it: We've arranged for two nights in Tel Aviv under advice [from Jesus], and it's probably a good idea at that....

Freddie is still sure of something behind loose stones at the back of the cave. He is sure the place is particularly holy because of it. I think he may be referring to the past, which your letter about the history of the area suggests....

So we'll be there shortly. I don't think we'll write after this week, because we could just as well bring the letters in person by that time.... And so you seem to have been right about our vacation after all. It will be lovely seeing you, though my own certainty stops there. Love—Helen

Bill added the following:

Dear Ken,

We received three letters from you this morning, which has indeed brightened our day.... Once we get the idea about "no order of difficulty in miracles," Helen and I should be well along toward accepting the peace and joy that radiates through your letters. We will have a great deal to talk about, and very soon, since our arrival will probably be shortly after you receive this. Love, and a happy reunion soon. Bill

August 17

Ken dear—

This should arrive pretty much along with us. Now that we have made the decision and have even paid for the tickets, it is slowly dawning on me that we are probably going to go. One of the more comforting things to me, a dedicated worrier by avocation, is that all the disasters I am gloomily anticipating on the way couldn't possibly happen. There won't be enough time. The thought isn't a really great comfort, though.

On the other hand, there is just a possibility it might be a wonderful trip—even a very important one. Anyway, the one thing I do know is that it will be lovely to be with you again.

354

And we do want to see your mountain, too, and hopefully the beautiful statue at Latroun [*see below*, p. 356]. So maybe, just possibly, all will be well. But did you really have to go so far away?

I guess it was a really inevitable trip, as you yourself suggested. Sort of closed in on us all, didn't it? We are still more or less keeping things fairly planless, although there's lots we'd like to see. I can just hear you say "There's lots of time." Hope you've heard from your other family by now, and that the news is good.

It's funny to say "see you soon" but there it is. Love— Helen (and some from Bill)

The New York entourage did arrive as scheduled, on August 29, and I met them at the Tel Aviv airport. We rented a car and I acted as chauffeur/tour guide for our two weeks together. I remember that one of the first things I did after their arrival was to shave off my "Israel" beard for Helen. After spending two nights in Tel Aviv, we drove north to Haifa. Leaving Louis for the day—he had no desire to go mountain climbing, let alone cave exploring—Helen, Bill, Chip, and I drove to the Arab village of Deir Hanna, at the base of the mountain.

I had made what I thought were definite arrangements for transportation up the mountain (walking up, the community's frequent means of "transportation," was out of the question for Helen), but a local school holiday had disrupted those plans. I managed, however, to prevail upon a member of an Arab family I knew to drive us up on his tractor. And so the ascent up the mountain began, with Helen and I sitting tightly together on the back of the cab, and Helen frightened she would fall off, but even more terrified that the bumps would dislodge her retina. Meanwhile, Bill and Chip were riding precariously on the attached wagon, up this almost one-mile dusty and very bumpy road to the monastery.

After a pleasant lunch with the two monks and a number of other community visitors—all of whom must have thought there was something very strange about us, not to mention this peculiar interest in the cave—I took Helen and Bill to the cave. A photograph remains of the three of us standing there (*see* p. P-7). Indelibly imprinted on my memory is the image of Helen, wrapped in my raincoat to protect her clothing, perched on the ledge of the interior entrance to the cave, not far from where I found the ring. Helen and Bill agreed with my thinking, incidentally, that I should not keep the ring, but rather should leave it in Israel. After all, the true gift was the ring's meaning to me, not the object itself: the content, not the form. We later visited a museum in Jerusalem, where the ring was dated from a period before the time of Jesus. We ultimately left the ring with the abbot, and I am not sure what has happened to it since.

We all returned to Haifa, and then made our way back across Galilee, visited the various holy sites, and then drove down along the Jordan to Jerusalem. On the way, I stopped the car by a little-known Moslem shrine where supposedly the tomb of Mary Magdalene is located, and Helen and I spent a few quiet minutes praying there. We then stayed several days in Jerusalem, visiting the various Christian and Jewish holy places. Helen and I also went to the Abbey of Latroun, the Trappist monastery in which I had spent three months. In the church was a truly beautiful statue of Mary (*see* p. P-11), to which I felt strongly attracted, and which Helen very much wanted to see. I shall discuss Helen's attraction to Mary in Chapter 16.

At one point during our Jerusalem stay, Bill became insistent that we visit Qumran, outside Jericho, the place where the Dead Sea Scrolls were found. They had been buried in the caves immediately adjacent to the home of the Essene community. A few months earlier I had driven with some friends past this site, and the decision to stop there was left to me. But I did not feel we should stop; perhaps some other time I would go there, I thought to myself, but not then. The "other time" had now obviously come, and so we all went to Qumran. The result was totally unexpected, and as with the Mayo Clinic episode years before—appropriately recalled by Bill over the summer (*see* Helen's letter of July 31)—the strange events of the summer finally received their explanation, as I shall now relate.

Almost from the moment we arrived at Qumran, Helen was visibly moved, most uncharacteristic of her. As we stood on the site of the ancient community, we looked across the roped-off area to a series of caves, including the one where the scrolls were found in cylinders not unlike what Bill thought might be in "my" cave. At some point Helen burst into tears, and told us that the cave in front of her was the exact cave she had seen in her vision of the "God Is" scroll. She then exclaimed that she was standing on the holiest place on earth.

Turning around to look at the Dead Sea, not far from Qumran, Helen remarked that the water level was too low, and that it should be considerably higher. Bill consulted his guide book, and sure enough it stated that two thousand years ago the water level had indeed been much higher. Helen and I then walked towards some of the ruins, and she told me of her strong impulse to walk over to the area which the Essenes had used as their cemetery. But then she felt an equally strong impulse from Jesus not to do so, hearing him say to her: "Let the dead bury the dead." And so Helen stayed away from what she almost certainly felt to be her own gravesite, nineteen hundred years ago.

Helen, Bill, and I later were discussing this rather emotional morning, when it occurred to all of us that it was this cave at Qumran, and what it represented for Helen, that was the true object of what had so preoccupied us during the summer. That preoccupation had been displaced to the cave at the monastery. Similar to Helen's and Bill's experience with the Mayo Clinic, we not only had the *content* wrong, but the *form* as well.

On another level, I think Bill's feelings about a scroll buried in a cylinder were displaced from the Qumran cave to the one on Mt. Netofa. Helen's thoughts about a chalice—such a holy symbol in Christianity, the Arthurian legends, as well as in *A Course in Miracles*, where as we have seen, it is identified with the Atonement—were likewise displaced from her experience at Qumran, "the holiest place on earth." As for me, I still feel there is something of value in the cave, but perhaps it was only of personal meaning, a meaning which was more than fulfilled by my experience in finding the ring. Of the chalice, scroll, or whatever is or is not buried there, we shall never know. The interior to the cave is sealed, and so, it seems, it should be. Let the dead bury the dead, as it were: the past—the form—is over; the content of love remains.

All in all, therefore, the experience was an exercise of faith, having trust with no concern for the outcome. And if nothing else, the cave episode had bonded Helen, Bill, and me ever more closely.

We left Israel for New York in September. As it turned out, it was a very timely exit, since it was only a few days before the outbreak of the Yom Kippur war. I arrived in New York without a place to live, let alone a job. For the first few days I stayed in Bill's apartment, until Father Michael arranged for me to stay at the Leo House, a Catholic hotel on West 23rd Street in Manhattan. I was to remain there for almost a year. A hiring freeze at Presbyterian Hospital made it impossible for me to get a job there, but since money was not an immediate concern, I was able to be up there *as if* I had a full-time position. It would not be for another year that a half-time position would become available to me, and that then provided me with the income I needed. In the interim, Father Michael had begun to refer a few nuns and priests to me for therapy, and before I knew it I had a regular practice. Michael also arranged for some psychological testing to be done by us on candidates for religious orders. Helen, Bill, and I collaborated on these, and the money generated from the evaluations paid for the costs of the final typing of the Course manuscript (actually, only the text needed retyping) and copying charges.

But I am getting ahead of the story, which awaits another chapter. I recall that as we landed in New York, I was feeling that I was about to embark on a journey whose direction I could not begin to understand, one which would take me places that at that point I was probably better off not knowing about. I had had hints in Israel of the ambivalent nature of Helen and Bill's relationship, not to mention during those ten weeks in the late spring and early summer when I was in New York, but it was not until now, when we would be together almost all of the time, that the full extent of this ambivalence would become clear to me. I shall return to Helen and Bill's special and holy relationship in Chapter 13, after the following chapter which discusses Helen's and my editing of the Course.

Chapter 12

THE EDITING (1973–1975)

I completed my first reading of *A Course in Miracles* during the ten weeks I spent back in the States in 1973. I read a copy of Helen's second retyping (at least of the text) which was presented to Hugh Lynn Cayce, and thus it was named by us, as mentioned earlier, the "Hugh Lynn Version." The text, incidentally, was divided at that time into four volumes, corresponding to the four thesis binders Bill had bought to house the manuscript. I read the text, workbook, and manual straight through, and then began the text again when I returned to Israel. Helen, Bill, and I agreed to do the workbook together, but only on Helen's condition that we start with Lesson 51, the beginning of the review for the first fifty lessons. Helen never liked the first fifty lessons, as was discussed in Part II. I completed my second reading of the three books, which I did much more slowly, sometime after our return to New York. Shortly afterwards I began again, partially in preparation for a glossary-index for the Course, something I thought would be useful. As it turned out, however, I did not seriously begin work on that book until 1977, when we were all in England, and even then it was not to be completed for another five years.

At any rate, I was reading the text again, and very carefully at this point. I commented to Helen and Bill that I thought the manuscript needed some additional editing. Some of the personal and professional material still remained, and seemed inappropriate for a published edition. The first four chapters did not read well at all, in large part because the deleted personal material left gaps in the remaining text, and thus required minor word additions to smooth the transition. Also, some of the divisions in the material appeared arbitrary to me, and many of the section and chapter titles did not really coincide with the material. (I later learned that Helen's usual methodology was to draw the section title from its opening lines, even if the subsequent material went in a different direction.) Finally, the paragraphing, punctuation, and capitalization were not only idiosyncratic, but notoriously inconsistent.

Helen and Bill agreed that it did need a final run-through. As Bill lacked the patience and attention to detail that was needed for such a task, we decided that Helen and I should go through it together. And so we did, never realizing just how long it would take us to complete the editing. I earlier quoted Helen's statement that she had come to think of *A Course in Miracles* as her life's work, and she approached the editing project with a real dedication. She and I meticulously went over every word to be sure that the final manuscript was right.

Helen was a compulsive editor, and an excellent one at that. She would not really edit a manuscript, however; she attacked it. While Helen had a pronounced writer's block, as discussed earlier, no such block existed when it came to editing something previously written. One day I was leaving the office for a luncheon appointment, and Helen was on the phone. I scribbled a two-line note telling her I was leaving and that I would be back later. Without batting an eye or losing the train of thought in her phone conversation, Helen picked up a pencil and began to edit my note. I always regretted not having kept it afterwards. It was therefore all the more remarkable that she was able to resist the great temptation, not to mention compulsive need, to edit the Course and "improve it." To be sure, some amount of editing was needed in the early chapters, and Helen felt that Jesus was helping her to do just that. But otherwise, she was basically able to leave the manuscript alone.

The editing was not without its humorous moments—despite Helen's obvious discomfort—and there were quite a few of them. Helen's now almost legendary anxiety surrounding the Course was probably never in fuller force. While she most definitely wanted us to complete the editing project, she nonetheless would find almost any excuse to distract us from *not* sitting down and doing it. The project took us considerably longer than it had to because of these delays, circumstances not too dissimilar from the dictation of *A Course in Miracles* itself, which clearly did not have to consume seven full years.

We did most of the editing either in Helen's offices at the

Neurological Institute and Black Building, at my studio apartment, or at Helen's apartment, the last being Helen's favorite place. Thus we would often sit together on her living room couch and work. Invariably, however, Helen would start to fall asleep. We would be editing, and suddenly I would look to my left, and there Helen would be, slumping in the corner of the couch, her usually very alert eyes practically closed. Very often the sleepiness would be accompanied by pronounced yawning jags that made speaking almost impossible. And then there were the times when Helen would *simultaneously* begin to cough, as if trying to expel some foreign agent stuck in her throat. At these moments Helen would begin to laugh at the obviousness of her ego's defenses, tears streaming down her face as she did so, in accompaniment to this very well orchestrated anxiety fugue of yawns, coughs, and laughter. I could not help thinking then of the end to Wagner's Prelude to *Die Meistersinger*, where three themes combine in a masterpiece of lighthearted contrapuntal writing. The good nature of Wagner's music was mirrored for me in the gentle humor of Helen's ego diversions, at least this aspect of them.

And then there was the time we were returning from the Medical Center, walking on 14th Street from Eighth to Third Avenues, on our way home to continue the editing. We were literally in the middle of Sixth Avenue when I brought up an editing question. I received no response and turned around, only to find Helen on the ground, again laughing heartily at herself. There were no potholes or crevices in the street that could have caused her to stumble, but there certainly were the inner potholes of fear that periodically reared their ugly head to trip Helen up. In this case, the only real victim was Helen's pantyhose that tore in the fall.

A major focus of our work was the early chapters of the text. We went through at least two complete edits of these, and many, many partial ones. As I indicated in Part II, the first weeks of the dictation were characterized not only by Helen's extreme anxiety and fear, but by the informality of Jesus' dictation to her. The conversational tone of these sessions, coupled with the personal material that was interwoven with the actual teaching, made the editing very difficult. As briefly mentioned above, stylistic gaps were left when the personal material was taken out. Incidentally, the miracle principles that properly begin the text did not come point by point, but were interspersed with considerable other material, as is apparent in the excerpts cited in Chapter 8.

I remember half-jokingly asking Helen at one point to suggest to Jesus that perhaps he might re-dictate the early chapters, but it was clear that this was not going to be done. We thus did the best we could in reorganizing this material into coherent sections and chapters that would fit in with the text as a whole. A discerning reader can sense the difference in tone and style as the text continues. Roughly the current fifth chapter of the text marks one such dividing line, after which the text was dictated pretty much as it is found now. Personal material that came afterwards did not present the same editing problem, as I commented above, for it was not so interwoven with the material of the text itself.

Our basic procedure was that early in the morning I would read through the material we would cover later that day, or review our previous day's work. I would pencil in those corrections and changes I thought were necessary. Helen and I would then go over these together, after which I would go back over what we had done, and re-present this to Helen. This procedure went back and forth in these early chapters, until we felt it was the way Jesus wanted it. We both felt his presence guiding us in this work, and it was clear for the most part that our personal preferences and concerns played no important role in these decisions. I added the qualifying phrase "for the most part," as Helen did feel that Jesus allowed her the license to make minor changes in the form, as long as the content itself was not affected. This license only extended itself to questions of punctuation, paragraphing, capitalization, and minor word changes (such as switching "that" for "which," and vice versa; *see* more below), but never to the inclusion or exclusion of important material.

Several times during our editing Helen would recognize a word that she had changed from the original dictation, and that she and Bill had not caught in their initial editing. And so we changed these words back to the original ones. I was impressed throughout by the integrity with which Helen went about the editing. I have already remarked on the ferocity of her editing when it came to professional writings, and yet she was able to resist such compulsivity during the editing of the Course. Any changes we made in the order of material (I've indicated earlier how certain paragraphs were moved around) we showed Bill, who likewise shared Helen's attitude of absolute integrity and fidelity to the original dictation.

Bill usually was most uninterested in form, but I remember two strong exceptions. Helen had told me how insistent he was that the final inspiring paragraph of the text—"And now we say 'Amen,'"—not be broken up, and that the full paragraph be on one page. He continued his insistence with the published edition, although it naturally fell that way in the typesetting. Second, Bill insisted that there be *fifty* miracle principles, even though in the original dictation there were only 43, later changed to 53 in the two re-typings by Helen. Again, this kind of insistence was unlike Bill. In these numbering changes, incidentally, no text was added or deleted; the material was simply rearranged.

A cute yet strange aspect to our editing recurred every once in a while, when after reading a particularly difficult passage Helen would turn to me in laughter, exclaiming that she did not have the remotest idea what the words meant. And so I found myself in the rather unusual situation of explaining the Course to the person who on another level understood what it was saying more clearly than anyone else possibly could. Thus began my first experiences of teaching this material.

Interestingly enough, when in the presence of someone else attempting to explain the Course, Helen would be quick to recognize the inaccuracies of the explanation; likewise, she was expert in helping other people understand, usually in a therapeutic context, the application of the Course's principles to personal situations. She, however, very rarely explained to others what the Course said, directly or indirectly, except for two instances that I recall. In one, Helen tried to help someone understand how God could not have created the beautiful lake setting we were in at the moment, and the importance of metaphysical teachings such as that for appreciating the message of the Course; and in the other, when at a family dinner party at the home of Louis' sister, Helen attempted to explain to her very Jewish relatives the importance of not judging Hitler and the Nazis. These were relatively rare examples, however, for in general, Helen's anxiety about its thought system caused her to leave the actual explanations of *A Course in Miracles* to me.

The paragraphing, punctuation, and capitalization, which rarely had any bearing on the teaching itself, nonetheless became a major focus of our work, one obvious reason being the distraction value they held for Helen. During her two retypings of the text, Helen imposed on the manuscript her peculiar idiosyncrasy of having most paragraphs be nine lines, almost always regardless of the content of the material. Helen thankfully did not object to our correcting these. More than one reader has commented on the Course's use of semicolons, which often were used in place of the more proper colon. This too was Helen's preference. And as we began to go through the text, I discovered that Helen had two comma philosophies: excessive and minimal. I cannot recall (denial sometimes serves a merciful purpose) how often—when Helen would suddenly decide on a comma-philosophy change well on into the editing—I would have to go back to the beginning of the manuscript to change the commas. In the end, we arrived at a decision to over-comma, in the hope that this would be of more help to a reader already having to struggle with the difficulty of the Course's concepts, not to mention its often complicated sentence structure. I am not sure to this day how consistent we were (there are still some changes I would be tempted to make, as I am sure many students feel should be made as well); however, the content of the Course was never jeopardized as a result of our editing.

Helen often had fits about the use of sentence splices or incomplete sentences, but knew that these were an important part of the Course's presentation, serving the stylistic purpose of added emphasis. We kept all these, despite Helen's "better" judgment, although at the urging of a friend who was a professor of linguistics, we did change in later editions some of the more glaring dangling participles.

Finally, there was the capitalization. One can see an

"evolution" in Helen's style as one traces the Course from its original dictation in the notebooks, through Bill's first typing and Helen's subsequent retypings. The process culminated in Helen's feeling that every word even remotely (a slight, but only slight, exaggeration on my part) associated with God should be capitalized, including pronouns and relative pronouns. I should mention that while here again Jesus left Helen with the freedom to do as she wished, he did make some exceptions. Under his specific instruction, all pronouns referring to him were to be lower case (in the earlier manuscripts Helen always capitalized them, as we have seen), to reflect his unity with us (more below). Jesus instructed Helen always to capitalize the term "Son of God," to emphasize the inclusion of all of us as part of God's one Son, in contradistinction to traditional Christianity's exclusion of all but Jesus from God's special Sonship. Pronouns referring to the Son, however, were to be lower case, to emphasize our separated state. The exception, of course, would be when "Son of God" refers to our true Identity as Christ, where the pronouns would be capitalized. Also, Jesus asked Helen to capitalize all pronouns referring to the Trinity—God, Christ, and the Holy Spirit—otherwise the reader might not always know for whom (or Whom) the referent was meant.

In the "Hugh Lynn Version," the one we were editing, Helen's capitalization was quite inconsistent. While I did originally try to talk her out of what I believed to be the excessive stylistic emphasis on God's divinity, I soon abandoned this fruitless enterprise and ended by saying to Helen that I would capitalize the Course words any way she chose to have them be, but that the capitalization should be consistent. This clearly appealed to her sense of logic, and so we set out in writing the rules of capitalization we would follow, and kept to these as best we could.

All in all, this part of the editing was a most valuable exercise in practicing the important principle from the Course of recognizing the distinction between form and content; namely, that it is the purpose or meaning that gives the form its importance, not the form in itself. In this case, the content of love was expressed in understanding that these minor manipulations of form had no importance when placed next to the value of joining with Helen. As the text itself says:

> Recognize what does not matter, and if your brothers ask you for something "outrageous," do it because it does not matter. Refuse, and your opposition establishes that it does matter to you (text, p. 206).

I shall return later to this important principle regarding Helen's relationship with Jesus.

Helen also felt the license to make the aforementioned changes of that to which and vice versa, an exercise that took quite a bit of time, another obvious illustration of Helen's attempt to control her anxiety over the content of the Course by focusing and manipulating its form. There was also the exercise Helen asked me to perform when she discovered that many times in the Course the word "know" was used in the popular sense, rather than Jesus strictly adhering to the word's more technical meaning as synonymous with the state of Heaven. Thus, for example, the Course teaches that spirit knows, but that the ego perceives. Helen thus asked me to change all the "popular" "knows" to other words, reserving "know" for its technical usage. I attempted to do as Helen asked, which presented no problems for at least the first half of the text. "Know" became variously "recognize," "perceive," "understand," etc. But then as the material became more poetic, and passages slipped in and out of blank verse, such changes became impossible without wreaking havoc on the meter, a cardinal sin in Helen's religion. I therefore stopped what I was doing and discussed the situation with Helen, who resolved the conflict by shifting her position and asking me to change back many of the words to their original "know." One side of Helen's defensive system—her need to be strictly consistent— thus gave way to the other, for which the poetry was sacrosanct.

I have already briefly mentioned that when Helen was writing down Jesus' words, she underlined all those that seemed to carry greater emphasis. In the typed manuscripts these words were all put in caps for ease of typing, but were obviously excessive in their number. Thus another part of our work was to leave only those words or phrases that seemed to require added emphasis. These are the italicized words in the published books.

The workbook and manual required very little editing work, other than our reading through them together to be sure that all was correct. Only punctuation, paragraphing, and the perennial capitalization were corrected, not to mention the "that's" and "which's."

Several times during the editing Helen would be obviously moved by what we were reading, although these moments were far fewer than one would have expected; Helen's defenses were always vigilantly upheld. When we had completed the sections on specialness in Chapter Twenty-Four—basically the last discussion in the text on this topic, although obviously its principles are expressed all the way through—Helen told me that when she had finished writing these down originally, she felt Jesus' gratitude for having completed them. The implication was that on another level—remember the Course's teaching that time is illusory: everything has *already* happened—she had attempted this but was not able to get through the material on special relationships. Helen's "prior" defense against having consciously to recognize before her eyes her own specialness thought system of guilt, fear, and attack, was thus simply to refuse to take the material down. Now, however, because of her commitment *to* scribing Jesus' Course, she did so, but without paying any attention to what it said, focusing on the form and style of the writing, ignoring as best she could the Course's content and meaning. And this was also her general policy during our editing.

Although Helen and I rarely discussed this, it *was* clear to her that Jesus' discussion of special relationships, the heart of the ego's thought system, was almost literally a description of her own mind. Thus, she was writing down words that described her ego self. To be sure, we all share the same ego thought system, but Helen's split mind contained blatant and extreme expressions of the dynamics of specialness. As a result, Helen's daily life was indeed a living nightmare, filled with anxieties, phobias, and attack thoughts that could have easily been the subject of any standard text on neurosis, let alone the model for Jesus' description of the ego. On the other hand, of course, Helen's mind also contained the extreme expression of God's Love, which the positive side of her relationship with Jesus represented.

The editing took over a year. My recollection is that we began near the end of 1973, and completed our work in early 1975. The text then had to be totally retyped, and this took time as well. We found an elderly Maryknoll Sister who felt it was a privilege to type the manuscript for us, although she did find some of the concepts to be rough going. A beatific experience, however, when she typed Chapter Fifteen—which among other things discusses the holy instant—ended all her doubts, and she was able to complete the typing in very good time and spirits. Near the end I, along with Helen and Bill, began to feel an urgency to complete our work, and so there was a kind of "push" to have it done. Finally, in the early spring of 1975 we had a completed manuscript of *A Course in Miracles* that awaited we-knew-not-what (or whom).

We found out the "who" on May 29, when we met Judith Skutch, and I leave this next segment of the story for the following chapter.

Chapter 13

HELEN AND BILL: THE SPECIAL AND HOLY
RELATIONSHIP, AND THEIR LATER LIFE WITH
A COURSE IN MIRACLES

Before continuing the story in sequence, let me backtrack
briefly from the completion of the editing of the Course to pick
up my relationship with Helen and Bill upon our return from
Israel in September 1973.

Helen, Bill, and I

It goes without saying that the initial weeks back in New
York were interesting ones, necessitating a major adjustment
in my orientation. As I have already indicated, I found myself
in the middle of Helen and Bill's very special relationship.
Each would speak to me of his and her grievances against the
other, and more than once I found myself reminded of the Buddhist story of two disciples who approach their master
separately to complain about the other, and to each the master
says: "You are right." A third disciple overhears the scene and
says to the master: "You have listened to two contradictory
points of view and agreed with both of them," to which the
master replies: "You are right, too." Both Helen and Bill were
correct on the "objective" level of enumerating the other's ego
dynamics. Where they were not correct, however, was in making these dynamics responsible for their own unhappiness.

At times it would almost seem as if both Helen and Bill were
vying for my attention, which merely compounded the situation. It was impossible to take sides, since as in the Buddhist
story again, both Helen and Bill were correct from their own
points of view. Yet neither of them was able to make the choice
of looking at the relationship differently. Although I had not
yet read the personal material contained in the original dictation (much of which I presented in Part II), where Jesus
repeatedly discussed this situation, and very specifically, it was

becoming quite obvious to me that there was indeed a clear distinction between Helen's and Bill's egos: one projected, the other denied. This did make it easier to discuss the situation with Helen, who never sought to deny her own angry perceptions of Bill (or anyone else, for that matter): she simply would not let them go. Bill, on the other hand, seemed unaware of the full extent of his hostility towards Helen. He seemed convinced, a belief reflected in the journal notes I quoted from in Part II, that if only Helen had been different their almost impossible situation would have been greatly alleviated. Once again, what Bill said about Helen was certainly true, as he and I often agreed. However, he was never able to accept responsibility for his *reactions* to Helen.

One morning the three of us were in Helen's office, in an atmosphere filled with the usual tension, to which we all had grown very accustomed. I was literally sitting in the middle, by the way: Helen sat in back of her desk by the window, I was in my usual seat on the other side of the desk near the door, while Bill sat by the doorway so the smoke from his cigarettes would not enter Helen's office. A typically angry interchange ensued between Helen and Bill, with both of them joining in an equal measure of hostility. They both then turned to me for substantiation of their positions, and I had no option at that moment but to say that *both* Helen and Bill seemed to be attacking the other. Bill became indignant at my statement that he was being hostile, as well as Helen, and walked angrily out the doorway and into his adjoining office. Helen turned to me and said, in effect: "Do you see what I am up against?"

I remember once during one of our California trips (*see below*), speaking directly to Bill about his relationship with Helen. Bill and I, incidentally, were both early-morning risers, unlike Helen and Louis, and so spent practically every morning of the month together, waiting for Helen and Louis to awaken and start their day. I referred to Bill's own wonderfully moving story of the healing of a relationship in the early years of the Course's transmission, where Bill had made a truly devoted effort to overlook a colleague's hostility. In time, the colleague's attitude toward Bill changed markedly, and they ultimately became and remained good friends. I asked Bill whether he could make the same effort now with Helen, but he retorted almost sharply that the situation was different. I knew then that I should not bring the subject up again. Later in the trip, Bill asked me to join him in confronting Helen about her specialness demands. I refused, not because Helen's demands were not filled with specialness, but because the meeting Bill proposed did not seem loving to me, nor did I think it would be particularly helpful.

Bill was thus never able personally to accept the Course's teaching that our problems rested in the decision *we* made to seek for grievances in others, in order to avoid responsibility for our own wish to be separate and therefore unhappy. As Jesus explained in the Course at one point:

> Anger always involves projection of separation, which must ultimately be accepted as one's own responsibility, rather than being blamed on others (text, p. 84).

Therefore, peace can never come until people change their minds from *desiring* conflict, realizing peace is all they truly want. This is the meaning of the Course's basic message of forgiveness, originally meant for Helen and Bill.

Helen, who was fully aware of her anger, could (or would) not let go of her grievances against Bill. Over and over she and I would discuss them. I even wrote little forgiveness poems for her, and prayers for her to say to Jesus, asking his help to forgive. I also very often prayed with Helen, asking Jesus in her name for help in looking at Bill differently. Thus despite the awareness of her own hostility, and the contradiction her position held vis à vis the Course, her understanding was to no avail. It was almost as if Helen intuitively knew she could (or would) not release these defenses, and she rested content with this awareness. One incident above all others is indelibly impressed on my memory. It did not specifically involve Bill, but the incident nonetheless illustrates Helen's need for her anger, against Bill or anyone else.

It was a rainy Saturday, and Helen and I were not able to go out, as we usually did. This particular afternoon Helen was incensed at someone whom in general she did not like, but this time more than usual. Her anger went on and on, and nothing I could say or do could convince her to let it go. As the day wore on in fact, her rage seemed to increase. But finally after dinner, Helen's fury abated enough to allow me to suggest a possible solution. I borrowed the imagery of Helen's experience with Jesus in the Elohim vision, and asked her to imagine herself kneeling before the altar with Jesus on one side, and this person on the other. She reluctantly agreed, and eventually was able to allow Jesus' presence to evaporate the anger, and she felt peaceful once again. I left for home shortly thereafter.

The following day when I came over, Helen greeted me at the door with an icy rage I did not often see in her, and certainly hardly ever directed at me. "Don't you ever do that to me again," she said sharply. I had no idea what Helen meant, but she promptly explained that after having gone to bed peacefully, she awakened in the middle of the night in a fury that almost equaled her London experience many years earlier. If that object of her unforgiveness had been available, she might have literally torn him limb from limb. Her rage was so all-consuming that she was unable to fall back asleep, and was still experiencing the effects of that forgiveness exercise. I assured her I would never "do that to her again." It was clear that Helen's anger was needed to "protect" her ego from the peace of God that was still so threatening, and I grew to respect that need in her.

Respect for Helen's ego was a lesson difficult for many to learn, for the temptation was always great in those who knew Helen to try to change her, to "save" her from her own ego. I remember that in the last year or two of Helen's life, some of her well-intentioned Course friends pressured her into going to California in an attempt to shake her out of her state of depression and withdrawal. They insisted she make the trip, made someone available to take care of her, and even placed her in a car, sitting in front of the steering wheel (she had not driven for quite a while). Thus, the attempt was made to change her mind by forcing changes in her behavioral patterns. This imposition of external changes on a person inadvertently depreciates the power of the mind that could choose differently, the *only* power that could truly help anyone. Helen made the trip with Louis (I was not able to go), and while she survived the good intentions, her ego also survived very well the attempts to save her.

While there was no question that Helen's judgmental attitude and phobic concerns brought her no peace, that state was preferable—*to her*—to the love that lay behind her defenses. I remember early in our relationship Helen quoting to me lines from Yeats: "Tread lightly on my dreams. They are dreams. Yet they *are* my dreams."[88] I never forgot that lesson, and later I shall discuss in more depth how Jesus treated Helen as well in this regard: love is strong when it *allows* the beloved to be weak in the presence of the mind's denial of its own strength. The strength of love, as the Course says of the Holy Spirit (text, p. 70), does not demand, command, or seek control. In its gentleness it simply reminds the mind of the strength of Christ it both has and is. Thus it reinforces the mind's power to choose again, whenever it so desires, knowing that the outcome of truth is certain. This is the ultimate meaning of patience, one of the ten characteristics of God's teachers that is discussed in the manual for teachers (pp. 13f).

During Helen's later years, I seemed to be increasingly in the role of her therapist, as she trusted me more than any other. Yet it had become clear to me after the first couple of years of our relationship that Helen would not change her mind-set, nor did she have to. My role thus became more and more a supportive and comforting one, and my love for her expressed itself in allowing her to choose as she did, in deep respect for the greater wisdom that I knew was the source of her life here, despite the ego side of her experience.

And so, loving both Helen and Bill, I grew to accept the unhealed nature of their relationship. My attempts to help them shift along the lines set forth in *A Course in Miracles*— given, after all, to help induce such a shift—evolved into gentle reminders. While my personal preference would clearly have

---

88. These lines were not remembered exactly by Helen. They are from Yeats' "Aedh wishes for the Cloths of Heaven," and the complete poem is as follows: "Had I the heavens' embroider'd cloth, / Enwrought with golden and silver light, / The blue and the dim and the dark cloths / Of night and light and the half light, / I would spread the cloths under your feet: / But I, being poor, have only my dreams; / I have spread my dreams under your feet; / Tread softly because you tread on my dreams."

been for them to have forgiven each other in the world of form, on a deeper level their apparent lack of forgiveness became irrelevant to the healing that had already occurred in the instant they joined together in June 1965.

One saving grace of this entire period, incidentally, was the keen sense of humor the three of us shared. Despite the ongoing and underlying tension, we laughed a lot. Our laughter was often able to express the ultimate purpose of our being together, a love often belied by the interpersonal squabbles. Looking back on this time, it is clear that there was never any question in any of our minds of the rightness of our having joined together. This recognition always allowed Helen and Bill to go beyond the unforgiveness to the love and commitment that was the true bonding of the relationship. And it was this commitment and fidelity that made their relationship truly holy.

I return our narrative now to where we left it at the spring of 1975, when we met Judith Skutch.

Judith Skutch and the Post-Publication Years

As Helen and Bill's relationship continued to worsen, the hopes we had once shared of one day living and teaching the Course together withered. Since the life of the Course for Helen and Bill was so inextricably intertwined with their own relationship—their joining was after all its birthplace—it stood to reason that their deteriorating relationship would adversely affect their relationship with the Course to which, almost paradoxically, they were both so faithfully dedicated. It was therefore obvious that our collaborating in the future as teachers would not be possible, and while we did not know what the future held, we certainly recognized that it did not hold the three of us together. And then we met Judith Skutch.[89]

---

89. The story of our meeting and the details of the subsequent developments involving the Foundation for Inner Peace and publication of the Course can be found in Robert Skutch's *Journey Without Distance* (Berkeley, CA: Celestial Arts, 1984).

In many ways, with the arrival of Judy the situation improved, at least externally. This was similar in one respect to my entry on the scene two years earlier, which had taken some of the pressure off the intensity of Helen and Bill's special relationship. Judy provided a clear external focus that served a needed distraction from the internal tensions and frustrations. For example, we met regularly two or three afternoons a week at Judy's apartment, and at Judy's request we did the work-book together for a year (the third time around for Helen and Bill). And most certainly Judy provided the direct stimulus for bringing Helen and Bill "out of the closet," as it were. Judy's infectious enthusiasm for the Course, and her large number of friends in the New Age community (Bill once jokingly remarked that we were about to attend a gathering to meet five thousand of Judy's closest friends), led Helen and Bill to consent to meet with groups of people to tell their story and present the Course. However, at first these meetings were not going to be held in New York, but three thousand miles away in California.

Within a month or two of our initial meeting, Judy arranged for us (Louis included, of course) to spend a month in the Bay Area of San Francisco (Judy's then second home, and now her permanent residence). There we met large numbers of very interested people, who seemed at times, however, more interested in the story of the Course's scribing than in the material itself. This fascination with the ostensible psychic elements to the story eventually paled, and many of these same people lost interest in the Course itself after a while, especially after recognizing what it truly said. The Course's profound metaphysical foundations—"There is no world! This is the central thought the course attempts to teach" (workbook. p. 237)—and spiritual commitment—"To learn this course requires willingness to question every value that you hold" (text, p. 464)—were certainly a far cry from the more worldly emphases and less demanding nature of many contemporary New Age approaches.

Several meetings were thus arranged throughout our stay. My role, in what we jokingly referred to as our vaudeville routine of presenting the Course, seemed to be to say after Helen and Bill had completed their stories and describing the circumstances of the Course's scribing: "You should all know that the inner voice that has been referred to was that of Jesus." It was very difficult, if not almost impossible, for either Helen or Bill to mention the obvious in terms of Jesus and his role with the Course. We repeated the California trip the following year, again for a month.

While Helen seemed to enjoy the change of pace that Judy provided from her relatively insulated New York life, the anxiety surrounding her role with the Course continued to increase. Helen and Bill, incidentally, did not believe that they should have any official part of the Course's public life. Before meeting us, Judy and her then husband Robert had established the Foundation for Parasensory Investigation, whose purpose was to investigate and provide funding for research in paranormal phenomena, healing, etc. The Foundation remained intact as a legal entity, but its name was changed to the Foundation for Inner Peace, the present owner of the Course's copyright. Judy retained her position as President, and Bob his position as Vice-President, with Helen, Bill, and I being informal consultants. I later became the third member—along with Judy and Bob—of the then three-member Board of Directors. Judy began by deferring decisions to Helen and Bill, but as they gradually pulled away from responsibility for the Course's public life, Judy filled in the vacuum. And in time Helen especially became quite uninterested with what the world was doing (or not doing) with the three books.

In the summer of 1977 we remained in New York, but in the early fall Judy arranged for us to travel to London for two weeks to meet people interested in the Course. The trip was not a happy one, to say the very least, certainly not from the point of view of Helen's situation. Despite being an Anglophile since childhood, Helen never really wanted to go. Judy was insistent, and as it did seem as if we had nothing to lose—the situation in New York was certainly not improving—off we went. Helen's usual anxieties about traveling were especially heightened, and these did not abate once we landed.

Helen, Louis, and I stayed in a hotel in the heart of the city, and Bill and Judy stayed in a house that belonged to one of

Judy's friends. Judy and Bill did most of the meeting with people, while my assignment was pretty much to remain with
Helen and Louis. Louis, for whom London was his second
favorite city (New York of course was first), thoroughly enjoyed
himself, often happily going off alone. Helen and I meanwhile
did our usual things together—shop, walk, and go to church.
We usually, however, got together with Bill and Judy at some
point later in the afternoon. To break things up, we all spent a
day together touring the lovely English countryside, and
another visiting Ina Twigg, a venerable member of the British
psychic establishment. It was very clear, however, that Helen
did not wish to meet with people to discuss the Course, and
with very few exceptions, did not. I believe that on one level
Helen was intuiting that most of these people were not really
interested in the Course's message, and on another level her
almost anti-social behavior reflected her gradually increasing
withdrawal from the world.

That was to be our last trip together, and basically marked a
watershed in terms of Helen's own involvement in the Course.
After this, she pretty much continued to withdraw from contact
with people who professed an interest in the three books. She
did meet with people from time to time, but the larger meetings she left to Judy, as well as to Bill who began to identify
more and more with Judy and her presentation of the Course.

To compound what was already a worsening situation,
Helen was forced by Columbia-Presbyterian's then mandatory
retirement policy to leave the Medical Center. Helen had
turned sixty-five in 1974, and was required to retire. However,
because Helen's birthday fell in July, Bill was able to negotiate
another year for her to remain on as an official member of the
department. And then for an additional two years, Helen continued as a volunteer consultant, which allowed her to go to the
Medical Center every day as before. But finally, somewhere in
the middle of 1977, the inevitable occurred and Helen left
Columbia-Presbyterian, never to return again. A year later
Bill retired, and sometime after that moved permanently to
California.

Therefore, the seeming improvement in the situation
between Helen and Bill after Judy's arrival on the scene, and

377

their increased public relationship with the Course, was short-lived. Even the ostensible shift in active interest was a two-edged sword, as the conflicting undercurrents merely intensified and widened the gulf still further. As *A Course in Miracles* repeatedly insists, seeking solutions through external circumstances never works, and the peace of God is not found outside us. Thus, despite all the well-intentioned purposes, the underlying unresolved conflicts within and between Helen and Bill became reinforced.

Helen's deterioration and withdrawal, which had already been slowly progressing, continued inexorably over time. What began as an almost imperceptible change, became increasingly noticeable as the months went by and the vacuum left by Helen's and Bill's fading leadership was increasingly filled by Judy. It was almost as if with Judy's coming, Helen (and Bill to a lesser extent) abdicated responsibility for the Course's life in the world. Helen certainly did not feel it was part of her "assignment" to demonstrate the Course's principles, nor to guide its public journey. For example, Helen supervised very closely the first printing of the Course, especially the color and design of the book, but did not do so afterwards with any of the subsequent printings. In the absence of Helen's supervision and guidance at the beginning of its public life, the Course has thus developed in a much less focused direction than it would have otherwise gone. Judy, I believe, represented an alternate "plan" for the Course's growth in the world, and one which involved its becoming quite popular, with approximately 700,000 sets sold as of this first printing in the summer of 1991.

As I have already mentioned, in the early years of our association Helen, Bill, and I spoke of one day living together and having a school or center where *A Course in Miracles* would be taught. In fact, Helen had seen in her mind a large country house near water, which she thought would be such a place. On a symbolic level Helen saw this center as a white temple with a gold cross atop it, representing the person and message of Jesus. Helen always maintained that the Course was for very few, the "five or six" mentioned earlier. Regardless of the actual number, what Helen was clearly expressing, with which I always agreed incidentally, was that *A Course in Miracles* was

378

not for the masses, at least not right now. It was clear to us that the magnitude of its thought system precluded the Course's ready acceptance by the general public in its complete form. One of the few specific guidelines Helen received from Jesus regarding the Course, moreover, was that the three books—text, workbook for students, and manual for teachers—should never be sold separately, and that they should not be abridged in any way. Thus it seemed clear to us that despite what the world might do with the three books, officially the Course should not be changed in form or its message diluted. And so we did think about a "hard core" group (Helen's expression for this small circle until we discovered it was a phrase usually associated with pornography) that would be together.

It therefore seemed as if on one level at least, Helen and Bill were waiting for this moment of meeting Judy. Although it was almost impossible to have known at the time, both Helen and Bill, as we have seen, had decided that their having taken down *A Course in Miracles* and preparing its final form completed the assignment and fulfilled their part of the "agreement" with Jesus. Aside from some relatively minor dictation (minor only by comparison with the monumental Course), Helen did little or nothing else with *A Course in Miracles* after its publication a year later in 1976.

Bill, on the other hand, when he left his rather isolated New York life and moved to California, became much more assimilated into the West Coast "community" of Course students, not to mention into the informal California lifestyle. It always remained a slight shock for me to see Bill in sneakers and blue jeans, he who while in New York was almost never without a jacket and tie. Bill died on July 4, 1988, and in his last years, with the Course's scribing, Helen, and the New York scene far behind him, seemed more peaceful than ever before. However, Bill, too, chose not to function in any leadership capacity regarding the Course. As I pointed out in Part II, Bill was an excellent public speaker who nonetheless found speaking to be extremely anxiety producing (remember the earlier material in the Course regarding Bill's fear of professing what he knew). And so he spoke only rarely; and then, only to tell his own story, but not to teach or "profess" the principles of the Course. He attended weekly and even daily groups on *A Course in Miracles* both in the San Francisco (Tiburon) and San Diego (La Jolla) areas, the two West Coast places he lived, yet there too he never assumed any kind of teaching function, a role with which he never felt personally comfortable.

On more than one occasion, Bill commented that he felt he and Helen had completed their assignment—the "sacred trust" I have already mentioned—when they handed the Course over to Judy. The conclusion that they had fulfilled their "assignment" was reached by Helen and Bill without asking Jesus first. I am referring not to the concrete decision to have Judy and the Foundation for Inner Peace publish the Course, but to the inner and not always conscious decision that, for all intents and purposes, they completed their involvement with the external life of the Course.

Helen's and Bill's inability to forgive each other, let alone identify with *A Course in Miracles*, made such a leadership role impossible. And this despite repeated assurances from Jesus of the important roles they each would play, above and beyond the scribing of the Course. The reader may recall Jesus' words to Helen that just as she had done something unexpected, so too would Bill do something equally unexpected. As I have already indicated, these past and present messages pointed to an even greater role for both of them, and one which definitely involved more of a teaching function, and themselves in a leadership capacity. In terms of Bill's new function, Jesus indicated that Helen would be as helpful to him with his, as he was to her with her scribal function. In conjunction with this "new" function, Helen saw a mental picture of Bill with headphones on. From time to time the three of us speculated on the meaning of this image, yet obviously nothing ever came of it.

It also seemed clear that there was more for Helen to do, as was seen in several informal messages to Helen from Jesus. One of these, dating from July, 22, 1978, said:

> There is no cause for fear. Make no decisions now. There is a plan for the future which is not what you expect. God knows what it is, and you do not. Do not try to figure it out.

In this more formal message of January 14, 1978 (later

incorporated in "The Gifts of God"), Jesus said to Helen:

> You still are needed in the world, to hear His Voice and share
> His messages of love with those who call in sorrow (*The Gifts of
> God*, p. 127).

I recall Helen and I discussing this specific passage, and her
emphatically stating to me that there was *nothing* more for her
to do. I responded with what I thought she (and Bill) could do
in terms of helping others with the Course and with their relationship with Jesus. If nothing else, I said to her, I believed
there were additional pamphlets "inside, waiting to be
birthed." However, Helen was adamant, and I knew that she
had made up her mind. Indeed, she did not "do more," at least
not anything that could be observed on this plane. Near the
end of her life she retreated more and more from her scribal
role, and from Jesus who represented her true Self, tending to
depreciate the importance of what she had done. Jesus, however, felt quite different, for also in that January 1978 message
he said to her:

> Be thankful for His Love and for His care, for in this world it
> has been given few to give a gift to God as you have done. Yet
> only few are needed. They suffice for all the rest, and they give
> thanks to you along with their Creator and with yours (*The
> Gifts of God*, p. 128).

To summarize, Helen and Bill's joining together was essential for this future function, as it was for the scribing of *A
Course in Miracles*, yet these two remarkably faithful and dedicated people chose otherwise. They thus remained estranged
from each other until the end, and so what might have been,
remained only within the realm of possibility and not actuality.

Helen's Relationship with *A Course in Miracles*

It is difficult indeed to describe Helen's relationship with *A
Course in Miracles*. That it aroused tremendous anxiety in her
goes without saying, that she fought with it tooth and nail and
determinedly chose, in the end, not to practice its teachings,
was also, for her, painfully true. Nonetheless, there remained

that part of Helen's mind that cared deeply about the Course and what happened to it. In fact, part of Helen's discomfort came not only from her usual fear of the Course's message and its author, but also from a more justified perception that the Course was not really being placed in its proper home, reaching its true audience. For example, the first published article on *A Course in Miracles* was slated to appear, with Helen's approval, in 1977 in a New Age magazine called *Psychic*. Helen was adamant, however, that *A Course in Miracles* was not to be written about in a magazine which she considered to have such an undignified title. Bill then came up with the name *New Realities*, a more appropriate fit, and editor and publisher James Bolen graciously agreed to the change.

There was thus a maternal aspect to Helen's relationship to the Course during this period, wherein she watched over its birth and infancy with the same care and concern a mother has for her child. I remember one day, shortly after the Course's publication, we were discussing the inevitable process of popularization and distortion that was already beginning to occur. Helen lowered her face between her hands, plaintively whispering: "My poor course; my poor course." She certainly did not mean this in the sense that *A Course in Miracles* was *hers*, but her statement did reflect the same concern a mother would feel for a child whose life seemed to be going awry.

Clearly admitting—to herself and to others—her inability to integrate the teachings into her own life, Helen's ego had little tolerance for the hypocritical stance of others who believed that they had understood and mastered the Course's profound message, nor who presented its inspired teachings in a superficial manner. Believing, as we have seen, that *A Course in Miracles* was for very few who would be able really to understand its message and successfully integrate its teachings into their lives, Helen knew the great difficulty the material would present to the world. It was clear to her that people's fearful egos would seek to prevent acceptance of the Course's radical message of forgiveness and truth. It therefore pained Helen in the very early years of publication to witness what was happening with the Course; however, she was not on the other hand, as we have seen, able to assume a role of spiritual leadership.

Yet despite the tremendous level of fear which led her to hold tenaciously on to the ego thought system, and her self-hatred over not being able to choose again—for God instead of the ego—Helen's underlying integrity allowed her to remain faithful to the Course and her function, albeit in her own "lopsided" way (recall the blue-gray bird of Helen's earlier dream). Helen's ego was such that she always had to be center-stage. Her dominant and compelling personality made it practically impossible for people in her presence *not* to have a strong reaction to her, positively or negatively. She was not one that others could easily ignore. Part of Helen's mind realized that such a situation regarding *A Course in Miracles* would have been a disaster, for it would have shifted people's focus from the inner Teacher to an external figure, a process of specialness directly antithetical to the Course's message of equality and unity. She was always clear that the central figure in the Course was Jesus (or the Holy Spirit), and both she and Bill were faithful to the position of not assuming a guru role. On one level I believe that they knew they were setting an example for others who would inevitably follow. Indeed, some people have already come along and given way to the temptation to set themselves up as guru figures.

Thus, because it did not seem possible for her to remain involved with the Course *without* her ego, I believe that on another level she chose to get out of the Course's way, rather than "contaminate" it with her ego's need to dominate. Her eventual physical and emotional deterioration was the ultimate expression of this "getting out of its way." Clearly, to paraphrase an already-quoted line from the Course (text, p. 20), this was not the highest level of problem-solving of which she was capable. However, it was the highest level of which she was capable *then*.

We have already seen how Helen could not avoid feeling bitterly resentful over a Course that one part of her mind believed had destroyed her very promising professional career, nor could she easily refrain from anger at Jesus for what was perceived as his failure to uphold his promises to her. Yet in another part of her mind she was able to remain true to what she considered to be her life's work, and to Jesus whom she loved more than any other. Therefore, to the end, as best she could, Helen demonstrated a remarkable integrity in preserving the purity of A *Course in Miracles* and her role with it.

In summary, then, the scribing of A *Course in Miracles* can be seen as having brought to the surface Helen's basic conflict. As with her dream of the blue-gray bird who was not even sure he *was* a bird, Helen on a conscious level could never successfully identify with who she really was: again, a child of God or a child of the ego. Her very strong ego-identification, and struggles to appear normal to the world, were very powerful defenses against accepting her true spiritual Self. However, once the Course began, this repressed conflict between her two selves was uncovered, as obviously Jesus could only have spoken through Helen's spiritual side. Helen was thus forced to deal with this problem, and her different and contradictory ways of coping were characteristic of her ego's very inefficient and ineffective problem-solving enterprises.

There was, moreover, Helen's ego that accepted no responsibility for her situation, which she bitterly perceived to be one of misery and imposition, if not outright persecution. In this state she felt only resentful and sacrificial, the exact opposite of the few moments of joy and gratitude the scribing of A *Course in Miracles* gave to her. As Bill later said of Helen's split mind: "The same process of dissociation that enabled Helen to take down the Course, also made it virtually impossible for her to learn it." Such conflict becomes intolerable, and it led to Helen's continued attempts *not* to deal with the anguish of its lack of resolution.

In the spring of 1968, while the Course was still coming through Helen, Bill took her to see Eileen Garrett, America's then leading psychic. Helen and Bill entered the room where she was to be speaking, and as soon as they walked in Garrett noticed them, immediately impressed by Helen. She called them over to her, and without anything being said about the Course, told Helen that she knew that she (Helen) had written something very important, and because of the light she saw around (or within) her, her Foundation would publish the book, if Helen and Bill so chose. (Such plans eventually fell through, however.) Garrett then said these very prophetic words to Helen: "If you go with what you have written down you will be the happiest person on the face of the earth. But if you fight it, you will be sick and unhappy the rest of your life."

Interestingly enough, people have used Helen's personal life and struggles with the Course as witnesses for *and* against its authenticity. The positive view was that Helen's ego was so dominant that in no way could she herself have written *A Course in Miracles*, and so Someone else must have. On the other side, often coming from a more traditional Christian view, others would argue that if Helen's experiences of Jesus were indeed valid, her life would surely have changed. The fact that it did not, therefore, invalidated the experiences and pointed up their ego nature. Actually, I myself sometimes used that idea with Helen, though without the purpose of discrediting her experience. When Helen would complain that nothing ever happened to her and that Jesus really let her down, I would remind her, first, of the Course itself, and then that if people had had one one-thousandth of her experiences of Jesus and the Love of God, their lives would have been changed forever. She of course could not disagree with me.

It is always instructive, especially in viewing Helen's life, to recall the lines from the text that refer to the Holy Spirit's plan of the Atonement (or forgiveness):

> Put yourself not in charge of this, for you cannot distinguish between advance and retreat. Some of your greatest advances you have judged as failures, and some of your deepest retreats you have evaluated as success (text, p. 357).

Thus, it would *appear* as if Helen's personal life were a failure: feeling "out of joint" in her worldly experience, she nonetheless ended up feeling equally "out of joint" in her "unworldly" life as well, at least judging by externals. Moreover, her relationship with Bill, the immediate stimulus for the Course's scribing, was from all external indications unhealed by Jesus' message.

It was not the case, however, that Helen's ego triumphed over Jesus in the end, and this fact is the principal burden of the balance of this book. Before developing this theme, however, I shall devote the next two chapters to a discussion of the rest of the material that Helen scribed from Jesus. I then turn to an in-depth discussion of Helen's special and holy relationship with Jesus, and her underlying identification with his reality that transcended the ambivalent world of her split mind.

Chapter 14

OTHER SCRIBINGS—A

"NOTES ON SOUND"; "PSYCHOTHERAPY";
"CLARIFICATION OF TERMS"; "THE SONG OF PRAYER";
SPECIAL MESSAGES

Helen's relationship with Jesus was not limited solely to scribing *A Course in Miracles*. As the earlier chapters have demonstrated, her relationship with him extended throughout her lifetime, and became more intimate and personal in the weeks preceding the actual beginning of the Course's dictation. It continued on for several more years after the completion of the scribing. Nor was *A Course in Miracles* the only material Jesus dictated to Helen, though it was by far the most extensive. The sole exception to these dictations is the "Notes on Sound," which is discussed below. In this chapter I discuss these other scribings chronologically, leaving for the following chapter the poetry, which constitutes, as it were, a special case insofar as Helen was more personally involved in the dictation.

"Notes on Sound" (1972,1977)

In October 1972, relatively soon after the scribing of *A Course in Miracles* was completed, Bill began to develop an interest in Kirlian photography. This was the Russian technique for photographing auras, the electromagnetic field around living things. He asked Helen to ask whether this was an important area to explore. A question from Bill thus once again acted as the stimulus for Helen, but this time with a totally different result, and with Helen being clear that the source of the writing was not Jesus.

The answer to Bill's question essentially was: No, light was not the important phenomenon; sound was. What followed was a highly technical treatise on the building of a device that would measure the physical effects of healing (not an actual healing device, as has been sometimes mistakenly believed).

387

This device operated under principles that converted light waves to sound waves. The dictation continued for about two months, and consisted of twenty-seven pages.

As was the case with *A Course in Miracles*, there was no way Helen could have written these "Notes on Sound," as we have called this document. However, unlike the Course as we shall see in Chapter 17 the "Notes" contained a subject matter that was totally alien to Helen's ego. Helen would not even have known how to change a light bulb, let alone understand something as sophisticated and complicated as this device. Scientists who later saw the document were quite impressed, especially with statements such as: "This is an aspect of the alignment of metals that is not yet known." This statement turned out to have been true; several years after Helen had written this down the unknown aspect was understood. It was also clear, however, that the information was not complete. Many scientists have attempted to construct this device, but to no avail. There is simply not enough information. In 1977 some interested people prevailed on Helen to write down some more. Helen was most reluctant, but did try to comply and in April eked out another two pages or so, but this too was not sufficient, and all subsequent efforts to have her complete the monograph failed. The "Notes on Sound," like Schubert's great symphony, remains unfinished.

Where did it come from? Except for one brief passage (to be quoted below), the tone of the "Notes" is obviously quite different from the Course and Helen's other scribed material, not to mention its content. *A Course in Miracles* is quite clear, for example, that healing is only of the mind, and has nothing whatsoever to do with the body, and yet here is a machine whose purpose is to measure the healing of the body. Bill had a theory which he once mentioned to me, that the source of the material might very well have been Helen's father, a brilliant metallurgist while he was alive. Helen's relationship with her father had never been healed, and as mentioned in Chapter 1, she always resented her father's detached and almost ruthlessly (at least from her perspective) objective fairness. It thus made sense that on another level, their joining together in this dictation would be an expression of forgiveness. I waited for quite some time before approaching Helen with this thought, as I knew her feelings towards her father. One day, however, I felt the timing was right, and was pleasantly surprised by Helen's almost matter-of-fact receptivity to the theory, for she thought too that it made sense, and perhaps it was true after all.

As I mentioned above, there is nothing in the material to suggest that the scribe of *A Course in Miracles* took it down, except for this very atypical passage from the document:

> The patient may, however, develop other symptoms, since physical healing represents a realignment of essentially local [i.e., bodily] forces rather than the total context [i.e., in the mind itself]. This is because they still occur in time, and therefore retain the illusory quality of time itself.... It does not matter in what part of the body the healing takes place, nor by what means it is brought about. From the theoretical point of view, it can be said that healing can only be the result of a change of mind which now accepts healing where it formerly accepted sickness. The change of mind alters the thought field around the patient, which seems to represent the place where he is. These changes cannot be different for a healing presumably brought about by medication, surgery, or faith. Healing can only be faith healing, for sickness can only be faith in sickness.

It would seem that here, as Helen later agreed, she had "tuned in" to Jesus for this brief passage so that students of *A Course in Miracles* would not be led astray by the "Notes'" sojourn into the "far country" of the body.

"Psychotherapy: Purpose, Process and Practice" (1973, 1975)

One day in the fall of 1973 I asked Helen if there were anything else she had taken down. Oh yes, she said casually, there are some pages on psychotherapy. I then learned that these notes had been taken down from Jesus in January 1973, in the same manner as was *A Course in Miracles*. It was obviously incomplete, only going so far as the bottom of page 13 in the published pamphlet, "Psychotherapy: Purpose, Process and

Practice." I could not wait to read the notes, and upon doing so very disappointedly said to Helen, "But this is just like the Course," not really paying attention to what I was saying. What else would I have thought this would be like? I was probably expecting something more specific, but a few more readings made it clear how perfect the pamphlet was, even in its incomplete form, in reflecting the application of the Course's principles of healing to psychotherapy.

From time to time I reminded Helen of the unfinished manuscript, but to no avail. And then in January 1975, while we were completing our editing of *A Course in Miracles*, Bill ran across a notice in the Newsletter of the Association for Transpersonal Psychology. It was placed by Jon Mundy, a non-traditional Methodist minister whom Helen and Bill had heard speak a few years earlier at a Spiritual Frontiers Fellowship Conference held in the South. Jon was a young man whose enthusiastic spiritual fervor had impressed Helen and Bill. In his note in the newsletter, Jon stated that he was doing a doctoral dissertation on spiritual psychotherapy, and was requesting any articles, books, or information from the transpersonal community that would be relevant for his study.

Bill quickly called our attention to it, and I think I might have been the one who said to Helen that this would be a wonderful opportunity to, in Bill's wonderful expression, "stone two birds." In other words, this would be the necessary stimulus to complete the psychotherapy pamphlet, as well as being an answer to the call for help. So Helen called Jon, who was living in New York City, and made a date for him to meet us one evening at my apartment. Helen told him she thought she would have something that would be of interest to him.

The meeting took place as scheduled, and we were joined there by Father Michael, who was interested in seeing how we presented the Course to others, at that point a very rare event. To this day I am not sure if Jon has entirely gotten over that fateful evening. Poor man! Jon and I subsequently became friends, and he frequently has remarked to me that he had no idea what he should have expected from this meeting, and certainly had no idea of the impact that evening would have on his life. Actually, there was of course no way Jon could have expected what he received. Interestingly enough, he had no clue as to why Helen had called him, since he had totally forgotten about the notice which he had placed months before; besides, he had no current plans for doing his dissertation on spiritual psychotherapy.

Nonetheless, Jon's notice provided the needed stimulus to Helen, who picked up the uncompleted manuscript where she had left off two years previously, and finally finished it in March. The pamphlet, again, is a wonderful summary of the Course's principles of healing, as specifically applied to the practice of psychotherapy, which essentially consists of two people joining together in the name of Christ. Helen felt little connection to the pamphlet, as I remember, although I always felt very close to it. I believed that its call for "special training" of therapists (p. 18) was something I would be responding to in the future.

"Clarification of Terms" (1975)

On occasion, Helen and I had discussed the possibility of a glossary that would define some of the terms used by *A Course in Miracles*, but nothing ever came from our discussions. Then Judy Skutch raised the idea again, feeling that it would be of great help to her, as well as others, especially in view of the Course's very non-traditional usage of Christian terminology; Judy was very much an identified Jew, whose father was a major figure in American and international Jewry.

Helen and I then sat down and drew up a list of terms we thought might be helpful, knowing full well that this glossary, later to be called a "Clarification of Terms," would not be written in that way. And of course it was not. Helen took it down from September through the beginning of December 1975, well in time for its inclusion in the printed books. As Jesus instructed us to do, we placed it as an appendix to the manual for teachers. Its beautiful closing passage, incidentally, was written at the beginning of the Advent season and thus reflects the Christmas theme. The "morning star" that is referred to at the end was taken from the final verses of the biblical book of Revelation, and traditionally has come to be a symbol for Jesus. This short piece of sixteen pages is a poetic gem, and provides as well some useful additional information for students of the Course. Its clarifications, however, will probably not be very helpful to people who do not already have some background in *A Course in Miracles* itself.

There is a cute story associated with Helen's scribing of the "Clarification of Terms," and one that fortunately has a happy ending. One afternoon while we were all at the Medical Center, Helen was complaining to me once again about Jesus and this dictation, and even brought up her past gripes about how *A Course in Miracles* had imposed itself on her life. She was not in the bitter state I had seen her in at other times, and so, having in front of me her notebook in which she was taking down the "Terms," I took it in my hands. Reminiscent of my boyhood basketball days, I then tossed it unerringly across the office into the wastepaper basket. My memory is not that precise, but I believe I exclaimed something to the effect: "So much for Jesus and his damn Course!" And that was that. I think Bill walked in at that point and Helen laughingly told Bill what had just happened. My memory again is a little vague, but I do know that we were then interrupted by something that distracted us totally from the notebook and Helen's complaints. Shortly afterwards we left for the day.

Early the next morning Helen called me in a panic, asking me if I knew where her notebook was, both of us totally forgetting the previous afternoon's basketball shot. Helen's misplacing her notebook was not an uncommon occurrence, and as I was usually very good at finding it, I reassured Helen that I would be over right after my 7:00 A.M. patient and would find it for her. My patient arrived soon afterwards, and in the middle of the session I suddenly remembered what had happened. But even before I had a chance to call Helen, she had remembered as well, and already telephoned Bill who was racing up to the Medical Center in a cab, hoping to beat the garbage collectors to the office wastepaper basket. He was too late, however. The garbage had already been collected, and the notebook now lay in one of about two or three dozen large plastic bags, soon to be burned. Many of the bags, incidentally, contained entrails of discarded experimental animals (the reader may recall that this was a research building). Bill prevailed upon the janitor to allow him access to the room, and was fortunately guided to the right bag almost immediately, finding the notebook safe and sound, and buried only in a mass of paper.

"The Song of Prayer" (1977)

The second and last pamphlet taken down by Helen is "The Song of Prayer: Prayer, Forgiveness, Healing," which was scribed from September through November of 1977. It is a beautiful summary of *A Course in Miracles'* teachings on forgiveness and healing in the context of prayer. Though it contains no new ideas, it does introduce some different terminology, notably "forgiveness-to-destroy." This is the false forgiveness the world has us hold out to each other, and which is described in several places in the Course itself, though never named as such. Even more important, however, the pamphlet addresses the meaning of prayer, including the issue of asking the Holy Spirit, and what in fact we should be asking *for*. It was this issue that provided the stimulus for the pamphlet, and was directly relevant to Helen's relationship with Jesus. I therefore will postpone further discussion of the circumstances of the pamphlet's writing and its contents until Chapter 17 when I discuss in greater depth the figure of Jesus, and Helen's relationship with him.

Special Messages (1975–1978)

There also is the group of small messages Helen took down over a period of time, that we came to refer to as "Special Messages." In the main, these involved "celestial pep talks," wherein Jesus offered us encouragement by guaranteeing a successful outcome to all things. Some of these even became quite specific as to *when* this success would or might come. None of these predictions, however, came to fruition, and on any kind of observable or experiential level, none of the positive more general predictions came to pass either. The reader may recall here Helen's statement in her letters to Bill about recognizing that it was not a good thing for her to become involved with specifics and the future.

Helen's true Self, from which she united with Jesus, existed in a dimension beyond time and space. It was from that Self, in which love united with itself, that *A Course in Miracles* originated. From that state of Mind there can be no concern for specific outcomes, or the times in which these outcomes would occur. That is why in *A Course in Miracles* itself there is no mention of specific outcomes, the forms in which the content of forgiveness would be expressed. In fact, it says of itself: "This is a course in cause [content] and not effect [form]" (text, p. 432.) Such specifics are irrelevant to the Atonement, which consists of only one outcome, which "is as certain as God" (text, p. 52). These special messages, therefore, while inspired in part, became contaminated by Helen's other self, which tried to help in a form *she* decided would be helpful. That is why Jesus taught: "Trust not your good intentions. They are not enough" (text, p. 355), and why in the earlier weeks of the dictation he was urging Helen to ask him *first* before she decided to be helpful to others.

Thus, Bill and I came to feel that these messages were highly influenced by Helen's own need to be encouraged, and to encourage others. This seemed to be especially the case, again, whenever the message became specific as to time, place, or person. Thus, we never felt that in the main, these had the same legitimacy or authenticity as did *A Course in Miracles* or the pamphlets, in none of which did it ever appear that Helen's ego had contaminated the information in any way. We realized that the same could not be said about these messages, and thus they have never been published. To borrow the language of the Churches, we did not feel they should be admitted to the scribal canon. Incidentally, it is important to note in this regard that all these messages date from Judith Skutch's arrival on the scene and our discussions about publication, etc. As I shall discuss in Chapter 17, this was the period when great emphasis was placed on receiving the answers to specific questions, leading inevitably to a concern for what was going to happen in the future. This emphasis and concern was largely absent before, and we shall see later how this adversely affected Helen's hearing.

Nonetheless, in a few of these messages, when they were more abstract, the authentic voice of Jesus seems quite manifest. We can find here still other examples of Jesus' attempts, not only to assuage Helen's fears—which was always a full-time job—but also to help her with specific forgiveness advice in the same manner as in the original dictations in 1965. I cite some of these messages now.

The first of these antedates by two years the specific message on asking that became Helen's introduction to "The Song of Prayer," which again, we will discuss in a later chapter. The first message cautions Helen—but really all the world as well—against believing that simply our *desire* to hear is sufficient to truly hear. As we have just observed: "Trust not your good intentions. They are not enough" (text, p. 355).

October 5, 1975

To God all things are possible, but you must ask His answer only of Himself.

Perhaps you think you do, but be you sure that if you did you would be quiet now and wholly undismayed by anything. Do not attempt to guess His Will for you. Do not assume that you are right because an answer seems to come from Him. Be sure you ask, and then be still and let Him speak. There is no problem He cannot resolve, for it is never He Who keeps apart some questions to be solved by someone else. You cannot share the world with Him and make half of it His while half belongs to you. Truth makes no compromise. To keep apart a little is to keep all separate. Your life, complete and whole, belongs to God or none of it is His. There is no thought in all the world that seems more terrible.

Yet it is only when this thought appears in perfect clarity that there is hope in peace and safety for the mind so long kept dark and twisted to avoid the light. This *is* the light. Step back and do not dwell upon the forms that seem to keep you bound. You *will* fulfill your function. And will have whatever you will need. God does not fail. But lay no limits on what you would give to Him to be resolved. For He can not offer a thousand answers when but one is all there is. Accept this one of Him, and not one question will remain to ask.

Do not forget if you attempt to solve a problem, you have judged it for yourself and so you have betrayed your proper role.

I interrupt the message to remind the reader of Helen's very inefficient way of solving the non-existent problem of the elevator strike, which stimulated the important message "I Need Do Nothing." This provides a wonderful example of the principle Jesus is teaching her here, and which he now continues:

Grandeur, which comes from God, establishes that judgment is impossible for you. But grandiosity insists you judge, and bring to this all problems that you have. And what is the result? Look carefully upon your life and let it speak for you....

What have you kept from God that you would hide behind your judgment? What have you concealed beneath the cloak of kindness and concern? Use no one for your needs, for that is "sin," and you will pay the penalty in guilt.

I interrupt again to point out that this last statement directly reflects the Course's teachings on special relationships. The message concludes:

Remember you need nothing, but you have an endless store of loving gifts to give. But teach this lesson only to yourself. Your brother will not learn it from your words or from the judgments you have laid on him. You need not even speak a word to him. You cannot ask, "What shall I say to him?" and hear God's answer. Rather ask instead, "Help me to see this brother through the eyes of truth and not of judgment," and the help of God and all His angels will respond.

For only here we rest. We cast away our little judgments and our petty words; our tiny problems and our false concerns. We have attempted to be master of our destiny and thought that peace lay there. Freedom and judgment *is* impossible. But by your side is One Who knows the way. Step back for Him and let Him lead you to the rest and silence of the Word of God.

This final statement is a direct reference to Lesson 155 "I will step back and let Him lead the way" (workbook, p. 284).

In the last part of the message Jesus is urging Helen to focus not on the answer, whatever it might be, but rather, to paraphrase the words of the introduction to the text, on removing the interferences to the awareness of love's wisdom. Judgment is a major ego defense against this wisdom—"the help of God and all His angels" that is symbolized for us by the presence of the Holy Spirit in our separated minds, "the One Who knows the way." Once again, we shall return in Chapter 17 to the very important issues raised by this message, and so we leave them for now.

The following, written for Helen as a New Year's message (with strong Christmas overtones, however), is reminiscent of the parallel references in a number of poems to Mary, the mother of Jesus:

January 1, 1978

You think the Child is stillborn, and you are in mourning now for Him. You do not understand what happened, nor the signs that still surround His birth. The star is there, and all attempts to call it something else will slip away in time. For it was so before, and will be so again. We cannot know when truth has come because it would be hard to see the Heaven where a manger stands. But when the truth has come, there is a light that finally shines through.

The mother waits. The Child has come, and has been born again. He is not dead. He is the sign of life, the gift of God, the Lord of peace, the King of all the world, the Son of man and you. There is a light surrounding you that you will see when you have ceased to fear to look on Him Who came to save you, and the world through you. How can you doubt that I will come and tell you just exactly what you need to do to let your function be fulfilled? Of all the world, how is it you who doubt?

There is no plan without your part, and it will be revealed as soon as you can see that life is there, and has been born to you. Be patient, Mother, for the end is not what you believe. I come in glory to the one who gave me birth, and I will stay and wait in patience for your waking. When you behold Me, you will understand. Till then we wait together, you and I.

Helen, of course, was Jesus' "mother" in the sense of giving birth to his Course. In Chapter 16 I shall discuss Helen's relationship with Mary, as well as Jesus' other references to her in that regard.

A week later this message came which speaks to Helen directly about her role: "You have been *given charge* of one way to God" (my italics). It is unclear how valid this message is; i.e., whether it truly came from Jesus or Helen herself—my discussions with Helen may have influenced her. Nonetheless, I do believe, as I discussed in the previous chapter, that Helen did have a potential leadership role with the Course's life in the world, and one that she abdicated.

January 7, 1978

There is an urgency that calls to you. You have a function. Do not now delay. In a little while you will understand. You have been given charge of one way to God. It is direct and sure and true, and there is need for it. You will be shown how it is needed, when to use it, and where it should be taught for continuity.

A very specific message came on October 2, 1976. Because of its special nature, I present it out of its proper chronological sequence. Helen and I were sitting on her couch, and she asked me if I believed in the physical resurrection of Jesus. I replied, not really, for if the body were not real and alive, how could it then resurrect? Besides, the definition of the resurrection basically given in the Course is that of the awakening from the dream of death, a process that occurs in the mind, not the body, since it is the mind alone that sleeps. However, I went on, it was certainly possible that Jesus' followers would have *experienced* this awakening as a physical event, given the level of their understanding, confusing form for content. I then suggested to Helen that she ask the "Boss" himself, since who better than Jesus could respond to her question. The following answer then came:

Was There a Physical Resurrection?

My body disappeared because I had no illusion about it. The last one had gone. It was laid in the tomb, but there was nothing left to bury. It did not disintegrate because the unreal cannot die. It merely became what it always was. And that is what "rolling the stone away" means. The body disappears, and no longer hides what lies beyond. It merely ceases to interfere with vision. To roll the stone away is to see beyond the tomb, beyond death, and to understand the body's nothingness. What is understood as nothing *must* disappear.

I did assume a human form with human attributes afterwards, to speak to those who were to prove the body's worthlessness to the world. This has been much misunderstood. I came to tell them that death is illusion, and the mind that made the body can make another since form itself is an illusion. They did not understand. But now I talk to you and give you the same message. The death of an illusion means nothing. It disappears when you awaken and decide to dream no more. And you still do have the power to make this decision as I did.

God holds out His hand to His Son to help him rise and return to Him. I can help because the world is illusion, and I have overcome the world. Look past the tomb, the body, the illusion. Have faith in nothing but the spirit and the guidance God gives you. He could not have created the body because it is a limit. He must have created the spirit because it is immortal. Can those who are created like Him be limited? The body is the symbol of the world. Leave it behind. It cannot enter Heaven. But I can take you there any time you choose. Together we can watch the world disappear and its symbol vanish as it does so. And then, and then—I cannot speak of that.

A body cannot stay without illusion, and the last one to be overcome is death. This is the message of the crucifixion: There is no order of difficulty in miracles. This is the message of the resurrection: Illusions are illusions. Truth is true. Illusions vanish. Only truth remains.

These lessons needed to be taught but once, for when the stone of death is rolled away, what can be seen except an empty tomb? And that is what you see who follow me into the sunlight and away from death, past all illusions, on to Heaven's gate, where God will come Himself to take you home.

So that students of *A Course in Miracles* do not become confused, it should be recognized that this message came to Helen in words she could understand at that time. Her mind was already in a fear state, otherwise she would not have asked *me* for an explanation instead of Jesus. And so the answer does carry with it the implication that Jesus actually did "return" in form: "I did assume a human form...." However, a careful reading of the message helps us to understand that speaking of such a return misses the point, as the overriding emphasis here is on the inherent illusory nature of the body. And so once again we have an example of Jesus speaking to Helen in a manner (the *form*) that she could accept without too much fear, at the same time placing the truth (the *content*) within the words themselves.

Chapter 15

OTHER SCRIBINGS—B

THE GIFTS OF GOD: HELEN'S POETRY

The Writing of the Poems

I mentioned in the preceding chapter my asking Helen in 1973 if there were anything else she had scribed, and her showing me the first part of what was to become the psychotherapy pamphlet. And that was it. Some time after that—probably in the late fall—during the course of an informal discussion Helen, Bill, and I were having, Bill made casual reference to the poems Helen had written down in 1971, sure that Helen had shown them to me. My ears perked up at the mention of these poems, and I said, "Helen, what poems?" She turned bright red in embarrassment, admitted the existence of such poems, but would not show them to me.

Helen's discomfort and refusal to show the poems to me was odd, given the intimacy of our relationship, all the more as she knew I loved poetry as much as she did, especially Shakespeare, her favorite. Whenever I mentioned the poems, which I irrepressibly did from time to time, she continued to blush in embarrassment, and still did not show them to me. Finally she told me her reason: "They are not much good, and I don't think you will like them." I persisted, however, sure that the poems were quite good, especially after Helen told me that they had come to her like the Course, and shared the same basic themes. "You know, Helen," I would say to her, "they would have to be at least halfway decent."

Our discussions went on for a while, and finally as Christmas approached—the first of many Christmases we would spend together—Helen relented and agreed that on Christmas Eve she would let me see these poems, her "guilty secret." It was extremely interesting to me just how uncomfortable Helen was. As distressed as *A Course in Miracles* made her feel, it was nothing compared to the anxiety set off by these poems. She had relatively little trouble, after a while, showing certain

401

people some of the more poetic and beautifully written sections of the Course. She took great pride in these, as a matter of fact, although it was clear to her she was not their author. But the poetry was something else again.

After dinner that Christmas Eve, the big moment came. Helen took out the poems, all neatly typed and kept in a file folder which had been buried in a drawer. Sitting with Helen at her dinette table I began to read them, and not surprisingly, liked them very much. There were fifty-eight poems in all. The earliest one, called "The Gifts of Christmas," was written on Christmas Day, 1969, while Helen was taking down the workbook. I had actually seen that poem before, as Bill had placed it in the beginning of the binder that held the first part of the workbook manuscript. The second poem, "The Singing Reed," was written in March 1971, while the remaining fifty-six were all written in a two-month period in the fall of 1971. While not great poetry, as I believe many of the later poems are, these early ones—all relatively objective in tone—were lovely little expressions of many of the themes found in *A Course in Miracles*. They were certainly nothing of which I felt Helen should have been ashamed. But of course it was not really the poems that caused such embarrassment for Helen, but what they represented about her. I shall explain this below.

As I was reading the poems, Helen watched me with bated breath to see my reaction, and she appeared very relieved when I obviously liked them. Helen then talked a little bit about the poetry, how she had written it down, etc., and I commented again how nice it was. I added that perhaps we should do something about publishing the poems and making them available to others. Helen, incidentally, never wished the poems— the early as well as the more sophisticated later ones—to be published during her lifetime, and relatively few people even knew of them. A year after her death, the Foundation for Inner Peace published them under the title *The Gifts of God*.[90]

That Christmas Eve was lovely, and I left shortly after reading the poems through a second time. I saw Helen the next

---

90. Glen Ellen, CA: Foundation for Inner Peace, 1982.

day, Christmas, and she greeted me at the door with a gift of the fifty-eight poems, which she retyped for me after I had left. But not only that, she had also written down three or four other poems, which she now presented me with as well. Two were Christmas poems, "Nativity" and "The Holiness of Christmas." This was the beginning of the second phase of Helen's poetry. Several poems followed, and between Christmas Eve and New Year's Helen wrote down ten poems in all. She continued to write poems on and off for the next five years, with the last poem, "The Second Easter," written for Easter, 1978. The prose poem entitled "The Gifts of God," which I shall discuss below, was completed shortly afterwards. And that, basically, marked the end of Helen's scribing.

Before proceeding, let me discuss the actual writing of the poetry. In one sense Helen wrote down the poems just as she had written down *A Course in Miracles*, and thus we can say that the poetry was scribed. In another sense, however, Helen considered the poems also partly hers, and that of course was the source of her embarrassment. Thus, because she always felt that her voice played a part in their transmission, one could describe the process of taking down the poems as a shared inspiration with Jesus, a collaborative venture as it were.

Many of the poems are written in the first person, with Jesus obviously being the voice. In some of these, especially the Easter poems, he speaks about his crucifixion and resurrection, and the voice is clearly the very loving and gentle one of the Course. However, in several poems the first person is Helen herself, though clearly not the person she experienced herself to be. Rather, it was a voice coming from a part of her self that she had successfully dissociated, but which broke through her defensive system. Occasionally this voice is pained, as we shall see in some examples below, expressing Helen's bitterness and disappointment over what she experienced as Jesus not keeping his promises. In other poems, the voice is filled with love and gratitude, as found in the Valentine's Day trilogy of love poems.

Thus the poetry gave voice to a part of Helen that she was not in touch with at all, and a part that certainly had no expression in her personal life. In this sense, then, many of

403

these later poems are clearly personal, while *A Course in Miracles* is not. Interestingly enough, Helen always loved poetry, especially the renowned poets of Great Britain, and as mentioned earlier, she once had aspirations of being a world-famous poet herself. Therefore, in distinction from *A Course in Miracles*, which was scribed directly from the voice of Jesus, and characterized by Helen as a process of internal dictation, we may simply characterize the writing process of the poems as inspired.

The poems would come at almost any time or any place, and Helen was not really in conscious control of them. She would start a poem on a bus, in a taxi, while we were walking, or when alone in her apartment. She would usually scrawl one or two lines at a minimum, in her notebook if that were handy, or if not, then on any scrap of paper that was available. And that would "save" the poem. She could then finish it later, even if "later" were months in the future, as occasionally happened.

Another major difference in transmission between *A Course in Miracles* and the poetry, however, was that the Course came through without any impediment at all. There was no difficulty in Helen's "hearing," and the Course material just flowed through her—especially after the first month or so of the process. Helen's anxiety, as we have seen, had no effect on the flow of the dictation. That was not the case with the poems, at least with the later ones. As far as I can gather, both from the ease and speed with which they were written, as well as Helen's own recollections to me, the early poems came rather quickly. However, many of the poems that followed that 1973 Christmas Eve were written down with a lot of difficulty— stanzas would be inverted, lines would be out of sequence, etc. Sometimes Helen could not really hear clearly between two phrases, so she would write both phrases down, and later on we would decide which one should be used. There was also a great deal of resistance to many of the poems, which we shall discuss later regarding Helen's personal relationship with them.

While Helen resisted the temptation to edit the Course, even though she was tempted to do that many times, she did not feel she had to resist that temptation with the poetry. Rather, Helen felt that it was her prerogative to make the poems better, and very often she would change words or phrases—though not to any great extent, to be sure. It was therefore clear that she felt a kind of a personal connection with the poetry which she did not believe she had with the Course.

As I have said, the process of taking down the poetry did not go nearly as smoothly as when Helen was scribing *A Course in Miracles*. Helen always kept steno notebooks in which she recorded the Course, and there is one notebook which contains some of the poems. For the most part, however, the poems were written on anything that was around: backs of envelopes, small notepaper, and the like. One of my assignments became to rescue these little pieces of paper, which could otherwise have very easily become forever lost in Helen's pocketbook, bureau drawer, or simply thrown out. Helen's anxiety led her often to absent-mindedness, and she was always misplacing things. While taking down the Course, she once left her notebook in a taxi, only to have the driver run after her to return it to her. Typed pages of the Course manuscript somehow ended up midst psychological reports, to be found later by an embarrassed secretary and returned to her. And so whenever Helen would write down something, I would quickly take it from her for safekeeping.

Sometimes poems would be written over a period of days. At other times, as already has been mentioned, Helen would write fragments of lines that would simply hang around. I kept these in a folder, and every once in a while I would take them out and say to Helen, "Here is a poem you haven't finished. Why don't you take the rest of it down?" Helen had a very strong will, and it was impossible to get her to do anything she really did not want to do, but there were times when she would protest and put up a fight that I knew was superficial. After a while I was able to tell the difference pretty well. When I felt that there was a part of her that was open to continue a poem, or even take one down, I would urge her to do that. I had the most success around Christmas and Easter, which is why there are several of these, as well as my birthday. Other occasions that seemed suitable for a poem would also come up for a try. Some of the poems that resulted from these efforts, and their circumstances, I will describe below. Occasionally I would be "subtle," like putting the notebook under Helen's pillow so that she would get the hint when she went to sleep. I even once wrote Helen a poem asking her to write me a special poem.

On the one hand, of course, the poems were not nearly as significant as *A Course in Miracles*. On the other hand, however, the poems—the later personal poems especially—had an important if not special place in Helen's experience, as they enabled her, again, to have access to a part of her mind that she had otherwise split off from her awareness. I believe this is why, despite her occasional protestations to the contrary, she was proud of the poems and agreed to let me "badger" her about taking them down. In addition, the poems have the obvious value of helping so many people relate to their own spiritual experience, and even more specifically, to their ambivalent relationship to Jesus. Jesus obviously valued them as well. One morning we were leaving Helen's apartment for the Medical Center, and Helen had her notebook with her as she was in the midst of taking down a poem. We were almost out the door when she stopped to express concern about not having taken with her a psychological report she was working on. Jesus replied to her: "That is not what you will leave behind you," referring to the important legacy of her poetry (not to mention *A Course in Miracles* itself), and *not* her professional work, which her ego of course considered to be of great value.

There was only one time when a fragment of a poem continually resisted all my efforts at convincing Helen to complete it. All the other fragments eventually found a home in a poem, but somehow Helen could never finish this particular one. The lines seemed particularly interesting, not to mention profound, yet my urgings were always in vain. Finally, after many, many months of this, Helen said to me that this fragment was not a poem at all, but belonged in the Course itself. It was dated June 15, 1971, while Helen was taking down the workbook, and shortly before the period when she took down a bevy of the "little" poems. But the fragment reflected a much more sophisticated level than these early poems, and one that was indeed more befitting of *A Course in Miracles*. And then Helen said to me: "Find the place for it."

And so I did, obviously with a lot of help. The challenge of finding the perfect fit involved both the form *and* content. The fragment was in blank verse, and so the setting had to fit in with the poetry, and of course, the theme of the fragment had to match the theme of the paragraph in which it would be placed. Where it clearly belonged comes near the end of Chapter Twenty-Seven in the tenth paragraph of the section "The Dreamer of the Dream." The fragment does seem to fit seamlessly in the middle of that paragraph. The eight lines, as Helen originally wrote them, are:

> There is a risk of thinking death is peace
> Because the world equates the body with
> The Self Which God created. Yet a thing
> Can never be its opposite. And death
> Is opposite to peace, because it is
> The opposite of life. And life is peace.
> Awaken and forget all thoughts of death,
> And you will find you have the peace of God.

I should also mention that almost all of Helen's poems are written in iambic pentameter, Shakespeare's meter. The only exception to this in the later poems is "The Invitation," wherein four lines are shorter than five meters (or measures). And, of course, as mentioned above, much of *A Course in Miracles* is also in the same blank verse. In fact, Helen did not consider any ametric poem to be a poem. I wrote a large number of poems myself, many of them for Helen, as I shall mention below. One of them was not in meter, and Helen disdainfully said, after a quick scan: "This is not a poem." We have already seen how Helen paid careful attention to the form or style of the Course, and how pleased she was with the high, poetic level of its language. She therefore considered this poetry to be Jesus' gift to her.

The Poems

One series of poems, called the "Personal Poems" in the collection, deals with Helen's relationship with Jesus. One of the real values of this particular group is its clear statement of the depth and intensity of Helen's relationship with Jesus—the positive and negative sides. As would now be apparent to the reader, Helen was hardly an unconscious and unknowing channel through which the words of Jesus passed. Her relationship with him was very real to her, and not without a great deal of emotion.

The personal poems thus exhibit a wide range of feeling. There is, first, the trilogy of three love poems, written on my urging for Valentine's Day. I suggested to Helen how nice it would be for her to tell Jesus how much she loved him, and these were the result: "Love Song" ("My Lord, my Love, my Life, I live in you"), "The Resting Place" ("My arms are open. Come, my Love, to me and rest upon my heart. It beats for you and sings in joyous welcome"), and "Deliverance" ("I go in glory, for you walk with me"). And then, on the other end of the spectrum, there are those poems that reflect bitter disappointment, as in "Prayer for a House," which ends with this quatrain:

> This was supposed to be a temple built
> To You who said the altar would be lit
> Forever. And I thought that You had said
> A holy altar cannot be a tomb.
>
> *(The Gifts of God*, p. 49)

The complete poem can be found in the next chapter.

These poems therefore reveal the unconscious depth of her love and longing for Jesus, coupled with the anger and despair at what she perceived to be his failed promises. It soon became clear to me after the personal poems began to come just why Helen was so embarrassed by the early ones: they pointed in the direction of this greater expression of feeling, a depth that she defended against so forcefully throughout her life. Thus, where *A Course in Miracles* in its entirety was a direct message to Helen from Jesus, many of the poems were, in effect, a direct message to Helen from herself. They revealed, as few other things about herself did, this deeper split that her relationship with Jesus represented. This split has been one of the principal themes of this book, and we shall return to it in the next chapter when I shall draw upon several of these Jesus poems.

Many of the poems have interesting stories about them. The Easter and Christmas poems had the obvious stimulus of the liturgical calendar, and it had been Helen's custom, once the poems began to come, to write down poems for these two holidays. Without question, I believe, the Easter poems are among the finest of the collection, and moreover, are among the finest of any religious poetry I have seen. The Easter themes, of course, represented the full spectrum of the split mind, ranging from the guilt and fear of the ego's thought system of crucifixion, to the resurrection hope of the Holy Spirit's Atonement message through Jesus.

One such poem is "The Place of Resurrection," written in 1974, almost a month before Easter. On Palm Sunday, which corresponded that year to the second day of Passover, Helen and I had supper with Father Michael on the Lower East Side with two very dear friends, Sisters Regina and Mercy. These nuns had left their very beautiful and quiet Maryknoll home in Westchester County to establish a prayer presence among the poor. Helen and Bill had been introduced to them by Michael, and Helen was very insistent that I meet them during my first summer back in New York. I did, and we quickly became good friends. As the Sisters lived not more than a 15–20 minute walk from Helen's apartment, she and I would on occasion pay them a visit, as Helen always liked to sit and pray with them. Our plan this Palm Sunday was to have a Seder meal, which I would lead, followed by Michael's saying Mass for us in the Sisters' chapel. Few priests I have known have said Mass as meaningfully and sincerely as did Michael, and he frequently said Mass for us and the Sisters.

I also brought along "The Place of Resurrection," which I thought would be nice to read sometime during the day. The Sisters at that point did not know about *A Course in Miracles*, but they had a deep love and respect for Helen, which was certainly reciprocated. I knew they would love the poem, as would Michael, who of course did know about the Course and was a great lover of Helen's poetry. One of us read the poem after the meal (I forget now if Helen or I read it), and then a stunning thing happened. We fell spontaneously into a deep and prayerful silence, and I think we all felt the loving and timeless presence of Jesus that was reflected in the poem's closing lines:

> And learn before an empty tomb to see,
> He is not dead Who here was crucified.
>
> *(The Gifts of God*, p. 99)

Eventually we "returned" to the room, and went quietly into the chapel for Michael's Mass.

On the way home, Helen and I were recalling that timeless instant, and ever vigilant for an opportunity for another poem, I suggested that Helen write down a poem about what had occurred. I could usually feel when Helen was pregnant with a new poem, and would act as a midwife, as it were. And sure enough the next day Helen presented me with "Transformation," one of her finest poems, I think. It begins:

> It happens suddenly. There is a Voice
> That speaks one Word, and everything is changed.

And closes with another Easter theme:

> By the tomb
> The angel stands in shining hopefulness
> To give salvation's message: "Be you free,
> And stay not here. Go on to Galilee."
>
> *(The Gifts of God*, p. 64)

Two other poems were related to Sisters Regina and Mercy. One year after they had been living on the Lower East Side, I suggested to Helen that an anniversary poem would be a lovely and meaningful gift for them. We were going to spend part of the day with the Sisters, and so Helen obliged with a sweet little poem that began: "A year is short. Yet given unto Me / It lasts forever." The second poem was also written in 1974, when Sister Regina's mother was dying. When we heard the news of her death, I encouraged Helen to write down a poem for Regina, and a lovely "Requiem" was the result. I remember feeling at the time that this would be Helen's Requiem for herself as well.

There were a large number of poems that Helen had written for me, and some of these, too, have interesting stories associated with them. I'll begin with the first one, "Awake in Stillness," written in January 1974. This was indirectly associated with the beginning of our editing. I have already spoken of the events leading to Helen's and my final editing of the

410

Course manuscript. I do not recall whether we had actually begun the editing, although I think we had, but certainly right around that time Helen said to me one evening that there was a dark cornerstone in my mind that must be healed. It was the first, and I think the only time she ever talked to me like that. There was an urgency in her voice as she spoke, certainly most atypical of Helen in relation to me. What she communicated, if not directly then certainly by implication, was that this block would interfere, not only with our editing, but with the work I would be doing in the future. The closing paragraph of the text states that "Not one illusion is accorded faith, and not one spot of darkness still remains to hide the face of Christ from anyone" (text, p. 622). Helen was saying to me that there must be nothing interfering with our work together, or mine later, and now was the time right at the beginning to remove all such "spots of darkness."

I replied that I did not know what this "spot" was, but certainly I was ready to proceed with uncovering it. It did not take too long for the darkness to surface, and it related to the death of my grandfather when I was six years old. I had been very close to him, at that time probably closer than to my parents, and had been devastated by his very sudden death in the hospital from complications arising from a relatively routine surgical procedure. That issue had surfaced for me about three years earlier in an unpublished short story I had written, and again, most unexpectedly, the previous year while I was in the Trappist monastery in Israel. Early one morning, while in the monastic church, I found myself reliving his death in my mind, and sobbing almost uncontrollably.

So Helen and I spoke of this, and spontaneously began a kind of visualization process. It was not anything I was accustomed to doing, before or since, but Helen was very visually sensitive, as we have already seen in her series of experiences prior to the Course's coming, and I was usually able to "tune in" to Helen's symbolism. We could therefore almost share the pictures in each other's mind. I will return to another example of this later in the book.

And so, a series of images began for me that extended over a period of days. Every evening after dinner, Helen and I would

411

share in the development of this series, with Helen leading me through it, as she was observing it herself. It began in a darkened room with a coffin in the corner, with my grandfather laid inside. Eventually he arose, stood up, and walked with me to the opposite corner, where, as I was gradually able to release him, he disappeared into the dark corner. The room suddenly began to brighten and fill with light. Windows and walls disappeared, and the room now opened out into an immense and open plain. It became clear to us that my grandfather was a symbol for Jesus, and the experience represented my resurrection, which the Course understands as the awakening from the dream of death's reality.

The light-filled note of joy and resurrection ended the experience, which was clearly most significant for me, and one for which I was always grateful to Helen. It was also basically the only time Helen was able to be of direct help to me, as I shall discuss in Chapter 16.

After I left that evening, Helen wrote down this poem for me: "Awake in Stillness." She gave it to me the next morning.

> Peace cover you, within without the same,
> In shining silence and in peace so deep
> No dream of sin and evil can come near
> Your quiet mind. And then in stillness wake.
> First there is silence; then awakening.
> Now is the time appointed for the end
> Of dreaming. Still the cradle where you come
> To be reborn. The Christ is stirring in
> The home that He has chosen as His Own.
> His vision rests upon your eyes, and soon
> You will behold His face, and will forget
> The fantasies that seemed to be so real
> Until the stillness came. The Son of God
> Has come to join you now. His shining hand
> Is on your shoulder. And God's silent Voice
> Speaks ceaselessly of Heaven. You will hear
> His single message calling to His Own
> From His abiding place, to wake in God.
>
> (*The Gifts of God*, p. 73)

My birthday, February 22, provided obvious occasions for poems, and I managed to convince Helen that I had a devoted and loving mother who was more than happy to give me material gifts for my birthday, but that I did not have a mother who could write me poems. (After a while, incidentally, I was able to reciprocate, and wrote poems for Helen for her birthday, Mother's Day, and Christmas.) I remember once being with my family at my uncle and aunt's house on Long Island for the second Passover Seder (Helen and Louis used to come to my parents' for the first night), and Helen was in her usual panic that I might suffer some incredible calamity and not return. I called her from the Island to tell her that I had arrived safely, and she related that Jesus told her that she was not my mother in that sense, and so did not have to feel responsible for my physical well-being. Helen told me once that she recalled being in the back of St. Francis Church in New York City, when an old and eccentric woman came up to her and told her that she was going to have a son. Helen obviously dismissed this as the words of a disturbed person, but she now thought that this occurred around my birth in 1942.

So although on the one hand Helen knew her relating to me as her actual son was inappropriate, on the other hand this did not stop her from buying me shoes, belts, sweaters, etc., and certainly did not cause her to stop worrying, but it did almost always lead to a poem for my birthday. Such seeming role confusion can best be understood as but another example of Helen's confusing form and content, wherein the content of my being her spiritual son—in providing the continuity for *A Course in Miracles*—was mistakenly translated by her into the role of being my material mother.

"Birthday" and "Name Day" were two specific birthday poems written for me, while the other two involved some interesting circumstances which I now relate. As my birthday approached in 1976, I began to "lobby" Helen for a poem specifically on Jesus. Aside from my obvious wish for such a poem, I also thought it was time that Helen be a bit more outspoken about him. She did not rule out the idea whenever I brought it up, yet it obviously made her uncomfortable. However, I felt her agreement on another level, and so I continued my efforts. As I have already mentioned, no one, including Jesus or me, could get Helen to do anything she had not

already agreed to do. But I could feel the poem already present
in her mind. Then one evening the thought came to me that
what would provide the stimulus for the poem's birth would be
my writing a poem for Helen. And so I quickly wrote what will
hardly go down in literary history as a poetic masterpiece, but
what nonetheless enabled Helen to give birth to one of her
finer poems. The poem I presented to Helen the next day was
called "A Birthday Request":

> You ask what you could do for me,
> Gift for my birthday soon to be,
> That would but make that day complete,
> And be for me as special treat.
>
> To be with Him is my desire,
> For of His presence who can tire?
> It is He who alone heals us,
> I'd love a poem to our Jesus:
>
> A poem that speaks of all He's done
> To teach us that we are God's Son;
> That speaks to Him of all we feel
> In love and gratitude so real.
>
> Jesus, Jesus, we do proclaim
> All that we do is in Your name.
> You are our hope, our life, our love,
> Our older brother from above.
>
> All this the poem I pray you'll write
> Will say to Him who is our light;
> For He it is who leads us home,
> Please, Mother dear, a Jesus poem.

A few days later I received "A Jesus Prayer," whose final
stanza speaks for all of us, ending with the wonderful line
taken from Cardinal Newman that would be everyone's prayer
who truly loves Jesus:

> A perfect picture of what I can be
> You show to me, that I might help renew
> Your brothers' failing sight. As they look up
> Let them not look on me, but only You.
>
> (*The Gifts of God*, p. 83)

The story associated with the other birthday poem,

414

"Heaven's Gift," is a longer one. When I first met Helen she had given me a gift of a Holy Spirit medal that she had owned for many, many years. I wore it for a while, and then, not really accustomed to wearing medals, took it off and placed it in my desk drawer. Some time after that my studio apartment was broken into while I was at the Medical Center, but while the desk drawers were taken out, except for a small amount of cash and postage stamps, nothing else seemed to be missing from the apartment. I straightened up and never thought of the burglary again.

Some time later, shortly before my birthday, I was looking for something in the desk drawer in which I had placed Helen's medal, and in the course of my search discovered that the medal was gone. Remembering the break-in, I concluded that the medal had been stolen, and was concerned that Helen would be upset. However, when I told her the next day she did not appear that troubled, and took me that very afternoon to a Catholic gift shop and bought me another Holy Spirit medal (which I wear to this day), and then wrote down this poem. It was originally entitled "A Birthday Gift," but as the poem itself does not deal with birthdays, I renamed it before publication. The poem is thus another illustration of how a specific circumstance can act as a trigger for a poem (or, as we have seen, a section in *A Course in Miracles*) that generalizes a greater lesson. In this case the lesson was that loss is impossible, as seen in these lines from the poem: "No one can rob infinity.... No one can take away from everything.... No one can lessen love.... Heaven can only give. This is the sign that losing is impossible" (*The Gifts of God*, p. 80).

"With Thanks" was a poem of gratitude Helen had written for me, while "The Gift" came at Christmas, when I again managed to convince her not to buy me a gift, but to write me a poem instead. And finally there was "Continuity." I forget the exact circumstances, but I think it came as a result of discussions Helen and I had about *A Course in Miracles'* life in the world, what Bill on occasion referred to as "Miracles Mischagass." Although in print less than a year, it was already clear, as I discussed earlier, how people were seizing the Course for themselves, using it as a means for self-aggrandizement, both psychologically as well as financially. Many students, in fact began to set themselves up as teachers, passing themselves off as representatives of the Course's holiness and wisdom, without any real understanding of what the Course was saying. None of this pleased Helen, although as I mentioned before, she was not in a position to do anything about it. I recall being asked by Jesus to quote to Helen from the biblical "Acts of the Apostles." The scene is where a number of the Jews are complaining to Rabbi Gamaliel about the miraculous and preaching activities of Peter and the other disciples. Gamaliel, the renowned rabbi who was St. Paul's teacher, wisely answered their concerns in this way:

> Refrain from these men, and let them alone: for if this counsel or this work be of men, it will come to nought: But if it be of God, ye cannot overthrow it (Acts 5:38f).

The point was to reassure Helen that what was happening with the Course was "the work...of men," not "of God," and so Helen need not be concerned about it. The fulfillment of the Course's role in the world was guaranteed by Jesus.

Incidentally, what was beginning in those early years as a trend, has now become, almost fifteen years since its publication in 1976, more solidified and widespread. It was a comfort for Helen to know that I was around, and would be around for some time to ensure that the Course message would be treated with fidelity, and that its life in the world would be a dignified and loving one. "Continuity" was a reflection of such feeling. It begins:

> Your life is like a jewel in the crown,
> The glowing light that Jesus promised me
> When my own little light is laid aside.
> Except your light is there my crown would be
> A thing of time, to end as all things must,
> Without an echo in eternity.

It later states:

> You are the light that stays behind a while
> To bring His stillness and His peace to all
> Who seek for Him in sorrow....

And closes with a sudden shift in tense and mood, from time to timelessness:

> He waits for me as I will wait for you,
> Standing with Him. In your unclouded sight
> The world will vanish. Now He leans to you
> And lifts you to your home. Behold how bright
> The crown He has for you. Come now, my child,
> And disappear with me into His light.
>
> *(The Gifts of God, p. 78)*

Some other poems worthy of mention are "Brother Swan," written for Gerald Jampolsky, whom we had met in 1975 through Judy Skutch. In his books and public lectures, Jerry has chronicled his sudden turnaround, through *A Course in Miracles*, from alcoholism, chronic back problems, and being a generally unhappy person. The reference in the poem of course is to the story of the ugly duckling who turns into a swan.

The oddest poem of all, in part because I do not think it is really meant to be a poem, is "Glory Train." As I mentioned in Chapter 2, from the time she was a little girl attending Georgia's Baptist church, Helen always loved Negro spirituals. In fact, during the 1970s there was a popular Broadway play called "Your Arms Too Short to Box with God," a gospel musical filled with spirituals. I took Helen to see it, and she had a wonderful time listening to the form of music she loved so much. Gospel music was certainly not an interest a person would have normally associated with Helen (whose great love, as I have already mentioned, was Gilbert and Sullivan). Given Helen's persona as an objective intellectual, such unabashed interest in the emotional outpouring of gospel music was indeed surprising. After Helen took down the poem, we felt it was more suited to be a song, as can be seen in this opening stanza:

> The glory train goes riding by,
> Hallelujah!
> A golden streaking in the sky,
> A gleam and whistling rising high,
> Above all souls that thought to die,
> Hallelujah!

Someone in fact once offered to put it to music, but nothing ever came of it. Helen would have rebelled against any of her poems being set to music, since a poem has its own metric rhythm with which music would interfere. However, Helen certainly approved of "Glory Train" as the exception.

I have already mentioned the Christmas and Easter poems, and these speak for themselves. "The Hope of Christmas" was specifically written as a Christmas present for Father Michael, of whom Helen was quite fond.

There is actually one poem that was not included in the published collection. This was a short little piece that was written, on my urging, for the printer and his staff who had worked so hard on rushing through the first printing of the Course in time for our own imposed summer deadline. It is called "In Gratitude."

> The time you spent is given back to you
> In shining hours and in quiet peace.
> The care you gave to God He saves for you
> With loving kindness so your sorrows cease.
>
> Your patience is His Own, and comes to you
> When you have need of it. But only look
> Upon His smile, and you will understand
> How very much He thanks you for His book.

About two years or so before Helen died, we were discussing the fate of the poetry. It seemed clear that the poetry phase had ended, and that in fact Helen was not going to scribe any more material. She had made her wishes quite clear that she, as I already mentioned, did not want the poetry to be published in her lifetime. I therefore said to her, in the same spirit as our earlier discussion of her autobiography, that when she died the poems would be my responsibility, and as I knew there were some words and lines she would want to change, that it would be best if she would go over them with me. I said that I basically knew what she wanted, and would certainly make any such changes, but that I would much prefer doing them with her. She was reluctant, but I finally convinced her that this would be a good thing.

And so we began, but after only a few poems I realized this editing project was a mistake. Helen's compulsive editing took over, often at the expense of the poems. I think Helen realized this as well, and gladly agreed that we stop. I apologized to her and promised never to bring the subject up again. She seemed comfortable with the unspoken fact that the poetry would be published after her death, and that I would supervise the process. As I have already said, the poems remain a wonderful witness to both sides of Helen's split mind, as well as being as beautiful a contemporary collection of spiritual poetry as one could find.

"The Gifts of God"

Finally, there is the prose-poem called "The Gifts of God," which requires some explanation. While it was not written *for* me, I was certainly the direct stimulus for it. Probably more than any other of the scribed material, this wonderful piece illustrates how something quite beautiful and inspiring can come from an almost hopeless ego situation. This was the circumstance of its origin: Once a month, early Sunday morning, I traveled by train to Ossining in northern Westchester County to spend a day and a half at the Maryknoll Cloister. This was a small community of cloistered nuns whom I met with individually, as well as addressed as a group. I was always back in New York early Monday afternoon. For this one particular Sunday (February 8, 1978), the weather forecast was for a blizzard to begin later that morning, and to continue on through the day and into the evening. I have already mentioned Helen's dependency on me, which would become greatly exacerbated whenever I would be out of my apartment and not with her. To alleviate her anxiety and perennial fears that I would never return, I would call her regularly, and also supply her with the telephone numbers where I could be reached.

Helen thus became frantic with anticipation of my almost certain demise in the blizzard, and asked me not to go. However, as I had canceled the previous weekend upon Helen's request, I did not feel I should do so again. I tried to assure Helen that since the storm was not expected to hit New York until *after* I arrived at Maryknoll, there was nothing to fear: I would be well taken care of, and would be sure to return safely on Monday. That seemed to relieve some of Helen's anxiety, at least temporarily. But then later that Sunday morning, as predicted, the snow began to fall, and fall, and fall. Helen's anxiety seemed to extend beyond her considerably extended boundaries, and I called frequently during the day and evening, and Helen called in between my calls. She was absolutely beside herself with worry. I continued to reassure her that the Sisters were taking very good care of me, I had lots to eat, the Cloister was warm, and I would be home the next day. But to no avail. And then to compound the situation, the switchboard shut off at 10 P.M., which meant there was no possible communication between us until morning.

I can only imagine Helen's anxiety at that point, and yet at what was probably its height, there was obviously another part of her mind that asked for help and allowed a different message to come through her from Jesus. Sometime late that evening began "The Gifts of God," which essentially contrasts the ego's gifts of fear with God's gifts of love. The first section (I added the titles and sections later) was "The Dream of Fear," followed the next morning by "The Two Gifts." Both were personal messages from Jesus, and were specifically aimed at helping Helen choose against her fear, saying in effect: "Turn over to me all *your* gifts of fear—your fearful dreams—and I will exchange them for the peace of God, *His* gifts." Unfortunately, these wonderful messages had no observable effect on Helen. I left Maryknoll later Monday morning, and it took me over seven hours to return, as train service had been adversely affected by the storm. By the time I arrived at Helen's apartment—around 7:00 P.M.—she was a nervous wreck, but obviously relieved to see me, and alive and well at that.

The crisis was now over, but two days later Helen picked up the writing where she had left off, and "The Ending of the Dream" was dictated to her. This section is a very powerful summary of the ego's world, and it, along with the rest of the piece, is a kind of miniature version of *A Course in Miracles*. We find here in this section an explanation of the ego, how it originated, the purpose of guilt, fear, and the physical world itself, and the effects of peace and love when we change our minds and turn the ego thought system over to Jesus.

The next section, "Our Gift to God," was written in the first week of March, and the beautifully inspiring final section, "The Father's Love," came on April 11, and actually is the last truly authentic scribing Helen ever did. It closes with this touching plea to us from God, our Father:

> Do not forget. Do not forget, My child. Open the door before the hidden place, and let Me blaze upon a world made glad in sudden ecstasy. I come, I come. Behold Me. I am here for I am You; in Christ, for Christ, My Own beloved Son, the glory of the infinite, the joy of Heaven and the holy peace of earth, returned to Christ and from His hand to Me. Say now Amen, My Son, for it is done. The secret place is open now at last. Forget all things except My changeless Love. Forget all things except that I am here (*The Gifts of God*, p. 128).

In the midst of this section, incidentally, I inserted another piece, which also requires some explanation. Earlier that year, on January 14, Helen had written down a beautiful and comforting special message, that although we had no way of knowing it then, was a foreshadowing of "The Gifts of God" that would come less than a month later. It certainly seemed on a different level from Helen's other "special messages." When I was visiting Bill in his California apartment the summer after Helen's death in 1981, and we were discussing the publication of Helen's poetry, and what we should do with "The Gifts of God," I recalled to him this message, and asked him his thoughts about it. He replied almost in the same words Helen had used several years earlier regarding the lines "There is a risk in thinking death is peace." Bill said: "Find a place for it" [i.e., in "The Gifts of God"]. And so I did, after the top paragraph on page 127 and before the second paragraph on page 128. The inserted passage begins with "The night is dark but it will have an end" and closes with "Be sure a mother does not fail the son she loves, nor will a Father cast away His child."

When it was clear that "The Gifts of God" was complete in 1978, we did not know what to do with it. At first we could not even be sure it all belonged together, although it became obvious after a while that it did. I remember discussing it with Helen, saying that it really should be published because it was so lovely, and that people would find it comforting and helpful. Yet, it was not really big enough to be published separately as a pamphlet, as were, for example, "Psychotherapy" and "The Song of Prayer." So we simply kept it aside. Yet when we were planning for the publication of the poetry after Helen's death, that volume seemed a perfect place for it. It is interesting to note that in "The Gifts of God" the specific and personal circumstances of its beginnings do not appear at all. Clearly it was ultimately meant, just as with *A Course in Miracles* twelve years earlier, for the world at large.

"The Gifts of God" remains, again, a wonderful witness to how silk (Jesus' gift of his loving message) can be made from a sow's ear (Helen' "gift" of fear). It also is yet another example of the split within Helen's mind: she was able to get her ego out of the way sufficiently to take down this message, but was not able to integrate her mind sufficiently to be able to benefit from it. To recall again Bill's insightful words: "The same process of dissociation that enabled Helen to take down the Course, also made it virtually impossible for her to learn it." In the words of the pompous Polonius from *Hamlet* (II,ii):

'tis true 'tis pity, and pity 'tis 'tis true.

Chapter 16

JESUS: THE WAY, THE TRUTH, AND THE LIFE

These next two chapters deal specifically, though not necessarily chronologically, with the nature of Helen's relationship with Jesus. In this first of two chapters I focus on Helen's *experience* of Jesus, drawing upon my personal experiences with her regarding Jesus, which illustrate the different facets of her relationship with him. In the following chapter I discuss the true *nature* of Jesus—the content behind the form—and of his reality in Helen's mind.

The title for this chapter comes, of course, from the famous statement attributed to Jesus in John's gospel (14:6), that he is the way, the truth, and the life. This was one of Helen's favorite quotations, and is referred to four times in the Course (text, pp. 86,108; workbook, pp. 143,475), once in the pamphlet, "Psychotherapy" (p. 1), and two times in *The Gifts of God* (pp. 47,54). Interestingly enough, Helen frequently mis-wrote the phrase, substituting "light" for "life." For Helen, Jesus was clearly the way, the truth, and the life; yet, as we have seen, she fought bitterly against him. This ambivalence ranged from overt hostility, passive indifference, and total dismissal on the one hand, and on the other to a devotion, dedication, and love that was as intense as was the hostility.

While it was often difficult for Helen to talk directly about her ego, she was nonetheless able to express her yearning to have a positive relationship with Jesus. Quite regularly we would pray together, with my speaking aloud to Jesus what I knew to be Helen's thoughts. These times would usually come at the end of a long day, either at the Medical Center, or more characteristically, after an afternoon's shopping expedition. Helen's mind would eventually quiet, becoming more receptive to experiencing the loving comfort of her Lord, as she referred to Jesus in the poetry. This was a side of Helen rarely seen by others, and probably not at all, yet one which touched another part of her mind, unaffected by the frantic ego maneuverings that were committed to maintaining her conflict. Often during these moments of quiet Helen would weep, allowing herself to experience her gratitude to Jesus, not to mention being able to experience his for her.

As Helen's relationship to Jesus was very much correlated with her ambivalence to the Roman Catholic Church, I begin this chapter with Helen's lifelong love-hate relationship with the Church.

Catholicism—Mary

Though Helen never subscribed to the doctrines and dogmas of the Roman Catholic Church (or any formal religious teaching for that matter), she never abandoned her fascination with it. She seemed to find a strange comfort in some of its rituals, notably Mass and the rosary. In fact, it was Helen who first taught me to say the rosary, and when particularly anxious, she found our reciting it together comforting, as she did attendance at Mass. Very often she would be able to hear helpful messages from Jesus while at church, during periods of being otherwise blocked in her hearing. Interestingly enough, right after she died, Louis asked me to remove from the apartment, along with the Course, two purses bulging with Catholic medals and rosaries accumulated by Helen over many years and "hidden" in a bureau drawer.

Helen and I frequently attended Mass together, one of her favorite churches being the aforementioned St. Francis Church, down the street from Pennsylvania Station in midtown Manhattan. When the Saturday weather was nice, part of our afternoon ritual was to go to St. Francis to attend the high Mass which served to fulfill the Sunday obligation for Catholics. Yet the already-discussed curious attraction Helen had to the Roman Catholic Church since childhood was not without its sharp edges, for Helen also hated the Church—in part for it not being able to provide her with the peace she so desperately desired, in part too because of its distortion of the person of Jesus and his teaching. On another level, Helen recognized the futility of seeking outside herself for salvation, yet she continually sought to deny this fact by blaming the Church for the inevitable disappointment she experienced. This feeling of futility can be seen in one of her letters to me while I was in Israel (*see above,* p. 349).

I have already discussed how early in Helen's life her interest in the Roman Catholic Church began to develop. While this attraction, as I have mentioned, clearly served the defensive purpose of distracting her mind, there were certainly many other forms in the world she could have chosen. And thus one would be ill-advised to dismiss Helen's interest as simply part of her neurotic character armor. The Church was a good vehicle for remaining close to the *content* of Helen's mind—the love and devotion to Jesus—at the same time affording her the *forms* through which she could, paradoxically, defend herself from this love and not identify with it.

Helen went to church very frequently in her life, and during certain periods would attend daily Mass, perform Novenas (a series of nine daily rosary recitations for a specific prayer intention), and often recite the rosary. She even carried in her purse a "pocket rosary," which allowed her to say the rosary while walking, riding a bus or taxi, even if Louis were present, for no one could see the activity of her hands within her pocket: another of Helen's secrets that she held from the world.

In addition, Helen knew the Bible very well, and could quote passages from it almost as readily as she could from Shakespeare. She was most familiar of course with the New Testament, but also felt at home with the more well known books and verses from the Old Testament, especially Isaiah and the Psalms. As would be expected, on one level Helen's attraction for the Bible was due to the beautiful Elizabethan language of the King James version, the only translation she knew. On another level, the Bible—the Old Testament prophecies supposedly relating to Jesus, and the New Testament—was the so-called testimony that related accounts of Jesus, and so herein lay her underlying attraction to it. At the same time, of course, her love-hate relationship with Jesus, not to mention with traditional Christianity, was projected onto its books. So for Helen, the Bible was both a literary masterpiece as well as being a symbolic reminder of Jesus, thereby making it subject to the same ambivalence she felt for him.

The negative side of her ambivalence towards the Bible and Christianity or Roman Catholicism did not always show. However, I remember one time when it *did*. Helen was helping me to edit my pamphlet, "Christian Psychology in 'A Course in Miracles.'" This pamphlet was written in 1977 to assist identified Christians to bridge the gap between their religious understanding and the Course. Thus, it quoted frequently from the Bible in explaining the Course's principles, and referred as well to some of the traditional Christian beliefs.

One section in the pamphlet consisted of a re-examination of quotations from the New Testament in light of the Course teachings. I have rarely seen Helen so furious. Reading these passages brought up so much anger in her it was impressive even to me, who had already frequently observed Helen at her "worst." All the repressed anger at the Churches—which purported to teach the gospel of Jesus and yet in truth corrupted it—flared up. This was not an issue that Helen usually related to, but it obviously was there. Even deeper of course was Helen's own guilt stemming from her self-accusations over having also not been faithful to Jesus. The disappointment, rage, and hatred at Jesus for his "broken promises" that Helen usually kept below the surface (although barely) suddenly flared up wildly, and she lashed out at him for not living up to his word. The Church likewise, though somewhat secondarily, received its share of abuse for its confusion of form and content, trapping its believers in a web of ritual and dogma. These feelings expressed towards Jesus were not too dissimilar from what is found in some of Helen's poems that I discuss later in this chapter, though they lacked the more controlled expression that is contained in the poetry. Her rage this time even kept her up through the night, Helen later told me, as she could not quiet her hurt and vengeful mind.

Nonetheless, for the most part Helen's conscious relationship to the Church was a positive one. I have already indicated Helen's affection for Father Michael, shared by all of us. During one period of our friendship, Michael would pick Bill up once a week at his apartment early in the morning, drive to the Medical Center, where Helen and I would meet them. Michael would then say Mass in Helen's office for the four of us. While

426

Bill was the least comfortable with religious rituals of any kind, let alone a Catholic Mass, he, along with Helen and me, enjoyed this peaceful time of intimate sharing. Incidentally, Michael departed somewhat from the traditional, by having me choose the Mass readings instead of following the daily Church liturgical schedule. Thus the "epistle" came from the Course, with the gospel selection following the same theme found in the Course reading. Every once in a while we would gather in my apartment for Mass, and then a light supper (for which Louis usually joined us—*after* Mass). Michael's obvious sincerity and devotion to God was the content with which we joined, since we did not subscribe to the Catholic dogma that the bread and wine literally became the body and blood of Jesus.[91] Helen used to joke with Michael about this and say, "After all, Mike, bread is bread." But I suggested to Helen that perhaps she not kid him like this, since the Mass was quite serious and real for him.

Michael was close to Mother Teresa, and whenever she came to New York, he chauffeured her around at the request of the Cardinal. On a number of occasions Michael arranged for us to meet with her, once even at our offices at the Medical Center, and Helen and she shared a mutual respect. Mother Teresa was particularly struck by Helen's work with retarded children, and assertively told Helen one winter that next year she (Helen) would be in India lending her talents on behalf of the poor children. Mother Teresa may have caused bishops to quake when she came to their dioceses, and had Jesus on her side to boot, but not even she could get Helen to do something she chose not to do; nor could Jesus, as we have seen. Thus, even saints can be mistaken!

---

91. In the original dictation of the Course, Jesus made several comments to Helen about the Eucharist: "The idea of cannibalism in connection with the [Blessed] Sacrament is a reflection of a distorted view of sharing. I told you before that the word 'thirst' in connection with the Spirit was used in the Bible because of the limited understanding of those to whom I spoke. I also told you not to use it.... I do not want to share my body in communion because this is to share nothing. Would I try to share an illusion with the most holy children of a most holy Father? But I do want to share my mind with you.... Yet would I offer you my body, you whom I love, knowing its littleness? Or would I teach that bodies cannot keep us apart? Mine was of no greater value than yours.... Communion comes with peace, and peace must transcend the body."

Keeping within her psychological identification as a Catholic, Helen held an exalted opinion of priests and nuns, magically believing that they were more spiritually advanced than others simply by virtue of their vocations. Her experience with this group offered her many opportunities to see the opposite, and yet, on one level at least, she never really abandoned this naive position. This otherwise anomalous attitude, given Helen's great worldly (not to mention other-worldly wisdom), made sense in light of Helen's substitution of form for content: the *form* of religious life in place of the *content* of the Love of God. And so she liked to meet many of the nuns and priests with whom I worked, many of whom did express a dedication and commitment to God that the forms of their lives reflected. Occasionally, Helen accompanied me to convents where I would be speaking or counseling sisters, and obviously enjoyed being with people she believed had made a commitment that she consciously was too fearful of doing.

Helen was thus a very closet Christian. The reader may recall Helen's "guilty-secret" attitude already present in her childhood, when she would sneak out with her Catholic governness to go to church on Sundays. Later, as a married woman, Helen went through a period when she would again sneak out of the house—at night while her husband Louis was asleep—to walk to St. Patrick's Cathedral to attend late night services. So devoted was she, at least on one level, that Michael was certain that at the moment of her death Helen would ask him to baptize her. And Louis' one great fear, as I mentioned in Part I, was that he would wake up one morning to find out that Helen had become Catholic. He obviously knew what we were doing in my apartment before he joined Helen, Bill, Michael, and me for supper, but characteristic of him, he chose not to pay attention, and would accept instead Helen's lame accounts of our "praying together."

There was also Helen's affinity for Mary, called the Blessed Mother by the Catholic Church. While Helen was never shy about sharing her angry feelings towards Jesus or even God, I never once heard her say anything negative about Mary. In fact, she would hardly speak of her at all. And yet, there was no question of a strong underlying attraction to the mother of

428

Jesus, regarded by Catholics as "the holiest of women." This attraction can be traced as far back as Helen's experiences as a little girl inside a Catholic Church when she accompanied her governness, but had to wait in the vestibule, sneaking glimpses of the "beautiful woman dressed in blue." The experience of "God's miracle" when she was twelve years old occurred at Lourdes, the place where Mary appeared to little Bernadette in 1858.

Interestingly enough, however, one of my first serious talks with Helen did focus on Mary. It came in the summer of 1973, as Helen and I were first becoming acquainted. We spent the day in the Bronx Zoo, and I remember Helen's asking me about Mary and my feelings about her. I thought that the question had some importance for Helen, and I responded by relating my experiences at the Trappist Abbey of Latroun in Israel, where I felt a very deep connection with Mary, through the lovely statue the monks had at the head of the sanctuary. It was a connection I found quite odd, since growing up Jewish, I had no background in Marian devotion. In fact, my very favorite part of each day in the monastery came at its close, when the last thing the monks would chant before retiring was the hauntingly beautiful Trappist Gregorian hymn "Salve Regina" ("Hail Holy Queen"). We would all kneel in the darkened church, with the only visible light emanating from the larger-than-life statue of Mary. It was always a special moment for me.

I shared these experiences with Helen, who was fascinated by it all. However, because Jesus was always the specific object of my spiritual experience, and not Mary, we never really discussed the subject again. Moreover, the clear ambivalence of Helen's relationship with Jesus seemed to require more attention. If I had pursued the subject of Mary, I am sure Helen would have spoken much more about her own feelings and experiences of her, and probably these discussions would have stimulated more poems with Marian themes than she took down.

Thus there was in Helen, on one level, the usual Catholic mentality of venerating Mary, especially in saying the rosary, but there was a deeper level in Helen as well. During the scribing of *A Course in Miracles*, Jesus made occasional references to Mary, comparing Helen to her in terms of function—Mary's bringing forth the person of Jesus, Helen's bringing forth his message through *A Course in Miracles*—with intimations of the same degree of holiness. In one short special message to Helen, probably dictated in 1978, Jesus began with the words: "Peace, Mother." It was always clear to Helen, by the way, that in no way was she an incarnation of Mary: she knew that Jesus was referring to *content*, not *form*. There were thus intimations, as just stated, that Helen shared the same inner radiance and purity as did Mary, and likewise, that Helen was as intimately one with Jesus as was Mary. And so we can say that the figure of Mary, the mother of Jesus, would not only be comparable but identical in *content* to the ancient priestess of Helen's vision. The mind of God's Son is one, and so each of us carries within us this Thought of the absolute purity of Christ that the historical figures of Jesus and Mary represent. In the various messages and inner experiences Helen had, Jesus was helping her to identify once again with the love that was her true Self.

An extremely powerful and important vision Helen had of Mary reflects the great respect, if not love, she had for this woman who was every bit the equal of Jesus. It was a vision of Michelangelo's great statue, the "Pieta," which depicts Mary holding the crumpled and dead body of her son. Helen saw this figure of Mary in front of her, and heard her say: "This means nothing." Imagine the depth of love and spiritual awareness that would allow a mother to say these words, and *fully mean them*. The figure of Mary represented the same content for Helen as did the priestess of her earlier vision, not to mention the "past life" image of Helen as an ancient priestess who was barely in the world, remaining at its "edge," healing those who were brought to her. I think it is safe to state that for Helen, Mary represented a being who shared the same rarefied mind as did Jesus, and was probably one of the very, very few who truly understood his message. It is a mind, as I shall discuss in the Epilogue, that Helen on another level also shared.

A number of poems likewise make reference to Mary, although some of these are admittedly strange references, to say the least. The first of these, "Mother of the World," was written on February 23, 1974, along with two other poems that related to Jesus. Helen originally called the poem "Earth Mother," but we realized afterwards that the pagan connotations of this term ill-fitted the poem, and so we changed it first to "Holy Mother," and finally to its present title. Here it is in its entirety:

> Peace is a woman, mother to the world,
> Whom God has sent to lay a gentle hand
> Across a thousand children's fevered brows.
> In its cool certainty there is no fear,
> And from her breasts there comes a quietness
> For them to lean against and to be still.
>
> She brings a message to their frightened hearts
> From Him Who sent her. Listen now to her
> Who is your mother in your Father's Name:
> "Do not attend the voices of the world.
> Do not attempt to crucify again
> My first-born Son, and brother still to you."
>
> Heaven is in her eyes, because she looked
> Upon this Son who was the first. And now
> She looks to you to find him once again.
> Do not deny the mother of the world
> The only thing she ever wants to see,
> For it is all you ever want to find.
>
> (*The Gifts of God*, p. 84)

After the opening stanza's reference to an almost archetypal mother, the second and third stanzas are clear allusions to Mary, the mother of Jesus. These stanzas also carry along with them the fervent appeal to listen to the mother's call for peace, and for us frightened children to be like Jesus, her "first-born Son."

One of Helen's last poems, written on New Year's Day, 1978, is "The Resurrection and the Life." It is an odd poem indeed, and combines both the Christmas and Easter messages. It has seven stanzas, but in one sense is actually two poems, and Helen specifically asked that only the first four stanzas be printed as the actual poem. (The poem, unfortunately, was printed in its entirety.) Helen in fact had asked me to draw a

431

line between these two poems (stanzas 1–4,5–7) on the sheets on which we originally typed them, reflecting the clear distinction in her mind between the two. Structurally, however, they are similar, as each stanza shares the same number of lines and rhyme scheme: abcbdb. This "first poem" is a beautiful Christmas and Easter message, as seen in the second stanza:

> So still the birth you did not understand
> Who came to you. Before your frightened eyes
> The Lord of light and life appears to fail
> His promises of Heaven's grace, and dies
> Forever on a cross. Nor can you see
> The Child of hope Who in a manger lies.
>
> (*The Gifts of God*, p. 100)

And it ends with this exhortation for Helen to look upon Jesus' resurrected life:

> Then look again on Him,
> And join His benediction, "It is done."
>
> (*The Gifts of God*, p. 100)

The second poem not only combines Christmas and Easter themes, but also images of Helen and Mary, Jesus and Christ.

> He held you in His arms as He arose,
> And death was overcome. Yet on the hill
> Of dying you had fixed your eyes, it seemed
> As if forever. Now you wait until
> You look beyond the end you thought you saw,
> And see the Child Who is your first-born still.
>
> Think of this Child Who comes again. He is
> The Son Who seemed to die. He offers you
> The motherhood the shadow of a cross
> Appeared to take away. Yet round it grew
> The lilies of rebirth. Accept again
> The deathless One, the holy Son you knew.
>
> See not an ending where beginning is,
> Nor dark in sunlight. You who came to mourn,
> Remember now the ancient song of birth,
> And lay aside the signs of grieving worn
> By childless mothers. Lift your heart to Him,
> For once again to you a Child is born.
>
> (*The Gifts of God*, pp. 100f)

This poem made Helen most uncomfortable, as did its companion "Mother of the World." It was a discomfort born of the ego fear of the Self beyond both "Heaven and Helen," the Self identified with the ancient priestess, and here with Mary. The call of the poem was for Helen to identify with this Self, and remember that within her holy mind was indeed reborn the holy Child of Christ. Her function as scribe to Jesus, giving birth to his Course, was merely the reflection of this more abstract rebirth of the presence of Christ in her mind. The Easter message of resurrection and rebirth is understood in *A Course in Miracles* as the awakening from the dream of death to the truth of Christ's ongoing birth in our mind. As Christmas Lesson 303 states: "The holy Christ is born in me today."

Two other poems—"Stabat Mater" and "Waiting"—carry with them a suggestion of Mary, in a theme immortalized in the great Church hymns as the "Stabat Mater": the *mother* (Mary) in John's gospel who *stands* sadly beneath the Cross. Here then Mary is seen as an ego symbol of hopelessness and despair. Helen's "Stabat Mater" poem conveys this hopelessness of believing that the Love of God has indeed been killed by the ego's hatred and fear. The poem begins and ends this way:

> Who stands beside a cross is all alone,
> For sorrow such as this cannot be shared....
> She stands
> Upon the edge of eons without hope.
> Here is forever. Here is timelessness.
> Who could believe the time of dying ends?
> (*The Gifts of God*, p. 92)

After Helen wrote down this poem (also, it should be noted, at Christmas time), I wrote her a similar poem but with a different ending: "Stabat Mater II."

Over a month earlier Helen had written down "Waiting," which while not specifically referring to the Cross, certainly conveys the same sense of waiting. Yet here faith wins out against the almost hopeless hope that in the end God's Word is true, and the ego's false. It is an important poem as it reflects Helen's inner journey, and in the fourth stanza there is a direct reference to the unbelieving part of Helen's mind, that at another "time"—this really means another part of her mind—

433

had chosen illusion over truth. It may also be a reference to a memory of Helen's actual fleeing from the scene on Calvary—"when I fled." In all, "Waiting" points to Helen's resurrection and the end of her dream of death, as will be discussed later in the book. Here is the poem in its entirety:

> Waiting is terrible. And yet I know
> That I have waited many times before.
> In vanity and hopelessness I go
> From dark to darker and to darkest door.
>
> And yet there is a difference. For I hear
> Another voice, still faint, perhaps, that sings
> An ancient melody. The cries of fear
> Are slightly softened by the stir of wings.
>
> Maybe there is an end to waiting. He
> Who promised to return may yet arise
> From what appeared as death. He still may be
> What never was begun and never dies.
>
> Perhaps there was a time, so long ago
> It is not half remembered, when I fled,
> Too soon to see the fearful shadows go,
> And look upon the living, not the dead.
>
> Let me not lose the tiny spark of trust
> That sprang to sudden life so lately born.
> Perhaps the living never fell to dust.
> Perhaps there never was a need to mourn.
>
> Let me remember. For it yet may be
> It was not as I thought. The dying rose,
> And maybe, in my haste, I did not see
> A circle not begun needs not to close.
>
> (*The Gifts of God*, p. 52)

This would be the appropriate place to address briefly an issue that is frequently raised these days from the feminist students of *A Course in Miracles*: its masculine language. In the Course itself there does not appear a single feminine reference (the sole exception is in the Course's appendix, the "Clarification of Terms," where a comparison is made between the miracle's gentleness and "a loving mother [who] sings her child to rest" [manual, p. 78]). The three Manifestations of the

Trinity, in line with traditional Christian usage, are masculine, as are the pronouns referring back to Them. In keeping with grammatical convention, pronouns referring back to the neutral "person" or "one" are kept in the masculine.

Finally, there is the phrase "Son of God," used to designate all of us seeming fragments of the unified Christ. The term has been specifically used in the Course to emphasize the unity of ourselves with Jesus, as discussed previously. Throughout the two-thousand-year history of Christianity, "Son of God" was exclusively used for Jesus, "God's only begotten Son." The rest of humanity was designated (by St. Paul, Ga 4:5) as adopted sons. Since *A Course in Miracles* is quite emphatic about our true Identity being spirit and not the body, the use of the term "Son" and its accompanying pronouns clearly have no meaning as to gender.

It is important to note, incidentally, that the sexist issue had no meaning for Helen, who never raised any question or concern about it. In fact, we were all quite surprised when after the Course's publication, people began to object to the language. It had never occurred to any of us that this language was a problem.

We turn now to a discussion of some specific aspects of Helen's ambivalent relationship with Jesus. This next section will focus on my personal experiences with Helen, which will serve as illustrations for what by now will be readily familiar themes to the reader.

Helen's Ambivalence Towards Jesus

1. The Journey Home to Jesus

One evening while Helen and I were praying, she told me that she saw a picture of the two of us standing midst ruins and rubble, she in a tattered white dress, and I as a little boy. The relationship could have been mother-son, or if not literally so, certainly in spirit. The description and Helen's feelings about it strongly suggested Qumran, during the time immediately following the destruction of the Essene community by the

Romans in 70 A.D. But this was clearly symbolic, as the reader may recall Helen's experience at Qumran where she distinctly felt she (in a past life) was buried there.

I was able to envision myself standing there with Helen, and then began a symbolic series of inner events that seemed to reflect a process in Helen's mind. She and I set out on a journey northward toward Galilee, along the Jordan river. Not all of the events remain with me, yet one in particular, as well as the conclusion of the series, I shall never forget.

While we walked along the shore, which at that point resembled a sea or ocean, and not the Jordan, Helen stopped before three objects: a shell, an urn, and a starfish. The starfish captured her attention as it had a broken arm, and was still very much alive. Helen knew that it would surely die, however, if it remained too much longer on the beach. And so she gently lifted up the broken starfish and returned it to the water, where it happily swam away. Helen felt this was significant, and could almost hear Jesus thank her as she saved the little one's life.

The theme of this segment of the series did not seem too different from some of Helen's earlier dreams, where she attempted to save helpless animals. Saving or helping the children was a thread of love that ran through Helen's life. In the early deleted material from *A Course in Miracles*, Jesus made a number of references to helping the children, and as discussed above, Helen's great professional love was helping families of retarded children. Again, Helen was always accessible to help others, regardless of her own personal (i.e., ego) feelings about the person. On the deepest level, moreover, her agreement to take down the Course was an expression of this same willingness to be of help to all those who wander "in the world, uncertain, lonely, and in constant fear" (text, p. 621).

Some days after this segment, I was riding home one evening on the subway, thinking of Helen and the starfish, and the beautiful gift she was giving to the world. I thought how nice it would be if someone could write *her* a poem in gratitude, seeing as she had given others so much, and specifically now with the poems she was writing down. I thought that that was something I should do for Helen, but did not see myself as a poet.

Then suddenly, sitting on the train, the following poem came into my mind. I doubt if very many other things I have done gave me as much joy as this poem. In fact, this poem became the first of the many I subsequently wrote for her.

The Starfish

Christ comes to us as we would come to Him;
A broken bit of life that washed ashore,
In seeming pain and darkened throes of death,
A dying starfish on the sandy floor.

And yet His light shines forth from every tip.
His love for us denies what eyes would see
When blinded by illusion's fearful grasp,
In chains forgiveness tenderly sets free.

Your gentle hand bent down to bless and heal
Two broken bits which are rejoined as one.
Where once stood death stands now a risen life.
The work forgiveness came to do is done.

The starfish blesses you in gratitude
For your great gift of love replacing sin.
The starfish in you joins in blessing you
For what was two is joined in God again.

Helen had a recurring experience which shared this same theme. She reported it to me as a dream, but I think the experience was more than likely an expression of another part of her mind—the home of the priestess—that she usually successfully repressed. Helen saw herself standing by a gate, at the end of a vast and open plain. A steady stream of people came to the gate, and to each she would say: "In the Name of Christ, pass through this gate in peace." Readers familiar with *A Course in Miracles* would recognize the symbolism of the lawns of the real world leading up to the gate of Heaven: the Course's purpose being to lead people to the gate, "beyond which learning does not go" (text, p. 369), after which "God leans to us and lifts us up" (workbook, p. 313).

After the starfish episode, the series depicting this northward journey continued with a number of different events, which I have largely forgotten, but the sequence culminated with Helen and I reaching our goal, a lovely grove of trees in what appeared to be lower Galilee, the biblical site of Jesus' childhood and of a good part of his ministry. I have rarely seen Helen so moved. She began to weep at the sight of this grove, saying: "I never thought I'd see those trees again." Through the trees could be seen the figure of Jesus, and joyfully we knew we had reached the end of our journey and would soon be with him again.

The sequence seemed symbolically to represent the spiritual journey, beginning with the devastation that is the ego's world (Qumran), continuing up through learning the meaning of forgiveness and selfless interest (the starfish), and finally culminating in the attainment of the real world (returning to Jesus in Galilee). For Helen personally it seemed to represent the same state reflected in many of her poems: the apparent destruction and end of her life and hope, her dreams shattered, and then the sudden fulfillment of Jesus' promises. We shall return later in this chapter to these poems that speak so eloquently of Helen's relationship with Jesus.

2. Resistance and Shame

But clearly there was another side to Helen's relationship to Jesus as well, characterized alternately by outright resistance and shame.

One afternoon—I was not with her at the time—Helen was crossing 14th Street on her way home, and passed Mays, an inexpensive department store known for its bargains. Helen and I would occasionally go in there for odds and ends. As Helen stood in front of the door planning to enter to buy some lingerie, she clearly heard Jesus tell her not to go in. Indignant at his nerve of telling *her* what to do, she threw back at Jesus: "What do you know of women's underwear?" and walked right in, probably at that point more in defiance than necessity.

Within moments she realized that her pocketbook had been stolen, which by the way was a constant fear and preoccupation with Helen, as she was *always* misplacing this important symbol of her self. Furious, she accused Jesus of not protecting her. But she heard his gentle voice comforting her with the words that she would get *everything* back. That infuriated Helen even more, and by the time I saw her later that afternoon she

438

was beside herself, more in anger at Jesus than at the loss.
However, he was right. Within a few hours Helen's pocketbook
was returned, with everything in it except the cash she was
carrying around with her. Helen was not satisfied, however, as
once again, she felt, Jesus lied to her because not *everything*
came back. And then a few days later in response to Helen's
relating this story (though *not* the part about Jesus), a friend
told her to check her insurance policy, because she might be
covered for such a theft. And sure enough Helen was, and so
she did in fact receive everything back, just as Jesus promised
would happen.

It would be nice to report that this experience strengthened
her faith in Jesus, but aside from a momentary wave of
gratitude, the incident appeared to have no effect. It was in
response to situations like this that I was led every once in a
while to make the aforementioned comment to Helen—pointing
over to her bookshelf where the Course was kept—that if others had had even a fraction of her experiences they would have
been changed forever. She would laugh, saying that she could
not really dispute what was so blatantly true. However, the
fact remained that Helen's life, at least from the vantage point
of her own ego experience, did not change for the better as a
result of her relationship with Jesus.

Another time, during the early months of taking down the
Course, Helen pulled out all the stops in her attempts to attack
and denigrate Jesus. She let down her guard and directly
accused him of all the psychological problems she could think
of, saying to him in effect: "What authority do you have? You
are a paranoid schizophrenic, filled with delusions of grandeur,
thoughts of religious persecution, and are of uncertain
psychosexual development."

"Oh, I don't know about that," Jesus gently replied to her.
"After all, all power in Heaven and earth was given unto me."

Helen could not argue with his response, and retreated from
her position in stunned yet humble silence.

I remember still another occasion when Helen was in an
absolute fury regarding Jesus and something he was asking of
her, which she stubbornly resisted. At some point in the midst
of her tirade, she was able to hear his clear, though gentle

response: "This is one battle you will never win." In addition, during our editing of Chapter Twenty-Three in the text, Helen recalled to me her anger when after Jesus described the insane thought system of the ego, he stated: "And God thinks otherwise" (text, p. 452). Helen's anger reflected her attitude: "Who does He think He is!" This was an ego defense that was usually very difficult for Helen to set aside.

Shortly after we began editing the Course together, Helen and I came to the line currently in the third paragraph of "Revelation, Time and Miracles" in Chapter One. This is how it read in the "Hugh Lynn Version":

> An elder brother [Helen incidentally capitalized these two words in her notebooks] is entitled to respect for his greater experience, and *a reasonable amount of* obedience for his greater wisdom [my italics].

I said to Helen that the qualifying "a reasonable amount of" did not seem quite right; after all, one would either be obedient to Jesus or not. Helen's face turned red as she laughingly confessed that she had originally heard only the word "obedience"; however, she could not bring herself to write that word in her notebook without first lessening the commitment to Jesus that it represented. She of course knew it did not belong, and so she gladly consented to removing the phrase. One could not ask for a clearer example of Helen's resistance to holding back nothing from her Lord. Jesus addressed this issue a bit later in these words, currently found in the eighth paragraph of "Love Without Conflict" in Chapter Four.

> Watch carefully and see what it is you are really asking for. Be very honest with yourself in this, for we must hide nothing from each other (text, p. 56).

A moving experience (for Helen and for me) powerfully illustrated her inner conflict with Jesus. This experience directly reflected her shame over her love for him, and shifted the "battleground" to a level deeper than her anger. It occurred one afternoon while we were sitting on her living room couch, musing over Helen's rather unusual life. Helen that day was in a particularly angry mood, bitter over what she felt—with considerable justification from her point of view—to

440

be the inequity of having kept her promise of doing Jesus' work for him, while he had not kept his promises of help to her. Helen was specifically referring to Jesus' assurances that she would find peace, as she frequently heard him tell her. Helen went on and on for a while that afternoon, in a hostile tirade against Jesus' betrayal of his promises to help her, using language that would seem most *un*befitting a scribe of *A Course in Miracles*.

Finally, I suggested to Helen that she might do better with this situation if she brought up her anger directly to Jesus, rather than using me as a middle-man. She finally agreed, and so quieted her mind sufficiently to ask Jesus very specifically: "Why have you not helped me more?" His answer, hardly what she was expecting, was also very specific: "I cannot help you more because you are so ashamed of me." Recognizing the truth of Jesus' words, Helen broke down in tears. She understood that she had never really asked him for help to undo her basic conflict, always striving to limit his assistance to non-personal or extraneous matters.

Shame, of course, is an aspect of guilt; a guilt which resulted, in part, from these persistent attempts to exclude Jesus from her life so that she could be in charge. As mentioned before, Helen had to be in control, preferring to be right with her ego rather than happy with God.

Indeed, her relationship with Jesus was a guilty secret for Helen, as indeed was *A Course in Miracles*, a secret that was shared with practically no one. To this day, less than a handful of people at the Medical Center know anything about Bill's typing the previous day's Course notes from Helen's dictation to him, an event that went on almost daily behind locked office doors. Thus, practically no one of Helen's friends, colleagues, or family knew anything about the Course or her "other life."

A humorous though at the time highly embarrassing incident for Helen occurred while we were in Israel. A couple whom Helen and Louis had been friendly with for many years had moved to Jerusalem several years earlier, and they kept in touch through occasional letters. The last thing in the world Helen wanted was to meet them, however, and so she never notified them of our visit: how could she possibly explain what we were all doing there? We had even joked about this possibility, since Helen had expressed her guilt over not informing them of our trip. And then sure enough, one evening as we were walking into a restaurant near the King David Hotel, we bumped right into them.

I have never seen Helen more flustered, she who was almost always so perfectly composed in public. She did not know what to say, as her friends gently reprimanded her for not telling them of the trip. Helen sputtered out something about this being a kind of top-secret enterprise, implying a connection to government intelligence agencies. Thus, she was not free to reveal the nature of the trip, but would be able to talk more at a later time. The couple had an appointment and so, fortunately for Helen, could not stay any longer. One of the funniest moments of my life then followed. We all sat down for dinner, and then Bill and I began to kid Helen about not telling her friends the truth. And so we told the *true* story about why we were in Israel, beginning with Helen's 1965 visions and experiences, the scribing of the Course, and continuing on through the cave episode. The contrast between all that we said, which was absolutely true, and the way we knew it would sound to a "normal" person, which included Helen's circle of personal and professional acquaintances, was uproariously funny.

This circle of the "unknowing" extended to my parents as well, at least at first. Surprising enough, since they were so different, Helen and my mother developed a reasonably close friendship, at least from my mother's point of view. My mother felt a real connection with Helen, and almost from their first meeting—a dinner at my parents' apartment, with Louis and Bill also present—respected and trusted Helen. Helen liked my mother, and feeling her pain, attempted to be of help to her. The fact that she was my mother was certainly a major factor as well. As Helen's ego would reason, being close to my mother was simply another way of keeping close to me.

And so my two mothers would have occasional lunches together, and as mentioned previously, Helen and Louis later on even became regulars at our family's annual Passover Seders. But of course, Helen never said anything about *A*

Course in Miracles, and certainly not its scribing. At this point in their relationship the Course was not yet published, and all that my parents knew was that I was deeply involved in this spiritual and psychological book, which Helen and Bill had "written." As I have already indicated, Helen had asked me never to speak of the true nature of the Course unless she felt absolutely comfortable with the circumstances.

But as the months went by, and my parents asked the usual questions about what I was doing, and more specifically, about this book, it became increasingly difficult for me to keep the conversation general. I spoke to Helen about this, and explained how the situation was beginning to sound somewhat strange and mysterious, as if there were something I was trying to hide, a circumstance I knew Helen would not want, in terms of her relationship with my mother, not to mention my own. She therefore agreed that it would be best to tell my mother the story, and on my urging, that she be the one to tell it.

The big day finally came, and Helen was prepared to tell my mother at a lunch they were going to have together in Manhattan. I was planning on seeing my parents in Brooklyn that evening, and so I waited for Helen to return from the luncheon to find out how it went, before I traveled to Brooklyn. When we spoke, Helen told me with great embarrassment that she just could not say anything to my mother. The words would not come out. The discrepancy between her public persona as a normal psychologist and her hidden life as a scribe for Jesus was simply too great for her to bridge. And so she said nothing. She agreed that at this point I should tell my parents myself. The split in her mind was not anything Helen was able to undo. The guilty secret, for her, remained just that.

While Helen was extremely protective of *A Course in Miracles* during the period preceding its publication, and generally wished that Bill and I not share it with anyone, she did at times make exceptions if she felt the person would be accepting of it. Thus a number of my friends were "allowed" to see the manuscript, even though a few of them had already been exposed to many of its ideas, albeit in modified form. And even after its publication, when Helen herself was able to talk to

Course students about the material, she hardly discussed Jesus, unless she felt that these students also shared a relationship with him.

To practically all who knew her, then, Helen was a brilliant research psychologist, witty conversationalist, a friend eager to be of professional help to those in distress, a woman immaculate in appearance and prone to excessive shopping (with a weakness for jewelry and shoes), and a somewhat neurotic person preoccupied with sickness and the threat of inclement weather; but hardly one whose internal life centered on religious concerns that directly involved Jesus: a well-kept secret indeed.

3. Doubt and Inconsistency

Another form in which Helen manifested her ambivalent relationship with Jesus was in experiences of doubt. Doubt, of course, as with anger and anxiety, was simply Helen's defense against the certainty of the love that united her and Jesus, and that she *knew* as reality. I believe that one of my important functions with Helen was to provide her with the steadfast certainty of Jesus' presence that softened the anxiety that came from her defense of doubt. One example illustrated nicely Helen's need for "proof" that there was a Jesus, and that her "hearing" was not the product of her imagination.

I had made arrangements with Helen one Sunday afternoon to come over after my dinner guests left. Shortly before I was to leave, it began to snow, not heavily, but enough to make the New York streets slushy and messy. I left my apartment and was on my way to the elevator when the thought came to me very clearly that I should return and put on my rubbers. I knew this was Jesus' idea and not mine, since I hardly ever put on rubbers, and so understood that this was for Helen's benefit, who always, always, was worrying about me.

I thought nothing more about it, put my rubbers on, and walked the short block and a half to Helen's apartment house. As she opened her apartment door for me, she did not so much as even greet me, but immediately looked down at my feet. She seemed almost to be in tears as she thanked me, saying that Jesus had promised her that I would have my rubbers on. The

444

fact that I had indeed worn them was almost as if Jesus had passed a test for Helen. And if he kept his word with my rubbers, then perhaps he could be trusted to keep his word regarding other matters as well.

Still another form in which Helen's anxiety manifested itself was in her great inconsistency of jumping back and forth between her wrong- and right-minded selves. Bill would comment frequently to me about this disconcerting phenomenon, and there was no question he was correct. Although Helen's ego was usually prominently displayed, one would never know from one minute to the next when it would be the voice of fear or of wisdom speaking, the ego or Jesus. And when it was clearly his voice speaking through her, her words reflecting a truth that could not be denied, Helen could just as quickly—in a matter of a second or two—switch back to her ego. So one minute you could be discussing with her an important question regarding the Course, or some situation that needed serious attention, and the very next Helen would be back into her ego state worrying about a temperature shift, Louis' latest cold, or the like.

This curious inconsistency (or perhaps "instability" is a better term) manifested itself in some humorous ways. My favorite involved Helen's manner of walking, an activity in which we spent many, many hours. As we made our way along the sidewalks of New York, Helen's steps would never hold to a straight line, as she continually veered to and fro, sometimes resembling a broken-field runner on a football field trying to avoid tacklers. We usually walked at a leisurely pace, and often the freneticism of many other New Yorkers would lead them to try to pass us. But their attempts were frequently frustrated and thwarted by Helen's back and forth weavings. And so I would take her arm and hold her until the person had successfully gotten through. I told Helen that perhaps my greatest contribution to the world, albeit an unnoticed one, was to the pedestrians of Manhattan, whom I continually saved from the dangers of her broken-field antics.

4. Shopping

I have already mentioned Helen's use of shopping to defend against Jesus, and we have seen Jesus alluding to it during the early weeks of the dictation. It was a masterful defense, for it almost totally preoccupied Helen, succeeding in its purpose of keeping Jesus safely away from Helen's attention. In the years before my coming on the scene, jewelry was Helen's major shopping focus, with each weekend seeing another pair of earrings being added to her collection. Shoes also played a major part of this defensive plan, and this carried over into the years of our shopping together. Often we would walk down Fifth Avenue, starting at Lord and Taylor's on 38th Street, covering all the shoestores until we hit 34th Street, and then the fun started. There seemed almost to be one shoestore after another in the two blocks that spanned Fifth and Seventh Avenues. Often in the past, Helen would buy shoes that did not fit, thereby necessitating yet another trip to exchange them, and the process would begin all over again. This particular ploy had largely ceased during the years we shopped together, although it did happen occasionally.

It was very instructive for me to observe Helen's experience of how gently Jesus dealt with her defense. She never once felt his censure or disapproval, and far more often than not, she experienced that Jesus was actively helping her to find what she was looking for. Of course, she did not always ask him, for if she had, the amount of time spent on these shopping expeditions would have been greatly diminished, but so too would have their defensive value of distracting her from his peace and love. Nonetheless, I know it meant a great deal to her that she experienced Jesus accompanying her as she shopped. It was a wonderful example of his important teaching in the Course, already quoted above:

> Recognize what does not matter, and if your brothers ask you for something "outrageous," do it because it does not matter (text, p. 206).

And then some one hundred pages later:

> I have said that if a brother asks a foolish thing of you to do it. But be certain that this does not mean to do a foolish thing that would hurt either him or you, for what would hurt one will hurt the other (text, p. 308).

One afternoon as Helen and I were leaving the Medical

Center, I asked her which stores she wanted to go to (Lord and Taylor and B. Altman were among her favorites), but she told me that Jesus had said that she should not go shopping anymore (obviously this did not mean shopping for necessities), as it would now prove to be harmful to her. Helen accepted this without a trace of resistance. I then suggested to her that with the rest of the afternoon still ahead of us, perhaps she might want to visit our friends, the Maryknoll Sisters on the Lower East Side. Helen readily agreed and so we went. Visiting the Sisters at this time was another dear friend of ours, Doris Yokelson. While there, Doris spontaneously gave Helen a set of gold bracelets from India that Helen had previously admired. These bracelets had great personal value and spiritual meaning to Doris, but she now presented them to Helen as a gift. Incidentally, I knew that Helen always intended that they be returned, and so after her death I gave them back to Doris. The synchronicity of this gift with Helen's ready acceptance of Jesus' request not to shop anymore did not escape Helen or me. She therefore accepted the gift with the same love with which it was offered, and when we prayed together afterwards, she thanked Jesus in her heart as well.

Defenses Against Jesus and Against Love: Special Hate (Judgment) and Special Love

Trapped in a morass of contradictory feelings from which she could never consciously be free, Helen believed in her earlier years at Columbia-Presbyterian Medical Center that she had finally succeeded in pushing this "intruder" Jesus from her life. And then, suddenly, with the beginning of *A Course in Miracles*—triggered by her joining with Bill to find "another way" of relating—there Jesus was again: "I was a stranger and you took me in, not knowing who I was" (text, p. 396). This line, incidentally, was one of the few in the Course that never failed to bring tears to Helen's eyes.

The process of scribing *A Course in Miracles*, not to mention the teachings themselves, was the undeniable proof that Helen's defenses against Jesus and his love would ultimately

447

fail. And yet she steadfastly held onto them. One of her ego's primary defenses was judgment (an expression of what the Course refers to as special hate), and I have rarely been in the presence of someone with the degree of criticalness possessed by Helen. Her fear—the actual defense against love—was supported by a heightened perception of the external world that saw practically everything and everyone as a threat (thereby justifying her fear). This was the basis of all her judgments, whether in the form of a subtle change in temperature which made her physically uncomfortable, or much more to the point, her judgments of others that necessitated her "self-protection" of anger and criticism. This successfully kept the perceived threat at a distance, and obviously people remained separate from her.

The same outcome of separation occurred even when the judgments were helpful and kindly meant, as when Helen functioned as a psychotherapist. This acute awareness of what was going on around her and in other people's minds made Helen a very insightful and wise therapist, even though her therapeutic stance reinforced thoughts of separation. She intuitively *knew* the truth of what was happening in another person's mind, regardless of the overt words or behavior. Helen's therapy was therefore not a process of true joining, as is discussed in the pamphlet on psychotherapy, but rather one of her pointing out what was going wrong in a person's life, and giving very specific recommendations about what to do about it. In the text Jesus commented on this quality of Helen's therapy, here stated in the context of teaching. He said to her:

> You have taught well, and yet you have not learned how to *accept* the comfort of your teaching. . . . You *have* taught freedom, but you have *not* learned how to be free. . . . Does not the fact that you have *not* learned what you *have* taught, show you that you do *not* perceive the Sonship as one? And does it not also show you that you do not regard *yourself* as one? . . . You have *taught* what you are, but have *not* let what you are, teach *you* [slightly edited from the original; the passage is currently found in the text, pp. 311f].

The reader may also recall this previously quoted statement to Helen in the original dictated material, which emphasizes the same point of reinforcing separation:

Bill was right in saying that you have learned to be a loving, wise, and very understanding therapist, except for yourself. That exception has given you more than perception of others because of what you saw in them, but less than knowledge of your real relationships *to* them because you did *not* make them part *of* you.... It is possible, with great effort, to understand someone else and to be helpful to him, but the effort is misdirected. The misdirection is quite apparent. It is directed *away* from you.

I was with Helen on a large number of occasions when she would be counseling someone, and her advice—again, always accurately to the point—would be totally based on the principles of the Course, and I knew, very relevant to her own personal situation. How helpful it would be to Helen, I would think to myself, if she could listen to what she said. When the person would leave and we would be alone, I would then ask Helen if by some chance she had remembered her words, or even paid attention to them. She would laugh embarrassingly and confess that she had not listened to a word of her advice. And I knew that that was true. I never attempted, however, to impose her own inner wisdom on herself, for I understood that on another level she *knew* what she was doing, even if the results *appeared* to be so painful for her.

Helen's criticalness also extended itself on behalf of Jesus and his Course. Despite all of her ambivalent feelings, she, as we have seen, was passionately devoted to the Course and to its author. In earlier chapters I have discussed Helen's observations of Course students. She knew what *A Course in Miracles* said and who it was who said it, and her ego at times became intolerant of all those who pretended to this knowledge. Helen could see right through these students, and they became the object of her scorn and wrath, although she almost never expressed this to their face unless she knew them well. Her belief that *A Course in Miracles* was only for "five or six" was born—figuratively if not literally—of her inner knowledge of its depth and source. It was as if Helen had an inner barometer that could measure where people were, relative to that depth.

As we have seen, Helen herself had difficulty in talking about the Course, let alone explaining it to others, but she certainly understood it. Thus she very rarely assumed the role of teacher of the Course to anyone. Once again, Helen was not averse to sometimes giving people advice if they solicited it of her, but she never actually "taught" the Course principles *per se*. Occasionally people spoke of Helen's value in their lives as a teacher, but they usually—and not very lovingly—meant by that the value of observing her ego in action and attempting to look beyond it. This of course was an example of the false forgiveness termed "forgiveness-to-destroy" in the aforementioned "Song of Prayer" pamphlet. There the process is clearly described wherein sin and the ego are first made real, and then overlooked and "forgiven."

So while Helen's criticalness of others was based on truth, her attitude of disdain certainly was not. One afternoon as she was ranting and raving in her mind about someone on another spiritual path she believed to be inauthentic, she suddenly heard the non-judgmental voice of Jesus say to her, cutting through *her* judgments: "Don't take another's path as your own, but neither should you judge it." In the presence of this loving and gentle correction for her judgment, Helen's anger quickly dissipated. Jesus' statement, incidentally, as we have already seen near the end of Part II, paralleled a much earlier message to her that is now found in the section entitled "I Need Do Nothing" in the text.

I found myself, by the way, almost never disagreeing with Helen's objective judgment about other people's relation to the Course, and their understanding and appreciation of it, or lack of it. But on most occasions it was difficult to help her let go of her anger. Once she "smelled out" people's inauthenticity regarding their "devotion" to the Course and "lip-service" love for it, she became most unforgiving. Helen always knew what it took for a person to follow *A Course in Miracles*, recognizing its call for selfless dedication to Jesus and to the depth of his teachings of forgiveness. Again, to her great credit, she never pretended to others to be an exemplar of what it said. In effect, she would say: "Do what I *scribed*, not what I *do*."

On the other hand, this critical acumen also made it impossible for her to get close to another. I was perhaps the person with whom she allowed herself to become the most intimate;

the one from whom she allowed herself to receive affection and love, as well as to whom she could offer it. Yet her specialness needs served as a major line of defense against this love, too. Helen had become so dependent on me, that it was impossible psychologically for her to be of assistance to me, with the one exception involving my grandfather that I related in Chapter 15. Helen's ego reasoned: if she helped *me*, who would there be to help *her*.

I remember once returning from a visit to my parents, commenting to Helen how sick my father appeared. He had a bad heart, and even though his health eventually improved and he lived considerably longer than doctors had predicted, at that point his condition did not seem favorable to a long life. Helen's immediate response, which practically blurted forth from her mouth, was: "What about me?" In other words, her mind quickly jumped to my father's dying, and my having to spend more time with my mother and thus less time with her.

Thus, while Helen could be, and indeed was, extraordinarily helpful to many, many people, she was not able to give of herself to me in that way. In fact, one afternoon she was bemoaning that situation, apologizing for being so self-centered that she could not be more of a help to me in my work. I reassured her that I did not really need such help then, but—anticipating a future I was not specifically aware of at that point—later on after she had died, I would need her help for all that I would be doing. I therefore told Helen that I knew then, after her death, she would be more than available to me. And over these past years I have certainly felt Helen's loving presence, as has my wife Gloria. We both have experienced Helen's gentle and guiding support in all we have been doing with the Foundation for "A Course in Miracles" and its Conference and Retreat Center in Roscoe, New York.

The form Helen's special love for me usually took was a mother-son relationship, as I have discussed earlier. I was indeed the son Helen never had. In its ego forms, of course, Helen's maternal concerns for me appeared rather neurotic, and on this level she certainly did not know how to love. It was always a blessing, I think, that she and Louis never had children. She could never keep plants in the house, for example, as she would always water them to death, neurotically worrying whether they had enough water. In her later years, Helen would occasionally be given plants as gifts, and she would gladly let me "rescue" them by taking them home. Helen and I used to think laughingly of what she would have done with a child of her own. In this connection I would tell her how fortunate it was that I came to her, as in the birth of Venus, fully grown. But when the real content of love was allowed to be itself, our relationship was one of true devotion to each other, which reflected our devotion to Jesus, and more specifically, to *A Course in Miracles*. The poems written for me, discussed earlier, came from that love.

Helen was more than aware of the specialness aspects of her relationship with me, and yet she chose to hold on to them. There was one time I had gone to visit someone in Manhattan and knew that I would be returning home late at night. Helen almost always asked me to take a taxi home instead of the subway, which was my usual means of transportation, and would even insist on giving me money for the fare. I would of course then call her as soon as I arrived home so she would know I was safe and sound. When I spoke with her this one evening on my return, she told me that she realized earlier what a terrible thing she was doing, to herself and to me. What if, she told me, I had gotten into a cab because of her request, and then the driver mugged or even killed me. It would be all her fault. And to this I added: the very fact that she had such thoughts would reflect an underlying wish to kill me, murder being the ultimate goal of specialness. Yet, as often happened after discussions like this, we would drop the topic and it would have no impact on Helen's future anxiety and "outrageous requests." We both silently understood that this was the way the relationship would be, and that its so very short time span here would have no effect on the eternal nature of the love that could never be changed, nor diminished by specialness.

Thus, despite the rare lowering of the ego barriers of specialness and judgment, Helen's defenses were almost always intact and in full operation. All of her special love and hate relationships were but the reflection of her defensive posture towards Jesus. But just as she occasionally allowed the barriers to fall between us, so too did they fall between her and her "lovely Lord of Life," as the poems so poignantly show. To them we now turn.

The Jesus Poems

Nowhere is Helen's ambivalence regarding love more clearly expressed than in the poetry, where, as briefly commented on in the previous chapter, the reader is allowed to see deeply into Helen's split mind. Here one finds the love and fear (hate) of Jesus that Helen did not often allow into her ordinary consciousness. Thus, these poems express, as few other things regarding Helen can, the depth of her love for Jesus, counter-balanced by the hate, disappointment, and rage that defended against the intensity of her identification with him as God's innocent and beloved Son. We shall look at some of these poems now.

In "Bright Stranger" Jesus is described as an "intruder on my peace," whose gifts were not perceived: "I tried to shut Him[92] out with locks and keys that merely fell away before His coming." These locks and keys can be understood as Helen's defensive system, which included her fear and hatred, as is seen in "The Second Chance." Though not one of Helen's best poems, I nonetheless quote it in its entirety because of the clear statement of the role Helen's hatred played in keeping the love of Jesus away from her. The reader, incidentally, may note the use of the star symbolism in the second stanza, an important personal symbol for Helen. As noted earlier, in addition to its use in the Course to denote Christ or the light-filled presence of God, the star represented Jesus to Helen as well. In fact, Helen had been told by Jesus to go to a jewelry store in New York where she would find a gold star he wanted her to have. It was not the store she would have personally chosen, but she

---

92. I might mention that the capitalization employed in the poetry differs from what is found in the Course. Jesus had instructed Helen regarding the Course not to capitalize any pronouns referring to him, in order to emphasize his inherent sameness with us, even though in her original notebooks and typing the pronouns were capitalized. However, in the poems Helen felt the liberty to capitalize as she wished, and so all words relating to Jesus begin with a capital letter.

followed instructions, and sure enough found just what she wanted. The star meant a great deal to Helen, and she frequently wore it on a chain, as I do now along with the Holy Spirit medal that Helen had bought for me. Here, then, is the poem:

> I have betrayed my God in many ways,
> Throughout the bitter nights and secret days.
> My hate drove deep into my mind, and tore
> Away the little love I had in store.
> I watched it go without regret, for I
> Did not perceive how much I lost thereby.
> With hatred as a friend, I did not fear
> To lose it for a god I held more dear.
> For now I seemed secure, by hate held fast,
> And feeling I was safe from love at last.
>
> The eyes of Christ looked steadily on me
> As if my secret hate He did not see.
> I hugged it tight and hid it in my heart,
> And still I held it from His Love apart.
> Until one day my eyes met His, and then
> My fingers opened and my heart. And when
> I looked away a star was in my hand;
> Another in my heart. I listened, and
> His voice said silently to me, "Now go
> And hate no more." And I said, "Be it so."
>
> *(The Gifts of God*, p. 45)

The fear in Helen's mind that would "protect" her from Jesus' love found consummate expression in "Stranger on the Road," perhaps her most moving poem. Here, more than any other place in the poetry, we see how the presence of Jesus represented the undoing of her ego's thought system of guilt, misery, and death. Helen clung to this misery with the same level of ferocity with which a falling person clings to an extended branch, or a dying person tries to retrieve a failing breath, desperately striving to ward off the inevitable end. The poem describes Helen's struggle *not* to believe in the risen Jesus, as a way of preserving her own ego life. The context is drawn from the famous resurrection narrative in Luke's gospel (24:13–35), where two disciples on the road to Emmaus (a

454

village outside Jerusalem) meet a stranger whom they do not recognize as Jesus. They relate to him the recent events of the crucifixion and the empty tomb. It is only when the stranger breaks bread with them and blesses it, that they recognize him. And then he disappears as suddenly as he had come: "And their eyes were opened, and they knew him; and he vanished out of their sight" (v. 31).

"Stranger on the Road" is Helen's longest poem, and was by far the most difficult for her to write down, with the stanzas coming in a different order than in the printed poem. In addition, three stanzas were removed, since Helen and I agreed that they were clearly redundant and detracted from the powerful flow of the poem. As I recall, it took some time for the finished poem to emerge, as Helen would write down a stanza or two, and then put down her pen. And then it took us a while until the "jigsaw puzzle" was complete. I excerpt some relevant lines here, in prose form:

> The dead are dead. They do not rise again. And yet I see in You a look I knew in One so recently destroyed...I will not lift my eyes, for fear has gripped my heart, and fear I know—the shield that keeps me safe from rising hope; the friend that keeps You stranger still to me.... Do not disturb me now. I am content with death.... Now I go in certainty, for death has surely come. Do not disturb the ending.... Do not arouse the dead.... my eyes are sealed against the slender thread of hope that cuts into my calm despair. O let me go! (*The Gifts of God*, pp. 103f).

Yet it was a struggle Helen knew she would lose in the end, as she had recognized many years earlier when she angrily left the church on hearing God "tell" her that she would not receive the grants *she* wanted.

Thus the poem reflects the powerful theme of *A Course in Miracles* that our fear is not really of crucifixion, but of redemption (text, p. 225). The "I" that knows fear is the ego, and its existence is guaranteed as long as we are fearful. God's Love, that *is* our redemption, is the ego's greatest fear, and a threat that must be defended against. Letting go our fear thus is directly related to the decision to accept Jesus' love for us. This decision is reflected by our choosing to forgive, which is why Jesus said to Helen on Palm Sunday, already quoted above: "I was a stranger and you took me in, not knowing who I was. Yet for your gift of lilies [i.e., forgiveness] you will know" (text, p. 396). In that gift is the ego gone, and all its fear and hatred with it. This shift is symbolized in the Course, as in this poem, in the choice between accepting the crucifixion or resurrection, death or life, the ego or God. John Dunne, a contemporary theologian, wrote a line the source of which I cannot locate: "Don't you know that what died on the cross was fear?" And so this wonderful poem closes with these three stanzas that reflect the now welcomed good news of the resurrection:

> Lord, did You really keep Your lovely Word?
> Was I mistaken? Did You rise again?
> And was it I who failed, instead of You?
> Are You returned to save me from the dead?
>
> Dear Stranger, let me recognize Your face,
> And all my doubts are answered. They are dead
> If You are living. Let me see again,
> And hope will be transformed to certainty.
>
> The dead are dead, but they do rise again.
> Let me remember only that. It was
> The rest that was the dream. The light has come.
> My eyes are opening to look on You.
>
> (*The Gifts of God*, pp. 104f)

Other poems focus more on the hopeless and bitter despair that attended the seeming fact of Jesus' death, symbolic of the ego's "fact" of its separation from God and destruction of Heaven's peace. In "The Ancient Love" we read:

> Love, You are silent. Not one shining word
> Has reached my heart for an eternity
> Of waiting and of tears....
>   Sometimes I believe
> I knew You once. And then again I think
> You were a dream that once I thought was real....
>
>   Is silence what You gave
> In golden promise as the Son of God?...
>   You promised that You will
> Forever answer. Yet, Love, You are still.
>
> (*The Gifts of God*, p. 44)

How many others have felt that our pleas for help have been met only with silence? On occasion when Helen would complain that Jesus never really helped her nor answered her desperate prayers, or that nothing ever happened to her, I would again point to the bookcase in her living room where the Course was kept, and ask: "Are you sure?" Incidentally, the above poem contains an interesting line: "Sometimes I believe I knew You once." While its actual meaning, as in the poem "Waiting" that is discussed earlier in this chapter, relates to a timeless experience within Helen's mind, the line could also be interpreted as reflecting a memory from a past life. As I have already mentioned, an English psychic once told Helen that she had never gotten over the crucifixion. And although in the period following the Course's scribing Helen never admitted to believing in reincarnation,[93] her experience of Jesus, not to mention her occasional outbursts against him, certainly did point to an earlier and intimate connection with him. We have already seen in her letters to Bill, dating from 1965, that Helen did most certainly believe in past lives and their helpfulness in explaining, at least on one level, certain contemporary problems or conflicts.

The bleakness of life without Jesus is movingly, if not painfully expressed in two poems written within two days of each other, in May 1974. Their ability to evoke this hopeless state of emptiness leads me to quote them both in full. The first poem, "Prayer for a House," actually had its origin in Bill's move from one apartment on the upper east side of Manhattan to another. I suggested to Helen that perhaps she write a poem for the occasion. The result was this "dark night" poem of despair that literally had nothing to do with Bill's move, but with life in a house (i.e., the mind) bereft of love's presence. I quoted its closing lines in the previous chapter. Here is the complete poem:

---

93. *A Course in Miracles* itself does not take a position on the subject, since belief in the concept is irrelevant to salvation, time being illusory anyway. On the other hand, many passages in the Course that reflect *our* experience of time do suggest reincarnation. Furthermore, in many of his personal messages to Helen, Jesus referred to her other lifetimes, in addition to the references to Helen's past life experiences that came to her during the summer that preceded the beginning of the Course.

> Enter my house. Its holiness is Yours,
> And it must wait for You who are the home
> Of Holiness Itself. Its altar stands
> Darkened as yet, but open to the light
> That You will bring. I have forgot the glow
> Of diamonds and the glittering of gold
> That once I thought would lighten up the dark
> And bring me comfort. Silvered drapes are gone,
> And floors are empty of the heavy rugs
> That once concealed their bareness with designs
> That Eastern hands had woven carefully
> In thick obscurity. Their bareness is
> The sign the Guest that was to come is yet
> Not ready to appear, and bring the peace
> That He has promised those who dwell with Him.
> My ringless fingers hold a lamp long since
> Gone out and cold. The wind sings bitterly
> A chant of fear that echoes round the walls
> And enters ceaselessly into my heart.
> This was supposed to be a temple built
> To You who said the altar would be lit
> Forever. And I thought that You had said
> A holy altar cannot be a tomb.
>
> (*The Gifts of God*, p. 49)

Helen, obviously representing all of us, is here reflecting on the bitterness of having given up the world's offerings ("I have forgot the glow of diamonds...") yet being left only with the bareness of empty floors, symbolizing the seemingly empty promises of Jesus. "Holy Saturday," written several months later as part of the Easter trilogy, depicts the same bleak mood of death's darkness having triumphed over the light of life. It ends with these words addressed to Jesus:

> You said You would redeem
> The world. Yet I can only see a cross.
> The resurrection seems to be a dream.
>
> (*The Gifts of God*, p. 108)

The second of these May 1974 poems is "The Wayside Cross," which again reflects the bleak hopes of what is perceived as a failed promise, closing with a poignant quotation from psalms 13 and 89:

I tarry by the wayside. Homeless I
Return each evening to an empty house
But to awaken and return each day,
To wait again in silence and despair.
How long, O Lord, did You ordain I be
A dweller in a ghost-house? Shadows come
And fall across my eyes at night, to bring
A parody of sleep. By day I go
In an illusion that I am awake
To my appointed round of bitterness.
The cup from which I drink is empty. And
The crumbs allotted me will not sustain
My little life but shortly. I retain
A hope so frail it stifles in the dust
Of waiting on an ancient way that seems
To lead to nowhere. I have not forgot
Your promise. I will wait until You come.
But I must wait in sorrow, with the song
Of dying all around me on the road
On which I stand and wait for Your return.
How long, O lovely Lord of Life, how long?

(The Gifts of God, p. 50)

Helen occasionally spoke to me of her bitterness of being in what she experienced as a "Catch-22" situation with Jesus. On the one hand she was told that the way she would know and trust his love was by giving up her fear and judgment. On the other, she could not give up her ego without his love. In like manner, we can say that Jesus waits for our invitation, and yet it is his presence that enables us to offer it. "The Invitation" expresses this seemingly paradoxical process, although within a positive framework. The poem incidentally is one of the very few in the collection, as I mentioned briefly above, that departs from a strict iambic pentameter. Jesus is the speaker here:

I came to you.
I saw your tears and knew
That you were ready. You had asked Me in
The instant that you understood that sin
Is an illusion. You were poor indeed.
I saw your grasping hands and watched them bleed
From golden nails; a heavy jewelled crown
Around your head, as sacred as My Own.

459

> I needed you
> As much. Yet till you grew
> In understanding, I could only wait
> In silent patience beyond Heaven's gate.
> My Father's house stood empty. For as we
> Are part of Him, so are you part of Me.
> We enter in together. We are one.
> And so I finish what I had begun.
>
> *(The Gifts of God,* p. 90)

We have already seen the other side of this ambivalence in the love poems. For although Helen could feel hatred towards Jesus for betraying his promises, she would become even more furious at others who would speak negatively of him. It was as if her intimacy with Jesus allowed her the prerogative and freedom to yell at him, similar to what sometimes occurs in relationships where two people are very close to each other, yet fight constantly. But let an "outsider" speak ill of the other, and quickly the underlying love sweeps aside the more superficial hate. I appropriately close this chapter on Helen's relationship with Jesus—her way, truth, and life—with one of her lovely Valentine love poems to him.

The Resting Place

> My arms are open. Come, my Lord, to me
> And rest upon my heart. It beats for you
> And sings in joyous welcome. What am I
> Except your resting place and your repose?
>
> Your rest is mine. Without you I am lost
> In senseless wanderings that have no end,
> No goal, no meaning, on a road that goes
> In twisted byways down to nothingness.
>
> Come now, my Love, and save me from despair.
> The Way, the Truth, the Life are with me then.
> The journey is forgotten in the joy
> Of endless quiet and your kiss of peace.
>
> *(The Gifts of God,* p. 54)

Chapter 17

THE REALITY OF JESUS:
INTO CHRIST'S PRESENCE

Helen, *as* Helen, always experienced Jesus as separate from her, a person to be loved, hated, or ignored. It was only when she was in the state of mind symbolized by the priestess that she could transcend the ambivalence of her relationship with Jesus and become one with the love that was their shared identity. Helen's experience of the priestess during the summer of 1965, as we have seen, began with an experience of separation, but with the clear recognition of the essential unity that was truly there. Thus the conflict of what Helen usually experienced as her life, revolved around hating and loving Jesus; the ultimate solution came in transcending the ambivalence entirely and becoming one with him. In the language of the early text, right-mindedness corrected wrong-mindedness, leaving the One-mindedness of Christ.

The previous chapter examined Helen's ambivalent relationship with Jesus. Here, I shall discuss Jesus, and Helen's relationship to him, from the perspective of the priestess; i.e., from the point in Helen's mind *beyond* "Heaven and Helen." It is from this point that we are able to identify Jesus, not as a person with a definite personality who speaks to us or specifically guides our lives, but as the symbol within our separated minds of the abstract and universal love of Christ. The pamphlet "The Song of Prayer," in its discussion of prayer, by implication addresses this issue of Jesus as reality and symbol. We therefore begin with the pamphlet and the interesting and important circumstances of its writing.

"The Song of Prayer": Special Message

The origin of "The Song of Prayer" in the fall of 1977 bears directly on the different levels of relating to Jesus, and therefore warrants presentation before we consider the actual teachings of the pamphlet.

461

For some time I had been feeling uneasy over our manner and practice of "asking." This discomfort referred first of all to Helen's and Bill's meditating and asking Jesus or the Holy Spirit[94] for very specific help in matters such as times to meet, street corners to stand on for taxi-cabs, whether to attend certain meetings, and the like. On joining Helen and Bill, I naturally joined with them in this activity of asking as well, although, again, something never seemed to me to be quite right with it.

After we met Judy, this practice of asking for specifics continued, and if anything, seemed to increase with all the practical decisions that needed resolution. Quite frequently during our afternoon meetings at Judy's apartment, the four of us would sit quietly and "ask" specifically what we should do regarding the Course. While we frequently would receive answers, and often the same ones (after all, minds *are* joined), I continued to feel uncomfortable with the process. It all seemed so magical, and while I did not believe the phenomenon in and of itself was necessarily invalid, it did seem to be somewhat less than what we were capable of doing, especially Helen. The meetings seemed to miss the whole point of developing a meaningful relationship with Jesus, for relating to him obviously involved much more than simply asking very specific questions. I increasingly felt that there was some self-deception involved, insofar as it did not seem to me that this prayer activity was really what it appeared to be. I especially felt this in regard to what I believed was the confusion between psychic ability and true spirituality. Something indeed was missing in all of this, and it had to do with the absence of Jesus' love and peace.

I knew that Helen understood, and so from time to time I shared my thoughts with her. Helen did not disagree with me, but as she had already begun to withdraw from active involvement with the Course, I recognized that there was not much to be done in terms of changing our practice. In addition, I understood the implications of this discussion regarding her

---

94. As mentioned earlier, Bill never did get over his discomfort with the person of Jesus, and preferred to speak of him as "J.C.," the Holy Spirit as "the H.S.," or more often than not he simply used the more impersonal term "Guidance."

relationship with Jesus. As I shall discuss below, Helen's relegating Jesus to being not much more than an information-giver defended nicely against the abstract love that was their mutual reality, this reality truly representing the end of the ego thought system. Nonetheless, I did feel this issue of asking was itself important for us to talk about. And so from 1973 on, Helen and I would discuss the subject of "asking" from time to time, and our talks became more serious as the years went by.

One such discussion in the fall of 1975 led to the special message of October 5, which I presented in full in Chapter 14, pp. 395f. This message dealt with the subject of asking for specifics, and the reader may recall that it emphasized, among other things, the importance of removing the judgments that would interfere with our "hearing," and did not emphasize at all *what* we would specifically "hear."

These discussions between Helen and me culminated one afternoon in 1977, the details of which I only vaguely recall now, though I do remember Helen's concern. Soon afterwards she began to scribe a special message from Jesus on the specific subject of asking and prayer. It formed the basis for the present opening pages of the pamphlet, which followed shortly after the personal message to Helen. I shall first present the message in its entirety, along with my comments, followed in the next section by the relevant passages from the beginning of the pamphlet.

Jesus began by addressing an issue that was increasingly arising in our circle. Besides Bill and Judy asking Helen for specific advice and answers to questions, others were demanding this of her as well. Helen generally felt uncomfortable with this role, and frequently told me how annoyed Bill would get with her if she were not able to give him an answer he wanted, as he felt that she was withholding from him. While Helen did at times hear answers from Jesus for people, and often for Bill, she understood intuitively the potential trap in this, for herself as well as for others. It is always tempting to mistake the *form* as the answer instead of the *content* of experiencing Jesus' presence. This experience of his peace alone was the Answer, for it alone could be generalized to *all* problems. And so the message begins by referring to this issue of asking, relating specifically to the importance of joining through unity, rather than upholding separation which maintains the illusion of differences, the heart of the ego thought system.

> Asking is holy, and it is holy because it is a way of reaching God. He is the Answer because you are in need of an Answer. You can ask for another and receive the Answer for him. But you can, and indeed you must, help him by offering your love and support that his asking be holy and his true need recognized. That is prayer; it is the same for yourself or for another. There is no difference. If only you received the answers for another, there would be a difference.
>
> This does not mean that you cannot get messages for another, if it is God Who chooses this way of reaching him. This will usually happen unexpectedly, generally in the form of a sudden feeling that you have something to tell him; a message to deliver. You have not been wrong in the past about how you have asked, but you are ready for a step ahead now. There are joint decisions in which unanimity of response is a good indication of authenticity. This should not be abandoned. But asking is a lesson in trust, and no one can trust for another. He can only strengthen another's trust by offering it to him and having faith in his ability to hear for himself.

Thus, on more than one occasion, as I have already pointed out in Part II, Helen would suggest to those who were asking her for help that they pray together, and that she, Helen, would reinforce their ability to receive the answer within themselves. Helen always maintained that what she could do, all people could do as well; in fact, until they were able to accept that power of their minds, salvation would remain an empty concept. Jesus thus was reinforcing in this message the importance of what Helen was already practicing, at the same time sanctioning the receiving of messages for others if it would be helpful and was a reflection of God's Will. But clearly what is essential in this teaching is recognizing the basic unity among all Sons of God, especially where their differences appear to be real, as in one's ability to "hear" Jesus' or the Holy Spirit's Voice, as opposed to another's inability. Helen clearly understood this, and this was the cause of her discomfort in "hearing" for others.

However, despite Helen's understanding the important

principle of not asking for another, she did not allow herself to generalize this to herself. Just as Helen's asking for others would emphasize separation from them and the reality of differences, so too her continually asking Jesus for specific answers to her specific questions emphasized her separation from him as well. While there is certainly a benefit in this activity, as we shall discuss below, in Helen's case it was becoming a hindrance. She was already at a stage far beyond the need to establish a relationship with Jesus, which asking him specific questions would foster. She was ready now, near the end of her life, to begin acceptance of the oneness of spirit and love that truly united them. In reality, she and Jesus were *not* different. She was thus ready for this next step, with which the message continues:

> Asking is the way to God because it offers you His Will as He would have you hear it. We will have a series of lessons [i.e., the pamphlet] on asking because you have not understood it. But do not think because of that, that you have been mistaken in your attempts. You have done well and will do better.

This completed the first part of the message, which specifically and gently addressed the issues I had been raising with Helen. The reader may note the total absence of blame or fault-finding in Jesus' message: "You have not been wrong in the past about how you have asked, but you are ready for a step ahead now." And then the same gentle tone again in the last paragraph, where his attitude, characteristic of the tone of *A Course in Miracles* as well, is that Helen had done her best, and her mistakes will now be corrected: "You have done well and will do better." I am reminded here of the statement Helen heard once from Jesus: "If you do my will I will uphold it. If you do not do my will I will correct it." The clear meaning is that we cannot lose either way, and all we are asked to do is simply our best. "Mistakes," which can come only from our fear of Jesus' love, will always be corrected at a later opportunity when we are less fearful. In fact, choosing to be less fearful *is* the correction of the mistake, whose origin, regardless of the form it takes, is always fear.

The second half of the message begins the more formal

teaching with the idea that specific questions inevitably place limitations on God:

> Any specific question involves a large number of assumptions which inevitably limit the answer. A specific question is actually a decision about the kind of answer that is acceptable. The purpose of words is to limit, and by limiting, to make a vast area of experience more manageable. But that means manageable by *you*.

The Course student is reminded of this statement from the manual for teachers:

> God does not understand words, for they were made by separated minds to keep them in the illusion of separation (manual, p. 51).

The statement in the message about managing a "vast area" is an important point, for it emphasizes Helen's underlying ego purpose in continuing to ask for specifics ("the purpose of words"), which was to place a limit ("make...more manageable") on Jesus and the experience of his love. We shall return to this phenomenon below.

The message continues:

> For many aspects of living in this world that [making "more manageable"] is necessary. But not for asking. God does not use words, and does not answer in words. He can only "speak" to the Christ in you, Who translates His Answer into whatever language you can understand and accept.

The aforementioned message of October 5, 1975, quoted in Chapter 14, made the same point:

> Step back and do not dwell upon the forms that seem to keep you bound....lay no limits on what you would give to Him to be resolved. For He can not offer a thousand answers when but one is all there is. Accept this one of Him, and not one question will remain to ask.

To understand this very important teaching, let us consider a glass of water. For the purposes of this example, we shall think of water as abstract and formless, thereby having the properties of spirit. Thus water will here symbolize for us the abstract and formless nature of God's Love, which alone is reality, and which is a reality we truly share as God's Son. As the Course states: "Complete abstraction is the natural condition of the mind" (workbook, p. 297). This reality as Christ, however, is beyond our limited and separated ego self, to which we give a name, history, anticipated future, etc. It is therefore impossible for us to *know* God in this world, because as the Course explains, this world in general, and bodies and brains in particular were made to fulfill the ego's purpose of keeping knowledge of God, Christ, and Their unity away from us ("Thus were specifics made" [workbook, p. 297]).[95]

When we call upon the Love of God, turning to Him as our Self, we are in effect able to transcend our ego identification, if only for an instant. In that holy instant which transcends time and the entire ego thought system, we remember our reality and Identity as God's Son. Thus we become that Identity, abstract and formless as our Creator. Love has rejoined itself, and that Love is one. Again, I am using water as a symbol for that unity of self and Self, love and Love.

That part of our minds that chooses to return to where we never truly left is "where" God "speaks" to us. However, when our minds return to their belief in separation, and we once again experience ourselves as a personal self in relation *to* our Creator—as opposed to being one *with* Him—the "speaking" is mediated through our separate minds and comes out as words, which our minds *can* understand. It is thus *our* separated minds that structure the unstructured, shape the shapeless, and form the formless. It is not God Who does this, because He does not know of shape and form. His Love, which simply is, supplies the content; our minds supply the shape or words. Returning to our image of the water and glass, we understand that the Love of God is the water, and the separated mind is the glass which gives shape to the water, limiting its accessibility to what the glass can hold, or what our minds' fear can tolerate.

To restate this, in the holy instant our minds have chosen to become one with God's Love, which is not a state our egos allow

---

95. A full discussion of this dynamic is beyond the scope of this book, but the interested reader may consult my book, *Love Does Not Condemn*, pp. 425-37.

us to continue with, since it means the end of the ego itself. As the Course explains:

> Sometimes a teacher of God may have a brief experience of direct union with God. In this world, it is almost impossible that this endure.... All worldly states must be illusory. If God were reached directly in sustained awareness, the body would not be long maintained (manual, p. 61).

And so the mind chooses to return to the ego identification, yet it brings the Love of God with it. To the extent to which fear remains in the mind, however, the body's words will obscure and distort the purity of the love; the less fear, the more transparent are the words, which then but serve to express the love in a form that can be accepted without fear. Using the analogy of a picture of light and its frame, the Course speaks of the Holy Spirit's purpose (content) for relationships (the form) in the world:

> [The Holy Spirit's picture of light] is framed for perfect clarity.... [It is] lightly framed, for time cannot contain eternity.... The picture of light, in clear-cut and unmistakable contrast [to the ego's dark picture], is transformed into what lies beyond the picture. As you look on this, you realize that it is not a picture, but a reality. This is no figured representation of a thought system, but the Thought itself. What it represents is there. The frame fades gently and God rises to your remembrance, offering you the whole of creation in exchange for your little picture, wholly without value and entirely deprived of meaning (text, p. 336).

Thus it is not the frame that is important, but the picture of light that it contains; likewise, it is not our words that are important, but the content of love that they express. And so it is not really the person of Jesus that we seek and yearn for, but the love that he expresses, and even more to the point, the love in us as Christ that he reflects back to us. For us in the Western world, however, and certainly for Helen, Jesus is the greatest symbol of God's Love:

> The Name of Jesus Christ as such is but a symbol. But it stands for love that is not of this world.... It becomes the shining symbol for the Word of God, so close to what it stands for

468

that the little space between the two is lost, the moment that the Name is called to mind (manual, p. 55).

Jesus then, and the specific ways we experience him for ourselves, is the glass which allows us to experience God's Love in a form that we can grow to accept. The form is *not* God's Love, yet it will ultimately blend into that Love, as we all will.

Returning now to the special message to Helen, the Love of God—the only answer to any of our problems, concerns, or questions—is beyond all words or thoughts. As *A Course in Miracles* states: "We say 'God is,' and then we cease to speak, for in that knowledge words are meaningless" (workbook, p. 315). Yet does this Love of God reflect itself to us in the form that we can accept, a form that we establish for ourselves. In metaphoric language, the process is explained to Helen in the message as Christ translating for us: "Christ...translates His [God's] Answer." In the Course itself, this "translation" is a function usually accorded to the Holy Spirit. It is stated metaphorically to correspond to what our experience is, not because it is reality itself.

Another useful analogy that can help our understanding is to consider our perceptions of sunrises and sunsets. We all, to a person, observe the sun seeming to rise and set each day. Many people, in fact, report profound spiritual or aesthetic experiences surrounding these perceptions. Yet, almost all of us have been taught that it is not the sun that rises or sets, or even moves at all. Rather, it is the earth's rotation on its axis that causes the sun to "rise" and "set," while the planet's revolution around the sun causes the change of seasons. Thus, the *appearance* is really an illusion that belies the *reality*. Likewise, our experience that Jesus or the Holy Spirit do things *for* us, or say things *to* us, is the illusion that belies the reality that we are the true agents of our words and actions. It is essential to realize that we are the ones who choose to move away from the presence of love and light in our minds, referred to as the Holy Spirit or Jesus. Thus we are the ones who must choose to return to this *stationary* source of light. The mind's movement—wandering off from love and then returning to it—is our responsibility.

Therefore, all of our questions have their origin in our

having chosen to move away from our Source in the mind—
that is why the Course teaches that questions are of the ego
(manual, pp. 73,78)—and they find their answer in our return
to the mind's decision to separate, choosing now for God
instead of against Him. Focusing on specific needs or questions
thus becomes the reinforcer of what the ego would have us
believe: that we truly have moved away. A response from outside our minds, which is how we usually experience Jesus,
simply then continues the illusion of our separation. Thus,
Jesus is urging Helen to return to the Love of God for her
answer, as he urges us similarly in this very beautiful Lesson:
"I call upon God's Name and on my own":

> Think not He [God] hears the little prayers of those who call on
> Him with names of idols cherished by the world. They cannot
> reach Him thus. He cannot hear requests that He be not Him-
> self, or that His Son receive another name than His....
> Turn to the Name of God for your release, and it is given
> you. No prayer but this is necessary, for it holds them all
> within it. Words are insignificant, and all requests unneeded
> when God's Son calls on his Father's Name....
> All little things are silent. Little sounds are soundless now.
> The little things of earth have disappeared. The universe con-
> sists of nothing but the Son of God, who calls upon his Father.
> And his Father's Voice gives answer in his Father's holy Name.
> In this eternal, still relationship, in which communication far
> transcends all words, and yet exceeds in depth and height
> whatever words could possibly convey, is peace eternal. In our
> Father's Name, we would experience this peace today. And in
> His Name, it shall be given us (workbook, p. 335).

We continue now with the balance of the message, picking
up with the idea I have already discussed; namely, that words
can serve either the ego's fear or Jesus' love. Once again, it is
not the form that is important, but the underlying content.
God's "Voice," without form, is silent, as we shall see.

> Sometimes words will limit fear; sometimes not. That is why
> some people hear words, some receive feelings of inner convic-
> tion, and some do not become aware of anything. Yet God has
> answered, and His Answer will reach you when you are ready.
> Answers are not up to you. Any limit you place on them
> interferes with hearing. God's Voice is silent and speaks in

470

silence. That means that you do not phrase the question and you do not restrict the answer [meaning that it is best for us not to do so].

Asking is a form of prayer. It is not a demand. It is not questioning. It is not limitation. The only real request is for God's Answer. This needs the humility of trust, not the arrogance of false certainty. Trust cannot lie in idols, for that is merely faith in magic. Trust requires faith that God understands, knows, and will answer. It means a state of peace. For this you can safely ask. In fact, if you do not feel that you have it, asking for it is the only real request that you can make.

Another expression of the same idea is the oft-quoted statement in *A Course in Miracles* that our one and only function is to accept the Atonement for ourselves. We do not ask or demand; we simply *accept* the peace and truth that is already present in us. Thus we find clearly stated what will be presently reiterated, that our true requests should be for peace, and that is the only prayer that makes sense.

This concludes Jesus' special message to Helen, after which came the notes that belong more properly to the pamphlet itself. These notes had no precise dates written on them and so I do not know exactly how many days elapsed between the message and the pamphlet. However, I do recall that the time span was relatively short.

"The Song of Prayer": The Pamphlet

In the first two pages of "The Song of Prayer" we find the following statements that bear on the same subject of praying for specifics:

Prayer is the greatest gift with which God blessed His Son at his creation. It was then what it is to become; the single voice Creator and creation share; the song the Son sings to the Father, Who returns the thanks it offers Him unto the Son....

Prayer thus is used as a synonym for the state of perfect unity between God and Christ, Creator and creation. It is the memory of that unity in our split minds that the Course refers to as the Holy Spirit, and which is manifest for us in the dream of this world by Jesus. And yet, again, since we are not ready to set aside our fear to accept the love of who we are, we need to accept this love in the forms we can accept:

> To you who are in time a little while, prayer takes the form that best will suit your need. You have but one.... [Prayer] is not merely a question or an entreaty. It cannot succeed until you realize that it asks for nothing.... True prayer must avoid the pitfall of asking to entreat. Ask, rather, to receive what is already given; to accept what is already there.

However, we should not forget that such asking is illusory, and therefore it can tempt us to forget that the truth is already present within us and need only be accepted.

The pamphlet then continues:

> You have been told to ask the Holy Spirit for the answer to any specific problem, and that you will receive a specific answer if such is your need.[96] You have also been told that there is only one problem and one answer.[97] In prayer this is not contradictory.... it is not the form of the question that matters, nor how it is asked. The form of the answer, if given by God, will suit your need as you see it. This is merely an echo of the reply of His Voice. The real sound is always a song of thanksgiving and of love.

Here we find the same teaching as in the special message, but presented now in a more generalized manner. We also find here the principle that would explain the form in which *A Course in Miracles* comes; namely, that the form of the teaching adapts, just as Jesus has been explaining above, to the specific teaching need of the section in question. In the context of prayer as a *process*, what Jesus says reflects the end of the process where we understand that there is only one problem— the separation—and one solution—the acceptance of the Atonement; at other times he is reflecting the early stages of the process, where we *experience* the Holy Spirit as solving problems for us. The true solution to our problems, however, always

---

96. *See,* for example, text, pp. 196,404, as well as Jesus' personal words to Helen, as we have seen in his special message to her on December 14, 1965 (p. 293 *above*).

97. *See* workbook, pp. 139–42.

rests in the one Answer that is God's Love, that is the "real sound" of the song of prayer. As Jesus will now explain to us, it is the experience of the song that we truly want—his love—not the illusory forms in which we may experience its reflection:

> You cannot ask, then, for the echo. It is the song that is the gift. Along with it come the overtones, the harmonics, the echoes, but these are secondary. In true prayer you hear only the song. All the rest is merely added. You have sought first the Kingdom of Heaven, and all else has indeed been given you.

In other words, in continuing the theme of his special message to Helen, Jesus is here cautioning all students of his Course that what they truly want is the peace of God, not its specific reflections. The reality of love is our heart's desire, not the illusory manifestations; it is the wondrous song of God's Love that is what we yearn to remember, not the various echoes that deflect through our fearful minds. The purpose of Jesus in our lives is not to grant our specific requests nor to answer specific questions, but rather to remind us of the one Answer to all these concerns that rests quietly within our minds, patiently awaiting our welcome. As the Course states: "Love waits on welcome...and the real world is but your welcome of what always was" (text, p. 238).

Therefore, once we have reunited with this love, have taken the hand of Jesus which reminds us of Who we truly are, all our concerns inevitably disappear. Since the content of our problems was the separation from love, their undoing simply lies in joining with it again. That is the meaning of the allusion to the biblical statement that when we have sought the love of the Kingdom of Heaven, all else "has indeed been given [us]": we have remembered the peace and love that is our only Answer.

"The Song of Prayer" continues, becoming even more specific:

> The secret of true prayer is to forget the things you think you need. To ask for the specific is much the same as to look on sin and then forgive it.

"True prayer" is Jesus' term here for the upper reaches of prayer, the real meaning of joining with the Love of God. A bit later in the pamphlet he compares the process of prayer with a ladder. Praying for specifics, or seeking guidance for specific answers, reflects the lower rungs of the ladder. This is referred to as "asking-out-of-need," and always involves "feelings of weakness and inadequacy, and could never be made by a Son of God who knows Who he is" ("The Song of Prayer," p. 3). Therefore, anyone uncertain of his or her Identity cannot help praying in these forms.

Jesus' purpose here clearly is not to make people feel guilty as they lapse into this magical form of prayer, but simply to remind them of what they truly want. One must always begin at the beginning, and *A Course in Miracles* would never suggest that its students should skip over the steps necessary to reach their goal of true peace. It is these steps that allow God to take His "final step" of lifting His children back unto Heaven— "God will take this final step Himself. Do not deny the little steps He asks you take to Him" (workbook, p. 359). However, here in the early pages of the pamphlet, Jesus is attempting to correct the errors his students, as well as Helen, were making right at the beginning of the Course's public life. He is reminding people that they are tempted to be content with the little crumbs the ego holds out to them, when they can have instead the beautiful song of their Identity as Christ: "The Son of God ask[s] not too much, but far too little" (text, p. 517). This point becomes clearer in the next passage:

> Also in the same way, in prayer you overlook your specific needs as you see them, and let them go into God's Hands. There they become your gifts to Him, for they tell Him that you would have no gods before Him; no Love but His. What could His answer be but your remembrance of Him? Can this be traded for a bit of trifling advice about a problem of an instant's duration? God answers only for eternity. But still all little answers are contained in this.... There is nothing to ask because there is nothing left to want....

Thus when we feel indecisive or unsure of a situation, unknowing about what we are to do, we are asked to lift our mind's attention from the battleground below in which we believe we exist, and where we continually seek "a bit of trifling advice about a problem of an instant's duration."

Leaving the battleground, we rejoin the loving presence of Jesus or the Holy Spirit, and are thus reminded that all we want is the peace of God. From that place of peace and love within our minds, we then return our attention to the situation confronting us. Once more on the battleground, but now carrying the memory of our true goal, we shall inevitably recognize what we should do. We have done our part by removing our fear of joining—the interference to our awareness of love's presence—and the Answer will then flow through our minds in the form we need to hear: "There is nothing to ask because there is nothing left to want." Thus Jesus has posed the question to all his students: Is the little answer you receive to a specific question what you really want, when in its place you can have the peace of God, *and* the certainty of your next steps in this illusory world? The little answers are contained in the one Answer, but not vice versa; we bring illusions to the truth, not truth to the illusions.

This teaching then comprises the "series of lessons" that Jesus mentioned to Helen in his preliminary message to her. He was reminding her, again in this final period of her life, to recall who she was, and that it was no longer necessary to pretend she was someone she was not. Her life as Helen could then express her reality as love. As we have already seen, however, these lessons had no observable effect. In fact, Helen would choose to delay this step until the moment of her death.

We come back now to the pamphlet, where Jesus returns to people's experiences on the ladder's lower rungs, and the need for help:

> This is not a level of prayer that everyone can attain as yet. Those who have not reached it still need your help in prayer because their asking is not yet based upon acceptance. Help in prayer does not mean that another mediates between you and God. But it does mean that another stands beside you and helps to raise you up to Him ("The Song of Prayer," pp. 1f).

The reader may recall here Jesus' words to Helen before "The Song of Prayer" began (*see above*, p. 464), reinforcing her joining with others by strengthening their own ability to "hear" for themselves. To quote again Jesus' reminder to us early in the text: "All my brothers are special" (text, p. 10).

475

Commenting once more on the different levels of prayer, we can extrapolate the different levels of understanding Jesus, including what it means to relate to him. In *A Course in Miracles*, Jesus explains that we cannot even think of God without a body, or in some form we think we recognize (text, p. 364). Therefore, as an important passage explains later in the text:

> Since you believe that you are separate, Heaven presents itself to you as separate, too. Not that it is in truth, but that the link that has been given you to join the truth may reach to you through what you understand. Father and Son and Holy Spirit are as One, as all your brothers join as one in truth.... It is the Holy Spirit's function to teach you how this oneness is experienced, what you must do that it can be experienced, and where you should go to do it.
>
> All this takes note of time and place as if they were discrete, for while you think that part of you is separate, the concept of a oneness joined as one is meaningless.... [Thus this Oneness must] use the language that this mind can understand, in the condition in which it thinks it is (text, pp. 483f).

Thus, we must speak of Jesus on two levels: the first is the metaphysical, wherein his love and presence is abstract and non-specific, as is known by the priestess, and which can be symbolized by the water in our example of the glass; the second reflects our experience within the dream, where Jesus is known by us as a body with a personality, since we believe our identity is rooted in the corporeal realm. Jesus' love and presence are therefore mediated through our separated minds that believe we are in bodies, and so our experience of him as a person is determined by the particular shape of the glass that is our own learning needs.

Correspondingly, the bottom rung of the ladder described in "The Song of Prayer" consists of asking for things, because we believe our reality is here in the world:

> At these levels prayer is merely wanting, out of a sense of scarcity and lack ("The Song of Prayer," p. 3).

As we grow in forgiveness and ascend the ladder of prayer, however, we become increasingly aware of the abstract and formless nature of love's presence, until it [prayer] reaches its formless state,and fuses into total communication with God ("The Song of Prayer," p. 3).

This concludes our discussion of "The Song of Prayer," and our brief digression to consider the nature of prayer and of Jesus, contrasting the illusion and reality. In this next section we return to the subject of Helen, and the implications of our discussion for her own relationship with Jesus.

Helen and Jesus: The Illusion and the Reality

We begin with the process by which *A Course in Miracles* was scribed. Up to now in the book we have discussed the scribing from the perspective in which Helen experienced Jesus and the dictation. Here, in view of our discussion in the previous sections, we can take another step in understanding the true nature of the Course's scribing.

About a year or so after the Course was published, an obviously sincere woman approached Helen and asked how Jesus could have possibly written the Course, as he did not know English. While on the one hand the question might appear to be simplistic, on the other hand it helps focus the inquiry on the role Jesus actually played in the scribing of *A Course in Miracles*. At first blush, and as the story of the scribing is usually told, it would seem as if the person of Jesus stood within Helen's mind with a microphone, dictating to her—word for word, in English!—the three books of the Course. It must be remembered, of course, that on one level this was Helen's experience. But similar to the misperception of the sun's rising and setting every day, one's experience, though valid for the individual, nonetheless, should not be taken for the actual truth, let alone as a model in form for other people's experience. Before continuing my comments on the Course's scribing, I should like to relate a relevant incident involving Helen and Jesus. This incident, perhaps more than any other, illustrates the two levels with which one can describe one's relationship with Jesus: the appearance and the reality. I shall first relate the circumstances as they occurred, and then discuss them in the context of our relationship with Jesus.

477

One afternoon during our San Francisco trip in the summer of 1975, Helen and I visited a lovely chapel that had been built by the brother of a Maryknoll Sister who was a dear friend of ours. As Helen and I sat quietly, an eyelash fell into Helen's eye. She related to me how this was not an uncommon experience for her, as her eyelashes were long. However, she continued, this was never a problem because Jesus always took the eyelashes out for her. Helen then described to me how she would close her eyes and pray, and when she opened them the eyelash would be out. And so sitting in the chapel, we proceeded to close our eyes and pray together. Sure enough, moments later, there was the eyelash resting on Helen's cheek.

Clearly, Helen's *experience* was that Jesus took the eyelash out of her eye, but this really makes no sense unless one is prepared to believe that Jesus plucked the eyelash from Helen's eye with his finger, or variations thereof. Since I knew that discussion of this magical Jesus would only make Helen anxious, I refrained from bringing it up, although I did indirectly a couple of years later in the discussion on prayer that led to the scribing of "The Song of Prayer." What I believe did happen with the eyelash is as follows.

Consider again that Jesus literally does not do anything. He remains an abstract presence of love in our minds, analogous to a lighthouse that simply shines its light into the dark night. Those ships that are lost at sea perceive the light and sail towards it. The light itself does not actively call to them, but its presence reminds them of where safety lies. So does Jesus (and the Holy Spirit) serve as a reminder. As is obvious from this book, Helen spent a lifetime attempting to run away from Jesus, continually turning from his light and using the darkness of her ego concerns and judgments as a hiding place. That is why early in the dictation Jesus told her, relative to the two stages involved in escaping from darkness: "The first is the recognition that darkness *cannot* hide.... The second is that there is nothing you *want* to hide, even if you could." Incidentally, this statement, from which I have already quoted, is currently found in slightly edited form in the first paragraph of the section "The Escape from Darkness" from Chapter One of the text.

One of the ways Helen expressed this running away was by attacking her eyes. Vision has always been a major symbol in spirituality, and *A Course in Miracles* is no exception. It would therefore stand to reason that Helen's ego would attack her eyes as symbolic of her attempts not to *see* what Jesus was teaching her. In fact, while Helen was taking down the Course, she went through a period when she was sure she was losing her eyesight. Panic-stricken, she checked into the Eye Institute that was part of the Medical Center. But she was released after a couple of days when all the tests came back negative. Soon afterwards, her eyesight returned. And for many, many years Helen was "meditating" on developing a detached retina, since her fear of this was so great. And, indeed, near the end of her life she did "succeed" finally in detaching her retina.

Another example of Helen's resistance to sharing in Jesus' vision came in the context of a series of efforts he asked her to make to look at him on the cross, presumably so that she would be able to see that he was not suffering. Very often I would try to help Helen in this, praying with her as she "saw" the cross. But she would always shift Jesus to the lower left-hand corner of her visual field, thereby avoiding seeing him full face. She was never able to see him as he asked.

On a much smaller scale, then, Helen's "detached eyelashes" also can be understood as reflecting her resistance to seeing what Jesus would have her see. Thus, on a level she was not in touch with, she would make a decision to separate from his love and therefore from the vision of Christ that is the goal of the Course. This decision, coming from fear, was essentially as non-specific as the love that Jesus represented, even though it manifested in specific forms. In this case, the eyelash in the eye was the *effect* of the *cause*: Helen's decision to separate from Jesus' love. When Helen decided to let Jesus help her with the eyelash, she was reflecting on this bodily level the decision made in her mind to move closer to Jesus and to join with his love. Thus she undid the cause of the eyelash in the eye—being separate from Jesus—by choosing to join him. At this point, with the cause undone, the effect was undone as well, and so the eyelash ended up on Helen's cheek.

The point in all this is that Jesus in reality did nothing.

Helen did all the work; first in moving away from Jesus (leading to *her* putting the eyelash in her eye), and then in moving back to him (leading to *her* removing the eyelash from her eye). Yet her experience, similar to the aforementioned example of the sun rising and setting, was that Jesus helped her. In reality, just as the sun remains relatively stationary as the earth rotates and revolves around it, Jesus' love and light remained still, while Helen moved away and then towards him.

Returning now to Helen and the Course, while her experience most definitely was of Jesus—a person *outside* herself—relating to her and dictating to her, in truth the reality was much different. Helen was able to return her mind to that memory of God's Love—her true Identity—symbolized by her as Jesus. By uniting with him, she united with love. That union has no form or specifics, for love, as we have seen, is abstract and beyond all divisions of the ego. This love, of which Jesus was the manifestation, flowed through the separated mind we know as Helen (the water taking shape in the glass) and came out to the world as the three books we know as *A Course in Miracles*. Thus, it was Helen's mind that gave the Course its *form*; the *content* came from outside her ego mind, from a love that nonetheless is within her mind, as indeed it is in all of us. Recall Helen's own description, given in Part II, that Jesus made use of her "educational background, interests and experience, but that was in matters of style [i.e., form] rather than content."

As one looks at the particulars of the Course's form and structure, one can find almost exact parallels with Helen's own life. Helen was American and obviously English speaking, the idiom and language of the Course. She was a Freudian psychologist and educator, and the Course contains a sophisticated psychodynamic study of the ego, coming within a curricular format: text, workbook for students, and manual for teachers. Its goal, moreover, is that we learn from our inner Teacher, the Holy Spirit, so as to become teachers of God. Despite her clear ambivalence, Helen nonetheless identified with the Christian tradition, more specifically Roman Catholicism, and was very well versed in the Bible. *A Course in Miracles* falls within the traditional Christian framework, correcting the distortions and misunderstandings of this two-thousand-year-old tradition, in addition to containing over eight hundred quotations and allusions to the Bible. Helen was a lover of Shakespeare as well as the great English poets, and the writing of the Course is quite Shakespearean in form, with large portions of the material coming in blank verse and iambic pentameter, the poetic meter of Shakespeare. Helen possessed a keenly logical mind—the reader may recall her love if not worship of logic as a college student—and the Course's theory is presented with a rigorous logic, that once its basic premises are accepted, cannot be argued with. Finally, Helen had great respect and love for Plato, and a number of specific allusions to Plato's work are included. In addition, as I pointed out in *Love Does Not Condemn, A Course in Miracles* comes within the philosophical tradition that, even though it traces its beginnings to the pre-Socratics, more properly begins with Plato, the true father of Western philosophy, along with Socrates.

The one seeming exception to this list in terms of the formal characteristics of the Course is the strong Gnostic theme that runs throughout the material, not to mention usage of specific Gnostic terminology.[98] Helen and I never discussed the subject (my interest in it did not really begin until after her death), but to the best of my knowledge she had no conscious awareness of this important philosophical and religious movement. However, since Platonists were among the leading Gnostics, and Platonic Gnosticism is reflected in much of the Course's teachings, there must have been part of Helen's mind that was familiar with this tradition.

Therefore, again, Helen was responsible for the Course's specific form; the abstract love of Jesus—the source—for its content. To a question raised by a North Carolina group that we had once visited, Helen responded that naturally *A Course in Miracles* was psychological and set up as a curriculum, since she was a psychologist and educator. I reminded her afterwards, however, that she became a psychologist and teacher because of a decision she had made prior *to*, and on a level

---

98. These are discussed at length in my aforementioned book *Love Does Not Condemn.*

different *from* her conscious existence as Helen Schucman. This was similar to the fact that the three people closest to the Course—Helen, Bill, and I—all had Ph.D's in Clinical Psychology. The Course teaches that time is not linear, and choices are made on the level of the mind—outside time— independent of the brain and body with which we identify.[99] Therefore, our choices to become psychologists, and Helen's to become an educator as well, were hardly accidental. Helen's becoming a psychologist and teacher was necessary so that her brain could accept the Course's teachings in that form. The difficulty in understanding this phenomenon, as mentioned briefly above, comes from our linear-programmed brains which cannot go beyond their own programming, to understand the mind's non-linearity.

However, Helen's experience, as we have seen, was that Jesus used her particular talents and abilities, just as she experienced him as specifically helping her. In fact, the reader may recall these lines from the original dictation, omitted in the published Course:

> You must have noticed how often I have used your own ideas to help *you*.

And then in the context of how the Holy Spirit teaches us "to use what the ego has made to *teach* the opposite of what the ego has *learned*" (found in slightly modified form in the published text, pp. 109f, and presented in Part II of this book), Jesus said to Helen:

> You could not have a better example of the Holy Spirit's unified purpose than this course. The Holy Spirit has taken very diversified areas of your past learning, and has applied them to a *unified* curriculum.

In truth, once again, it was really the mind beyond Helen— called here the Holy Spirit—that took the "diversified areas" of her life and "applied them to a unified curriculum."

Therefore, we can now better understand, on a more

---

99. The interested reader may consult my *A Vast Illusion: Time According to A COURSE IN MIRACLES* for an in-depth treatment of the Course's understanding of time.

sophisticated level, the true nature of Helen's relationship with Jesus. An abstract and non-specific presence, Jesus remains a thought of perfect love within the minds of all people who still believe in the reality of the dream. The thought we know as Helen rejoined the thought we know as Jesus. Within the dream of the world, this union of love manifested itself as *A Course in Miracles.* The Self of Helen we have described as the perfectly objective and impersonal priestess is the more complete expression of this union, as it more directly reflected the abstract impersonal nature of this love.

Given this reality, we can now also understand the motivation behind the pamphlet "The Song of Prayer" and its preceding message. By focusing on the specifics of her ego's concerns, Helen was virtually able to bury the love of her Self; the miracle of this love became sacrificed for the magic contained in the demands for answers to her questions. Returning to our earlier analogy, instead of holding an almost infinite container to the flowing waters of Jesus, Helen presented him with the narrow thimble of her ego needs, that he might fill only that. In this sense, again, the love of Jesus was made more "manageable." To repeat part of the message:

> A specific question is actually a decision about the kind of answer that is acceptable. The purpose of words is to limit, and by limiting to make a vast area more manageable.... Answers are not up to you. Any limit you place on them interferes with hearing.

All the questions about specifics thus came to symbolize the limitation placed on love by fear. At first, at the lower rungs of our ladder of prayer, they can represent our attempts to join with Jesus in an acceptable way that would minimize our fear of uniting with his love. However, it is an easy temptation to become seduced by the "answers" and thereby avoid the true Answer. Getting beyond this temptation, again, was the purpose of Jesus' message to Helen. It is always helpful, therefore, to be reminded of the difference between symbol and reality, appearance and truth: the forms of the world only have meaning to the extent that they help us to move beyond them to the content of God's Love that is our only desire and goal.

From the perspective of this discussion on the meaning of

prayer, we can return now to the "prayer" meetings with Judy, Bill, Helen, and me, and our practice of asking for guidance with decisions regarding the worldly life of the Course. There is a danger in attributing everything that occurred in the early Foundation years to inspiration. The "danger" comes in presenting an ideal to the world that makes it extremely easy to set up a specialness model, wherein students of *A Course in Miracles* end up feeling like failures because they do not "measure up" to the example we supposedly set. Mistakes were made during those early years, and there was nothing sacred or sacrosanct about how we proceeded. That we were well-intentioned there is no question, but students of the Course are familiar with these very important cautionary words, already partially quoted above:

> Trust not your good intentions. They are not enough. But trust implicitly your willingness, whatever else may enter (text, p. 355).

This last reference, of course, is to the little willingness we are asked to give to the Holy Spirit to abandon our belief that we are correct in our perceptions and values. So often when people ask for specific answers to specific questions they are really asking the Holy Spirit or Jesus to provide them with the answers for which they have already unconsciously wished. Thus they are bringing truth to illusion, rather than illusion to the truth as we are asked repeatedly to do in the Course. Since we made the world—the illusion—specifically to exclude the Love of God, it is the height of the ego's arrogance then to ask God (or His symbolic manifestations) to enter it to help solve a problem He knows nothing about. That is why, again, *A Course in Miracles* asks us to bring our illusory beliefs and perceptions to the truth that is within our minds, where in the presence of its light the darkness of our fears and concerns simply disappears.

The ego thought system is almost all unconscious to us, and so for the most part we are unaware of the silent investments we have in the outcome of events. This is the advantage to moving beyond specifics: there is far less likelihood of one's hearing being "contaminated." In the section on Helen's "Special Messages," I mentioned Helen's unreliability when it came

484

to specifics. To restate this important point, unconscious ego conflicts and demands most easily surface when one's attention is riveted on specific questions, needs, and outcomes. When one is at rest in the peace of God, there is no serious concern with outcomes, and the answer is always known and understood. This does not mean, certainly, that decisions are not necessary. As Jesus states in "The Song of Prayer":

There are decisions to make here, and they must be made whether they be illusions or not (p. 2).

And in the psychotherapy pamphlet, Jesus reminds us that "Even an advanced therapist has some earthly needs while he is here" (p. 21), meaning that some attention needs to be given to money. The point is that the problem lies in placing emphasis on *hearing* the specific answer to a question, for such concern draws away from the real Answer.

Thus, when the Course was being taken down by Helen, part of her mind rested with Jesus, and his message of love and truth passed through her mind purely and without impediment. Concern with decisions regarding the Course, however, was always a product of a split mind that was invested in what was done, and so the "answers" lacked the purity of the Course itself. Once again, it is essential not to forget the crucial distinction between form and content. It was the love of Jesus alone—the content—that was the source of *A Course in Miracles*, but the guidance regarding its life in the world of form came, I believe, from minds that were often too involved in the answers of the world, and not necessarily always the Answer of Heaven.

Part of the special message of October 5, 1975 is deserving of a repeat quotation:

To God all things are possible, but you must ask His answer only of Himself.

Perhaps you think you do, but be you sure that if you did you would be quiet now and wholly undismayed by anything. Do not attempt to guess His Will for you. Do not assume that you are right because an answer seems to come from Him. Be sure you ask, and then be still and let Him speak.

This extremely important caution against believing that the

inner voice is God's simply because one experiences it as such, was underscored by this statement in the manual for teachers: "Only very few can hear God's Voice at all" (manual, p. 30).

Before continuing on, I should like to introduce a slight digression to tell a story that points up the mistake of holding Helen (or any of our "holy" group) as an example of impeccable hearing regarding specifics. Some time ago I received a telephone call from a very distraught man, who related to me how he had been receiving specific guidance from the Holy Spirit over the past few years. I do not recall most of the details of our conversation, but I do remember that he was being told very specific things regarding places, dates, etc. One piece of this guidance stated that he was going to die on a specific date, which was due now in three days. And this man was calling me the day before he was supposed to enter the hospital for minor surgery, which was to take place on the very day the Holy Spirit told him would be his last.

I explained to him the confusion of form and content, using Helen's hearing mistakes as examples, including her errors in the death dates of Louis, Bill, and herself. Fortunately, he understood, and feeling relieved, entered the hospital for his surgery. A week or so later he called to tell me that he was safely home, the operation a success, and he was obviously very much alive. I frequently caution students of *A Course in Miracles* about this kind of mistake, urging them to be suspicious of any specific guidance they receive, even more so when Jesus and the Holy Spirit sound urgent or demanding. Love is always patient, since it knows not of time. The content may be from the Holy Spirit, but the form always is the product of the individual's separated mind.

A good example of this confusion of form and content is the "explanation" Helen received about the Course's timing, the "celestial speed-up" message (*see above*, pp. 200f). Unfortunately, this story is frequently taken by students of *A Course in Miracles* to be the literal truth. Rather, it should be understood as a set of symbols that were adapted to Helen's conceptual level of understanding at the time, and the meaning of which is beyond all concepts. Thus, this "explanation" was the form in which Helen could best understand the startling

486

events of that summer of 1965. In an important passage, already alluded to, Jesus teaches:

> The value of the Atonement [by which is meant here any expression of love from the Holy Spirit] does not lie in the manner in which it is expressed. In fact, if it is used truly, it will inevitably be expressed in whatever way is most helpful to the receiver. This means that a miracle, to attain its full efficacy, must be expressed in a language that the recipient can understand without fear. This does not necessarily mean that this is the highest level of communication of which he is capable. It does mean, however, that it is the highest level of communication of which he is capable *now*. The whole aim of the miracle is to raise the level of communication, not to lower it by increasing fear (text, pp. 20f).

Again, Helen's ego was not able at that point in her life to understand the illusory nature of time, which would have been too fearful for her; it did not get discussed in the Course until much later. Therefore, as Helen's thinking was still subject to the belief in time as linear, the level of explanation she could accept was commensurate with this belief. If she required an explanation later on, which she did not, it would doubtlessly have come in a more sophisticated fashion.

I conclude this chapter with some comments and examples regarding Helen's wisdom. I cite these as evidence for the holiness of the Self that was always present in her, though well-hidden most of the time.

The Unconscious Priestess

There was a wisdom about Helen throughout her entire life, almost like a knowing or pre-knowing the workings of the mind that the Course would later expound. And it was as if that wisdom, indicative of the underlying priestess Self in Helen, were already firmly in place in her mind—before the Course—and I believe it was. She seemed always to be someone to whom others naturally gravitated for help. While she was still a young woman an incident occurred that exemplifies this, and at the same time reflects the bitterness Helen felt towards her father. At a family gathering, one of Helen's aunts sought her out for

487

help, and Helen and she spent some time together. At the conclusion of the evening, Helen's father inquired as to the purpose of this extended conversation. Helen explained, and her father responded incredulously: "Why would anyone want to speak with you. You are the littlest and the least?" Helen never consciously forgave him for what she perceived as an egregious insult, but in "Deliverance," her poem to Jesus, she wrote down:

> I am the least and yet the greatest. I
> Who hold your hand have Heaven's might with me.
> I go in glory, for you walk with me.
> Deliver me into my Father's Arms.
>
> *(The Gifts of God*, p. 55)

It would indeed seem that with these words, coming from a deeper part of Helen's mind, she had forgiven her father at last. Interestingly enough, the context of the poem is Jesus' leading Helen back to her Father's Arms. The reader may also recall the strong possibility that Helen's father was the source of the material dictated on sound to her (*see above*, pp. 388f), an expression of Helen allowing her father to join with her.

I return now from this slight digression related to Helen's father. Helen related to me three isolated incidents from her life, each of which exemplifies her innate wisdom in recognizing the power of the mind, and the powerlessness of anything external to affect that mind. Both of these ideas, by the way, are essential to the thought system of *A Course in Miracles*. I should also mention that while awareness of the truth of these ideas is certainly not in and of itself an expression of a state of advanced holiness, I believe that in Helen's case such awareness was indeed reflective of this deeper wisdom that came from her true Self. The first incident occurred when Helen was a child. The other two occurred in Helen's adulthood.

Helen's brother Adolph was fourteen years older, and although they were never close (and, in fact, never became close), he did enjoy tickling Helen, whose squeals and screams made the activity quite appealing to him. Recognizing that while there was nothing she could do physically to stop him, Helen knew she could control her reactions to the tickling. And so she decided that she would no longer be ticklish. The next time Adolph began to tickle Helen he was met with no squeals or screams. With all the fun gone, he very quickly abandoned this activity. Helen had done nothing to stop the external source of her distress, but was able to do something about its internal source, her own mind.

The same principle was applied many, many years later when a woman moved into the apartment above Helen and Louis. She had only the bare floor in her bedroom, which was directly above Helen's bed. Late at night, while Helen was attempting to sleep, the woman would walk in her bedroom in high heels. And Helen would lie in bed fuming, experiencing this apparently insensitive and thoughtless person as walking on her head. As she lay in bed this one evening, it suddenly occurred to her that the problem was actually very simple: she *believed* that the woman was walking on her head. Always the visual person, Helen saw a string attached from the woman's heels to her head, and understood that the string or connection was the problem, not the woman's heels. Once Helen perceived the problem as existing in her mind, the solution was clear. Still visualizing the string connecting the shoes and her head, Helen reached into her imagination, took out a scissors, and cut the string. And she promptly fell asleep. Again, Helen had done nothing to change the external situation, nor did she have to *do* anything with the woman in terms of forgiving her. She simply changed her mind, and forgiveness was accomplished.

This example, by the way, is important to correct the mistake many students of *A Course in Miracles* make regarding forgiveness, believing that some behavioral expression is necessary for the process of forgiveness to be complete. While sometimes such behavior is called for, it need not be. This was taught to Helen very clearly during the early months of her scribing the Course, in an incident I alluded to in Part II. In the context of what is now miracle principle 25, Jesus used the example of a colleague of Helen who had not done the best job possible on an important report. Jesus explained to Helen how in correcting the report, with the person never knowing (to this day!) of the mistake, she was performing a miracle by undoing the effects of the colleague's "sin."

Miracles are part of an interlocking chain of forgiveness, which, when completed, is the Atonement. This process works all the time and in all dimensions of time. A very good example of how this is accomplished is the time you rewrote the entire report for X....X had hurt something you love, by writing a report you regarded as very bad. You atoned for him by writing one in his name that was very good. Actually, it was not your responsibility professionally to do this but...you recognized in this case that you *are* your brother's keeper. While you did not cancel X's sin [later defined as "lack of love"], you *did* cancel out its *effects* [which ultimately does cancel—i.e., undo—the sin].

Someday I want to tell X that not only is he forgiven, but that the effects of all his sins are canceled. This is what I have already told you. When I can tell him, he will be afraid for a long time, because he will remember many things, consciously or unconsciously, including the...report, a sin [i.e., lack of love] which you canceled out in advance by a miracle of devotion.

The final example involved Louis. One evening, Helen and Louis had an argument, which was not resolved by the time Louis retired to the bedroom to take his usual evening nap. Helen was still fuming, and in the course of her stompings, walked into the kitchen and for some reason opened the breadbox. And there, beside whatever bread and cake was stored, was a pair of Louis' very much used socks. The passive aggressiveness behind Louis' absent-mindedness did not escape Helen (Louis never felt he was a match for Helen's anger, and so this was not an uncommon way for him to "get even"), and she became even more enraged. Suddenly, in the midst of her mental tirade, during which she was probably on the verge of storming into the bedroom, armed to kill, the thought occurred to her: "I am angry because I believe that I am a breadbox, and that Louis did this *to me*." Her anger immediately subsided as she realized the silliness of her position.

This situation with Louis, as well as the one with the high-heeled lady, antedated the Course. Again, they illustrate Helen's intuitive understanding of the important principle from *A Course in Miracles*, already cited, that we are never angry at a fact, but only an interpretation of a fact (manual, p. 43); in other words, our anger only comes from our misperception (the interpretation) that our unhappiness is caused by events or circumstances external to us and beyond our control. In these two situations, the facts were that the lady was walking on her bare floor with her high heels, and that Louis placed his socks in the breadbox. The interpretation was that these facts were being done *to* Helen. And while this might have been Louis' unconscious intent (I cannot actually vouch for this regarding the woman), this would have nothing to do with Helen unless she shared in these attack thoughts. Thus she did not change the facts; she simply reinterpreted them. Helen did not need the wisdom of *A Course in Miracles* to teach her this principle; she *was* that Wisdom.

Chapter 18

HELEN'S FINAL MONTHS AND REQUIEM

Returning now to our chronological view of Helen's life, we come to her final months in 1980 and 1981. It did not require a trained eye to observe the continuation of Helen's physical and emotional deterioration. Aside from its obvious effects on Helen, her worsening condition succeeded in isolating her from practically all of her friends. I can think of two people in particular, both students of *A Course in Miracles* and very fond of Helen, who became so upset over seeing her as she was that they were compelled abruptly to curtail their visits (one had actually traveled quite a long distance to see her). The discrepancy between the Helen they knew—impeccably groomed and socially appropriate, wise and helpful, not to mention the one who was Jesus' close companion and the scribe of *A Course in Miracles*—and the Helen they now were experiencing—physically disheveled, preoccupied with her own disturbing thoughts, and totally unresponsive to anyone beside herself—was so glaring as to be disturbing, painful, and even frightening.

As I have already indicated, during her final year Helen never left her apartment, except to go to the doctor or hospital. We did not know it until much later, but she was already experiencing the emotional and physical effects of pancreatic cancer. Incidentally, of all the malignant forms of the disease, this is the most "desirable" as it generally carries with it the least pain. On the other hand, because of the location of the pancreas behind the liver, the cancer almost always goes undetected until the tumor has grown to such an extent that there is little that can be done for it. Often the tumor's growth impinges on the liver, interfering with that vital organ's functioning. This developing liver malfunction thus can become— on the level of the body[100]—the cause of emotional and physical

---

100. *A Course in Miracles*, of course, teaches that *all* distress is the result of unforgiveness—a choice made in the mind—seeming appearances to the contrary.

distress, and then ultimately death, as it was in Helen's case.

That final year was a difficult one, especially for Louis, as Helen increasingly and demandingly focused her attention on him. The dependency that at varying times in her life had been placed on her mother, Bill, and more recently me, Helen now transferred to Louis, as mentioned earlier in the book. He could not leave the apartment without Helen's becoming quite upset. They eventually worked out an arrangement whereby Louis would be able to go out for periods each day, while I would usually remain by Helen's side, along with a day nursing companion and Evelyn, Helen and Louis' very faithful housekeeper, the successor to Georgia.

During this final period, virtually nothing of any consequence would ever be spoken between Helen and me regarding *A Course in Miracles*. Whereby in the past Helen and I would regularly pray together, talk about Jesus, or speak about what I was doing related to the Course, we now with very rare exceptions discussed any of these things. It was clear that Helen was preparing herself for death, although we still labored under the assumption that she would die at the age of seventy-two, despite our past experiences of Helen's unreliability regarding specific predictions; the number seventy-two had seemed to be so clear and certain for her. Therefore, even though the end came quickly, up until the final day or two I still felt Helen would hold out for several more months, on into the summer of 1981.

Bill would call her every day from California, but their conversations would be brief and innocuous, as they had been for quite some time. Their relationship had lost all expression of the emotional volatility of the past, and had fallen into the ritualistic adherence to form that nonetheless still reflected the inner connection, however limply it did so.

I had long ago abandoned any thought that on the level of Helen's conscious mind there would be any healing regarding her relationship with Bill, Jesus, or the Course. It therefore came as no surprise to me that when any of these subjects would arise, there would be a noticeable absence of any positive expression on Helen's part, to put it mildly. Thus, Helen's conflict between her two selves never *appeared* to be resolved.

Symbolized above all by her relationship with Jesus, the conflict that had raged for years—now in the final period of her life—again lapsed into the seeming oblivion of inattention or outright forgetfulness. However, the internal dis-ease and lack of peace—the inevitable result of any unresolved conflict—remained with her, even though there were no longer any overt emotional expressions of this conflict.

And yet even though it did not *appear* to be so, I was certain that at the actual moment of her death Helen finally reached a peaceful resolution to her lifelong conflict with God. The following account of her death provides the final punctuation to this wonderfully inspiring, if not somewhat sad story of her life. I might mention that while this resolution occurred at Helen's death, it need not have waited that long. Physical death, as the Course teaches, is not the answer to any problem. The reader may recall the opening line from the fragment Helen asked me to insert in the text: "There is a risk of thinking death is peace" (text, p. 541).

On Sunday, February 8, 1981, I kept a long-standing speaking engagement in upstate New York. While Helen's condition was deteriorating, we again did not suspect how imminent her death actually was. I called during the day, and forget now if I had even spoken to her. Upon my return in the evening I saw Helen and Louis, and decided to stay overnight. Helen would constantly cry out "Louis" in her delirium, and I thought I should remain close at hand. I believe there was also a nurse's aide present. I left early the next morning to see some patients. My last memory of Helen's conscious state was my saying good-bye, realizing she did not even know who I was. Closing the door behind me, I was to hear her call out "Louis" for the last time. Her condition remained the same throughout the morning, and I left my apartment for a luncheon appointment uptown. When I returned home, there was a message on my answering machine that Louis was taking Helen to the emergency room of New York Hospital, where I met them.

Helen had already lapsed into a coma. This was about 3:00 in the afternoon, as I recall, and Louis and I remained with Helen as they brought her to her room. I had a class on the Course that evening, which I canceled, recognizing now that

Helen's death was near, and that she might not survive the night. Louis and I remained until around 8:00 P.M., and Helen's condition appeared to be stabilizing. On the recommendation of the medical staff, believing that she would most likely live a while longer, at least until morning, Louis chose to return home. I accompanied him, only to have the hospital call about three hours later, shortly after 11:00, that Helen had indeed died. We returned to the hospital, and Helen was still in her bed. Her face had a remarkably quiet expression of peace, so different from the tortured disquiet we had grown so accustomed to seeing these many months. I suddenly recalled what Helen had shared with me on several occasions, a thought that always brought her great comfort. Jesus had told her that when she died, he would come for her personally. Who can really know what was in her mind in those closing instants? Yet, her peaceful face was unmistakable, and spoke convincingly for an experience of knowing, at the very end, that her beloved Jesus had indeed kept his promise, as she had kept hers. The priestess had returned home.

As I stood over Helen's dead body in the hospital I knew she was free at last, and different lines from the aforementioned "Requiem" poem, originally written for Sister Regina's mother, went through my mind. And I gave thanks. The complete poem is as follows:

> You came but for a while. When Jesus called
> You were content to go. For who would stay
> To watch the dreary cycle of the nights
> Turn coldly gray with each return of day?
>
> This world was not your home. Would God allow
> His child to wander long without a home
> Which He Himself makes bright? Your tired eyes
> Closed gratefully when He at last said, "Come."
>
> You have forgot all this. All thoughts that hurt,
> All sorrow, all regret, have ceased to be
> In your remembrance. He Who called to you
> Has loosened all your chains and set you free.

Because I love you I would have you go.
Because I love Him I can scarcely weep.
Because He loves you glory goes with you,
And in that glory you but seem to sleep.

He came in mercy. Let me give Him thanks
You stayed with us until you saw Him smile
And tell you it is finished. He will come
For me that way in just a little while.

It is for this I wait, in certainty
That He Who made the stars will not forget.
I will be glad to see Him smile at me,
Or if He choose, to wait a little yet.

(The Gifts of God, p. 109)

Louis and I returned to his apartment where I called Bill, Judy, and other friends and family. As I have already mentioned, Louis lost no time in having me remove from the apartment copies of the Course, and Helen's Catholic medals and rosaries—that very night!

Helen's funeral was two days later on February 11, the Catholic feast of Our Lady of Lourdes, commemorating the Blessed Mother's appearance to Bernadette, a fitting date given Helen's feelings about Mary, and her childhood experience at Lourdes. The people assembled at this traditional Jewish funeral roughly fell into two categories: those who were students of the Course, and those consisting of family, friends, and colleagues, almost all of whom knew absolutely nothing about Helen's "other life," let alone the existence of *A Course in Miracles*.

I delivered the eulogy, in such a soft voice I was told, that many of the large crowd had trouble hearing me. Louis wanted me to omit any mention of the Course, or anything Christian for that matter, and yet he wished me to speak of Helen's strong spiritual nature. To the surprise of many, therefore, I spoke of Helen's religious devotion, describing how that led her to help all those she believed God had sent to her. As deftly as I could, I tried to describe her spiritual commitment to God and His work that more properly belonged to the Course and Jesus. My principal focus was the degree to which Helen had dedicated herself to helping others, a fact to which the great majority sitting in the chapel could gratefully attest.

But my task that day, as even in this book, was really an impossible one, for how truly to describe this remarkable woman, whose very human self could not ultimately conceal the love of the transhuman Self that so faithfully was allowed to flow through her hands? Heaven's gift of love, through the union of Jesus and Helen, thus became immortalized in *A Course in Miracles*, the three books for which the world will be forever grateful. And so, whatever words I actually used to close the eulogy, my heart was instead singing these to Helen, based upon Horatio's tender farewell to his beloved Hamlet (V, ii):

> *Now cracks a noble heart. Good night, sweet mother;*
> *And flights of angels sing thee to thy rest!*

Epilogue

BEYOND HEAVEN AND HELEN: THE PRIESTESS

My primary focus in this book has been the two sides of Helen's personality—"Heaven and Helen." But there was another dimension as well, that I have noted throughout, especially in Chapter 17. This dimension existed beyond both the right- and wrong-mind division, and was represented by the priestess of Helen's visions.

Very infrequently, Helen spoke to me of another level of "hearing" that transcended her experience of Jesus' voice. On certain rare occasions (I doubt if it happened more than four or five times), I was with Helen when she allowed herself and me to experience this other dimension. It was indeed a movement beyond hearing Jesus, to a state of mind even beyond the individuality of Jesus himself. At these times Helen appeared timeless, transformed into a state in which she seemed to merge finally with the priestess of her vision. In these truly holy instants I was vouchsafed a glimpse into Helen's real Identity, an egoless Self that was barely here. The words she uttered spoke through her during these times from a source that was clearly not of this world, but rather reflected an ancient, eternal wisdom. Her face lacked all feeling, and the closest I was ever able to come in describing it to myself was in recalling descriptions of the void of human emotion reported in Beethoven's death mask. The twentieth-century German poet Rilke referred to this mask in *The Journal of Malte Laurids Brigge*,[101] in words that reflected the other-worldly peace of the great composer's inner life at the hour of his death. Rilke wrote:

> The mouleur [maker of plaster casts], whose shop I pass every day, has hung two plaster masks beside his door. The face of the young drowned woman, which ... smiled so deceptively, as if it knew. And beneath it, *his* face, which knows (p. 76).

---

101. New York: Random House, 1982.

499

This egoless, *knowing* Self was the real Helen, although the name "Helen" does not quite fit here. It was clear to me that the Helen the world recognized, with whom I related most of the time, was totally unrelated to this other Self. In order to "hear" the voice of Jesus and have his love be translated into *A Course in Miracles*, it was necessary that she have a mask, a "life mask," as it were. The mask was remarkably successful, for no one could ever have known what lay behind it.

To be sure, the elements that went into this ego mask came from Helen herself. In the context of her "past life" experiences, it would certainly seem as if in another part of her mind she had misused the spiritual power so that it became self-serving rather than God-serving. And yet my own experience of Helen was that during this lifetime she could easily have shaken off this ego part whenever she chose. Over and over during these final years, I thought of Prince Hal and the wonderful scene near the end of Shakespeare's *King Henry IV, Part II*, where the former prince has shed his profligate lifestyle to become King Henry V. Visited by his erstwhile drinking companion, Falstaff, the new and mature king says:

> Presume not that I am the thing I was;
> For God doth know, so shall the world perceive,[102]
> That I have turned away my former self (V,v).

Indeed, I believe, God *doth* know, and now the world also can perceive that Helen has turned from her former ego self, and reassumed her ancient One. On a number of occasions Helen mentioned to me that Jesus told her that the "next time you come you would be different," reminiscent of the lines in Lesson 157—"Into His Presence would I enter now"—originally meant for Helen herself:

> The time will come when you will not return in the same form in which you now appear, for you will have no need of it. Yet now it has a purpose, and will serve it well (workbook, p. 290).

Incidentally, this was one of Helen's favorite lessons. Her

---

102. Note, incidentally, Shakespeare's interesting contrast of *know* for God and *perceive* for the world, identical to the distinction made by the Course, a similarity hardly accidental.

understanding of these lines, even though the subject of reincarnation usually made her very uncomfortable, was that the
next time she "came"—her next life—she would be ego-free, as
was the priestess of her earlier vision. Thus, Helen would shed
the final chain around the priestess' wrist, and stand within
the world as the light she truly was, having at last united with
her Self. One of Helen's lovelier poems, "The Soundless Song"
written in March 1974, reflects this shedding of her false self:

> I walk in stillness. Where my rest is set
> Is Heaven. And the silence of the stars
> Sings in a soundless circle. For the song
> Of Heaven is past hearing, and ascends
> Beyond the tiny range the ear can catch,
> And soars into a spaceless magnitude
> Where sound and silence meet in unity.
> Holy am I, who bring my Father's Name
> With me and who abide in Him, although
> I seem to walk alone. Look carefully,
> And you may catch a glimpse of He Who stands
> Beside me. And I lean on Him in sure
> Unswerving confidence. It was not thus
> Before, for I was bitterly afraid
> To take the Help of Heaven for my own.
> Yet Heaven never failed, and only I
> Stayed comfortless, while all of Heaven's gifts
> Poured out before me. Now the arms of Christ
> Are all I have and all my treasure is.
> Now I have ceased to question. Now I come
> From chaos to the stillness of my home.
>
> (*The Gifts of God*, p. 76)

Thus, Helen's life cannot be truly evaluated from the outside, without doing violence to her mind's true purpose.
Helen's ego experiences, when we look at her life in total,
amounted to nothing. When another part of her mind chose to
join with Bill and Jesus—reflecting the choice to rejoin her Self
and become *Its* instrument of love and peace, rather than the
ego's instrument of hate and power—that choice canceled out
all the others. It makes no difference whether one has a mon-
strous ego or a sliver; an illusion remains what it is, and all of
them can disappear in one true holy instant. This principle

was in fact enunciated by the recorder in Helen's dream (*see above*, p. 81), who told Helen in response to her question about how well she was doing:

> I never indulge in speculation.... In my work it would be a waste of time. Over and over I've seen a person suddenly decide to do something very unexpected,—something that changes the whole picture of his accounts. He's quite likely to do it up until the very last minute.

Helen's continuous efforts on behalf of others can therefore be understood as a reflection and ongoing reminder of this deeper presence of love within her. It is not the *form* of her behaviorally helping those in need that is the significant factor, but the *content* of joining with Jesus and therefore with others in a love that totally transcended the superficial ego thoughts of her worldly self. This presence of love more properly belongs to the symbolic identity of the ancient priestess, who in Helen's vision helped all those who came to her, totally indiscriminately and with equal love and devotion. And we may recall this same content expressed in Helen's recurring "dream" of standing by the gate of Heaven, greeting those returning with the words: "In the Name of Christ, pass through this gate in peace."

When Jesus told Helen that the next time she came she would be different, he was reflecting Helen's having finally resolved the "Heaven-Helen" conflict. As one does with an old garment, she discarded her ego, leaving only her true Self present. This is the state of mind *A Course in Miracles* refers to as the real world, the reflection within the separation dream of the reality of our true Self. In this sense, therefore, Helen's ego was a shield that hid her holiness, as well as expressing her ancient conflict. The final piece in her Atonement path of undoing the ego was accomplished when she chose to join with Bill and collaborate on *A Course in Miracles* (symbolized by the last vestige of chain on the priestess' wrist, reflected, again, in the dream of "The Recorder" with its shoehorn symbolism). Although more could have been done in the world, on completion of the scribing, Helen's task was indeed complete. And now has the garment slipped off, revealing the radiance of the ancient priestess and spiritual companion of Jesus. This resplendence alone is what remains.

Thus, Jesus *did,* in fact, "come" for Helen, though in their home of light they were always one and unseparated. Together now they—along with all the others who have passed through the gate—welcome those who make their way home: Christ gathering His own unto His Self. *A Course in Miracles* is one of the means that guide the sleeping world of darkness back to the awakening light of Christ shining through the gate. From there, all of God's children are welcomed at last into the Light beyond, into which they disappear as One.

As the Course's birth was accomplished through love joining with itself, Helen's gift to the world, may its light of love now ever extend throughout the darkness—even as the Love of God extends throughout His Heaven—gently calling us back to the remembrance of our one reality as Christ.

> Now is Helen's most holy purpose done.
> For she has come. For she has come at last.
> Into Christ's Presence has she entered now,
> And be us glad and grateful it is so.

AMEN

APPENDIX

A COURSE IN MIRACLES – What It Says

In 1977, in response to many requests for a brief introduction to *A Course in Miracles*, Helen wrote/scribed a three-part pamphlet entitled: *A COURSE IN MIRACLES: How It Came, What It Is, What It Says.** The first two parts Helen wrote herself, the final part—*What It Says*—was scribed from Jesus. It provides a wonderful summary of the Course's principles, and is reproduced here in its entirety.

* * * * * * *

Nothing real can be threatened.
Nothing unreal exists.
Herein lies the peace of God.

This is how *A Course in Miracles* begins. It makes a fundamental distinction between the real and the unreal; between knowledge and perception. Knowledge is truth, under one law, the law of love or God. Truth is unalterable, eternal and unambiguous. It can be unrecognized, but it cannot be changed. It applies to everything that God created, and only what He created is real. It is beyond learning because it is beyond time and process. It has no opposite; no beginning and no end. It merely is.

The world of perception, on the other hand, is the world of time, of change, of beginnings and endings. It is based on interpretation, not on facts. It is the world of birth and death, founded on the belief in scarcity, loss, separation and death. It is learned rather than given, selective in its perceptual emphases, unstable in its functioning, and inaccurate in its interpretations.

From knowledge and perception respectively, two distinct thought systems arise which are opposite in every respect. In the realm of knowledge no thoughts exist apart from God, because God and His Creation share one Will. The world of perception, however, is made by the belief in opposites and

---

* It is now included as a Preface to all published editions of the Course.

separate wills, in perpetual conflict with each other and with with God. What perception sees and hears appears to be real because it permits into awareness only what conforms to the wishes of the perceiver. This leads to a world of illusions, a world which needs constant defense precisely *because* it is not real.

When you have been caught in the world of perception you are caught in a dream. You cannot escape without help, because everything your senses show merely witnesses to the reality of the dream. God has provided the Answer, the only Way out, the true Helper. It is the function of His Voice, His Holy Spirit, to mediate between the two worlds. He can do this because, while on the one hand He knows the truth, on the other He also recognizes our illusions, but without believing in them. It is the Holy Spirit's goal to help us escape from the dream world by teaching us how to reverse our thinking and unlearn our mistakes. Forgiveness is the Holy Spirit's great learning aid in bringing this thought reversal about. However, the Course has its own definition of what forgiveness really is just as it defines the world in its own way.

The world we see merely reflects our own internal frame of reference—the dominant ideas, wishes and emotions in our minds. "Projection makes perception." We look inside first, decide the kind of world we want to see and then project that world outside, making it the truth *as we see it*. We make it true by our interpretations of what it is we are seeing. If we are using perception to justify our own mistakes—our anger, our impulses to attack, our lack of love in whatever form it may take—we will see a world of evil, destruction, malice, envy and despair. All this we must learn to forgive, not because we are being "good" and "charitable," but because what we are seeing is not true. We have distorted the world by our twisted defenses, and are therefore seeing what is not there. As we learn to recognize our perceptual errors, we also learn to look past them or "forgive" them. At the same time we are forgiving ourselves, looking past our distorted self concepts to the Self that God created in us and as us.

Sin is defined as "lack of love." Since love is all there is, sin in the sight of the Holy Spirit is a mistake to be corrected, rather than an evil to be punished. Our sense of inadequacy, weakness and incompletion comes from the strong investment in the "scarcity principle" that governs the whole world of illusions. From that point of view, we seek in others what we feel is wanting in ourselves. We "love" another in order to get something ourselves. That, in fact, is what passes for love in the dream world. There can be no greater mistake than that, for love is incapable of asking for anything.

Only minds can really join, and whom God has joined no man *can* put asunder. It is, however, only at the level of Christ Mind that true union is possible, and has, in fact, never been lost. The "little I" seeks to enhance itself by external approval, external possessions and external "love." The Self that God created needs nothing. It is forever complete, safe, loved and loving. It seeks to share rather than to get; to extend rather than project. It has no needs and wants to join with others out of their mutual awareness of abundance.

The special relationships of the world are destructive, selfish and childishly egocentric. Yet, if given to the Holy Spirit, these relationships can become the holiest things on earth—the miracles that point the way to the return to Heaven. The world uses its special relationships as a final weapon of exclusion and a demonstration of separateness. The Holy Spirit transforms them into perfect lessons in forgiveness and in awakening from the dream. Each one is an opportunity to let perceptions be healed and errors corrected. Each one is another chance to forgive oneself by forgiving the other. And each one becomes still another invitation to the Holy Spirit and to the remembrance of God.

Perception is a function of the body, and therefore represents a limit on awareness. Perception sees through the body's eyes and hears through the body's ears. It evokes the limited responses which the body makes. The body appears to be largely self-motivated and independent, yet it actually responds only to the intentions of the mind. If the mind wants to use it for attack in any form, it becomes prey to sickness, age and decay. If the mind accepts the Holy Spirit's purpose for it instead, it becomes a useful way of communicating with others, invulnerable as along as it is needed, and to be gently laid by when its use is over. Of itself it is neutral, as is everything in the world of perception. Whether it is used for the goals of the ego or the Holy Spirit depends entirely on what the mind wants.

The opposite of seeing through the body's eyes is the vision of Christ, which reflects strength rather than weakness, unity rather than separation, and love rather than fear. The opposite of hearing through the body's ears is communication through the Voice for God, the Holy Spirit, which abides in each of us. His Voice seems distant and difficult to hear because the ego, which speaks for the little, separated self, seems to be much louder. This is actually reversed. The Holy Spirit speaks with unmistakable clarity and overwhelming appeal. No one who does not choose to identify with the body could possibly be deaf to His messages of release and hope, nor could he fail to accept joyously the vision of Christ in glad exchange for his miserable picture of himself.

Christ's vision is the Holy Spirit's gift, God's alternative to the illusion of separation and to the belief in the reality of sin, guilt and death. It is the one correction for all errors of perception; the reconciliation of the seeming opposites on which this world is based. Its kindly light shows all things from another point of view, reflecting the thought system that arises from knowledge and making return to God not only possible but inevitable. What was regarded as injustices done to one by someone else now becomes a call for help and for union. Sin, sickness and attack are seen as misperceptions calling for remedy through gentleness and love. Defenses are laid down because where there is no attack there is no need for them. Our brothers' needs become our own, because they are taking the journey with us as we go to God. Without us they would lose their way. Without them we could never find our own.

Forgiveness is unknown in Heaven, where the need for it would be inconceivable. However, in this world forgiveness is a necessary correction for all the mistakes that we have made. To offer forgiveness is the only way for us to have it, for it reflects the law of Heaven that giving and receiving are the same. Heaven is the natural state of all the Sons of God as He created them. Such is their reality forever. It has not changed because it has been forgotten.

Forgiveness is the means by which we will remember. Through forgiveness the thinking of the world is reversed. The forgiven world becomes the gate of Heaven, because by its mercy we can at last forgive ourselves. Holding no one prisoner to guilt, we become free. Acknowledging Christ in all our brothers, we recognize His Presence in ourselves. Forgetting all our misperceptions, and with nothing from the past to hold us back, we can remember God. Beyond this learning cannot go. When we are ready, God Himself will take the final step in our return to Him.

DATES
Helen Schucman

1909 (July 14): Birth
1921 (Summer): Experience at Lourdes, France
1922: Baptism as a Baptist
1931–1935: New York University (B.A.)
1932 (Fall): Meets Louis Schucman
1933 (May 26): Marries Louis Schucman

1938 ca.: Subway experience
1952–1957: New York University (Ph.D.)
1958 (Early): Meets William Thetford
1965 (June): "There must be another way" speech
1965 (June–October): Pre-Course visions and experiences
1965–1972: Scribing of *A Course in Miracles*
    text: October 21, 1965–October 10, 1968
    workbook: May 26, 1969–February 18, 1971
    manual: April 12, 1972–September 7,* 1972
1969,1971 (December 25, 1969, March 12, 1971 –
    November 11, 1971): Early poems
1972 (October), **1977** (April): "Notes on Sound"

1972 (November 25): Meets Kenneth Wapnick
1973 (January), **1975** (January, March): "Psychotherapy:
    Purpose, Process and Practice"
1973 (December 24)–**1978** (March 20): Later poems
1973 (late)–**1975** (early): Final editing of *A Course in Miracles*
1975 (May 29): Meets Judith Skutch
1975 (Summer, Fall): Distribution of 300 photo-offset copies of
    A Course in Miracles
1975 (September–December): "Clarification of Terms"
1976 (June): Publication of *A Course in Miracles*
1977 (September–November): "The Song of Prayer"
1978 (February 8–April 11): "The Gifts of God"
1981 (February 9): Death
1988 (July 4): Bill's death

---

* This is the last date given in the urtext, but it almost certainly was not the final date of the dictation, which probably came a week or so later.

INDICES

The purpose of these three indices is to provide the reader with a handy means of finding some of the more important names, places, and themes in the book. They are not intended to be exhaustive listings. Thus, there are no main entries for some names and terms—e.g., God, Jesus, and *A Course in Miracles*—which ordinarily would appear in comprehensive indices. Listings not found in the Index of Names or in the Index of William Thetford may be found in the more complete Index of Helen Schucman.

INDEX OF NAMES

Adolph (Helen's brother), *see* Index of Helen Schucman
Aesculapius, 112
Altman, B. (store), 236, 447
Asbury Park, 150

Bolen, James, 382

Cayce, Edgar, 115, 136, 295, 296, 298
Association for Research and Enlightenment (Virginia Beach), 126–27, 176
Cayce, Hugh Lynn, 115, 127, 176, 359
Charlotte, 122–24, 178
Chesterton, G.K.
The Man Who Was Thursday, 149
Chip, 7, 119, 139, 153, 223, 226, 313, 314, 340, 355
Cohn, Rose and Sigmund (Helen's parents), *see* Index of Helen Schucman
Columbia University, 161, 269–80

Diamond, David, 189, 193–96, 218, 242, 243

Evelyn, 494

Foundation for Inner Peace, 374n, 376, 380, 484

Freddie (x-ray technician), 340, 343–44, 345–47, 350, 351, 354
Freud, 3, 163, 257
and the genetic fallacy, 295–96

Gamaliel, Rabbi, 416
Garrett, Eileen, 384–85
Georgia, 33–37, 40, 41, 43, 50, 51, 494
Gilbert and Sullivan, 417
The Gondoliers, 138

Hatcher, Cal, 316–17, 321–22

Jampolsky, Gerald, 417
Journal of Abnormal and Social Psychology, 315, 316n, 318

Kafka, Franz, 64, 68, 76
Klein's (store), 236

Lord and Taylor (store), 236, 446

Mary, Mother of Jesus, 28, 31, 43, 233, 345, 356, 397–98; *see also* Index of Helen Schucman: Roman Catholic Church
Mary Magdalene, 345, 356

Maryknoll Cloister, 419–20
Mays (store), 438
Mercy, Sister, 409–10, 447
Michael, Father, 7, 8–11, 358, 390,
    409–10, 418, 425–26
Michael-Smith, Harold, 85, 86
Morristown, 168, 175
Mundy, Jon, 390–91

Newman, Cardinal, 414
New York Times, The, 209–210

Pelleas et Melisande, 117
Plato, 38, 349, 481

Regina, Sister, 409–10, 447, 496
Richardson, Miss, 27-29
Rockwell, Dr. William, 83, 237n

S (friend of Bill), 135–39, 222, 224,
    226, 253
St. Francis Church, 413, 424
Shakespeare, 11, 21, 407, 425, 481,
    500
    Hamlet, 2, 4, 155, 422, 498
Shield Institute for Retarded
    Children, 87, 188
Skutch, Judith, 374–80, 391, 394,
    417, 462–63, 484, 497
Skutch, Robert, 374n, 376

Teresa, Mother, 427

Unpublished Writings of Helen
    Schucman, 13n

Wapnick, Kenneth, see also, Index of
    Helen Schucman
    "Birthday Request, A" (poem for
        Helen), 414
    "Christian Psychology in 'A
        Course in Miracles,'"
        426
    Gethsemani, Abbey of, 7, 12,
        336–37
    Israel, 10, 11, 335–36, 339–58
    Latroun, Abbey of, 10, 356, 429
    Lavra Netofa, 10, 336
    Love Does Not Condemn, 467n,
        481n
    parents, 351, 442–43
    "Stabat Mater II" (poem for
        Helen), 433
    "Starfish, The" (poem), 437
    Vast Illusion, A: Time According
        to A COURSE IN
        MIRACLES, 482n
    Watermill (New York), 135, 137,
        143–46, 168, 178
    Wolff, Harold, 87

Yeats, William Butler, 373
Yokelson, Doris, 447

INDEX OF WILLIAM THETFORD

appointment as head of Psychology Department, Presbyterian Hospital, 87, 277

fear of public speaking, 161, 188, 269, 379–80

fear of teaching, 188, 190, 273–80, 305

homosexuality, 89

Jesus, relationship with, 239, 462n
    prayer from Jesus, 197, 197n, 225, 266–67

last years and death, 379

letters to Kenneth Wapnick, 346, 348–49, 351, 353, 354

move to California, 377, 379

parents, relationship with, 164–67, 269–72

Princeton meetings, 299–301, 322

Professor, meaning of, 230, 277

punning, 161, 187, 224, 228, 230, 239, 240, 263, 268

strawberry mark, 238–39

INDEX OF HELEN SCHUCMAN

Adolph (Helen's Brother), 33, 40,
    163, 290, 488–89
agnosticism, 97
astrology, 164–67
atheism, 32n, 52, 115, 166, 206, 212
autobiography, *see also* DREAMS; EX-
    PERIENCES AND INCI-
    DENTS; PSYCHIC EXPERI-
    ENCES; VISIONS
    editing of, 1–2, 13, 17–18, 198–99
    quotations from, 17, 27–44,
        49–55, 83–91, 93–97,
        124n, 126–27, 198–208,
        211, 328–30

baptism, 36
Baptist religion, 33–36
Bible, The
    favorite passages in, 35n, 423
    knowledge of, 223, 229, 232,
        425–26, 480

capitalization, 32n, 49, 109n, 179,
    187n, 198, 226n,
    364–65, 453n
"celestial speed-up," 197, 200–201,
    245–46, 282, 298,
    486–87
chalice symbolism, *see* VISIONS,
    chalice
Christian Science, 37, 69
"Clarification of Terms," 391–93,
    434
    wastepaper basket incident,
        392–93
Columbia-Presbyterian Medical
    Center, 64, 85–91, 93,
    153, 338, 377, 426–27,
    441, 447
    Black Building, 207, 361
    Eye Institute, 479
    Neurological Institute, 195, 196,
        207, 290, 322, 361
    Psychiatric Institute, 8, 207, 290

Psychology Dept. (Presbyterian
    Hospital), 86, 87, 88,
    89, 90, 93–94, 346
Cornell University Medical Center,
    87, 93–94, 191
Course in Miracles, A
    belief in, 173, 206–207, 212–13,
        381–86
    favorite passages in, 11, 204, 347,
        447, 500
    form and content, 199, 210–11,
        225, 232, 480–82,
        485–87
    masculine language of, 434–35
    miracle principles
        "cobwebs of iron," 227–28
        "flat feet," 225–26, 234
crown, 189
"crucifixion," misspelling of, 189,
    267

DREAMS
    animals, 220
    Blue-Gray Bird, The, 22–24, 383
    diagnosing child's illness, 221
    dispossession by "the man,"
        146–48
    Gentleman, The, 56–59, 75, 148
    Greatest Experience of My Life,
        The, 69–72
    green and red rubber ball, 140–41
    Heaven's gate, *see* VISIONS
    Hen and the Pot, The, 59–61
    Puppy, The, 61–64
    Rabbit, The, 64–68, 75–76
    Recorder, The, 78–82, 284, 502
    Witch/Angel, The, 77

ego contrasted with Bill's, 89,
    160–63, 222, 223–24,
    231, 249–50, 255, 268,
    276, 282–87, 303–306,
    310, 370

elevator operators strike, 326
England
    fondness for, 156n
    trip to, 376–77

EXPERIENCES AND INCIDENTS
    anger toward Jesus, 440–41
    Atlantic City, in, 127–28, 156
    correcting colleague's report,
        489–90
    darkened theater, in, 128
    eyelash in eye, 478–80
    fur coat - Klein's dept. store,
        235–36
    gold bracelets, 447
    gold star from Jesus, 453–54
    grant proposals rejected, 84–85
    Greatest Experience of My Life,
        The, 68–76
    London, in, 20
    looking at Jesus on the cross, 479
    Louis' socks in breadbox, 490
    Mays dept. store, 438–39
    meeting friends in Israel, 441–42
    meeting with British psychic, 49,
        457
    meeting with Eileen Garrett,
        384–85
    scribing
        grammatical "error" by
            Jesus, 255–56
        "I will to do it," 230, 244
        Lord's Prayer, the, 324–25
        "perfect shaft of pure light,"
            19, 232–33
        "reasonable amount of obedi-
            ence," 440
        scalding of hand, 254
        time, insignificance of, 129–30
    southern France, in, 20, 107, 117,
        128
    subway, in, 51, 52–55, 107, 127,
        177
    squabble with Louis, 182–84
    tickling by brother, 488–89
    Wapnick, Kenneth
        anger - Elohim altar, 371–72

"broken-field" walking, 445
fall on 14th Street, 361
rubbers, 444–45
St. Francis Church - eccentric
    woman, 413
woman in high heels, 489

eyesight—visual problems, 142, 170,
    177–78, 179–80, 183–84,
    281–82, 478–80

France, ambivalence about, 117

hospitalizations
    appendectomy, 29
    gall bladder surgery, 41–43
    final illness, 495–96

Israel
    cave (Lavra Natofa), 339–57
    Qumran, 124n, 356–57, 435–36

Judaism, 27, 28, 29, 39–40, 497
    tablet symbols, 110–11

logic, 38–39, 155, 481
    syllogisms, 229
Louis (Jonathan), 207–210
    attitude toward scribing, 207–208
    book about New York City, 154,
        175
    book business, 40, 41, 50
    and decision to go to graduate
        school, 50
    dependence on, 175–76, 494
    marriage to, 39–41

Mayo Clinic, *see* PSYCHIC EXPERIENCES
mother-in-law, 150–51, 243

Negro spirituals
    love of, 34n, 417
New York University
    graduate school, 50–51, 56n,
        83–84
    term papers, 17–44, 83–84,
        257

519

undergraduate school, 39–40
   "God and Elizabeth Jane,"
      30–31
   "He All Alone Bewept His
      Outcast State," 21–22
"Notes on Sound," 387–89

parents
   father, 27–30, 39, 40, 43, 50, 53,
      140–41, 151, 388–89,
      488
   mother, 27–31, 33, 37, 39–40, 43,
      140, 141, 149, 150–52
phobias
   name, 27, 189, 193, 237n, 240–41,
      264
   reading, 83, 155
   writing, 38, 83–84, 360
POETRY
   "Ancient Love, The," 456–57
   "Awake in Stillness," 410–12
   "Birthday," 413
   "Bright Stranger," 453
   "Brother Swan," 417
   "Continuity," 415–17
   "Dedication For An Altar," 108
   "Deliverance," 408, 488
   "Gift, The," 415
   "Gifts of Christmas, The," 402
   "Gifts of God, The" (prose
      poem), 381, 419–22
   "Glory Train," 417–18
   "Heaven's Gift," 415
   "Holy Saturday," 458
   "Hope of Christmas, The," 418
   "In Gratitude," 418
   "Invitation, The," 459–60
   "Jesus Prayer, A," 414
   "Love Song," 408
   "Mother of the World," 431, 433
   "Name Day," 413
   "Place of Resurrection, The,"
      409–10
   "Prayer for a House," 408,
      457–58

"Requiem," 410, 496–97
"Resting Place, The," 408, 460
"Resurrection and the Life, The,"
   431–33
"Second Chance, The," 453–54
"Second Easter," 403
"Singing Reed, The," 402
"Soundless Song, The," 501
"Stabat Mater," 433
"Stranger on the Road," 454–56
"Transformation," 410
"Waiting," 433–34, 457
"Wayside Cross, The," 458–59
"With Thanks," 415

prayer and meditation, 28–31, 41–42,
      141, 157, 159, 176–77,
      178, 192, 242, 246, 263,
      266–67, 287, 289, 302,
      423–24, 462, 479; see
      also "Song of Prayer"
priestess, 19, 77, 86, 107, 117, 141,
      144, 156–58, 189, 246,
      297, 430, 433, 437, 483,
      487, 496, 499–503; see
      also VISIONS, priestess
   evil, 20, 160, 171

PSYCHIC EXPERIENCES
   Bill and the gold pin, 119
   Bill out of town, 118–19
   Joe - Chicago, 118, 315
   Mayo Clinic, 119–24, 347, 356,
      357

"Psychotherapy: Purpose, Process
      and Practice," 389–91,
      448, 485

reincarnation, 99, 115–16, 136, 166,
      180, 295, 457, 500–501
Roman Catholic Church
   lighting candles, 33, 40, 85
   Lourdes, 31–32, 33, 158, 429, 497
   Mary, 28, 31, 32–33, 42, 43, 233,
      345, 35⁚, 356, 397–98,
      428–33

Roman Catholic Church *(continued)*
    Pieta, 430
    Mass, 27, 31, 41, 345, 349–50, 424,
        425, 426–28
    Eucharist, the, 427n
    medals, 42, 43, 415, 424, 497
    Novenas, 41, 425
    relationship with, 25, 32–33,
        424–28
    rosary, 27, 31, 33, 424, 425, 497

sacrificial helping ("one or the
        other"), 101–102, 140,
        166–67, 189, 197, 218
sexuality, 89–90, 252–53
smoking, 142
"Song of Prayer, The," 393, 450
    origin of, 461–63, 478, 483
    pamphlet, 471–77, 485
    special message, 463–71, 483
Spiritual Eye, 238
star symbolism, 107, 453
statistics, love of, 159–60, 170, 237-
        38, 241

Top Sergeant (Jesus), 168–74, 191,
        250, 257

VISIONS - IMAGES
    boat - Jesus, 108–14
        "receiving and sending set,"
            109, 113, 159, 200
        stork, 112
        treasure chest, 112–14, 344
    Bride of Christ, 251
    cave: "God is" scroll, 124–25, 174,
            220, 313, 357
    chalice, 128, 222, 253–54, 339,
            357
    Elohim altar, 106–108

girl - 18th century France, 116
girl - 12th/13th century, 116
girl, joyous and innocent, 117–18
Heaven's gate, 437, 502
journey to Galilee, 435–38
laurel wreath, 157
Mary - Pieta, 430
nun - France, 116–17
one star in dark sky, 164
past lives with Bill, 99–107
plants in desert, 129, 220–21
priestess, 19, 97–99, 103–105,
        246–47

WAPNICK, KENNETH
    and the "Clarification of Terms,"
            391
        wastepaper basket incident,
            392–93
    and Elohim altar, 107–108,
            371–72
    gift of medals to, 415, 454
    and gold star, 454
    and grandfather's death, 411–12
    letters to, 342–55
    and poetry, 401–403, 405–406,
            409–22, 433
    praying with, 107, 371–72, 423,
            435, 462–63, 479,
            484–85
    and "Psychotherapy," 389–91
    shopping with, 446–47
    and "Song of Prayer, The,"
            461–63
    vision with (journey to Galilee),
            436–38

"Was There A Physical Resurrec-
        tion?" 398–400
wisdom of, 133, 143, 144–45, 162–63,
        172, 196, 449, 487–91

Foundation For "A Course in Miracles"
Conference and Retreat Center

In 1982, Kenneth and Gloria Wapnick began the Foundation for "A Course in Miracles," and in 1988 they opened a Conference and Retreat Center in upstate New York. The following is their vision of the Foundation and description of the Center.

In our early years of studying *A Course in Miracles*, and of teaching and applying its principles in our respective professions of psychotherapy, teaching and school administration, it seemed evident that this was not the simplest of thought systems to understand. This was so not only with respect to the intellectual grasp of its principles, but perhaps even more important, in the application of these principles to one's personal life. Thus, it appeared to us from the beginning that the Course lent itself to teaching, paralleling the teaching of the Holy Spirit in the daily opportunities within our relationships that the manual discusses in its early pages.

One day several years ago while Helen Schucman and I (Kenneth) were discussing these ideas, she shared a vision that she had of this Center as a white temple with a gold cross atop it. Although it is clear that this image was symbolic, we understood it to be representative of what the Conference and Retreat Center was to be: a place where the person of Jesus and his message in the Course would be manifest. We have sometimes seen an image of a lighthouse shining its light into the sea, calling to it those passers-by who sought it. For us, this light is the Course's teaching of forgiveness, which we would hope to share and learn with those who are drawn to the Center's form of teaching.

We have always believed, moreover, that there was not to be *one* form or place of teaching, as this would be antithetical to the Course's principles. As the Course says in another context: "Are other teachers possible, to lead the way to those who speak in different tongues and appeal to different symbols? Certainly there are" (manual, p. 56). The Center thus reflects our personal vision of *A Course in Miracles*. This vision entails the belief that Jesus gave the Course at this particular time in this particular form for several reasons. These include:

1) the necessity of healing the mind of its belief that attack is salvation; this is accomplished through forgiveness, the undoing of our belief in the reality of separation and guilt.

2) emphasizing the importance of Jesus and/or the Holy Spirit as our loving and gentle Teacher, and developing a relationship with this Teacher.

3) correcting the errors of Christianity, particularly where it has emphasized suffering, sacrifice, separation, and sacrament as inherent to God's plan of salvation.

In light of these statements, therefore, we view the Center's principal purpose as being to help students of the Course deepen their understanding of its thought system, conceptually and experientially, so that they may be more effective instruments of the Holy Spirit's teaching in their own lives. Since teaching forgiveness without experiencing it is empty, one of the Center's specific goals is to help facilitate the process whereby people may be better able to know that their own sins are forgiven and that they are truly loved by God. Thus is the Holy Spirit able to extend His love through them to others.

To help achieve these goals, we offer workshops on various topics, ranging from a general overview of the Course's thought system to concentrated studies of specific sections or themes such as special and holy relationships, healing, and time. Classes also are offered for those who wish to study the Course in the context of preparing to teach it to others. In addition, we welcome students who wish to stay at the Center for a period of time for private study and retreats.

The Center is situated on ninety-five acres in the Catskill Mountains, about 120 miles from New York City. The property surrounds beautiful Tennanah Lake, which is suitable for swimming, boating, fishing, and ice skating in the winter. There is a tennis court, an indoor swimming pool, sauna, and ample wooded grounds and trails for leisurely walking. All in all, our Center's country location and comfortable accommodations provide a peaceful and meditative setting in which students may carry out their plans for study and reflection.

RELATED MATERIAL ON *A COURSE IN MIRACLES*

By Kenneth Wapnick

Books and Pamphlets

A VAST ILLUSION: Time According to *A Course in Miracles*. This book weaves together various passages from the Course to present a coherent statement of time, including its metaphysical nature, the role of the miracle and forgiveness in collapsing time, and finally the end of time. (This is an edited and expanded transcription of the tape album "Time According to *A Course in Miracles*.")
ISBN 0-933291-09-4 • Paperback • 301 pages $12.

LOVE DOES NOT CONDEMN: The World, the Flesh, and the Devil According to Platonism, Christianity, Gnosticism, and *A Course in Miracles*. An in-depth exploration of the non-dualistic metaphysics of *A Course in Miracles,* and its integration with living in this illusory world.
ISBN 0-933291-07-08 • Hardcover • 614 pages $25.

FORGIVENESS AND JESUS: The Meeting Place of *A Course in Miracles* and Christianity. This book discusses the teachings of Christianity in the light of the principles of the Course, highlighting the similarities and differences, as well as discussing the application of these principles to important areas in our lives such as injustice, anger, sickness, sexuality, and money.
ISBN 0-933291-01-9 • Paperback • 348 pages $16.

A TALK GIVEN ON *A COURSE IN MIRACLES*: An Introduction. Third edition, revised and enlarged. Edited transcript of a workshop summarizing the principles of the Course; includes the story of how the Course was written.
ISBN 0-933291-00-0 • Paperback • 128 pages $4.

AWAKEN FROM THE DREAM. Gloria and Kenneth Wapnick. Presentation of the Course's major principles from a new perspective. Includes background material on how the Course was written.
ISBN 0-933291-04-3 • Paperback • 144 pages $10.

GLOSSARY-INDEX FOR *A COURSE IN MIRACLES*. Third edition. Summary of the Course's theory; more than 125 terms defined and indexed; index of over 800 scriptural references; line-gauge included to assist use of index.
ISBN 0-933291-03-5 • Hardcover • 308 pages $16.

THE FIFTY MIRACLE PRINCIPLES OF *A COURSE IN MIRA-CLES*. Combined and edited transcript of two workshops; line-by-line analysis of the fifty miracle principles, with additional material.
ISBN 0-933291-02-7 • Paperback • 153 pages $8.

CHRISTIAN PSYCHOLOGY IN *A COURSE IN MIRACLES*. Discussion of the basic principles of the Course in the context of some of the traditional teachings of Christianity.
ISBN 0-933291-06X • Pamphlet • 36 pages $3.
Audio tape of pamphlet, recorded by Kenneth Wapnick. $5.

THE OBSTACLES TO PEACE. Edited transcript of tape album; line-by-line analysis of "The Obstacles to Peace" and related passages.
ISBN 0-933291-05-1 • Paperback • 296 pages $12.

Video Tape Albums

SEEK NOT TO CHANGE THE COURSE. Reflections on *A Course in Miracles*. Talk given by Gloria and Kenneth Wapnick, including questions and answers, on some of the more common misunderstandings about the Course.
135 mins.   VHS $30.   Audio tape version $15.

FOUNDATION FOR "A COURSE IN MIRACLES" Conference and Retreat Center. Gloria and Kenneth Wapnick speak about the Course's beginnings, the origin and purpose of the Foundation, and their vision of its development in the future. A visual and verbal portrait of the Center.
24 mins.   VHS $10.

Audio Cassette Albums

RECORDED SEMINARS AND WORKSHOPS

THE SIMPLICITY OF SALVATION. Intensive overview of the Course. 8 tapes $65.

HOLY IS HEALING. Psychotherapeutic applications of the Course. 8 tapes $65.

ATONEMENT WITHOUT SACRIFICE. Christianity, the Bible, and the Course. 2 tapes $15.

THE END OF INJUSTICE. Overview of the Course. 6 tapes $45.

THE EGO AND FORGIVENESS. Introductory overview of the Course. (Album consists of first two tapes of "The End of Injustice.") 2 tapes $15.

THE GIFTS OF GOD. A discussion of the inspired poetry of Helen Schucman, scribe of the Course; includes personal reminiscences about Helen. 3 tapes $24.

THE ORIGIN OF *A COURSE IN MIRACLES*. The story of the scribing of *A Course in Miracles*; reflections on Helen Schucman and William Thetford. 1 tape $6.

I WILL BE STILL AN INSTANT AND GO HOME. A collection of two talks and a meditation by Kenneth Wapnick, and one talk by Gloria Wapnick and Kenneth—given at various Sunday services. 1 tape $6.

LOVE DOES NOT OPPOSE. The importance of non-opposition as the basis of forgiveness in special relationships. 8 tapes $65.

JESUS AND THE MESSAGE OF EASTER. The Course's view of Jesus and the meaning of his crucifixion and resurrection. 8 tapes $65.

THE AUTHORITY PROBLEM. The authority problem with God and its reflection in our everyday life. 5 tapes $40.

OUR GRATITUDE TO GOD. Our gratitude to God, to Jesus, and to each other; the obstacles and resistances to this gratitude. 5 tapes $40.

SICKNESS AND HEALING. Discussion of the cause and purpose of sickness in the ego thought system; analysis of healing as occurring in the mind—the healing of the belief in guilt, by turning to the Holy Spirit and forgiving. 8 tapes $60.

WHAT IT MEANS TO BE A TEACHER OF GOD. Discussion of the ten characteristics of a teacher of God, magic, and healing. 6 tapes $48.

OVEREATING: A DIALOGUE BASED UPON *A COURSE IN MIRA-CLES*. The ego dynamics involved in food addictions and weight problems; forgiveness through the Holy Spirit as the solution. 1 tape $6.

TO JUDGE OR NOT TO JUDGE. The Course's teachings on judgment; the process of recognizing our need to judge, and letting Jesus or the Holy Spirit judge for us. 4 tapes $32.

HEALING THE UNHEALED HEALER. The characteristics of the unhealed healer; healing through joining with Jesus in understanding all forms of sickness and problems as calls for love. 8 tapes $65.

THE REAL WORLD: OUR HOME AWAY FROM HOME. A discussion of our true home in Heaven, the ego's home in the world, and the Holy Spirit's correction of the ego's world: the real world. 8 tapes $65.

TRUE EMPATHY: THE GREATER JOINING. The world's version of empathy contrasted with the Holy Spirit's true empathy. 8 tapes $65.

LINE-BY-LINE ANALYSIS OF KEY SECTIONS IN THE COURSE

THE FIFTY MIRACLE PRINCIPLES OF *A COURSE IN MIRACLES*
3 tapes $24.
THE WORLD ACCORDING TO *A COURSE IN MIRACLES*
3 tapes $24.

THE OBSTACLES TO PEACE - 6 tapes $48.

SPECIAL RELATIONSHIPS—PART 1 - 8 tapes $65.

SPECIAL RELATIONSHIPS—PART 2 - 6 tapes $48.

TIME ACCORDING TO *A COURSE IN MIRACLES* - 6 tapes $48.

JESUS AND *A COURSE IN MIRACLES* - 5 tapes $40.

CAUSE AND EFFECT - 8 tapes $65.

PSYCHOTHERAPY: PURPOSE, PROCESS AND PRACTICE
7 tapes $56.

THE SONG OF PRAYER - 10 tapes $80.

Ordering Information

Prices include shipping if mailed in the U.S. For orders *outside* the U.S. only, please add the following: for books and tape sets, $3.00 for the first item, $1.00 each additional item; for pamphlets add $.75 per item.

New York State residents please add local sales tax. VISA and MasterCard accepted.

Order from:

Foundation for "A Course in Miracles"
R.R. 2, Box 71
Roscoe, NY 12776-9506
(607) 498-4116 • FAX (607) 498-5325

A COURSE IN MIRACLES and other scribed material may be ordered from:

Foundation for Inner Peace
Box 1104
Glen Ellen, CA 95442
(707) 939-0200

A COURSE IN MIRACLES: Hardcover: $40   Softcover: $25

PSYCHOTHERAPY: PURPOSE, PROCESS AND PRACTICE: $3.00

THE SONG OF PRAYER: PRAYER, FORGIVENESS, HEALING: $3.00

THE GIFTS OF GOD: $21.00